Multiple Perspectives on Play in Early Childhood Education

SUNY Series, Early Childhood Education: Inquiries and Insights
Mary A. Jensen, Editor

Multiple Perspectives on Play in Early Childhood Education

Olivia N. Saracho and
Bernard Spodek, Editors

State University of New York Press

Published by
State University of New York Press, Albany

For information, address State University of New York
Press, State University Plaza, Albany, N.Y., 12246

Production by E. Moore
Marketing by Hannah J. Hazen

Library of Congress Cataloging-in-Publication Data

Multiple perspectives on play in early childhood education / Olivia N.
    Saracho and Bernard Spodek, editors.
        p.   cm. — (SUNY series, early childhood education)
    Includes bibliographical references and index.
    ISBN 0-7914-3615-2 (hc : alk. paper). — ISBN 0-7914-3616-0 (pbk.
    : alk. paper)
    1. Play. 2. Early childhood education. I. Saracho, Olivia N.
    II. Spodek, Bernard. III. Series.
    LB1139.35.P55M85 1998
    155.4′18—dc21   97-12087
                                                                      CIP

10 9 8 7 6 5 4 3 2 1

Contents

Acknowledgments

Editing a work such as these requires the help and support of many people. We would like to acknowledge those that have been of the most help to us. First, we would like to thank Priscilla Ross, acquisitions editor for SUNY Press, and Mary Jensen, series editor, for the encouragement and support they have given to our project since it was first proposed. We would also like to thank the colleagues who helped review the manuscripts that are included here. Their critical sense and their feedback to the chapter authors and to us helped to improve the quality of this volume. These persons include Doris Bergen, Alice Honig, Mary Jensen, Jan McCarthy, Michealene Ostosky, Judith Schickedanz, and Kelvin Seifert. All these individuals have made significant contributions to this volume.

Introduction:
Play in Early Childhood Education

Olivia N. Saracho and Bernard Spodek

The field of early childhood education has undergone significant changes in recent decades. The number of early childhood programs, the number of early childhood practitioners, and the number of children enrolled in early childhood programs have all increased. In addition, the field has received increased attention from scholars and policymakers. One indication of the increase in attention is the increase in publications relating to early childhood education, both books and periodicals.

Parallel to the increased interest in the field of early childhood education has been the increased attention given to research in the field. A body of empirical and theoretical knowledge has been created that can inform practice. Too often, however, research in the field has only reported to other researchers and does not achieve its potential of informing practice. There has been, on the whole, an inadequate attempt to present the available research in a meaningful, integrated fashion that would be understood by a wide ranging audience of early childhood educators. This audience includes practitioners— administrators and teachers, students at the undergraduate and graduate level, teacher educators, and policymakers. Among the research studies that have been conducted is a broad range of research on children's play in educational settings.

Play has been a part of early childhood programs since the initial kindergarten developed by Friedreich Froebel more than 150 years ago. While play in the Froebelian kindergarten was highly teacher directed, a freer form of educational play evolved in the Macmillan Nursery School and in the reformed kindergarten that was constructed during the progressive education era.

While teachers value children's play, they often do not know how to guide that play to make it more educational. Too often, in reflecting the value of child-initiated activities, teachers set the stage for children's play and observe it, but hesitate to enrich that play. They may fear that to intervene is to create a developmentally inappropriate set of educational practices. However, the lack of intervention may limit the educational outcomes of this play. A large body of research exists on different forms of children's play in educational settings that could inform teachers of young children and help them to improve their practice and support more educational play.

OVERVIEW

This book aims to collect and communicate the research and theoretical knowledge that exists regarding play as a medium of learning and development in the early childhood years. Each chapter provides a different perspective on some aspect of children's play. Each includes a review of research and theory related to that aspect of play as well as implications for practice. The references included with each chapter could point the way to further study on the part of the reader.

In the first chapter we present a brief historical overview of the theories that have been developed to help individuals understand play and to justify its use as a form of education of young children. These theories, both classical and contemporary, provide the reader with a context for the current discourse on play and provides the context for understanding the ideas presented in the chapters that follow.

In Chapter 2, "Playing with a Theory of Mind," Angeline S. Lillard uses children's pretense, or make-believe play, to gain insight into children's theory of mind. Children's play is seen as mental as well as physical activity. Lillard suggests that observations of play can be used to probe how children represent their world and how they think about internal states and social order.

Larry Smolucha and Francine Smolucha analyze post-Piagetian perspectives on play in Chapter 3. They present an historical-social overview of the decline of the Piagetian paradigm for studying children's play and describe the events leading to the reemergence of Vygotskian theory in its place. The Vygotskian framework provides a strong basis for the use of guided pretend play in early education. The Smoluchas suggest that this framework may have especially great significance for the study of the education of infants and toddlers.

David H. Uttal and his colleagues discuss a different aspect of cognitive development in young childen in relation to play. They look at the way that children understand the symbols they use. Since symbolic play is typical of children in the early childhood period, this understanding has significance for teaching young children through play. In addition, the use of hands-on activities to support children's learning through the primary grades is based on the notion that children's manipulation of symbolic materials leads to a greater understanding of the concepts underlying these symbols and their manipulation. While the authors conclude that play is essential in young children's cognitive development, they provide an important caveat: that just because children play with an object does not mean that have learned from that experience.

Robert D. Cavanaugh and Susan Engel, in Chapter 5, extend our understanding of symbolic thought as it emerges in children's play. Their chapter focuses on pretend play and narrative in young children. They identify the continuity between children's make-believe play and adults' responses to works of art. Thus they argue that children use their capacity for make-believe as they mature into adulthood.

In Chapter 6, Kathleen Roskos and Susan Neuman explore the relationship between literacy and play in terms of the interaction of pretense play and literacy-related discourse and the environmental forces that elicit literacy-related behavior in the play context. After reviewing research relating to these themes, they identify research needs, including research to examine the efficacy of play activities for supporting emergent literacy in children, changes in children's literacy behavior in a play context over time, and the adult strategies that facilitate literacy behavior in play.

Gary L. Creasey, Patricia A. Jarvis, and Laura E. Berk look at the role of play in the development of social competence in Chapter 7. They review theories of social competence development from the perspectives of Piaget and Vygotsky. They also see young children's play as reflecting their attachment to their caregivers, the child-rearing practices of their parents, and their peer relations. Since research suggests that adults can promote social competence by guiding young children's play, the authors suggest the need for more studies on play intervention techniques of teachers and the consequences of using these techniques.

In Chapter 8 Kenneth H. Rubin and Robert J. Coplan focus and the developmental aspect of various forms of social and nonsocial children's play. They explore the origins of individual differences in children's social play as well as the developmental outcomes of social and nonsocial children's play. They also suggest future directions of research in children's play, including looking more closely at sex differences in relation to children's social play and at the influence of culture on children's social play.

Fergus P. Hughes reviews the research on the play of children with special educational needs in Chapter 9. He analyzes studies related to preterm infants, those exposed prenatally to drugs, and children with impairments.

These include children with visual and hearing impairments, cognitive and language delays, attention deficit hyperactivity disorders, autism, and children who are victims of abuse. Too often the social environment of children with such disabilities does not support engagement in play. Even the inclusion of these children in classes for normally developing children may not be enough to encourage play unless specific interventions are offered. Hughes concludes that teachers and others who work with these children need to provide the necessary scaffolding to enhance their play activities.

In Chapter 10, Jaipal L. Roopnarine and his colleagues examine the cultural context of children's play. They argue that most studies of children's play are grounded in Western, and especially North American cultures. They suggest that we need to consider play in the context of diverse cultures and provide theoretical underpinnings for such a consideration. They review research on parent-child play as well as play among children in different social contexts. They look at traditional forms of play and at the changing social context of children's play. They suggest that introducing play into a school curriculum must be done with attention to the sociocultural context. Such initiatives should embrace culture specific and societywide goals. Traditional forms of play should be preserved in an effort to search for universal forms of play.

In Chapter 11, on play and the assessment of young children, Anthony D. Pellegrini looks at the relationship between these two important elements in early childhood education: play and assessment. He begins by providing definitions for both terms: play and assessment. He then looks at the use of play as a context for assessment. He presents two observational instruments that can be used for this purpose. He concludes his chapter by raising some caveats regarding the observation of children's play as an assessment technique.

Olivia Saracho, in Chapter 12, looks at the relationship of cognitive style and young children's play. She focuses primarily on the field dependent-independent dimension of cognitive style. After reviewing research in the area, Saracho suggests that teachers use play to help children develop competency in both cognitive styles. She also recommends continued study of the relationship between play and children's cognitive styles

Chapter 13, by Joe L. Frost, Dongju Shin, and Paul J. Jacobs focus on understanding the effects of the physical environment on children's play. They identify the physical characteristics of play environments, including spatial arrangements, density, and the availability of play props. They especially look at the characteristics of playground environments, including play materials and equipment. In concluding their chapter the authors provide guidelines for developing physical environments in support of children's play.

Since the beginning of this century, controversy has ranged over whether young children confuse fantasy and reality. Montessori did not include play activities in her curriculum. She argued that children confuse fantasy with reality and she believed that children at this age should focus on understanding reality. Brian Vandenberg, in his chapter, "Real and Unreal: A Vital Developmental Dichotomy," asserts that children communicate their intent to play and then enter into play situations that require them to mutually understand what is real and what is unreal. The ability to suspend reality allows children to preserve the mythic playful aspects of childhood while enhancing their cognitive and social skills. He warns that heavy-handed adult guidance can destroy the freedom and joy of play for children.

Taken together these chapters reflect a broad view of the current state of knowledge regarding children's play. They provide suggestions for researchers studying children's play. They also identify the implications of our current state of knowledge for teachers and others who work with young children. We believe that the materials presented in this volume should open new horizons, especially for those in early childhood education, a field that for many generations has venerated play as a medium for the education of young children.

Chapter 1

A Historical Overview of Theories of Play

Olivia N. Saracho and Bernard Spodek

For centuries play has been a phenomenon that has piqued the interest of educators, psychologists, philosophers, and others who have attempted to define it, explain it, understand it, and relate it to the individual's activities. Play is difficult to understand because it appears in such diverse forms. Play is also an activity of young children, adults, and nonhuman animals. Children, adults, and nonhuman animals engage in play; consequently, play must be considered in the context of the individual's development and education (Spodek & Saracho, 1988). A quality of mystery shaded with humor is found in the imaginative play of children. For example, in a nursery school, the following play situations are observed.

Situation 1
    The children run into the playground area. Two children, Nikki and Elizabeth, head immediately for the sandbox. They each grab a bucket and a shovel, and sit down next to each other.
    "Let's make mudcakes," says Elizabeth.
    "OK," replies Nikki.
    The girls work quietly, digging in the sand, filling their buckets. Elizabeth gets up and walks over to the teacher. "Would you like a mudcake?" she asks. The teacher answers, "Oh, how wonderful," and pretends to taste the mudcakes. When Elizabeth returns, Nikki is no longer in the sandbox. Instead, Nikki is sitting in the middle of the sandbox. Elizabeth says, "Nikki, move! You're in the way."

    One can contrast this type of play with the comparable situation of two other children.

Situation 2

Two children, Matthew and Bobby, are pretending to be Robin Hood. They both are crawling on the floor, pretending to hide from the enemy. Every once in a while, they reach for an imaginary bow from their backs, and shoot an arrow at the oncoming enemy.

Matthew screams, "I got you, Prince!"

Bobby hollers, "Watch out, Robin, they're coming behind you!"

Matthew rolls around the ground, pretending to fight with the enemy. Bobby comes to the rescue and pretends to scare away the enemy.

The children's play experiences present elements that add or modify their knowledge through the integration of new and familiar experiences. The children's fantasy play generates their different patterns of thought (Freud, 1937; Lewin, 1935; Luria, 1932; Piaget, 1962).

Make-believe play usually has a social quality in the symbolic sense. Its interpersonal transactions, events, and adventures summon many characters and locations in space and time. Although make-believe play occurs in pairs or groups of children, additional invisible characters or inanimate objects may be introduced to portray the absence of people or animals. Children's play also manifests a social quality when children imitate adults' activities or an adventure others have read to them or they have seen on television.

Play is a critical element of the early childhood curriculum. It influences children's social, emotional, physical, and cognitive development. Play allows children to communicate their ideas and feelings and to verify their knowledge of the world. Play is intrinsically motivated, interpreted for its own sake, and conveyed in a relaxed manner providing a positive outcome. Play is free and unconscious. Play activities or their origins have always been integrated in the early childhood educational curriculum.

DEFINING PLAY

The word "play" is used in many ways (Spodek & Saracho, 1988), making it difficult to define. It is observed in many aspects of life such as a dramatic performance, a person making music with an instrument, and people's "kidding around" or making a pun. Striving to define the word "play" in everyday use is a challenge. Some observers (i.e., Lorenz, Thorpe) recommend that play should not be defined because interobserver consensus on what is or is not play is extremely high (cited in Dobbert, 1985). On the other hand, Fagen (1981) disagrees and tries to distill a comprehensive definition of play from an extensive review of the literature. The definition of play, however, varies among educators and philosophers. For example, Mitchell and Mason (1948) offer a comparison of these definitions:

SEASHORE: *Free self-expression for the pleasure of expression.*
FROEBEL: *The natural unfolding of the germinal leaves of childhood.*
HALL: *The motor habits and spirit of the past persisting in the present.*
GROOS: *Instinctive practice, without serious intent, of activities which will later be essential to life.*
DEWEY: *Activities not consciously performed for the sake of any result beyond themselves.*
SCHILLER: *The aimless expenditure of exuberant energy.*
SPENSER: *Superfluous actions taking place instinctively in the absence of real actions. . . . Activity performed for the immediate gratification derived without regard for ulterior benefits.*
LAZARUS: *Activity in itself free, aimless, amusing, or diverting.*
SHAND: *A type of play directed at the maintenance of joy. Dulles: An instinctive form of self-expression and emotional escape value.*
CURTI: *Highly motivated activity which, as free from conflicts, is usually, though not always, pleasurable. (pp. 103–104)*

Each definition implies a distinctive understanding and interpretation of play. Therefore, researchers are continuing to define play (Schwartzman, 1978), to identify "paradigm cases" of the phenomenon, to delay definitional problems to a later time (Matthews & Matthews, 1982), and to disagree on a definition of play. The problem of defining play, however, needs to be resolved soon to circumvent definitional confusions. Smith and Vollstedt (1985) believe that play can be defined by merging the attributes of play activity rather than by surveying the literature for the presence or absence of one definitive trait. Such conviction suggests the use of criteria to identify play behavior (Sokal, 1974). Researchers (e.g., Rubin, Fein, & Vandenberg, 1983; Spodek, Saracho, & Davis, 1991) have identified various criteria of play. Krasnor and Pepler (1980) propose four criteria to identify a play activity: flexibility, positive affect, intrinsic motivation, and nonliterality. Sutton-Smith and Kelly-Byrne (1984) disagree with the Krasnor and Pepler (1980) criteria. They argue that some patterns of play are not only involuntary or inflexible but also depict a negative affect. Rubin et al. (1983) have offered a broader set of criteria:

1. Play is personally motivated by the satisfaction embedded in the activity and not governed either by basic needs and drives, or by social demands.
2. Players are concerned with activities more than with goals. Goals are self-imposed and the behavior of the players is spontaneous.
3. Play occurs with familiar objects, or following the exploration of unfamiliar objects. Children supply their own meanings to play activities and control the activity themselves.

4. Play activities can be nonliteral.
5. Play is free from the rules imposed from the outside and the rules that do exist can be modified by the players.
6. Play requires the active engagement of the players.

Indicating a set of criteria assists in identifying play behavior; nonetheless, some vital play episodes may be dismissed. A set of clear criteria can facilitate the understanding of play, but does not explain why people and children play. Since no empirical study justifies the use of any set of criteria to identify a play episode, Smith and Vollstedt (1985) took several sets of criteria that were proposed by researchers and empirically explored which criteria individuals applied to depict a play activity. They tested several sets of criteria and found that the combination of nonliterality (Krasnor & Pepler, 1980; Rubin et al., 1983), positive affect, and flexibility (Krasnor & Pepler, 1980) were used most often to identify a play activity. Apparently, play is joyful, flexible, and imaginative. Although other criteria relate to play, the definition by Smith and Vollstedt (1985) can be acknowledged as a tentative definition of play. Since research evidence shows that play is vital for the individual's development or education, a reliable definition may help to identify play behavior, but a valid definition must also be tied to developmental theories.

HISTORICAL PERSPECTIVES

Play has been a part of early childhood programs since the establishment of the kindergarten by Friedreich Froebel more than 150 years ago. The original Froebelian kindergarten curriculum consisted of the manipulation of *gifts*, engagement in craft activities or *occupations*, and the children's participation in the mother's *plays and songs* (Spodek & Saracho [1994] provide a description of Froebel's gifts). Children, however, were not free to express themselves within these different activities, although the activities were manipulative and derived from children's free play. Observing the natural play of German peasant children, Friedrich Froebel abstracted the essential elements of the play and systematized them into his kindergarten activities to guarantee that they would be presented to all children. While play in the Froebel kindergarten was highly teacher directed, a freer form of play was found later in the Macmillan Nursery School and in the reformed kindergarten of the progressive era.

Play also was integrated in the early childhood curriculum of Maria Montessori. When she developed her educational method, she also drew its essential elements from the children's natural play activities, reconstructed them, and systematized them in an instructional method. The activities in the early childhood curricula of Friedrich Froebel and Maria Montessori, however, were used to accomplish dissimilar instructional goals. Froebel's purpose was to help children acquire the spiritual meanings symbolized by the materials and the activities. In contrast, Montessori's purpose was to help children obtain a better understanding of the properties of the objects and acquire specific skills by manipulating the objects. In both cases, the aspects of the activity regarded as educational were abstract and various features of play were discarded.

In the first quarter of the twentieth century, the emergence of the reform kindergarten movement and the modern nursery-school movement brought the acceptance of children's organic play as a vehicle for learning. These educational systems supported and nurtured the children's natural play activities as being educationally meaningful in their own right, although neither of these innovative educational systems considered play to be the only way for children to learn. Increased concerns about educational play and its effects in young children's education stimulated numerous studies that explore the effects of young children's play. With increased concerns about the quality of young children's education in early childhood programs, alternative approaches to using young children's play to educate them also developed. A review of the emerging definitions and the theories of play should provide a better understanding of the influence of this historical movement.

THEORIES OF PLAY

Relevant theories of play have been proposed for the last two decades to assist in understanding the nature of children's play behavior. Mellon (1994) described two types of theories: classical and modern. Classical theories were initiated in the nineteenth century while modern theories generated after 1920. Spodek and Saracho (1994) included dynamic theories among the modern theories. Classical and dynamic theories are summarized in the sections below.

Classical Theories

Classical theories strive to explain the reason that play exists and its function. Gillmore (1971) summarized the surplus energy, relaxation, recapitulation, and pre-exercise classical theories of play as follows

1. The relaxation theory proposes that through play individuals restore their energy that they exhaust during their work. Hence, after working for a period of time, individuals need to play to relax and to generate and reserve sufficient energy to continue working again.

2. The surplus energy theory proposes that, as organisms, individuals constantly produce energy, that they exhaust through their work. Excess energy left over beyond what individuals need to work can be eliminated through play.
3. The recapitulation theory proposes that individuals proceed through personal developmental stages that parallel those stages that the human race experiences. Play is an inherent manner of discontinuing primitive skills and drives that individuals have inherited from the epochs of civilization. When individuals use play to migrate through these primitive stages, they become prepared for the endeavors of modern life.
4. The pre-exercise theory proposes that play is an instinctive manner of preparing children for the endeavors of adult life. Young children's play experiences are similar to those experiences they will encounter as adults. This process permits children to employ play to rehearse those skills they will need in adult life.

Each of these theories has a definite appeal, but none of them serves to define children's play. The first two theories (surplus energy and relaxation theory) perceive play as a means of energy regulation. The last two theories (recapitulation and pre-exercise) relate play to instincts. Each pair of classical theories offers opposing explanations of the way play expresses energy or instincts (Mellon, 1994). The classical theories are "armchair" theories that are rooted in philosophical meditation rather than in experimental research (Ellis, 1973). To a substantial degree, they embody the nineteenth-century concept that in order to generate a symbolic representation of the world, children convert reality into play experiences (Groos, Schiller, Spenser). This early belief, advocated by the surplus energy, pre-exercise. and recapitulation theories, is evident still in the contemporary theories and research (Piaget, 1962; Singer, 1973; Vygotsky, 1967). Although the classical theories have profound deficiencies such as discredited beliefs regarding energy, instincts, and evolution, they are important, because they have provided a foundation for modern theories of play (Rubin, 1982).

Dynamic Theories

Dynamic theories of play are less concerned with understanding why children play, accepting the fact that children play. These theories make an effort to explain the content of play. Dynamic theories of children's play include those of Sigmund Freud and Jean Piaget (Spodek & Saracho, 1994). They are summarized below:

1. The psychodynamic theory of play evolved from the psychoanalysis of Sigmund Freud. He believed that play permits children to communicate

and to eliminate their fears and anxieties by forcing those fears and anxieties to a level of consciousness and then articulating them in their play. Children employ fantasy play to cope with those elements of reality that are difficult for them. Problems in everyday events are reduced through play. Children may be able to manage problems in their play that they are not able to cope with in real life. During play, situations can be modified to the degree that problems can be overcome. Since play can help children to express conflicts and problems, psychoanalysts utilize play as a form of therapy. The language of play serves a similar purpose for children that verbal language serves for adults in psychoanalysis.

2. Constructivist theory is based on the work of Jean Piaget (1962), who viewed individuals as using two complementary processes to gain knowledge: assimilation and accommodation. Assimilation lets individuals adapt the information they acquired through their experiences into the individuals' already developed sense of understanding. When new information cannot be adapted into existing frameworks of understanding, because it contradicts what they know or their past understandings, individuals must modify how they perceive and understand the world. To do this, they use accommodation to modify what they know in relation to newly acquired information and establish a new balance or equilibrium. Through play, individuals take information from the outside world and adapt that information to their already developed schemes of understanding.

Dynamic theories of play propose that play activities have a strong influence on children's development. This influence is congruous with the basic goals of early childhood education, implying that play activities provide an important educational purpose. It is essential that the content of play and how to guide it in an appropriate way be considered. Freud believed that the content of play has a strong affective tone, whereas Piaget believed that play has a strong cognitive tone. Play can promote learning in both of these domains. Play also serves an important role in the socialization process, which has been supported by other theories (e.g., Parten).

Within the last several decades additional theories have emerged to explain children's play and its consequences. Theories by Vygotsky (1967), Singer (1973), Ellis (1973), and White (1959) also assist in interpreting several facets of play. Vygotsky (1967) believed that through play children use their ingenuity to create imaginary events that originate from real life circumstances. Play also liberates individuals from the constraints of the real world that surrounds them. This process gives children more control over a situation than they would have in reality. Such freedom from reality allows children to play with meanings and objects. Therefore, they use higher-order thought processes in their play. Vygotsky (1967) speculated that play builds mental structures through the use of signs and tools that promote language and thought development.

According to Singer (1973), individuals use their physical and mental abilities in imaginative play to arrange their experiences. Through play, individuals explore the world, develop the ability to cope with the world, and cultivate their creativity.

Ellis (1973) views play as a way to process information. Since human beings typically are mentally active, they endlessly attempt to make sense out of the information they accumulate. When they have too much or insufficient information to process, they feel uncomfortable and need a proper balance. Thus, they neglect some things in their environment that appear overwhelming. If they have insufficient information, they get bored and daydream. Play creates that balance. Children formulate information internally through fantasy play.

White's (1959) theory of competence motivation also explains play. Individuals do not need rewards to play; they play for play's sake. Individuals acquire personal satisfaction from feeling competent. The ability to accomplish something well or to influence the surrounding world provides its own rewards. Through play, individuals behave on their own in a productive way. Consequently, play activities become the rewards.

An integration of these theories can define the multifaceted functions of play. Play is a natural activity and assists individuals in understanding and depicting their world, at both thinking and feeling levels. Play provides individuals with a sense of mastery or control over some facets of their world. It requires them to use symbols, actions, or objects that represent something other than themselves. Fantasy is play that is free from reality, and it can also promote the individual's understandings and creativity.

SUMMARY

Theories of play seek to explain play as it exists. Most theories suggest that play behavior is voluntary, enjoyable, and pleasurable to children. An understanding of these theories can provide guidelines to researchers and educators hoping to promote educational play in young children. For example, children in the dramatic play area may acquire personal satisfactions from playing out a specific role, interacting with children in other roles, or using various play properties in innovative ways. Children continue to play because it is a most enjoyable experience for them. Young children spend many hours participating in play activities because play is their way of interacting with themselves and the world (Mellon, 1994). The merit of play is that it assists children in exploring and understanding various role and interaction patterns, thereby supporting their understanding of their social world and facilitating their efforts to build a realistic sense of self (Spodek & Saracho, 1994). Play seems to serve as an information-seeking process for the children and as a means to interact with their environment. In addition, play helps children learn how to learn.

Educational play may take many forms. The fundamental role of the teacher is to use the natural spontaneous play of children in a way that it has educational value while continuing to maintain its qualities as play. Educational play activities should be evaluated by the degree of children's involvement and its effectiveness in helping children reach educational goals.

REFERENCES

Dobbert, M. L. (1985, Summer). Play is not monkey business: a holistic bioculture perspective on the role of play in learning. *Educational Horizons, 63*(4), 158–163.

Ellis, M. J. (1973). *Why people play?* Englewood Cliffs, NJ: Prentice Hall.

Fagen, R. (1981). *Animal behavior.* New York: Oxford University Press.

Freud, A. (1937). *The ego and the mechanism of defenses.* London: Hogarth.

Gillmore, J. B. (1971). Play: A special behavior. In C. Herron & B. Sutton-Smith (Eds.), *Child's play.* New York: Wiley.

Krasnor, L. R. & Pepler, D. J. (1980). The study of children's play: Some future directions. In K. H. Rubin (Ed.), *New directions for child development: Children's play* (pp. 85–95). San Francisco: Jossey-Bass.

Lewin, K. (1935). *A dynamic theory of personality.* New York: McGraw-Hill.

Luria, A. R. (1932). *The nature of human conflicts.* New York: Liveright.

Matthews, W. S., & Matthews, R. J. (1982). Eliminating operational definitions: A paradigm case approach to the study of fantasy play. In D. J. Pepler & K. H. Rubin (Eds.), *The play of children: Current theory and research* (pp. 21–29). Basel: Karger.

Mellon, E. (1994). Play theories: A contemporary view. *Early Child Development and Care, 102,* 91–100.

Mitchell, E. D., & Mason, B. (1948). *The theory of play* (revised edition). New York: A. S. Barnes.

Parten, M. B. (1932). Social participation among preschool children. *Journal of Abnormal and Social Psychology, 27,* 243–269.

Piaget, J. (1962). *Play, dreams, and imitation in childhood.* New York: Norton.

Rubin, K. H. (1982). Early play theories revisited: Contributions to contemporary research and theory. In D. J. Pepler & K. H. Rubin (Eds.), *The play of children: Current theory and research* (Vol. 6, pp. 4–14). Basel, Switzerland: Karger.

Rubin, K. H., Fein, G. G., & Vandenberg, B. (1983). Play. In E. M. Hetherington (Ed।)., P. H. Mussen (Series Ed.), *Handbook of child psychology: Vol. 4. Socialization, personality, and social development* (pp. 693–741). New York: Wiley.

Schwartzman, H. B. (1978). *Transformations: The anthropology of play.* New York: Plenum.

Singer, J. L. (1973). Theories of play and the origins of imagination. In J. L. Singer (Ed.), *The child's world of make-believe* (pp. 1–26). New York: Academic Press.

Smith, P. K., & Vollstedt, R. (1985). On defining play: An empirical study of the relationship between play and various play criteria. *Child Development, 56,* 1042–1050.

Sokal, R. R. (1974). Classification: Purposes, principles, progress, prospects. *Science, 185,* 1115–1123.

Spodek, B., & Saracho, O. N. (1988). The challenge of educational play. In D. Bergen (Ed.), *Play as a medium for learning and development* (pp. 9–22). Portsmouth, NH: Heinemann.

Spodek, B., & Saracho, O. N. (1994). *Right from the start: Teaching children ages three to eight.* Boston: Allyn & Bacon.

Spodek, B., Saracho, O. N., & Davis, M. D. (1991). *Foundations of early childhood education: Teaching three-, four-, and five-year-old children.* Englewood Cliffs, NJ: Prentice Hall.

Sutton-Smith, B., & Kelly-Byrne, D. (1984). The idealization of play. In P. K. Smith (Ed.), *Play in animals and humans* (pp. 305–321). Oxford: Basil Blackwell.

Vygotsky, L. S. (1967). Play and its role in the mental development of the child. *Soviet Psychology, 12,* 62–76.

White, R. F. (1959). Motivation reconsidered: The concept of competence. *Psychological Review, 66,* 297–333.

Chapter 2

Playing with a Theory of Mind

Angeline S. Lillard

In recent years children's understanding of the mind has become an extremely active area of research within cognitive development, and there have been pleas to extend its methods and concerns more into social development as well (Dunn, 1995). The broader reason for this interest and activity is that understanding the mind is central to human interaction. In most of our social encounters, we at least implicitly draw on our knowledge of minds, for example, whether someone hears something, why someone is surprised, or how to inspire someone to work harder. This body of social knowledge is often referred to as a theory of mind, for two reasons. First, mental states are theoretical constructs: their existence cannot be proven (hence philosophers like Stich [1983] can argue that they do not in fact exist). We have a theory that there are minds and mental states, and we impute these to ourselves and others accordingly (Premack & Woodruff, 1978). The second reason is that our knowledge about minds takes the form of a theory: it makes certain ontological distinctions, has a causal-explanatory framework, and defines its constructs in terms of other constructs in the theory (surprise is defined with reference to belief, for example) (Wellman, 1990).

This area of knowledge has of course long been important to human survival. The impetus for its recently being brought to center stage in developmental psychology is a particularly striking finding: that young children typically fail tasks assessing their understanding of false belief (Wimmer & Perner, 1983). Young children's responses to such tasks are very counterintuitive yet very robust. These factors combined with the importance of the knowledge under scrutiny—that people can believe things that are not true—places it among the seminal findings of cognitive development.

In the original false belief task (Wimmer & Perner, 1983), children are shown a doll (Maxi), who hides a piece of chocolate in a blue cupboard. Then

Maxi leaves the scene. During his absence, his mother arrives, moves the chocolate from the blue cupboard to a white one, then also leaves. Maxi returns. The chocolate is not visible as both cupboards are closed, and Maxi has clearly not seen his mother move the chocolate. Children are asked, "Where will Maxi look for his chocolate?" One should say, "The blue cupboard" since that is where Maxi left the chocolate, and he has no way of knowing that it has been moved. But what Wimmer and Perner found is that children under four years of age tend to fail the test by claiming that Maxi will go to the white cupboard, where his mother put it. Possible problems with the paradigm (the story is hard for young children to follow, children do not understand the question, and so on) have been examined, and while the issue is not entirely resolved, most would agree that young children do have a genuine problem understanding that people can have false beliefs. Like many of Piaget's classic tasks, the false belief task brings into sharp relief how truly different the world is in some ways for young children as compared with adults. Also like many of Piaget's classic tasks, one can push down the ages at which children "pass" by altering the test situation, but the result with the original version is easily replicable and remains compelling in its own right.

Wimmer and Perner's (1983) study is credited with having begun the avalanche of work examining how children understand the mind. Researchers have studied a range of topics, such as children's understanding of emotion, thinking, perception, and desire (see Flavell & Miller, in press). One topic that has been of particular interest in this realm is pretend play. Indicative of this interest, at the March, 1995 Biennial Meeting of the Society for Research in Child Development (SRCD), more than a dozen presentations directly concerned the issue of pretense and the child's theory of mind (Amsel & Bobadilla, 1995; Bruell, Davis & Thomas, 1995; Davis, 1995; Dockett & Smith, 1995; Gerow & Taylor, 1995; Hickling & Wellman, 1995; Lillard, 1995; Lillard & Seja, 1995; Mitchell & Neal, 1995; O'Reilly, 1995; Ritblatt, 1995; Ruther & O'Reilly, 1995; Youngblade & Bandyk, 1995).

What might pretend play have to do with children's understanding of the mind? There are both theoretical and practical grounds for linking the two activities. On theoretical grounds, it has been claimed that both pretend play and understanding minds rest on understanding mental representation (Leslie, 1987). This has been the subject of most of the experimental work in this area, and it is taken up in the latter half of the chapter. On practical grounds, a number of studies have found positive correlations between pretending and social understanding. An underlying assumption in the field is that these correlations result from pretend play's improving social reasoning, such that pretending has a causal role in developing theories of mind (for discussion, see Harris, 1994; Lillard, 1996). Connolly and Doyle (1984), for example, found that preschoolers' social pretend play was related to affective role-taking and to other measures of social competence. Rubin (1986) reported that children who engaged in more sociodramatic play in kindergarten were rated higher on measures of perspective-taking and social problem solving in grades 1 and 2. More recently, Youngblade and Dunn (1995) found that children who engaged in more pretend role enactment at 33 months performed better on a standard false belief task and an affective perspective-taking task at 40 months of age. Taylor and Carlson (in press) found that 3- to 4-year-olds who score high on a fantasy scale (have imaginary companions, prefer symbolic to functional toys, and so on) excel at false belief and other "theory of mind" tasks (such as the appearance-reality task described later). Finally, Astington and Jenkins (1995) found that making explicit role assignments in pretend play was significantly related to false belief understanding in a sample of 3- to 5-year-olds. These results held in each study even when factors like language ability, verbal intelligence, and age were controlled for. What all these studies seem to have in common is pretending to be someone else. When one has an imaginary companion, one must act and speak for it. When one engages in social pretense, one also tends to take on roles. Supporting the possibility that these associations result from pretense role play having causal force in social understanding, Dockett (1994) found that children who are trained to engage in pretend play pass theory of mind tasks earlier than do those in a control group, corroborating an earlier training study by Chandler (1975) with respect to role-taking (but see Cole & LaVoie, 1985; Rubin & Maioni, 1975; and Rubin & Pepler, 1980).

The evidence weighs in favor of the notion that pretend play might facilitate mentalistic understanding. Below I consider five ways in which pretending might serve this end, focusing separately on its "within frame" and "out of frame" levels. Although this discussion refers to pretend play generally, some of the studies just mentioned found correlations specifically with fantasy predisposition, pretend role play, and social pretend play.

EXPLAINING THE RELATION

Pretending involves two levels: within frame and out of frame. At the out-of-frame level, children negotiate what they are going to pretend, for example, "You be the mommy, and I'll be the daddy," or "Let's say there was a fire in the house." The within-frame level is the level at which the pretense is actually carried out. Pretending and theory of mind are linked on both of these levels.

At the out-of-frame level, pretending might aid in the development of mentalistic understanding because pretending involves a sometimes intensive negotiating of different people's wishes. When pretending, children have multiple opportunities to rub up against the fact that someone else has a different viewpoint: "No, I don't want to be the mommy! I want to be the daddy!" As Garvey and Berndt wrote, "a great deal of speech is devoted to creating, clarifying, maintaining, or negotiating the social pretend experience" (1975, p. 10; see also Giffin, 1984). Negotiation is extremely important since the success of the pretense interaction is dependent on synchronizing the different players' desires. Repeatedly coming up against and needing to resolve different desires in the context of creating a pretend play scenario could help to lay the foundation upon which understanding others' minds might rest.

Particularly important here is that fact that of all the activities children engage in, play (including pretend play) is probably the one in which they are most left on their own to undertake such negotiations. As Piaget suggested, peer engagement might be an especially conducive circumstance for developmental advance. The intensive working-outs of pretending, in which another's desires or concepts must be accommodated or altered to fit with one's own program, therefore form a fine venue for learning about the fact that others do see the world differently (Garvey & Berndt, 1975; Matthews, 1977; Rubin, 1980. See Hartup, 1996 for more general discussion of the role of peers in social cognitive development).

However, although this negotiating of different desires might occur especially frequently in the context of developing pretense scripts, there is nothing in this out-of-frame level of pretending that is really unique to fantasy play. Children might as well be playing games with rules that they are inventing themselves. The really unique aspects of pretending come up at the within-frame level.

There are at least four within-frame ways in which pretending might assist the development of a theory of mind (the first three of these are also discussed in Lillard, 1993a). First, there is the fact of dealing with a world that is not the real, present one. Take the pretense that a bracelet is a piece of cake. At one and the same time, one views the bracelet both as a delectable piece of cake to stuff into one's mouth, and as a plastic bracelet.[1] This is analogous to what one must do when entertaining others' viewpoints, when one must in some sense entertain the idea (attributed to someone else) that the chocolate is in the blue cupboard at the same time as one holds it to be actually in the white cupboard. The ability to think of one situation in two ways at once—essentially decentration—is used both in pretending and in understanding minds (Flavell, Flavell, & Green, 1987; Rubin, Fein, & Vandenberg, 1983). Practicing this ability in pretending might facilitate a skill that could then be transferred to nonpretense domains like representing others' viewpoints at the same time as one represents one's own. This is congruent with the motivation for many pretend play training studies conducted in the 1970s, in which investigators sought to determine if pretend play training could enhance children's conservation skills via decentration (for a review of these studies, see Rubin et al., 1983).

Second, in pretense one thinks of one object or event as "representing" another. The bracelet is not simply a bracelet and a cake; the bracelet *designates* a cake. Exercising this capacity to see one thing as representing another might assist its use in the mental domain, leading to the (implicit) realization that my thought of a cake designates a real cake. As was mentioned earlier, much of the research on pretense and theory of mind is concerned with this parallel (although the factors described in both the previous and the next paragraphs are also central). Some have assumed that in pretense, children understand pretense mental representations as mental representations. As will be seen later, this assertion is controversial. But even if pretending does *not* involve seeing representations *as* representations, it nonetheless must involve using and manipulating one's own and possibly one's play partner's representation of a situation. Perhaps this practice leads to mental flexibility in dealing with mental representations, which then assists more mature thought regarding others' minds.

Third, pretend *role* play can involve social metarepresentation. A child pretending to be someone else may well represent the thoughts, desires, and perceptions of that other person. In pretending to be a firefighter, one both carries out the behaviors that a firefighter carries out and sees the world through the eyes of a firefighter: one hears the fire engine's roar, feels the heat of the fire, thinks about how to rescue the burning man, and so on. Practice at taking on others' perspectives by pretending to be them could assist in the development of a theory of mind (for similar ideas, see Bretherton, 1984; Harris, 1994; Miller & Garvey, 1984). This venue is congruent with one of the major theories of how children develop an understanding of the mind: the simulation theory (Harris, 1992). In this view, children come to understand minds by pretending they are in others' situations.

Finally, pretending could (within frame) assist in the development of a theory of mind by virtue of its content. Children often pretend about conflictful situations (Giffin, 1984), leading to negotiations within the pretend frame. They might have two dolls get into a fight and then seek resolution, for example. Pretending could also lead to additional experiences in dealing with emotions (pretend ones, but emotions nonetheless) and in how different situations evoke different emotions (Garvey, 1990). Real life emotion talk has been shown to be positively associated with later theory of mind performance (Denman, 1994; Dunn, Brown, Slomkowski, Tesla, & Youngblade, 1991); pretend play emotion talk might be associated with such performance as well.

To summarize, there are five ways in which pretending might lead to more advanced social understanding. Outside of the pretend frame, joint pretenders must negotiate the topic and script of their pretense, what different objects denote, and so on. This causes pretenders to face the fact that others have different views, and to go about synchronizing those views. Within the pretend frame, pretending involves seeing one entity as two things at once, seeing one entity as representing another, and representing others' mental representations by "being" another character. These are all skills that are involved both in pretending and in understanding minds, and practice at the one might facilitate the other. Finally, in pretending children often act out intense conflicts and other emotional situations, and this might also help develop the child's theory of mind. Whenever children engage in joint pretense activities there is potential for practicing all five of these skills, which could lay the foundations for or exercise skills relevant to a theory of mind. In these ways, pretending might assist in the development of this fundament of social understanding.

PRETENSE AND MENTAL REPRESENTATION

This section expands on a issue touched upon in the previous one: that of understanding pretense mental representations _as_ mental representations. It first discusses mental representation and its relationship to pretending and a theory of mind. Next it reviews three sets of studies examining whether children understand pretense (a) as a mental representational state, (b) as involving intentions, and (c) as involving the mind at all.

A preliminary issue is that of defining mental representation. Unfortunately, the term "mental representation" does not fare well under scrutiny: philosophers and psychologists are not far along in explaining how objects can also be ideas or how to characterize the relationship between real world objects and ideas. However, for the present purposes the term can be glossed as a mental model of some entity or idea, literally its "re-presentation" inside the mind. That mental model need not match a real world situation or object; there can be cases of misrepresentation, or of representations that are made up fantasy objects never seen to exist in the real world.

Mental representations are subjective: One person's mental representation of something will undoubtedly be somewhat different from another's. This subjectivity is an important feature of minds. People's interactions with the world are based on their subjective mental models of how the world is rather than on direct knowledge of reality. Because of this, a politician can make one group think she is for a certain law while making another group think she is against it, in effect creating two different representations of her position on a single issue. Understanding representational diversity, both between people and within the same person over time, is fundamental social knowledge. For this reason, it is often seen as being at the core of a theory of mind. The understanding is not only important to passing the false belief task;

it is vital to the basic understanding that everyone has their own realities. And it is also the point at which pretending and theory of mind have most commonly been linked by social cognitive theorists, because both skills appear to rely on understanding mental representational diversity.

Pretense clearly involves using mental representations. When one pretends, one projects one's internal, mental representation of something onto some real situation or object (Lillard, 1994). While pretending a pencil is an airplane, I mentally represent it as both these objects. I see it as an airplane and might make it fly, but in keeping with its actually being a pencil I do not try to enter it to fly to Hawaii. And were I to suddenly need a real pencil, I probably would not reject this one on account of its being an airplane. This maintenance of two representations for one entity is cognitively not a simple business, as Leslie (1987) pointed out. In order not to get confused about pencils and airplanes I must keep the pretense representation cordoned off or "decoupled" (Leslie's term) from that to which my airplane representation normally refers: a real airplane. Otherwise I might come to expect real airplanes to be wooden and filled with lead. This keeping separate of the mental representation used in pretense and the real entity (to which that representation normally refers) necessitates, in the minds of many theorists, understanding that our pretense mental representations are only representations, that we can apply them to different objects, and that we can apply multiple representations to the self-same object.

Pretense and understanding false beliefs—a benchmark for understanding the mind—are in a sense conceptually parallel (Leslie, 1987). When one pretends, one keeps a view of a situation in one's mind that is different from reality. For example, if I pretend my backyard is a beach, then I map a pretend representation of a beach on to the reality of my backyard. The pretense representation is a false one, and I entertain it with reference to a real situation: my backyard. Likewise, if I were confused about my whereabouts and I really believed that a beach was just out my back door, then I would be yet again mapping a false representation of a beach onto the reality of my backyard. This parallel has intrigued theory of mind researchers, for the simple reason that children appear to understand pretense long before they appear to understand false belief.

To summarize, then, pretending appears to rely on understanding mental representation. The mystery is that although by two years of age most children are ready and willing pretenders, not until age four do they appear to understand mental representation, at least in the belief domain. How is it that children appear to understand mental representation in pretense but not in belief domains?

The claim that children fail to understand mental representation in belief domains prior to age four is well founded (e.g., Astington, Harris, &

Olson, 1988; Flavell, Flavell, Green, & Moses, 1990; Frye & Moore, 1990; Lewis & Mitchell, 1994; although there are exceptions such as Chandler, Fritz, & Hala, 1989; Winner & Sullivan, 1993). The Maxi paradigm was described earlier; another popular test is the "Smarties" or "deceptive box" task (Gopnik & Astington, 1988; Perner, Leekam, & Wimmer, 1987). A child is shown a bandaid box and asked "What is inside here?" Most children say "bandaids." The box is opened, revealing that it actually contains a toy cow, and the child is asked, "When you first looked at this box, what did you think was inside?" Four-year-olds usually say "bandaids," but 3-year-olds usually claim they thought it contained a toy cow even when they first saw it. Further, they claim that anyone who saw that box, even for the first time, would initially think it had a cow inside (Lillard, 1993b). Many different versions of the so-called "false belief" experiment have been used over the past decade and the great majority have replicated the result that most of the time children under four fail such tasks. Most theorists believe that the reason for their failure is that young children do not understand diversity of representation, neither in themselves over time, nor across individuals.

Two other tasks, developed independently of the false belief work, appear to support the possibility that children fail the false belief task due to a failure to understand mental representation. One is the appearance-reality task (Flavell, Green, & Flavell, 1986). In this task, children are shown a deceptive object such as a candle that looks like an apple. The child is asked what the object looks like to their eyes, and what it really is. The child has to juxtapose two representations of one object: its appearance (apple) and the reality (candle). Children begin to pass this task around age four; prior to that age most children respond that the object appears to be and is a candle. The other task is a Level 2 visual perspective taking task (Flavell, 1990). A drawing of a some object, say a turtle, is placed on a table so its feet face the child and its back faces the experimenter. The child is then asked how it looks to each of them, upside down or right side up. Again, the task requires that the child juxtapose two alternative conceptions of the same reality (the turtle). Children must appreciate that our minds hold models of the world that are subjective, and hence might be unique to the individual. Again, children do not tend to pass until they are about four. Not only do 3-year-olds tend to fail all these tasks while 4-year-olds tend to pass them, but performance on the tasks is actually intercorrelated (Gopnik & Astington, 1988; Taylor & Carlson, in press), so that a given 3-year-old who passes one is quite likely to pass the others, and vice-versa. This lends support to the possibility that all three rely on the same underlying understanding, and that underlying understanding is commonly supposed to be mental representation.

Against this depiction of why children fail these tasks is the case of pretense. As reviewed earlier, to pretend is knowingly to represent reality as other than it is. Leslie (1987; Roth & Leslie, 1994) claims that engaging in pretense is tantamount to understanding mental representation, and that therefore children must be able to understand false belief when they engage in pretense. But if children do not understand mental representation until four, how is it that even younger children so freely and frequently engage in pretend play?

Three reasons have been given. Leslie (1987; Roth & Leslie, 1994) claims that even 3-year-olds must understand mental representation, because of their success at pretend play. He claims that children fail false belief tasks for other reasons, namely due to difficulty drawing inferences about what a person who had never seen a given box would think it contained, or difficulty following the story in the Maxi task. For Leslie, the problem is in the experimental procedure, not the child. However, Leslie appears to ignore that many of these tasks do not require that children draw inferences or follow complex stories. For example, in the Smarties or deceptive box task described earlier, children only need to recall their own past statement. Second, it is unclear how appearance-reality tasks require making an inference. Third, Flavell and his colleagues have found that children cannot pass a false belief task even when it requires only that they repeat back what both the experimenter and the child just said about someone else's belief (Flavell, Flavell, Green, & Moses, 1990; Lillard & Flavell, 1992). Lillard and Flavell (1992) showed 3-year-olds a doll and told them, "He thinks there is juice in that [closed] cupboard." As a control, they immediately asked, "What does he think?" The cupboard was then opened revealing a teddy bear to the child. Importantly, the doll was unable to see inside the cupboard. When asked again, "What does he think is in the cupboard?," 3-year-olds typically changed their previous answer and said "a teddy," failing to attribute a false belief. No inference is required to pass such a task; children need only repeat back what they just heard and said in response to the first control question: "juice." However, 3-year-olds do very poorly on such tasks, incorrectly claiming that the person's thoughts reflect reality. Furthermore, when given the exact same scenarios but with the word "pretend" substituted for "think," 3-year-olds are significantly more likely to correctly claim he is pretending there is juice. The task demands in these two conditions, aside from the demands created by the mental state in question, are identical, so one cannot make claims that the young child's failure is due to extraneous task demands. Because of these factors, Leslie's explanation for the pretense-belief décalage lacks force.

A second explanation is that children understand pretense prior to understanding belief because they are precociously able to understand "joke" or nonserious false mental representations—in other words that pretense mental representation is easier because pretenders do not truly believe in their alternative mental representation of reality (Flavell, Green, & Flavell, 1990; Forguson & Gopnik, 1988; Wellman, 1990). In line with this, Woolley (1995) finds that young children are able to attribute imaginings that do not coincide with reality earlier than they are able to attribute beliefs that do not coincide with reality. Perhaps children understand pretending similarly to how they understand imagining.

A third possibility is that there is no décalage in understanding mental representation in these two domains because in fact children do not have a mental representational understanding of pretense (Harris, 1991; Lillard & Flavell, 1992; Perner, 1991). Perner claims that young children construe pretending as a person's relating to an alternative external situation, rather than a mental situation (Perner, Baker, & Hutton, 1994). Harris has said children might understand pretending as acting as if something else were true, but again pay no heed to the mental aspects of pretending. Likewise, Lillard (Lillard & Flavell, 1992; Lillard, 1993b, 1994) has proposed that young children might construe pretending simply as its external manifestations, like actions and costumes. (For a discussion of these three positions, see Harris, Lillard, & Perner, 1994.) Some recent experimental evidence supports the position that children do not see pretense as a mental representational state, and even suggests that it is not until they are over 8 years of age that children appreciate that everyday acts of pretending are primarily mental processes (Lillard, 1996). (For discussion of the mental components of pretense, see Lillard, 1994.)

Prelude: Pretense With Action

Lillard and Flavell (1992) suggested that young children might understand pretense as action or acting-as-if rather than as a mental state. In this study, mentioned earlier, the experimenter presented children with dolls that were described, for example, as pretending or thinking there was juice in a cupboard, when in fact the cupboard contained a teddy bear. After the teddy bear was revealed to the children, they were asked what the doll had pretended or thought. For the think cases, children usually said the doll *thought* there was a teddy bear. In contrast, in pretense cases, children tended to say that the doll was *pretending* there was juice. This suggests, among other things, that children understand that pretenses can differ from reality earlier than they understand that beliefs can.

However, of critical importance here are two different conditions under which children were presented each mental state. For two of the four trials involving each mental state, the doll was shown to be carrying out an action consistent with the mental state. In the example just described, the doll was (for half the children) getting a cup. The hypothesis underlying this condition was that having an external reality for the child to "anchor" the mental state content would help children to perform better on all of the action cases. However, the action manipulation in fact only improved children's performance for pretense; for the nonaction cases of pretense, children performed no better than they performed on either of the think (action or nonaction) cases.[2] Thus although statistically pretense scenarios were easier overall, in fact that result was carried by the *action* pretense scenarios.

This was a puzzling finding. Why should action be helping children to relate that a pretense differed from reality, when that same action did not help them to see that a thought differed from reality? One explanation is that children do not see pretense as a mental state at all. In the action condition, upon hearing "She's pretending there's juice in the cupboard," children equate the juice-pretense with the action, "getting a cup." In contrast, in the nonaction condition, when the doll was not getting a cup, children perhaps could not process the pretense statement, because they could not conceive of pretending as simply mental representing one thing as another. This would lead to poor performance on the nonaction pretense condition and on both think conditions, which is exactly what was found.

Act I: Does Pretense Require Mental Representation?

Lillard (1993b) set out to address whether young children conceptualize pretense as action, without regard for mental representation. One method used to test this was to present children with dolls who were unable to mentally represent something (by virtue of their out-and-out ignorance of it), but who were nonetheless acting like that thing typically acts. In one experiment, a troll doll named Moe, described as being from "The Land of the Trolls," engaged in various actions, for example, hopping. Children were told that Moe did not know anything about rabbits, not even that rabbits hop, but that he was nonetheless hopping like a rabbit. Control questions were asked to ascertain that children accepted these premises: "Does Moe know that rabbits hop?" and "Is Moe hopping like a rabbit?" (in counterbalanced order). Children were then asked, "Would you say he is pretending he's a rabbit, or he's not pretending he's a rabbit?" Notice that the troll lacked the ability to mentally represent his own behavior as rabbit-like hopping, but he was engaged in the sort of action one would perform were one pretending to be a rabbit. Given these circumstances, 4- and even many 5-year-olds tended to claim Moe was pretending to be a rabbit: the action was more important to their judgment than the mental representational information. Additional experiments addressed various concerns, for example whether children were confused by the troll (since trolls are used to pretend with) and whether children simply could not understand lack of knowledge. The results converged with those of the experiment described above: Children claimed the protagonists were pretending even when the protagonists were other children, and even when the protagonists were not thinking about being the animals in question. Further, it was found that the same subjects who failed the pretense tasks passed a standard false belief task. This last finding, which was replicated in several experiments, suggests that children understand mental representation in belief contexts even earlier than they understand it in pretense contexts. To reiterate, although children appear to understand pretense as action earlier than they appear to understand belief (Lillard & Flavell, 1992), children also fail to understand the mental representational underpinnings of pretense at least until the elementary school years (Lillard, 1993b, 1996). Perhaps this is because children initially learn about pretending before they understand mental representation, and so they focus on the activity part of the construct. Not until many years later, when they have a competent understanding that minds represent, does it dawn on them that those very representations are at the crux of pretending (Lillard, 1993b). This would explain why children apparently understand the mental aspects of imagining prior to understanding the mental aspects of pretense: they were never able to conceive of imagining as action (Woolley, 1995).

It should be noted that these findings are controversial, and several of the recent SRCD presentations mentioned earlier contribute to that controversy (see also Custer, 1996). It is not within the scope of this chapter to provide a detailed analysis of these reports. It is notable, though, that children's success or failure in seeming to understand pretense mental representations in all these experiments seems to rest on a certain feature of presentation. When children are first told that someone is pretending, even older 3-year-olds are quite good at guessing what the person is thinking. However, when told about mental features of a character, such as what she is or is not thinking, and given contradictory behavior, children do not tend to fare as well in stating whether or what she is pretending. This implies that although children can guess what pretenders are thinking (perhaps by simply guessing that they think about what they pretend), they do not understand that pretending always crucially depends on underlying mental representations. Further work will confirm whether this is the case.

Act II: Does Pretense Require Intention?

The aforementioned work suggests that children do not understand the mental representational aspect of pretense until school age. However, there might be mental features of pretense that children do understand earlier, even if they do not understand them as mental features. One possible early acquisition is pretense intention. In pretense the actor always intends a certain pretense, such that the pretense representation is intentionally projected onto reality. In general, desires and intentions appear to be understood earlier than beliefs (Bartsch & Wellman, 1995; Bretherton & Beeghly, 1982; Lillard & Flavell, 1992; Moses, 1993; Wellman & Woolley, 1990). Wellman (1990) has suggested that this is because desires and intentions might be understood without resort to minds, for example, as propensity to get a desired object. Consistent with this, perhaps pretense intention, the fact that pretenders engage in their pursuit on purpose, not accidentally, is understood early.

In one experiment to test this, sixteen 4- and sixteen 5-year-olds were given scenarios similar to the Moe ones just described, but in which the premises referred to intention rather than to knowledge and thought (Lillard, 1995). As an example: "This is Suzy. Suzy is wiggling around. She's not trying to be like a worm—she's just wiggling. But she looks just like a worm— worms wiggle like that." Thus the troll doll had no intention to be worm-like, so adults would not think of her as pretending to be a worm. However, 4-year-olds claimed on 59% of trials that the troll was pretending, and 5-year-olds did so on 47% of the trials. In addition, individual children's response patterns were systematic over four trials, suggesting this was not chance performance. The level of performance was not notably better than that obtained in the Moe studies (Lillard, 1993b), in which the premises referred to the doll's knowledge state and thoughts rather than her intentions.

Perhaps the reason for children's poor performance in this experiment is not that they do not understand pretense intention, but rather that they do not understand the term "trying." A follow-up experiment therefore used a variety of phrases to convey intent. This experiment also sought to determine how performance on the intention task relates to performance on the knowledge and thinking versions. A within-subjects design was used to compare three conditions: a character who did not want to be like an *x*; a character who was not thinking about being an *x*; and a character who did not know about *x*-es. Twenty-four 4-year-olds were told two stories for each of the three conditions, for a total of six stories. An intention story went as follows: "This is Chris. He's a little boy. Right now, Chris is digging. Chris doesn't want to be like a dog. He doesn't like dogs. He's not trying to dig like a dog. But right now he is digging just like a dog—dogs dig just like that." Following two control questions (" Do dogs dig like that?" and "Does Chris want to be like a dog?"), children were asked, "Right now, is Chris pretending he's a dog?" A think story was similar but specified, "Jean isn't thinking about being a monkey. She doesn't have monkeys on her mind. She isn't thinking she's climbing like a monkey," and a know story specified, "Moe doesn't know what a pig is. He's never heard of a pig. He doesn't even know that pigs roll." The animal/action pairs used for each mental state were varied across subjects. The results indicated no significant difference in performance based on condition. Although children did moderately better on the want items (40% correct) than the know items (29% correct), they also did better on the thought items (42%

correct). Hence this experiment leads to the same conclusion as the first: Children do not appear to have a privileged understanding of the intention component of pretense. This is surprising given their generally precocious understanding of desire and intention. It provides further indication that their concept of pretense might be fixed, at least until the elementary school years, as externally manifesting (via action or perhaps costume) some other situation. Further work is investigating whether a pictorial representation of the mental state (a "thought bubble") improves performance.

Act III: Does Pretending Involve the Mind at All?

Given that children do not appear to understand that pretense rests on mental representation or intention, a subsequent question is whether they see it as a mental state at all. Lillard (1996) examined this issue by looking at whether children categorize pretending with other mental states like thinking, or, in contrast, with activities like hopping. Five experiments examining this are described below.

The method used in the first experiment draws on a finding of Johnson and Wellman (1982) that young children claim, in response to simple yes-no questions regarding various activities, that the brain is used for cognitive but not for physical tasks. If children appreciate that pretending is a cognitive activity one would expect them to say it requires a brain, but if they fail to appreciate its cognitive underpinnings they should cluster it with physical activities and deny that it requires a brain. Sixteen children in each of three age groups (3, 4, and 5) were simply asked if the brain was needed to think, imagine, pretend, hop, clap, and so on. Children's answers closely aligned with those of Johnson and Wellman's (1982) subjects for those activities that were asked about in both studies. For example, about 88% of 4- and 5-year-olds understood the brain was needed to think, but only about 12% understood it was needed to clap. Pretending, the mental state of most interest here, fell between the cognitive and physical activities, with about 40% of children at these ages claiming it was needed to pretend. It was unclear, given that each child just answered one pretense question, whether many children in the sample were uncertain and were simply guessing.

Experiment 2 remedied this by asking three pretense questions. It also employed a different method to address the question of whether children construe pretending as being basically mental or basically physical. Sixteen 4- and sixteen 5-year-olds were shown two boxes, and it was explained that one was for things one could do just inside one's head, without using one's body, and that the other was for things one could do just with one's body, without using one's mind.[3] Children were then read various descriptions of activities off of small cards, and were asked which box each card should go in. The descriptions detailed three different types each of thinking (such as think about a puppy, destined for the "mind" box), pretending (pretend you are a tree, a test item), and purely physical activities (fall over, destined for the "body'" box). In this experiment, and others (described later) using the box method, the cognitive and purely physical activities served as controls to ensure children understood the purpose of the boxes. Experiment 2 elicited results similar to those of Experiment 1: About 40% of children at each age treated pretending like thinking and the other mental states, and the remaining 60% denied that the mind is necessary to pretense. Further, most children responded in the same way to all three pretense questions, suggesting they were not simply guessing.

Experiment 3 used essentially the same method, but tested 4-, 6-, 7-, and 8-year-olds and adults on an expanded set of questions to (1) look for developmental trends and (2) see if children show different patterns of responding based on what sort of pretense is being enacted (object, animal, or person). The results gave no indication that children make different decisions about the need for using one's mind based on whether one was pretending to be an object, animal, or person. However, children did not appear haphazard in their choices, and there were distinct developmental trends, with 8-year-olds performing at adult levels on this task: about 85% appeared to view pretense as primarily mental. Four-year-olds were again at about 40% on this score, whereas 6- and 7-year-olds were at about 65%.

A fourth experiment in this line, testing only 4-year-olds, looked at whether children would make more mentalistic claims for other types of pretense (described later). It also incorporated a third box, which was described as being for activities that absolutely needed both a mind and a body. Children rarely chose this box for pretense items, and so it is not discussed further. As controls, there were three items for which adults would be expected to claim "mind" (think), three for "body" (physical process), and three for "both" (i.e., bake a cake). There were also three nonsense items (such as foss you are a feasehosh) to check whether children used the "both" box whenever they were uncertain. The pretense items used in this experiment varied in two ways. First, they ranged from very familiar to exotic (in terms of whether the referent was part of children's everyday reality), and second, they differed in whether the child was asked about pretending to be something else or to be in a different location. Examples of the "exotic" manipulation are "Pretend you are the Lion King" (identity) and "Pretend you are in a jungle" (location), whereas examples of the mundane items are "Pretend you are a puppy" and "Pretend you are in your bedroom." It was hypothesized that because imagining is more clearly involved, pretending to be in a different location and pretending to be more exotic things might elicit more "mind" responses.

Although the location/identity manipulation had no effect, the exotic/mundane manipulation made a significant difference in children's responses, such that 4-year-olds chose the mind box for exotic pretenses on approximately 70% of trials. Further, this difference appeared to hold for all the pretend items that followed an exotic item, even when those pretenses were mundane. Half the subjects always received the exotic Lion King item on their second trial, and overall these subjects chose the mind box for pretense items significantly more often than children who did not hear an exotic item until their final few pretend trials. Offsetting concerns that the two groups were different at the outset, on the one pretense item that all subjects heard prior to hearing an exotic item ("Pretend you are in an airplane," deemed to be intermediate on the exotic/mundane scale), the two groups were equivalent in percentage of "mind" choices (44%). Hence the difference between the groups appears to have been driven by the exotic items themselves clueing in children to a different view of pretense than did the more mundane items. This result has recently been replicated (Lillard & Sobel, unpublished data), and further work will attempt to pinpoint just what it was about the so-called exotic items that made children think about them more mentalistically than they thought about mundane items.

A fifth experiment concerns exactly what aspects of pretending children focused on in choosing their responses. When children pretend, they can be observed to engage in a planning phase in which they decide how various pretenses will be executed, and then in an execution phase in which they go on to execute the pretense. (Obviously these phases are not always distinct, with some further planning occurring during execution phases.) Six- and 8-year-olds were presented with a "Mind" and a "No Mind" box, and were asked in which box various instances of deciding how to pretend something, actually pretending it, thinking about doing something, and actually doing it, belonged. Children's replies indicate that although most 8-year-olds appreciate that the mind is used in planning pretense, less than half appreciate that pretenders use their minds to imagine the pretend situation all the while that they are pretending.

These five experiments, taken together with Lillard (1993b), suggest that young children do not in general think of pretending, at least in its execution, as entailing the mind. They appear instead to think of pretending as a mindless activity. However, the fact that children tend to invoke the mind more often for certain "exotic" pretense items is very intriguing and deserves more investigation. Perhaps it is via such sorts of pretense that children come to appreciate pretense's mental aspects.

CONCLUSIONS

The findings just presented at least suggest some basic difficulties in understanding the mental aspects of pretense. Early on, children do not generally appear to think about pretending as a mental state. However, even if children see pretending simply as its external manifestations, like actions, pretend play still has many connections to a theory of mind. The correlational and training studies support this. This paper discussed five possible origins of this connection. Outside the pretend frame, pretenders negotiate what they will pretend and how, thereby confronting and synchronizing diverse conceptualizations and desires. Within the pretend frame, children practice seeing one object or situation in two different ways at once, and seeing one object as representing another. They also practice taking on others' points of view when they pretend role play. Finally, because the content of pretense is often emotional and conflictful, pretending provides opportunity to practice dealing with such feelings and events. In all these ways pretend play is linked to a theory of mind. Further research should probe these connections to see which are most important for the correlations found between social pretend or role play and understanding minds.

Observing children's pretense can provide educators and psychologists insights into children's theory of mind. Pretend play provides a window on how children represent their worlds, on how they think about internal states and the social order. Watching children's pretending can provide information as to what their major concerns are, how they respond to certain events, and what they are working on. This can indicate what one can expect of a child, and how one might direct efforts at helping the child to further her understanding. Pretending can thereby provide information that adults can use in modifying their expectations and in educating children about minds and subjectivity.

ACKNOWLEDGMENTS

Preparation of this manuscript was supported by grant HD30418 from the National Institutes of Health and grant DGE-9550152 from the National Science Foundation. I am grateful to Jacqueline Woolley and an anonymous reviewer for comments on an earlier version of the manuscript.

NOTES

1. One assumes the two representations are held simultaneously because the pretender does not attempt actually to eat the bracelet, suggesting that she bears in mind that it is made of plastic.

2. For a later experiment in which such a manipulation did work for belief, see Mitchell and Lacohee (1991).

3. Experiment 4 employs a "both" box as well, but children rarely chose it for pretense items.

REFERENCES

Amsel, E., & Bobadilla, W. (1995). *Preschooler's identification of objects' true and pretend identities.* Paper presented at the Biennial Meeting of the Society for Research in Child Development, Indianapolis.

Astington, J. W. & Jenkins, J. M. (1995). Theory of mind development and social understanding. *Cognition and Emotion, 9,* 151–165.

Astington, J. W., Harris, P. L., & Olson, D. R. (Eds.). (1988). *Developing theories of mind.* New York: Cambridge University Press.

Bartsch, K., & Wellman, H. M. (1995). *Children talk about the mind.* Oxford: Oxford University Press.

Bretherton, I. E. (1984). *Symbolic play: The development of social understanding.* Orlando, FL: Academic Press.

Bretherton, I. & Beeghly, M. (1982). Talking about internal states: The acquisition of an explicit theory of mind. *Developmental Psychology, 18,* 906–921.

Bruell, M. J., Davis, D. L., & Thomas, F. J. (1995). *Young children's understanding of representational diversity in pretense.* Paper presented at the Biennial Meeting of the Society for Research in Child Development, Indianapolis.

Chandler, M. J. (1975). Egocentrism and anti-social behavior: The assessment and training of social perspective-taking skills. *Developmental Psychology, 9,* 326–332.

Chandler, M., Fritz, S. A., & Hala, S. (1989). Small-scale deceit: Deception as a marker of two-, three-, and four-year-olds' early theories of mind. *Child Development, 60,* 1263–1277.

Cole, D., & LaVoie, J. C. (1985). Fantasy play and related cognitive development in 2- to 6-year-olds. *Developmental Psychology, 21,* 233–240.

Connolly, J. A. & Doyle, A. (1984). Relation of social fantasy play to social competence in preschoolers. *Developmental Psychology, 20,* 597–608.

Davis, D. L. (1995). *Young children's understanding of pretense as a mental representation.* Paper presented at the Biennial Meeting of the Society for Research in Child Development, Indianapolis.

Denham, S. A. (1994). Socialization of preschooler's emotion understanding. *Developmental Psychology, 30,* 928–936.

Dockett, S. (1994). *Pretend play and young children's developing theories of mind.* Unpublished doctoral dissertation, University of Sydney.

Dockett, S. B., & Smith, I. (1995). *Children's theories of mind and their involvement in complex shared pretense.* Paper presented at the Biennial Meeting of the Society for Research in Child Development, Indianapolis.

Dunn, J. F. (1995, March). *Children's relationships: Bridging the gap between social and cognitive development.* Paper presented at the Biennial Meeting of the Society for Research in Child Development, Indianapolis.

Dunn, J., Brown, J., Slomkowski, C., Tesla, C., & Youngblade, L. (1991). Young children's understanding of other people's feelings and beliefs: Individual differences and their antecedents. *Child Development, 62,* 1352–1366.

Fein, G. G. (1975). A transformational analysis of pretending. *Developmental Psychology, 11,* 291–296.

Flavell, J. H. (1990). *Perspectives on perspective-taking.* Paper presented at the 20th Annual Symposium of the Jean Piaget Society, Philadelphia.

Flavell, J. H., Flavell, E. R., & Green, F. L. (1987). Young children's knowledge about the apparent-real and pretend-real distinctions. *Developmental Psychology, 23,* 816–822.

Flavell, J. H., Flavell, E. R., Green, F. L., & Moses, L. J. (1990). Young children's understanding of fact beliefs versus value beliefs. *Child Development, 61,* 915–928.

Flavell, J. H., Green, F. L., & Flavell, E. R. (1986). Development of knowledge about the appearance-reality distinction. *Monographs of the Society for Research in Child Development, 51,* (1, Serial No. 212).

Flavell, J. H., Green, F. L., & Flavell, E. R. (1990). Developmental changes in young children's knowledge about the mind. *Cognitive Development, 5,* 1–27.

Flavell, J., & Miller, P. (in press). Social cognition. *Handbook of child psychology: Vol. 2. Cognitive development.* (Damon, W., Kuhn, D., & Siegler, R., Eds.) New York: Wiley.

Forguson, L. & Gopnik, A. (1988). The ontogeny of common sense. In J. W. Astington, P. L. Harris, & D. R. Olson (Eds.), *Developing theories of mind.* (pp. 226–243). New York: Cambridge University Press.

Frye, D., & Moore, C. (Eds.) (1991). *Children's theories of mind.* Hillsdale, NJ: Lawrence Erlbaum.

Garvey, C. (1990). *Play* (2 ed.). Cambridge, MA: Harvard University Press.

Garvey, C. & Berndt, R. (1975). *Organization in pretend play.* Paper presented at the meeting of the American Psychological Association, Chicago.

Gerow, L. E., & Taylor, M. (1995). *Children's understanding that pretense is based on mental representation.* Paper presented at the Biennial Meeting of the Society for Research in Child Development, Indianapolis.

Giffin, H. (1984). The coordination of meaning in the creation of shared make-believe play. In I. Bretherton (Ed.), *Symbolic play* (pp. 73–100). Orlando, FL: Academic Press.

Gopnik, A. & Astington, J. W. (1988). Children's understanding of representational change and its relation to the understanding of false belief and the appearance-reality distinction. *Child Development, 59,* 26–37.

Harris, P. L. (1991). The work of the imagination. In A. Whiten (Ed.), *Natural theories of mind* (pp. 283–304). Oxford: Basil Blackwell.

Harris, P. L. (1992). From simulation to folk psychology: The case for development. *Mind and Language, 7* (1 & 2), 121–143.

Harris, P. L. (1994). The child's understanding of emotion: Developmental change and the family environment. *Journal of Child Psychology and Psychiatry, 35,* 3–28.

Harris, P. L., Lillard, A. S., & Perner, J. (1994). Triangulating pretence and belief: Commentary. In C. Lewis, & P. Mitchell (Eds.), *Children's early understanding of mind* (pp. 287–293). London: Lawrence Erlbaum.

Hartup, W. W. (1996). The company they keep: Friendship and its developmental significance. *Child Development, 67,* 1–13.

Hickling, A., & Wellman, H. M. (1995). *Preschoolers' understanding of others' mental attitudes toward pretend happenings.* Paper presented at the Biennial Meeting of the Society for Research in Child Development, Indianapolis.

Johnson, C. N. & Wellman, H. M. (1982). Children's developing conceptions of the mind and the brain. *Child Development, 52,* 222–234.

Leslie, A. M. (1987). Pretense and representation: The origins of "theory of mind." *Psychological Review, 94,* 412–426.

Lewis, C., & Mitchell, P. (Eds.). (1994). *Origins of an understanding of mind.* London: Lawrence Erlbaum.

Lillard, A. S. (1993a). Pretend play skills and the child's theory of mind. *Child Development, 64,* 348–371.

Lillard, A. S. (1993b). Young children's conceptualization of pretend: Action or mental representational state? *Child Development, 64,* 372–386.

Lillard, A. S. (1994). Making sense of pretence. In C. Lewis & P. Mitchell (Eds.), *Children's early understanding of mind* (pp. 211–234). London: Lawrence Erlbaum.

Lillard, A. S. (1997). *Wanting to be it: Children's understanding of pretense intentions.* Unpublished manuscript, University of Virginia..

Lillard, A. S. (1996). Body or mind: Young children's categorizing of pretense. *Child Development, 67,* 1717–1734.

Lillard, A. S. & Flavell, J. H. (1992). Young children's understanding of different mental states. *Developmental Psychology, 28,* 626–634.

Lillard, A. S., & Seja, A. (1995). *Children's understanding of the animacy constraint on pretense.* Paper presented at the Biennial Meeting of the Society for Research in Child Development, Indianapolis.

Matthews, W. S. (1977). Modes of transformation in the initiation of fantasy play. *Developmental Psychology, 13,* 212–216.

Miller, P. & Garvey, C. (1984). Mother-baby role play: Its origins in social support. In I. Bretherton (Ed.), *Symbolic Play* (pp. 101–158). London: Academic Press.

Mitchell, P., & Lacohee, H. (1991). Children's early understanding of false belief. *Cognition, 39,* 107–127.

Mitchell, R. W., & Neal, M. R. (1995). *Children understand their own before they understand another's pretense.* Paper presented at the Biennial Meeting of the Society for Research in Child Development, Indianapolis.

Moses, L. (1993). Young children's understanding of belief constraints on intention. *Cognitive Development, 8,* 1–25.

O'Reilly, A. W. (1995). *Elicited talk about mental states: Desire, belief, and pretense.* Paper presented at the Biennial Meeting of the Society for Research in Child Development, Indianapolis.

Perner, J. (1991). *Understanding the representational mind.* Cambridge, MA: MIT Press.

Perner, J., Baker, S., & Hutton, D. (1994). *Prelief:* The conceptual origins of belief and pretence. In C. Lewis & P. Mitchell (Eds.), *Children's early understanding of mind.* (pp. 261–286). Hillsdale, NJ: Lawrence Erlbaum.

Perner, J., Leekam, S. R., & Wimmer, H. (1987). Three-year-olds' difficulty with false belief: The case for a conceptual deficit. *British Journal of Developmental Psychology, 5,* 125–137.

Premack, D., & Woodruff, G. (1978). Does the chimpanzee have a theory of mind? *The Behavioral and Brain Sciences, 1,* 515–526.

Ritblatt, S. N. (1995). *Theory of mind in preschoolers: False beliefs, deception, and pretense.* Paper presented at the Biennial Meeting of the Society for Research in Child Development, Indianapolis.

Roth, D. & Leslie, A. M. (1994). *Solving belief problems: Toward a task analysis.* Unpublished manuscript, Rutgers University.

Rubin, K. H. (1980). Fantasy play: Its role in the development of social skills and social cognition. In K. H. Rubin (Ed.), *Children's Play. New Directions for Child Development* (Vol. 9, pp. 69–84). San Francisco: Jossey-Bass.

Rubin, K. H. (1986). Play, peer interaction, and social development. In A. Gottfried & C. Brown (Eds.), *Play interactions: The contribution of play materials and parental involvement to child development* (pp. 113–125). Lexington, MA: Heath.

Rubin, K. H., & Maioni, T. L. (1975). Play preference and its relationship to egocentrism, popularity, and classification skills in preschoolers. *Merrill-Palmer Quarterly, 21,* 171–179.

Rubin, K. H., & Pepler, D. J. (1980). The relationship of child's play to social-cognitive growth and development. In H. C. Foot, A. J. Chapman, & J. R. Smith (Eds.), *Friendship and social relations in children* (pp. 209–233). New York: Wiley.

Rubin, K. H., & Howe, N. (1986). Social play and perspective-taking. In G. Fein & M. Rivkin (Eds.), *The young child at play: Reviews of research* (pp. 113–125). Washington, DC: NAEYC.

Rubin, K. H., Fein, G. G., & Vandenberg, B. (1983). Play. In E. M. Hetherington (Ed.), *Handbook of child psychology: Socialization, personality, and social development* (Vol. 4, pp. 693–774). New York: Wiley. (P. H. Mussen, General Editor).

Ruther, N., & O'Reilly, A. W. (1995). *Do preschoolers understand the role of knowledge in pretense?* Paper presented at the Biennial Meeting of the Society for Research in Child Development, Indianapolis.

Custer, W. L. (1996). A comparison of young children's understanding of contradictory mental representations in pretense, memory, and belief. *Child Development, 67,* 678–688.

Stich, S. (1983). *From folk psychology to cognitive science.* Cambridge, MA: MIT Press.

Taylor, M., & Carlson, S. M. (in press). The relation between individual differences in fantasy and theory of mind. *Child Development.*

Vygotsky, L. S. (1978). *Mind in society.* Cambridge, MA: Harvard University Press.

Wellman, H. M. (1990). *The child's theory of mind.* Cambridge, MA: Bradford Books/MIT Press.

Wimmer, H. & Perner, J. (1983). Beliefs about beliefs: Representation and constraining function of wrong beliefs in young children's understanding of deception. *Cognition, 13,* 103–128.

Wellman, H. M., & Woolley, J. D. (1990). From desires to beliefs: The early development of everyday psychology. *Cognition, 35,* 245–275.

Winner, E. & Sullivan, K. (1993). *Young 3-year-olds understand false belief when observing or participating in deception.* Paper presented at Biennial Meeting of the Society for Research in Child Development, New Orleans.

Woolley, J. D. (1995). Young children's understanding of fictional versus epistemic mental representations: Imagination and belief. *Child Development, 66,* 1011–1021.

Youngblade, L. M., & Bandyk, J. (1995). *Pretending with a friend: Associations with early pretense, relationships, and social understanding.* Paper presented at the Biennial Meeting of the Society for Research in Child Development, Indianapolis.

Youngblade, L. M. & Dunn, J. (1995). Individual differences in young children's pretend play with mother and sibling: Links to relationships and understanding of other people's feelings and beliefs. *Child Development, 66,* 1472–1492.

Chapter 3

The Social Origins of Mind: Post-Piagetian Perspectives on Pretend Play

Larry Smolucha and Francine Smolucha

This chapter presents an historical overview of the decline of Piagetian theory as the dominant research paradigm for studies on children's play and recounts the events leading to the simultaneous reemergence of Vygotskian theory during the mid-1980s. A review of the research literature from the 1920s through the early 1990s reveals the principal conceptual and method-ological changes associated with this paradigmatic shift. Briefly stated, Piaget regarded early pretend play as a solitary activity which served only to con-solidate schema that the child already possessed, while Vygotsky, in contrast, regarded early pretend play as a formative activity directly associated with the development of the child's higher mental functions. In Vygotskian theory, play, and consequently the higher mental functions, originate from social interactions between the child and his/her caregivers. Devolving from this theoretical premise, neo-Vygotskian research offers important insights and implications for infant and preschool education, especially in regard to the importance of social interactions between infants and their caregivers as a for-mative influence affecting later cognitive development.

HISTORICAL OVERVIEW

The history of play research does not follow a simple linear develop-mental vector; instead, it is convoluted, twisting back upon itself as contem-porary play researchers look to the past in an attempt to reconstruct the Vygot-skian theoretical perspective of the 1920s and 1930s. Among Western researchers, the interest in reconstructing Vygotskian theory arose first during the 1960s following a belated interest in Piaget's early work of the same period. This reconstruction of Vygotsky's theory, however, has not been an easy task. Stalin banned Vygotsky's works on political grounds in 1936 and, for 20 years following his death, the manuscripts remained virtually inaccessible until Nikita Kruschev finally lifted the political ban against Vygotsky's works in 1956. Soviet researchers have faced similar problems in their attempts to reconstruct Vygotsky's theory from his original manuscripts.

As Vygotsky's works were reissued in Russian and eventually translated into English, various interpretations of his theory were advanced, each framed in accordance with the sociopolitical idealogies and intellectual predispositions of the principal interpreters. Western researchers, having embraced Piaget's assertion that pretend play is nonsocial in origin, suddenly found their basic premise being directly challenged by some "obscure" Russian psychologists who suggested in their sporadic publications that pretend play is learned through social interactions (Vygotsky 1928(29)/1978a, 1933/1967, 1933/1976, 1933/1978b; El'konin, 1966, 1967, 1969). So all-pervasive was the dominant Piagetian perspective that it occasionally biased not only the methodologies employed to test the two opposing hypotheses (Fein, 1975; Nicholich 1977), but even the reviews of the research literature (Rubin, Fein, & Vandenberg, 1983). The behaviorist perspective dominant in American psychology also led to an interpretation of Vygotsky's theory as just another Soviet S-R psychology (Cole, 1979). In the United States the political persecution of "Communist sympathizers" during the 1950s, exacerbated by continuing Cold War tensions, inspired cautious translators and researchers to maintain a prudent distance from Russian psychology.

Meanwhile, in the Soviet Union, Vygotsky's colleague Daniel B. El'konin and his students continued to research Vygotsky's theory of play. Soviet researchers, like their Western counterparts, were forced to rely on sporadic republications of Vygotsky's writings. Disputes arose concerning the proper interpretation of the author's works. To confuse matters further, the post-Stalinist political idealogy of the Soviet Union led to a selective reassimilation of Vygotsky's theory into Soviet psychology by researchers like A. N. Leontiev, V. Zinchenko, and others. Ironically enough, several significant writings by Vygotsky on the development of creativity in childhood and adolescence only reentered the international discussion of Vygotskian theory when an American researcher translated these papers in the 1980s (Smolucha & Smolucha, 1986, 1992; F. Smolucha, 1992a; Vygotsky, 1930/1990, 1931/1991).

Thomas Kuhn's description of scientific revolutions as involving a struggle for dominance between rival research paradigms provides an apt characterization of these historical events (see Smolucha & Smolucha, 1992). According to Kuhn, scientific theories as research paradigms include more than a set of testable hypotheses (Kuhn, 1970, 1977) having imbedded within them various *a priori* philosophical assumptions, cultural beliefs, and tacit analogies that not only influence research methods, but can also confound the outcomes of research in various subtle and unexpected ways. The following survey-analysis of the research literature provides many examples of how Piagetian research methods isolated children's play activities from interactions with their caregivers, thus perpetuating an erroneous assumption that social pretend play does not occur during the first 3 years of life (Piaget, 1923/1973, 1945/1962; Fein, 1975; Rubin, Fein, & Vandenberg, 1983).

JEAN PIAGET'S RESEARCH ON CHILDREN'S PLAY

In *Play, Dreams, and Imitation in Childhood* (1945) Piaget defines pretend play as an act of "pure assimilation" in which activities are repeated solely for the functional pleasure which the reenactment of a sensory-motor schema brings (1945/1962, p. 89). According to Piaget, just as an infant shakes a rattle to enjoy the sensory-motor pleasure of that repeated action, so too a child will use *ludic symbols,* such as using a stuffed animal as a pillow when acting out a play scenario of going-to-sleep, for the simple pleasure afforded by the experience of the reenactment. For Piaget, the simple repetition of the act is a source of pleasure in itself.[1]

Piaget went on to describe how the ludic symbol emerges from the child's own independent sensory-motor activity involving *ludic rituals,* instances of play-acting certain behaviors outside of their normal context (1945/1962, p. 100). An example of this behavior occurred when Piaget's daughter Jacqueline, at 18 months of age, closed her eyes and put her head upon a pillow as if she were going to go to sleep, though it was not time for bed and she did not actually appear intent on sleep. Such ludic rituals gradually come to be accompanied by signs of pretend play such as smiling, verbalizing, acting on an absent object (such as the well-known gesture of bringing one's hands to the side of the head to imitate a pillow), or using ludic symbols involving object substitutions (such as holding onto a toy donkey's tail as though it were the fringe of a pillow). Piaget stated explicitly that the ludic symbol evolved during the sensory-motor stage and was *not* a sign learned through social interaction (Piaget, 1945/1962, pp. 99–100).

Critics of Piaget's work have raised concerns about Piaget's methods of data collection, claiming that he was not sensitive to the social contexts in which he observed his children. Also, Piaget's periodic observations of children engaging in solitary play do not rule out the possibility that some of these play behaviors might have been learned *during previous interactions* with play partners or caregivers such as the child's mother, nanny, or an older sibling. Such criticisms gain further credence in light of the fact that Piaget completely disregarded his wife's activities when she was present during play sessions (1945/1962). In the words of Brian Sutton-Smith,

Piaget had probably seen his infants with Mrs. Piaget a great deal, and, though he usually leaves her out of the pictures, he would undoubtedly have learned to make discriminations of her relationships with the baby that made him feel that these particular examples were play ones. But by leaving her out he also neglects the role of her signals to the baby; that is, he leaves out the social context without which it is difficult to be sure when play occurs. (1986, p. 142)

According to Piaget there were three types of play: *sensory-motor play, symbolic play,* and *rule-governed play.* In the Piagetian scheme of things, sensory-motor play and symbolic play result from the child's own independent actions on the physical world and are not the result of social interactions with caregivers or peers. Piaget's (1945/1962) description of how the infant independently discovers how to shake a rattle (a form of sensorimotor play) can be clearly contrasted with the Vygotskian account in which the caregiver demonstrates rattle shaking to the infant, then assists the infant's attempts to shake the rattle (Moukhena, 1986).

Piaget's own analysis of the play activities of his three children in *Play, Dreams and Imitation in Childhood* (1945/1962) expanded the theory of play which he first introduced in 1923 in his book *The Language and Thought of the Child* (1923/1973). In that earlier work Piaget described play as an expression of egocentric thought forming a transitional stage between autistic thought and realistic thought (1973, pp. 63–66). Although Piaget does state that the concept of autistic thought was originally formulated by the famous psychoanalyst Eugene Bleuler, he neglects to mention that Bleuler introduced the concept to describe the thinking of schizophrenics (1973, p. 63). Piaget also fails to mention that Bleuler did not consider the thinking of normal children to be autistic (Vygotsky, 1932/1962). Apparently Piaget was never challenged to elaborate further on his implicit suggestion of a similarity between the thought processes of children and the autistic thinking of schizophrenics. In fact, most psychologists, with the notable exception of Vygotsky, overlooked the fact that Piaget had based his theory largely on psychoanalytic concepts which he had become acquainted with as a result of his studies with Carl Jung (Fancher, 1990, p. 413).

Piaget's belief that pretend play originated as a solitary activity on the part of the child was derived from his assumption that the child's first thought processes are nonsocial, unrealistic, and serve only to express personal fantasies—all characteristic features of the psychoanalytic concepts of *autistic thinking* and *primary process thought.* In *Language and Thought of the Child*, Piaget clearly stated that thinking begins as autistic or undirected thought which is "not adapted to reality, but creates for itself a dream world of imagination" (1923/1973, p. 63). Realistic or self-directed thought emerged years later as a consequence of increased experience and the socialization process. In Piaget's words,

To put it quite simply we may say that the adult thinks socially, even when he is alone, and that the child under seven thinks egocentrically, even in the society of others.

What is the reason for this? It is in our opinion, twofold. It is due, in the first place, to the absence of any sustained social intercourse among the children of less than 7 or 8, and in the second place to the fact that the language used in the fundamental activity of the child—play—is one of gestures, movement, and mimicry as much as of words. There is, as we have said, no real social life among children of less than 7 or 8 years. (1973, pp. 60–61)

Piaget based these conclusions on his observations of two boys, aged six-and-a-half years, who were attending a morning class at the Maison des Petits de l'Institut Rousseau over a period of one month (1923/1973, pp. 28–29). Piaget's assumption that "these school rooms supply a first-class field of observation for everything connected with the study of the social life and the language of childhood" remains, at best, a highly debatable claim. Since Piaget's theory of egocentric thought was based on observations made in a childcare facility operating according to Rousseau's *laissez-faire* philosophy of education, it should come as no surprise to anyone that a minimum of social learning was observed.

Nevertheless, in the decades following World War II, an impression spread among Western researchers that Piaget's theory on the solitary origins of pretend play had been confirmed through observation and, having only lately adopted the Piagetian perspective, many Western researchers prematurely dismissed Vygotsky's alternative theory, which was then being published in English for the first time (Rubin, Fein, & Vandenberg, 1983, p.717). Additional analyses would later show that early research on Piaget's theory often contained methodological biases (Fein, 1975; Nicolich, 1977) or unintentionally misrepresented research findings, as in the case of Rubin, Fein, & Vandenberg's (1983, pp. 728–729) erroneous description of the results of Dunn and Wooding (1977) study.

RESEARCH SUPPORTING PIAGETIAN THEORY— A CRITICAL REAPPRAISAL

Having thus sketched the overall contours of the situation, we can proceed to a critical reappraisal of the principal research studies often cited as supporting Piaget's theory of play. A close and careful analysis of these studies shows that they do not provide the kind of incontrovertible evidence for the solitary origins of pretend play that they are often cited as presenting.

Because none of them take into consideration the possibility that their results may have been confounded by play interactions occurring outside of the parameters of the study, their interpretations remain equivocal.

Mildred Parten (1932) developed the first formal definition of solitary play and the first actual assessment of it. Although Parten's writings make no reference to Piaget's theories, and it appears that her research arose entirely independently of Piaget, Partens studies are often cited as providing evidence for Piaget's claim that play begins as a solitary activity. A careful reading of Parten's publications, however, reveals that some of her findings are not consistent with Piagetian theory. Parten had observed 42 children, aged 1 year to 5 years, playing in groups at a daycare center where they were not directed by an adult. Parten identified six types of social participation, including: *unoccupied, onlooker, solitary play, parallel play, associative play,* and *cooperative play* (Parten, 1932). While solitary play appeared more frequently among the younger children, there was a significant amount of individual variation in the amount of solitary versus cooperative play observed. (One child demonstrated practically no solitary play at all.) Cooperative group play, however, was most frequently observed among the older children, as Piaget had claimed, and this fact alone is often cited to the exclusion of the other more equivocal data.

Both Parten's studies and Piaget's studies at the Rousseau Institute documented a shift from solitary-to-social play in group facilities where adults did not direct the play activities of the children. Consequently, many researchers assumed that these patterns also characterized the children's play interactions at home. It was not until the 1980s that Western researchers demonstrated that this was not the case and that children could—and did— play in a more sophisticated way when guided by caregivers at home (Dunn & Wooding, 1977; Dale, 1983; Dunn & Dale, 1984; Miller & Garvey, 1984; O'Conell & Bretherton, 1984; Dunn, 1986; Haight, 1989; Smolucha, 1991). These results of these studies are consistent with the findings reported earlier by Israeli researchers who used Vygotskian theory succesfully as a rationale for teaching pretend play in preschools (Smilansky, 1966; Feitelson, 1972).

Hermina Sinclair's (1970) study is also frequently cited in support of Piaget's theory. Sinclair (1970) documented object substitutions during solitary play sessions in infants aged 12-months to 26-months at a nursery school. The infants were seated individually for 15 minutes in front of a collection of toys. The experimenter was *the only other person present* and she interacted with the child *only if the child specifically asked for attention,* which raises the obvious question of how truly "solitary" such play activity could actually be. Three categories of play were identified, these being described as (1) exploratory, (2) combinatory, and (3) pretend play using object substitutions (Sinclair's study does not include any detailed information about the object substitutions, other than to to say that they occurred). At the risk of laboring an already obvious point, it should be mentioned that when a child performs an object substitution while playing alone, that fact does not, of course, obviate the possibility that the child's behavior was learned during previous play interactions with a caregiver outside of the immediate context of the experiment.

Lorraine McCune-Nicolich's (1977) study is of historical importance here, because her work has been cited as a definitive study confirming Piaget's theory of the solitary origins of pretend play (Rubin, Fein, & Vandenberg, 1983, p. 717). Five female subjects, who ranged in age at the beginning of the study from 14 months to 19 months, were observed on a monthly basis over a period of one year as they engaged in pretend play activities at home.

A careful reading of the instructions given to the mother reveals that this was not really a study of solitary play. "Mothers were instructed not to make play suggestions to the child, but to respond as naturally as possible to any child-initiated overtures inviting them to join in play" (McCune-Nicolich, 1977, p. 91). While the mothers were told not to direct the play activities, no report was made of the mothers' behaviors, so it is impossible to know to what extent, if at all, the mothers actually followed these directions. Several comments made by McCune-Nicolich indicated that the mothers did, in fact, initiate some of the object substitutions. It should be noted that one of the criteria used for assigning the level of play was "the source of the scheme, that is, whether it is derived from the child's own activity or from the observed activity of others" (McCune-Nicolich, 1977, p. 91). McCune-Nicolich also specified that,

> The complexity of the incident itself, whether it had been suggested by the mother earlier in the session, and the supporting occurrences [the amount of assistance provided] at that level would need to be considered for the child to be credited with that level of play. (McCune-Nicolich, 1977, p. 91)

Contrary to the popular misinterpretation of it, the McCune-Nicoloch study did not actually provide documentation of the solitary origins of pretend play but rather documented the *levels of the children's independent activities* when their mothers were no longer providing assistance.[2]

The methodology in *Greta Fein*'s (1975) study illustrates how the Russian theory of social interaction has been misinterpreted as a "theory of imitation." Fein (1975) studied how children aged 22 months to 27 months responded to object substitutions involving varied levels of abstraction: (1) feeding a 3-D stuffed toy horse from a cup, (2) feeding a 2-D metal silhouette horse from a cup, and (3) feeding the 2-D metal silhouette horse from a clam shell. The objects were presented to the subjects in three different ways: (1) presented without instructions along with other objects which were then removed by the experimenter, (2) "modeled" by the experimenter (who pretended to feed the horse, saying *yum-yum* and smacking her lips), and (3) presented along with the experimenter's direct verbal suggestion that the child feed the horse. In each case the subject's mother was present, but had been instructed not to interact with her child.

Fein concluded that the ability to perform the most abstract object substitutions (i.e., feeding the silhouette metal horse from a clam shell) became more frequent with age. Fein also found that the experimenter's "modeling" of the play behavior did not produce more substitutions than simply presenting the objects to the child with no instructions, a finding which Fein then interpreted as disproving the Russian theory that children learn to do object substitutions through play interactions with other people (El'konin, 1966). Significantly enough, El'konin's term *modeling* was misinterpreted in Fein's study to mean learning by imitating a role model—along the same lines as Bandura's use of the term *modeling* (Bandura, 1976). A more accurate portrayal of El'konin's theory, however, would have involved not merely acting out a play behavior in front of the child, but rather engaging the child in a play *interaction* in which the adult *demonstrated an object substitution* and then *assisted the child in his/her reenactment* of the adult's behavior (El'konin, 1978). This misinterpretation is understandable, however, since Western researchers in the early 1970s were unfamilar with Vygotsky's concept of assisted learning in the zone of proximal development (1934/1978) and most researchers were also unaware of the fact that El'konin's theory derived from his collaboration with Vygotsky on play research during the 1930s (1978).

As we have shown, the empirical basis for Piaget's theory—the idea that play originates from the child's own solitary activities rather than interactions with caregivers—was greatly overstated by researchers during the 1960s and 1970s. A careful reading of the research literature reveals that researchers appear to have ignored instances of caregiver-child interactions and restricted their observations to what the child could accomplish alone or with children of the same attainment level; thus, little evidence of early collaborative play was discovered.

ALTERNATIVE PERSPECTIVES ON EARLY PRETEND-PLAY INTERACTIONS

Western research on social pretend play in early childhood proceeded slowly since any suggestion that social pretend play might begin as early as the second year of life was likely to be dismissed out-of-hand by most traditional play researchers, virtually all of whom had adopted the Piagetian model. Mounting evidence, however, gradually established the fact that many, but not all, caregivers were actively involved in pretend play interactions with children as young as 12 months of age. Until the mid-1970s, however, many researchers remained hesitant to make the explicit claim that the children were actually learning how to do pretend play from their caregivers and more advanced peers; so strong was the prevailing Piagetian paradigm.

The research studies surveyed below all document pretend play as a *collaborative activity* of early childhood although the individual studies vary in the degree to which they analyze the data for evidence of the children's having learned how to play from more experienced play partners.

The work of Cambridge researchers *Judy Dunn and Carol Wooding* (1977) constitutes a turning point in Western research on the origins of pretend play, being the first study to report evidence of mother-initiated pretend play. (Even the early Russian studies reported by El'konin neglect the role of the mother, focusing instead upon interactions between children and their preschool teachers.) In Dunn and Wooding's study, 24 children aged 18 months to 24 months were observed at home with their mothers during periods when the mother did housework and while she was relaxing. Significantly enough, the researchers found that play periods were longer when the mother was paying attention to the child, indicating a social dimension to the play situation. Also of significance was the fact that while the majority of play sequences were initiated by the child, few were completed by the child without maternal assistance. Mothers initiated 42% of the play with representational objects, *39% of the pretend play,* and 29% of the sensori-motor play. As a consequence of these findings, Dunn and Wooding concluded that the Russian theory of symbolic play being social in origin must remain open for consideration.

Dunn and Wooding's 1977 study was misrepresented in Rubin, Fein, and Vandenberg's review of play research literature (1983, pp. 728–729) as failing to support the "social learning theory" that play originates in social interactions, a criticism inconsistent with the actual reported empirical data. The Rubin, Fein, and Vandenberg review further states that while there was research demonstrating that pretend play *can be taught in training sessions by researchers,*[3] there was no evidence that children learned how to do pretend play from their parents (Rubin, Fein, & Vandenberg, 1983, p. 728). The reviewers seem to dismiss the salient possibility that some children might have learned pretend play from their parents, or even that this possibility might warrant further investigation.

Subsequent research by Judy Dunn and her colleagues, however, has further documented that the time spent by children in collaborative pretend play with mother or sibling was far greater than the time spent in solitary play, but with very wide individual differences (Dale, 1983; Dunn & Dale, 1984; Dunn, 1986). These findings suggest that some mothers are better than others at teaching their children how to do pretend play.

Other researchers have published additional observations of early collaborative pretend play yielding data similiar to that reported by Judy Dunn and her colleagues. The publication of *Symbolic Play: The Development of Social Understanding* (1984, Ing Bretherton, editor) heralded the decline of the Piagetian perspective and the emergence of the social-origins perspective associated with Vygotsky's theory.

Gestures aimed at reconciling these two theories were overshadowed by three new studies in *Symbolic Play* that gave additional evidence of the fact that caregivers and siblings were guiding early pretend play. *Peggy Miller and Catherine Garvey* (1984) reported a discourse analysis that illustrated how mothers "guided, structured, modeled, and taught" their daughters how to play with a baby doll in observations made from 18 to 38 months of age. *Barbara O'Connell and Ing Bretherton* (1984) conducted a study with 15 girls and 15 boys observed at an average age of 20 months and again at 28 months in two different observational contexts: a 15-minute independent play session at the child's home and, 2 or 3 days later, a 5-minute independent play session with the mother in a laboratory setting. O'Connell and Bretherton found that the subject children demonstrated a greater diversity of play activities when paired in collaboration with their mothers than when they played alone. *Judy Dunn and Naomi Dale* (1984) likewise reported "evidence for collaboration in social role play by 18-month-olds and 24-month-olds" during interactions at home with mothers and older siblings. Individual differences in the participation of mothers and siblings appeared very marked (which confirms Dunn and Wooding's 1977 study).

As evidence for cooperative pretend play with caregivers during the second year of life grew, studies began to investigate the exact role of the caregiver in such interactions. Research attempted to clarify whether the caregivers were teaching the children how to play or merely supporting the children's play efforts. By the end of 1980s, research had shifted its emphasis to the benefits associated with a caregiver's guidance of the child's early pretend play. *Arietta Slade* conducted a longitudinal study of 16 children from 18 months to 30 months of age and found that "the level of play is highest when the mother both initiates play and actively interacts with the child while playing" (Slade, 1987, p. 373). Slade, however, interpreted her findings as supporting Werner and Kaplan's theory of symbol formation and made only a passing refence to Vygotsky's theory. In a longitudinal study conducted in the home, *Wendy Haight* (1989) found that the percentage of play involving the mother decreased from 87% at 12 months of age to 50% at 48 months, while pretend play with another child increased from 12% at 24 months of age to

50% at 48 months. This finding suggests that the role of the caregiver in play activities is later transferred to a sibling/peer play partner.

Patricia Zukow's (1989) cross-cultural study conducted in the United States and in central Mexico showed that children aged 11 months to 30 months performed at a higher level of play during interactions with their mother or an older sibling than when playing alone. Zukow interpreted this finding as supporting Vygotsky's theory that play interactions create a zone of proximal development where the child is able to perform at a higher level with the assistance of a more experienced play partner (Zukow, 1989, pp. 89–90). In a study of 57 toddlers, *Barbara Fiese* (1990) reported that the subject children performed more complex forms of symbolic play when engaged in reciprocal turn-taking play with their mothers than when playing alone. Fiese carefully qualified her conclusions by stating that "this study does not directly assess Vygotsky's proposed zone of proximal development (Vygotsky, 1978). It highlights, however, one way in which apprenticeship interactions may influence symbolic process" (Fiese, 1990, p. 1654). *Laura Biezer and Carollee Howes* (1992) have also found that mothers frequently guided the pretend play of toddlers, and that toddlers engaged in more elaborate pretend play with their mothers than when playing alone.

With a growing number of studies confirming that caregivers actively guided, structured, modeled, or taught children play activities, the next logical step from a methodological perspective would have been to test Vygotsky's theory in a formal experiment by manipulating caregiver-guided play as an independent variable—something that no researcher had actually done. The reason why this rather obvious next step had not been taken by this time is a complex one. None of the previous studies had done a sufficiently detailed analysis to provide experimenters with a clear operational description of exactly what sort of behavior(s) the caregiver should perform to stimulate children's play. Simply directing the mother to "play with her child" in a reciprocal turn-taking interaction was too ambiguous to provide a workable description of exactly what the mother was to say and do. Something more was necessary, but what exactly this involved no one could say with any real clarity. What researchers needed at this point were additional observations of the caregiver's scaffolding behaviors in order to pinpoint the salient activities involved in the mother-child play interaction.

The research of *Francine Smolucha* (1991, 1992b, 1992c) provides a description of the specific strategies used by caregivers to demonstrate, elicit, and interpret object substitutions during pretend play with children as young as 14 months of age. The graphed data from Smolucha's study illustrates how the novice play partner's skill level gradually approaches the performance level of the more expert play partner, a finding that supports Vygotsky's theory of teaching in the zone of proximal development (see Figure 3.1).

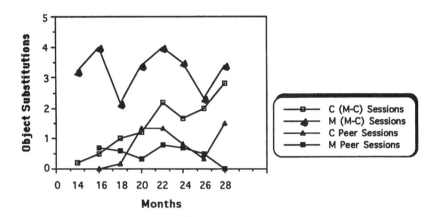

FIGURE 3.1
THE AVERAGE NUMBER OF CHILD- AND MOTHER-INITIATED OBJECT SUBSTITUTIONS
IN MOTHER-CHILD AND PEER SESSIONS

Beginning at 14 months of age, 6 mother-child dyads were observed during 30-minute play sessions at two month intervals. From 16 months on, a peer-play session was also added involving a second child. Both the mother-child and peer-play sessions were repeated at 2-month intervals until the subjects reached the age of 28 months.[4] The mothers were told to do whatever they would normally do if they had a half-hour free. The observations were made in a home environment, where replica toys were provided to be used as the principle play objects (dolls, table, and chairs). A variety of nonreplica items (bottle lids, buttons, blocks, boxes, handkerchief) were provided for use as supplementary props. The inclusion of nonreplica items was done to test Fradkina's claim that object substitutions originate when a supplementary replica toy is missing and another object has to be pressed into service in its place, as when using a button to serve as a toy dish (Fradkina's dissertation from the 1940s as cited in El'konin, 1978).

Once again, a wide variation was evident in the mothers' level of involvement in their children's play, the same finding also reported by Dunn and her colleagues. Evidence indicated that the more expert mothers were able to communicate their play skills to their children.[5] The children of the mothers who initiated the most object substitutions at the beginning of the study also initiated the most object substitutions by the end of the study ($p < .01$). Figure 3.1 compares the average number of object substitutions performed by the subject children and their mothers during the mother-child sessions and during the peer sessions.

During the mother-child play sessions, mothers initiated an average of three object substitutions per session, while the number of child-initiated object substitutions gradually increased, eventually matching the mothers' average by the end of the study. Fluctuations in the mothers' and children's behavior appear to be synchronized, suggesting that varied levels of expert assistance stimulated the performance level of the novice play partner (cf., Vygotsky's *zone of proximal development*). The fact that the subject children showed a preference for their own mothers as play partners during peer sessions, along with the absence of any cooperative play among peers, demonstrates further that subject performance improved with the availability of a more experienced play partner.

As Figure 3.2 shows, it was not until 26 months that child-initiated object substitutions surpassed the number of object substitutions made as immediate re-enactments of mother-initiated object substitutions.[6] Fifty-two percent of the child-initiated object substitutions imitated substitutions made originally by the mother during a previous play session. The earliest *original* child-initiated substitutions (i.e., those that could not be traced back to the mother's previous behavior) tended to involve overgeneralization of objects marginally different from each other: putting a stacking cup to the lips, using a tiny replica pitchfork or shovel as silverware, or bringing toy blocks to the mouth as if food.

In a separate analysis of play with invisible substances (e.g., pretending that there was food on an empty spoon), the children's actions at 24 months surpassed that of their mothers. Moreover, an analysis of the levels of scaffolding behavior occurring in the child-mother interactions found that at 28 months the children were *actively directing their mother's play behavior.* A discourse analysis of the children's private speech in the later play sessions

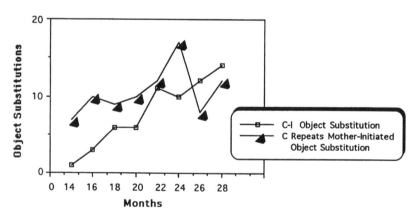

FIGURE 3.2
CHILD-INITIATED VERSUS CHILD-REPEATED OBJECT SUBSTITUTIONS
FROM ALL SESSIONS COMBINED

revealed a direct correspondance to the mother's verbal instructions from earlier play sessions (Smolucha, 1992a). All these data analyses are consistent with Vygotsky's concept of how assisted learning can elevate a learner's performance to a higher level of functioning, illustrating the concept of teaching in the zone of proximal development.

Table 3.1 lists the basic components of pretend play interactions observed between caregiver-child dyads during the second year of life (source: F. Smolucha, 1991).

Attempts to describe the discrete stages of social pretend play have produced two different models (Howes 1992; and Bugrimenko & Smirnova, 1994),[7] both of which are contradicted by the findings of F. Smolucha's study

TABLE 3.1
BASIC COMPONENTS OF PRETEND PLAY INTERACTIONS DURING THE 2ND YEAR OF LIFE

Caregiver Behaviors: (listed in increasing levels of assistance)

(1) Verbal prompts—*Imperative:* "Use this as food"
—*Interpretive:* "Are you pretending to cut the food?"
—*Elaboration:* "Yum, yum. That tasted good."
—*Suggestive:* "Let's pretend that this box is a bed."
—*Explanatory:* "These are really just bottle caps, but we can pretend that they are dishes on the table."
—*Reinforcing:* "That's right."
—*Corrective:* "Don't put that in your mouth!"

(2) Specific verbal directions—"Here, we can pretend this block is food. Put it on the table and cut it with your toy knife."

(3) Physical assistance—Use of pointing gestures to accompany verbal prompts, arranging or assembling things, holding things so that they do not fall over.

(4) Demonstrations—Acting out the play behavior while using verbal prompts.

Elementary Play Scripts:

Care of a baby (feeding, bathing, going to bed)
Playing house (cooking, setting table, washing dishes, bathing, going to sleep)

Elementary Object Substitutions

blocks → food, baby bottle   buttons → dishes
bottle caps/lids → dishes, pots   stacking cups → drinking cups, bathtub, pots
boxes → beds, bathtubs   handkerchiefs → blankets

Basic Replica Toys:

Baby doll, doll family, table and chairs

Source: F. Smolucha, 1991

(1991). These contradictory findings, however, may be due to the fact that social pretend play can be expected to vary under the influence of different sociocultural factors.

The stage model of *Carollee Howes* et al. (1992) proposes that at 21–24 months the mother's role changes from that of structuring the child's play to that of becoming a play spectator. This was not the case, however, in F. Smolucha's study (1991), where the mothers remained actively engaged in pretend play, but changed the ways in which they interacted with their children. Smolucha also found that the children introduced play scripts earlier than the 25 months of age identified in Howes's stages.

Elena Bugrimenko and Elena Smirnova (1994) have proposed five stages in the development of object substitution skills during symbolic play. These stages, briefly summarized below, span an age range from 18 to 30 months.

> *Stage 1 (occurring at age 18 months):* Children play only with realistic toys and show no interest in object substitutions performed by adults (a finding not corroborated by Smolucha's study [1991] as evidenced in Figure 3.2).
> *Stage 2:* Children automatically imitate adult-initiated object substitutions, but do not appear to understand that one object has been substituted for another.
> *Stage 3:* Children independently imitate object substitutions previously performed by an adult.
> *Stage 4:* Children initiate their own object substitutions, but do not rename the objects with substitute names. (Note: In Smolucha's study (1991), children used and renamed substitute objects as early as 18 months.)
> *Stage 5 (occurring at age 3 years):* Children originate and rename substitute objects.

The preceeding research literature has demonstrated that social pretend play occurs as early as 12 months of age. Moreover, an increasing number of studies have indicated that much of early pretend play is learned through play interactions with a caregiver; as a consequence, Vygotsky's cultural/historical theory has emerged as the principal theoretical paradigm in this research domain. In Vygotsky's writings, the child's learning how to do pretend play is not treated as an end in itself, but rather as a step in the development of the child's higher mental functions (Vygotsky, 1928(29)/1978a, 1930/1990, 1931/1991, 1932/1960, 1933/1978b). The following overview[8] of Vygotsky's theory can serve as a guide for future investigations into the role of social pretend play as a means of enhancing sociocognitive development.

SOCIAL PRETEND PLAY AND THE
HIGHER MENTAL FUNCTIONS

Lev Vygotsky provided a theoretical model describing how thought develops from an external social activity into an internal mental process. He referred to this process as the development of the *higher mental functions*, that is to say, those thought processes which an individual is able to consciously direct by means of *inner speech*. It is this silent inner speech that enables the individual to regulate her own thoughts as if she were directing the actions of another person. Vygotsky's theory of inner speech has been supported by decades of empirical research (Berk, 1992).

Vygotsky introduced his general theory in 1924. The first description of his research on play appears in a lecture given in 1928 or 1929, which was later published as *The Prehistory of Written Language* (Vygotsky 1935, 1928–29/1978a). In this treatise Vygotsky discussed the gestural-symbolic nature of the object substitutions made during pretend play.

The child's own movements, his own gestures are what assign a symbolic function to the corresponding object, that communicate meaning to it. All symbolic representational activity is full of such indicatory gestures; thus, a stick becomes a riding-horse for the child, because it can be placed between the legs and it is possible to apply a gesture to it, which will indicate to the child,[9] that a stick in this case designates a horse.

From this point of view children's symbolic play can be understood as a very complex system of speech with the help of gestures, communicating and indicating the meaning of different playthings. It is only on the basis of these indicatory gestures that playthings gradually acquire their own meaning, just as drawing, at first supported by gesture becomes an independent sign. Only from this point of view is it possible for science to explain two facts, which up to this time still have not had a proper theoretical explanation.

The first fact consists in this, that for the child anything can be anything in play. This can be explained thus, the object itself acquires an unction and a symbolic meaning only thanks to the gesture, which endows it with this. From here follows the idea that meaning consists in the gesture and not in the object. That is why it is unimportant what an object is in any given case. The object is only a point of support for the corresponding gesture.

The second fact consists in this, that it is only early in the play of 4- to 5-year old children that the verbal conventional symbol appears. Children agree among themselves "this will be a house for us, this is a plate" and so on; and at about this age extraordinarily rich verbal connections arise, indicating, explaining, and communicating the meaning of each movement, object, and action. The child not only gesticulates, but also converses, explaining his own play. Gesture and speech mutually intertwine and are united. (1935, pp. 77–78, F. Smolucha trans.)

Vygotsky goes on to describe the research that he conducted to determine what types of object substitutions a child would perform during play activity.

The object itself performs a substitution function: a pencil substitutes for a nursemaid or a watch for a drugstore, but only the relevant gesture endows them with meaning. However, under the influence of this gesture, older children begin to make one exceptionally important discovery—that objects can indicate the things they denote as well as substitute for them. For example, when we put down a book with a dark cover and say this will be a forest, a child will spontaneously add, "yes, it's a forest because it's black and dark." She thus isolates one of the features of the object, which, for her, is an indication of the fact that the book is supposed to be a forest. . . . Thus, the object acquires a sign function with a developmental history of its own that is now independent of the child's gesture. This is second-order symbolism, and because it develops in play, we see make-believe play as a major contributor to the development of written language—a system of second-order symbolism (Vygotsky, 1935, pp. 79–80, F. Smolucha trans.; cf. Vygotsky, 1978a, pp. 109-110).

In *Play and Its Role in the Mental Development of the Child* (1933) Vygotsky stated that play creates a "zone of proximal development" for the preschool child (1978b, p. 102). In another paper written at that time (1933–1934), Vygotsky defined the zone of proximal development as *"the distance between the actual developmental level as determined by independent problem solving and the level of potential development as determined through problem solving under adult guidance or in collaboration with more capable peers"* (italics in the original text, from Vygotsky, 1978c, p. 86).

Vygotsky's statement that play creates a zone of proximal development has been eccentrically interpreted by some researchers to mean that *solitary play* also creates a zone of proximal development (Gaskins & Goncu, 1988). This, however, is inconsistent with the basic premise of Vygotsky's general theory, which states that the higher mental functions result from the internalization of *speech interactions* with a more knowledgeable person. There is no indication in any of Vygotsky's writings that he later abandoned his earlier theory of social interactions, or that he regarded pretend play as an exception to the rest of his theoretical framework.

The interpretation of Vygotsky's theory of symbolic play as originating in social interactions is consistent with Daniel El'konin's interpretation of Vygotsky's theory of play (El'konin, 1978). (El'konin and Vygotsky began to collaborate on play research in 1932.) The writings of El'konin, as well as Bugrimenko and Smirnova (1994, p. 291), refer to extensive Soviet research demonstrating that adult guidance is necessary for the development of pretend play.

Vygotsky claimed that the child's use of object substitutions in play serves an important role in the development of creativity as well as in the child's development of the capacity for abstract thought. In *Imagination and Creativity in Childhood* (1930/1990) Vygotsky stated,

> Already at an early age we find children have creative processes, which are expressed in children's play. The child who straddles a stick imagining that he is riding a horse, or the girl who plays with a doll imagining herself the mother, or the child who in play changes into a highwayman, a Red Army soldier, or a sailor—all these playing children represent examples of early forms of creativity. (1930/1967, p. 7)

For Vygotsky, the simple object substitutions made during pretend play signal the beginning of the development of creativity as a higher mental function, a self-directed higher order mental skill that will eventually reach its full mature expression in adulthood. Vygotsky introduced his theory of creative imagination in his paper "Imagination and Creativity in Childhood" (1930/1967). The idea of creativity as a higher mental function was elaborated further in "Imagination and Creativity in the Adolescent" (1931/1991) and in "Imagination and its Development in Childhood" (1932/1960). The importance of Vygotsky's theory lies in its view of creativity as a higher mental function capable of maturing beyond the skill levels evident in childhood, thus Vygotsky removes creativity from the sphere of simple regressive behaviors.

IMPLICATIONS FOR RESEARCH AND EDUCATION

While many preschool educators already recognize the importance of guided pretend play (Gowen, 1995; Smolucha & Smolucha, 1996), pioneering work remains to be done on pretend play interactions with infants. It is expected that as infant enrichment programs become more common, the term *preschool education* will eventually be extended to cover the entire period from birth through 6 years of age.

Certainly the suggestion that infants only a few weeks old can engage in social pretend play interactions seems absurd under the Piagetian paradigm. And, indeed, while Piagetian theory dominated American child psychology, caregivers were not expected to engage in stimulating social interactions with infants and toddlers. The caregiver could be content with providing age-appropriate sensory-motor toys for the infant's own solitary exploration and manipulation. This *laissez-faire* approach was compatible with other societal trends including (1) the growing economic need for more mothers to work and, thus, spend less time interacting with their infants; (2) the increased workload of daycare workers and preschool teachers; and (3) the sale of educational toys, which has become a lucrative industry.

The alternative perspective represented by Vygotskian theory views caregiver-infant social interactions as essential for the children's cognitive development. Research has demonstrated that *language-based play interactions* can accelerate the sociocognitive development of normal infants as well as remediate developmental delays in at-risk infants (Fowler, 1995; Fowler, Ogston, Roberts-Fiati, Swenson, in press). Using a diverse sample of 160 infants, Fowler's intervention program consistently produced 20-point increases in IQ scores that have lasted well into the teen years. Caregivers in Fowler's program began by imitating the infants and encouraging their further vocalizations as early as 6 weeks of age. Objects were named during routine caretaking activities and during play with replica toys. Gradually, over the next 6 years, more complex grammatical structures were introduced.

While Fowler's program focused upon the conventional naming of replica toys, it did not utilize object substitution as part of the play scenario. Research needs to be done on how very young infants learn to use object substitutions during pretend play and how these influence later cognitive development. Object substitutions and their linguistic countpart *metaphors* become part of the infant's socialization experience from birth. Perhaps the most well known example being the pervasive metaphor of the cradle-as-ship (either of the sea or sky) found in many lullabies, nursery rhymes, and in the various decorative items intended for children's rooms. Early pretend play involving object substitution is also experienced when an infant is bounced upon a caregiver's knee—renamed as a *horse*—in what often becomes the first instance of sociodramatic roleplay. Cross-cultural research would reveal the relative frequency and variation in use of such metaphors and object substutions.

The design of effective language-based play enrichment programs is dependent upon certain general principles. In the two-volume *Potentials of Childhood* (Fowler et al, 1983), William Fowler emphasizes the complex interrelationship of earliness, duration, and intensity/frequency as primary variables affecting the outcome of cognitive-stimulation programs. The importance of these three variables are further corroborated by the failure of many Headstart programs to produce lasting gains in the ability levels of children who enter late (after the third year), remain in the program for shorter periods of time, or with less frequency of participation. As Fowler points out, however, data have indicated that earliness alone—the age at which a child starts the program—is not solely responsible for the cognitive gains regularly attained. Intensity/frequency of participation and duration of participation greatly magnify the cognitive effects. Behind this lack of participation is the erroneous belief, commonly found among the general public and in certain quarters of the professional community, that enrichment programs inherently traumatize the child emotionally because they accelerate learning. Contemporary research on infant development has revealed quite the contrary; it is the absence of social interactions, a form of child neglect, that is detrimental to normal infant development.

Caregiver-infant interactions can be enhanced by several factors, none of which require a labyrinthine bureaucracy heavily funded by tax dollars to implement. First, the increasing number of people who work at home has reduced the number of hours wasted commuting, thereby allowing parents to spend more time interacting with their infants. Second, the techniques for enriching infant sociocognitive development are easy to learn and play-like in their simplicity, which simplifies the training of caregivers. These enrichment techniques can be easily and inexpensively disseminated through videotapes broadcast on public television, circulated free through public libraries, or distributed along with textbooks. Free seminars could be offered at hospitals, park district programs, and schools. A minimal amount of money from government agencies, private foundations, or interested corporations could launch such initiatives. More elaborate training programs could be offered to families who are at risk for developmental delays.

Studies of the social origins of children's pretend play have yielded valuable insights into the processes of learning, symbol-making, and creative imagination. Within this context Vygotsky's research has played a pivotal role by establishing that the higher mental functions owe their very existance to social dialogues between the caregiver and child that become internalized as the child's self-regulatory inner speech. The implications of this discovery for early childhood education are profound. Early play interactions not only establish attitudes and values, but virtually create the child's higher mental functions—including logical thought and creative imagination. The fields of multicultural education, remedial education, and psychotherapy (Smolucha, 1994) can be expected to benefit from future research into the social origins of pretend play, as will future generations of children.

NOTES

1. The idea of reptition for the sake of the simple pleasure afforded by the experience of the reenactment derives from Karl Groos's concept of *function lust* (Piaget, 1945/62).

2. At the 1989 conference of the *Society for Research in Child Development*, Francine Smolucha asked Lorraine McCune about the seemingly paradoxical fact that her study has been cited by Rubin, Fein, and Vandenberg as confirming Piaget's stages of solitary pretend play and yet McCune's journal article refers to mother-child play interactions. Lorraine McCune replied that she had always regarded her study as a study of social pretend play.

3. During the 1960s Israeli researchers familiar with the writings of Soviet psychologists Vygotsky and El'konin had demonstrated the benefits of teaching preschool children how to do pretend play (Smilansky, 1968; Feitelson & Ross, 1973). Researchers in the West who took an interest in these Israeli "training studies" apparently did not realize that this research derived from Russian theories that had been dismissed as implausible.

4. The peer sessions began at 16 months.

5. When the study had been completed the mothers were asked to recall whether the mother or the child had initiated certain object substitutions. All of the mothers who had initiated object substitutions mistakenly thought that their child had initiated the object substitutions. This suggests that the mothers were not conscious of their role in teaching the child how to play pretend.

6. These totals include all object substitutions from both mother-child and peer sessions.

7. Howes et al. (1992) and Bugrimenko and Smirnova (1994) interpret their findings as supporting Vygotsky's theory that social interaction creates a zone of proximal development.

8. The interpretation of Vygotsky's theory presented here is based on Francine Smolucha's original translations of previously untranslated works by Vygotsky and El'konin.

9. The phrase "to the child" was omitted from the published English translation of this paper (1978a, p. 108). In the Russian publication of Vygotsky's lecture, *child* is in the dative case, which would be translated as the phrase "to the child" (1928–29/1935, p. 77).

REFERENCES

Biezer, L., & Howes, C. (1992). Mothers and toddlers: Partners in early symbolic play. In E. Howes, O. Unger, & C. Matheson (Eds.), *The collaborative construction of pretend*. Albany: State University of New York Press.

Berk, L. (1992). Children's private speech: An overview of theory and the status of research. In R. Diaz and L. Berk (Eds.), *Private speech* (pp. 17–54). Hillsdale, NJ: Lawrence Erlbaum.

Bugrimenko, E., & Smirnova, E. (1994). Paradoxes of children's play in Vygotsky's theory. In G. Cupchick & J. Laszlo (Eds.), *Emerging visions of the aesthetic process* (pp. 286–299). Cambridge: Cambridge University Press.

Bretherton, I. (1982). *Symbolic play: The development of social understanding.* New York: Academic Press.

Cole, M. (1979). Epilogue: A portrait of Luria. In A. Luria, *The making of mind* (pp. 189–198). Cambridge, MA: Harvard University Press.

Dale, N. (1983). *Early pretend play within the family.* Unpublished doctoral dissertation, University of Cambridge, Cambridge, England.

Dunn, J. (1986). Pretend play in the family. In A. Gottfried & C. Caldwell Brown (Eds.), *Play interactions* (pp. 149–161). Lexington, MA: Lexington Books.

Dunn, J., & Dale, N. (1984). I a daddy: 2-year-olds' collaboration in joint pretend with sibling and with mother. In I. Bretherton (Ed.), *Symbolic play* (pp. 131–158). New York: Academic Press.

Dunn, J., & Wooding, C. (1977). Play in the home and its implications for learning. In B. Tizard and D. Harvey (Eds.), *The biology of play* (pp. 45–58). London: Heinemann.

El'konin, D. B. (1966). Symbolics and its functions in the play of children. *Soviet Education, 8,* 35–41.

El'konin, D. B. (1967). The problem of instruction and development in the works of L. S. Vygotsky. *Soviet Psychology, 5*(3), 34–41.

El'konin, D. B. (1969) Psychological development of preschool-age children. In M. Cole & I. Maltzman (Eds.), *A handbook of contemporary Soviet psychology* (pp. 180–208). New York: Basic Books.

El'konin, D. B. (1978). *Psikhologia igri* [The psychology of play]. Moscow: Izdatel'stvo Pedagogika.

Fagot, B. I. (1978). The influence of sex of child on parental reactions to toddler children. *Child Development, 49,* 459–465.

Fancher, R. (1990). *Pioneers of psychology.* New York: Norton.

Fein, G. (1975). A transformational analysis of pretending. *Developmental Psychology, 1*(3), 291–296.

Feitelson, D., & Ross, G. S. (1973).The neglected factor—play. *Human Development, 16,* 202–223.

Fiese, B. H. (1990). Playful relationships: A contextual analysis of mother-toddler interaction and symbolic play. *Child Development, 61,* 1648–1656.

Fowler, W., Ogston, K., Roberts, G., Steane, D., and Swenson, A. (1983). *Potential of childhood,* 2 vols. Lexington, MA: D.C. Heath.

Fowler, W. (1995). Language interaction techniques for stimulating the development of at-risk children in infant and preschool day care. *Early Child Development and Care, 111,* 35–48.

Fowler, W., Ogston, K., Roberts-Fiati, G., & Swenson, A. (in press). Patterns of giftedness and high competence in high school students educationally enriched during infancy. *Gifted and Talented International.*

Fradkina, F. I. (1946). *Psikhologiia igry v rannem detsve (geneticheskie korni doshkol'noi igry)* [The psychology of play in early childhood (the developmental roots of preschool play)]. Unpublished doctoral dissertation, Moscow. Cited in El'konin, D. B. (1978). *Psikhologia igri* [The psychology of play]. Moscow: Izdatel'stvo Pedagogika.

Gaskins, S., & Goncu, A. (1988). Children's play as representation and imagination: The case of Piaget and Vygotsky. *The Quarterly Newsletter of the Laboratory of Comparative Human Cognition, 10*(4), 104–107.

Gowen, J. W. (1995, March). The early development of symbolic play. *Young Children,* 75–84.

Haight, W. (1989). *The social ecology of play.* Unpublished doctoral dissertation, University of Chicago.

Howes, E., Unger, O., & Matheson, C. (1992). The collaborative construction of pretend. Albany: State University of New York Press.

Kuhn, T. (1970). *The structure of scientific revolutions.* Chicago: University of Chicago Press.

Kuhn, T. (1977). *The essential tension.* Chicago: University of Chicago Press.

McCune-Nicolich, L. (1977). Beyond sensorimotor intelligence: Assessment of symbolic maturity through analysis of pretend play. *Merrill-Palmer Quarterly, 33*(2), 89–99.

Miller, P., & Garvey, C. (1984). Mother-baby role play: Its origins in social support. In I. Bretherton (Ed.), *Symbolic play* (pp. 101–130). New York: Academic Press.

Moukhina, V. S. (1988). Igrushka kak sredstba psikhicheskava razvitiya rebenka [The toy as a means of psychological development of the child]. *Voprosy Psikhologii, 2,* 123–128.

O'Connell, B., & Bretherton, I. (1984). Toddler's play, alone and with mother: The role of maternal guidance. In I. Bretherton (Ed.), *Symbolic play* (pp. 337–368). New York: Academic Press.

Parten, M. (1932). Social participation among preschool children. *Journal of Abnormal and Social Psychology, 27*, 243–269.

Piaget, J. (1962). *Play, dreams, and imitation in childhood* (C. Gattegno & F. M. Hodgson, Trans.). New York: Norton. (Original work published in 1945)

Piaget, J. (1973). *The language and thought of the child* (M. Gabain, Trans.). New York: World Publishing. (Original work published in 1923)

Rubin, K., Fein, G., & Vandenberg, B. (1983). Play. In P. Mussen (Ed.), *Handbook of child psychology, Vol. 4: Socialization, personality, and social development* (pp. 693–774). New York: Wiley.

Sinclair, H. (1970). The transition from sensory-motor behavior to symbolic activity. *Interchange, 1*, 119–126.

Slade, A. (1987). A longitudinal study of maternal involvement and symbolic play during the toddler period. *Child Development, 58*, 367–375.

Smilansky, S. (1968). *The effect of sociodramatic play on disadvantaged preschool children.* New York: Wiley.

Smolucha, F. (1991). *The origins of object substitutions in social pretend play.* Unpublished doctoral dissertation, University of Chicago.

Smolucha, F. (1992a). A reconstruction of Vygotsky's theory of creativity. *Creativity Research Journal, 5*(1), 49–67.

Smolucha, F. (1992b). The relevance of Vygotsky's theory of creative imagination for contemporary research on play. *Creativity Research Journal, 5*(1), 69–76.

Smolucha, F. (1992c). The social origins of private speech during pretend play. In R. Diaz & L. Berk (Eds.), *Private speech.* Hillsdale, NJ: Lawrence Erlbaum.

Smolucha, L. (1994). Levels of discourse in psychotherapeutic interactions. *Journal of Literary Semantics, 23*(1), 1–41.

Smolucha, L., & Smolucha, F. (1986). L. S. Vygotsky's theory of creative imagination. *Siegener Periodicum Internationalen Emprirschen Literaturwissenschaft, 5*, 299–308.

Smolucha, L., & Smolucha, F. (1992). Vygotskian theory: An emerging paradigm with implications for a synergistic psychology. *Creativity Research Journal, 5*(1), 87–97.

Smolucha, L., & Smolucha, F. (1996). *Developmental psychology: A synergistic approach.* Unpublished manuscript.

Sutton-Smith, B. (1986). *Toys as culture.* New York: Gardner Press.

Vygotsky, L. S. (1935). Predistoria peismennoy rechi [The prehistory of written language]. In *The mental development of children during education* (pp. 73–95). Moscow/Leningrad: Uchpedgiz. (Original work written in 1928 or 1929)

Vygotsky, L. S. (1960). Voabraszeniye i yeva razvitie v destkom vozraste [Imagination and its development in childhood]. In *Razvitie vysshkih psikhicheskikh finkstii* [The development of higher mental functions] (pp. 327–349). Moscow: Izdatel-l'stvo Akademii Pedagogicheskikh Nauk RSFSR. (Original work presented as a lecture in 1932)

Vygotsky, L. S. (1967a) Play and its role in the mental development of the child. *Soviet Psychology, 5*(3), 6–18. (Original work written in 1933)

Vygotsky, L. S. (1967b). Voabraszeniye i tvorchestvo v destkom vosraste [Imagination and creativity in childhood]. Moscow: Prosvescheniye. (Original work written in 1930)

Vygotsky, L. S. (1976). Play and its role in the mental development of the child. In J. Bruner, A. Jolly, & K. Sylva (Eds.), *Play—its role in development and evolution..* New York: Basic Books. (Original work written in 1933)

Vygotsky, L. S. (1978a). The prehistory of written language. In M. Cole, V. John-Steiner, S. Scribner, & E. Souberman (Eds.), *Mind in society* (pp. 105–119). Cambridge, MA: Harvard University Press. (Original work written in 1928–29)

Vygotsky, L. S. (1978b). The role of play in development. In M. Cole, V. John-Steiner, S. Scribner, & E. Souberman (Eds.), *Mind in society* (pp. 92–104). Cambridge, MA: Harvard University Press. (Original work written in 1933)

Vygotsky, L. S. (1978c). The interaction between learning and development. In M. Cole, V. John-Steiner, S. Scribner, & E. Souberman (Eds.), *Mind in society* (pp. 79–91). Cambridge, MA: Harvard University Press. (Original work written in 1933–34)

Vygotsky, L. S. (1990). Imagination and creativity in childhood (F. Smolucha, Trans.). *Soviet Psychology, 28*(1), 84–96.

Vygotsky, L. S. (1991). Imagination and creativity in the adolescent (F. Smolucha, Trans.). *Soviet Psychology, 29*(1), 73–88.

Yogman, M. W. (1981). Development of the father-infant relationship. In H. Fitzger-ald, B. Lester & M. W. Yogman (Eds.), *Theory and research in behavioral pediatrics* (Vol. 1, pp. 221–279). New York: Plenum.

Zukow, P. (1989) Siblings as effective socilizing agents: Evidence from central Mexico. In P. Zuckow (Ed.), *Sibling interaction across cultures*. New York: Springer-Verlag.

Chapter 4

Seeing through Symbols: The Development of Children's Understanding of Symbolic Relations

David H. Uttal, Donald P. Marzolf,
Sophia L. Pierroutsakos, Catherine M. Smith,
Georgene L. Troseth, Kathryn V. Scudder,
and Judy S. DeLoache

The idea that children learn best through play has become almost a truism in research on cognitive development and education. Materials and books are designed to encourage children's play and hence their comprehension of specific ideas. For example, many children are encouraged to play with alphabet or number blocks to help them learn to recognize letters or numbers. Educators and researchers almost universally view play as a positive force in cognitive development.

In this chapter, we raise the possibility that there may be another side to the role of play in cognitive development: Children may have trouble treating objects simultaneously as toys *and* as representations of something else. Playing with an object may engage children's interest but it may simultaneously make it hard for them to grasp the relation between the object and a concept or fact. For example, playing with letter blocks may raise children's interest in letters, but this interest does not guarantee that they will learn anything about the relations between letters, sounds, and words. In fact, having played with a letter block may make it *harder* for children to treat the letter as a symbol of a sound. Similarly, children may enjoy playing with mathematics manipulatives, but doing so may not help them learn arithmetic.

Our perspective on play is based on the results of our research on the development of early symbol use. The ability to use symbols is a hallmark of human cognition. The capacity to communicate and learn from others depends upon knowledge that one thing can stand for another. Not surprisingly, almost all theories of cognitive development have stressed the importance of acquiring an understanding of symbols. Initially, young infants are not privy to the information symbols can provide; they learn primarily through interacting directly with the world. The development of symbolic skills fundamentally changes the way children learn and communicate.

The early development of symbolization occurs in the context of an abundance of symbolic representations. In addition to language and symbolic gestures, children in every society encounter numerous cultural artifacts. Virtually all American toddlers and preschool children are exposed to television, and many have experience with home videos as well. Pictures are found everywhere in our culture, from the illustrations in children's books to the sports heroes on cereal boxes and the advertisements on billboards. Many children learn the meaning of icons in computer games, and what American child does not know the significance of the Golden Arches?

Given the ubiquity of symbols in the lives of young children and the importance of symbols in human culture and communication, one might suppose that a basic understanding of the nature of symbols would come quite early and relatively easily—that children could readily "see through" at least some symbols to what they represent. Our research indicates that this is not the case; one can never take for granted that a young child will appreciate the representational nature and role of any given symbol. This is not surprising with respect to abstract, arbitrary symbol systems, such as letters and numbers; however, as our research shows, young children often fail to detect the relation between even highly iconic symbols and their referents. Children's play with symbolically related toys does not always help them gain insight into the relations between symbols and their referents and may, in fact, sometimes be counterproductive.

In this chapter, we first discuss briefly what is involved in understanding a symbol-referent relation and using information provided by a symbol. We then describe some of the evidence for the above claims about the nontransparency of symbols to young children. Finally, we discuss the implications of our research for some aspects of educational practice with young children and for the role of play in cognitive development.

SYMBOL UNDERSTANDING AND USE

What is involved in understanding and using symbols? First, one must realize *that* a given entity is a symbol; that is, one must appreciate that it is intended to stand for something other than itself and that it should be responded to and interpreted primarily in terms of its referent rather than itself. Second, one must know *what* the symbol represents. In other words, one must understand something about the relation between the symbol and its referent. Third, one must know *how* the symbol and its referent are related, that is, how the symbol is to be mapped onto the referent.

To illustrate these three aspects of symbolic functioning, consider a family on a holiday in Chicago. The parents might want to find the Art Institute, and the children are demanding to see the Shedd Aquarium and the Lincoln Park Zoo. The children win out, and the family decides to head for the zoo. They pull out their city map and note that the zoo is just a few miles to the north. They plan their route and head for the nearest train station.

To use their map, the family must understand (1) *that* the map they hold is a symbol—a representation of something other than itself, (2) *what* it represents (Chicago), and (3) *how* to apply the lines, shapes, words, and other symbols on the two-dimensional map to the real landmarks in the city. The children, depending on their age and experience, might share their parents knowledge of all three or none of these features of the map.

These three aspects are always involved in symbol use, but they are not always neatly separable in research addressing children's symbolic understanding. The child's knowledge of them can be explicit and statable, or it can be implicit and tacit. Preschool children's knowledge of symbol-referent relations is probably usually implicit. Such children are capable, however, of explicit understanding in some domains, as evidenced by one preschool subject in our lab. When the experimenter admired the Batman logo on his shoes, commenting, "Oh, it's Batman," this child corrected him—"No, it's just a symbol." In this chapter, we will explore the developmental origins of this sophisticated understanding.

RESEARCH ON SYMBOLIC UNDERSTANDING

Photographs

We begin our discussion of research with a symbol-referent relation that seems, at least initially, to be transparent and obvious. As adults, we know that photographs of objects are only representations. Although we may kiss a photograph of an absent loved one, we realize that the photograph is not the actual object of our affection. The results of our research suggest that infants and toddlers may not share this understanding; they do not fully appreciate the representational nature of photographs. As with all symbols, children must learn *that* photographs are representations and *how* these representations function.

Our research on this issue was motivated in part by anecdotes reported by parents and some informal accounts by researchers. The claim was made that infants sometimes treat photographs of objects as if the photographs were the objects themselves by, for example, attempting to grasp or otherwise manipulate depicted objects (Murphy, 1978; Ninio & Bruner, 1978).

We designed a series of studies to determine whether these reports could be validated in a controlled setting. In our first study (DeLoache, Uttal, Pierrout-sakos, & Rosengren, 1993), we examined 9-month-old infants' manual responses to pictures, focusing particularly on behaviors that appeared to be attempts to grasp or pick up the depicted objects. We presented the infants with specially constructed picture books with a highly realistic color photograph of a single object on each page. The pictured objects were small enough (ca. 3.8 x 2.5 cm) that a 9-month-old could have picked them up, had they been real objects.

The results were surprisingly clear. As shown in Figure 4.1, every infant attempted, at least once, to manually investigate a pictured object, by grasping at, hitting, or rubbing the depicted object. Some infants were remarkably persistent, making repeated and concerted efforts to pluck the objects from the pages. Thus, these infants did not comprehend fully the representational nature of the photographs. Instead, they treated the photographs as if they were the objects themselves.

In subsequent studies, we have shown that children's confusion of photographs and represented objects declines in the second year of life. As Fig-

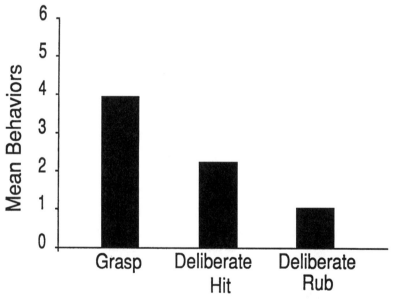

FIGURE 4.1
MANUAL INVESTIGATION OF COLOR PHOTOGRAPHS BY 9-MONTH-OLD INFANTS

ure 4.2 shows, older children (15-month-olds and 19-month-olds) attempt to grasp or otherwise manipulate the photographs substantially less than 9-month-olds do. Instead, older infants tend to point to the pictures, often vocalizing to another person as they point. They show substantial interest in the photographs and attempt to communicate their interest, but they rarely attempt to manually explore the represented objects.

It is important to note that the younger infants' frequent attempts to grasp or manipulate the photographs do not stem from difficulty distinguishing *perceptually* between objects and photographs of objects. Several prior studies have shown that even young infants can reliably distinguish between two- and three-dimensional objects and photographs of stimuli (e.g., DeLoache, Strauss, & Maynard, 1979). Hence we believe that the problem for the young infants is not perceptual, but rather *conceptual*; the infants can perceive the difference between objects and photographs of objects, but they do

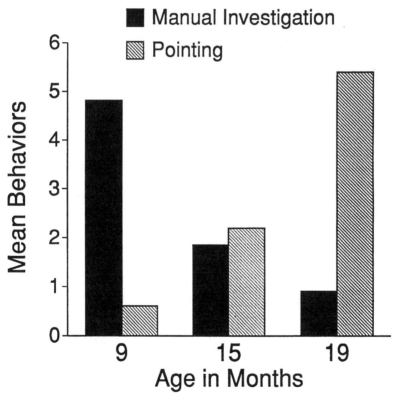

FIGURE 4.2
MANUAL INVESTIGATION AND POINTING TO PHOTOGRAPHS AS A FUNCTION OF AGE

not yet know the implications of this perceptual difference.

In the next section, we document that problems with understanding symbols continue well beyond infancy. In addition to understanding that something is a symbol, and should be responded to as such, one must understand the specific symbol-referent relation and how to use it. Like infants, young children often respond to a symbol more in terms of the object itself than in terms of what it represents.

Scale Models

Much of our research on the development of early symbolic functioning has focused on very young children's understanding of scale models as representations (DeLoache, 1987, 1989, 1991; DeLoache, Kolstad, & Anderson, 1991; Marzolf & DeLoache, 1994). Specifically, we have investigated young children's ability to use a scale model as a representation of a larger space (i.e., a full-sized room). To do this, we use an object-retrieval task in which children are required to find a toy hidden in a room based on where they see a miniature version of the toy hidden in a scale model of the room. Success in this task indicates that the children appreciate something about the symbolic relation between the model and the room.

There are several benefits to this scale model paradigm. First, very young children (such as the 2½- to 3-year-olds that we study) are relatively unfamiliar with scale models as representations of specific entities. While they frequently play with dollhouses and farm sets, they typically do not relate them to specific houses or farms that exist in the real world. Thus, we are able to observe children's developing appreciation of scale models as specific representations from their very first exposure to them. Two additional benefits of the scale-model paradigm stem from the object retrieval aspect of the task. Because finding a toy in a room requires little verbal skill on the part of our young subjects, we avoid confounding symbolic understanding and verbal competence. Also, most children find the hide and seek nature of the task very enjoyable, so even notoriously uncooperative toddlers remain highly motivated throughout testing.

The room used in the standard model task is furnished with familiar objects, such as a couch, a chair, and a dresser. The objects in the model are very similar to their counterparts in the room (e.g., same color and texture), with the obvious exception of size. Further, the objects in both spaces are arranged in the same way, and the model is always aligned with the room. The model is always located outside of the room so that the children cannot see the interior of both spaces at the same time.

During an extensive orientation, the experimenter emphasizes the correspondence between the model and the room by directly comparing each miniature object from the model with its counterpart in the room. On each of the subsequent trials, the children watch as the experimenter hides a miniature toy in the model. The toy is hidden behind or under one of the items of furniture (e.g., behind the chair), and a different hiding place is used on each trial. The experimenter then tells the child that she is going to hide a large toy in the same place in the room. When the experimenter returns, she reminds the child that the large toy is hidden in the "same place" as the miniature toy. The child then searches for the large toy in the room. This *symbol-based retrieval* is the key dependent variable. If the child is consistently able to find the large toy, we conclude that he or she appreciates the relation between the model and the room. Without this awareness, the child has no way of knowing where to search for the larger toy in the room. After retrieving the large toy, the child returns to the model and retrieves the miniature toy that he or she had seen hidden. This *memory-based retrieval* is important for interpreting the performance of children who have difficulty finding the large toy in the room. If children remember where the miniature toy is hidden, yet still fail to find the large toy in the room, then we conclude that they do not appreciate that the two spaces are related.

The analysis of symbol use that we presented above is relevant to understanding what children must do to succeed in the model task. First, they must understand *that* the model is a symbol; they must know that it represents something and is more than simply an object. Second, the children must understand *what* the model represents; they must know that the model represents the room. Third, the children must understand *how* the model-room relation works; they must know that the toy can be found in the room by searching in the location corresponding to the one that was indicated in the model. Our research suggests that children can have problems with each of these three aspects.

The results of the standard model task are quite dramatic, and have been replicated several times in our own lab as well as by others (DeLoache, 1987; Dow & Pick, 1992). As shown in Figure 4.3, 3-year-old children are very good at retrieving the large toy in the room. They clearly appreciate that the model and the room are related and they use what they know about one to make an inference about the other. In contrast, 2½-year-old children are very unsuccessful at finding the large toy in the room. In assessing their poor performance, it is important to note that they *do* understand several key components of the task. First, they understand that they are to find the large toy in the room, as evidenced by their enthusiasm during the symbol-based retrieval. Second, they are very good at remembering where the original toy was hidden in the model. Their memory-based retrieval performance is always near ceiling, on par with that of the 3-year-olds. Thus, their inability to find the toy in the room is not because they fail to remember where the miniature toy is

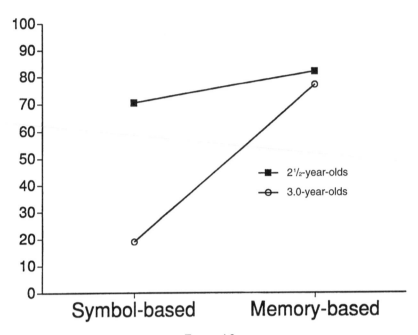

FIGURE 4.3
PERCENTAGE OF ERRORLESS RETRIEVALS BY 2½- AND 3-YEAR-OLD CHILDREN
IN THE SCALE-MODEL TASK

hidden in the model. Finally, 2½-year olds can match the corresponding objects (e.g., large and small chairs) in the two spaces. In a recent study (Troseth & DeLoache, 1996), children were presented with an item from the model and told: "Show me the one in the big room that looks like this." They were quite successful at doing this (79% correct). Nevertheless, the same children subsequently failed to exploit those object correspondences in the standard model task (symbol-based retrieval = 21%). We believe that the 2½-year-old children who fail the standard model simply do not realize that the model and the room are related, and therefore they have no basis for using what they know about one to make an inference about the other.

Why is it so difficult for these young children to understand the model-room relation? Our research has revealed several factors that influence children's appreciation of symbol-referent relations. Two factors are particularly relevant to this chapter: the salience of the symbol as an object and experience. We consider each of these in turn.

Salience of the symbol as an object. DeLoache (1987, 1991; DeLoache & Marzolf, 1992) has proposed that young children find the model task difficult because it requires thinking of the model in two different ways—as an object in its own right and as a representation of something else. To succeed, the child must interact with the model as an object (i.e., hide and retrieve toys in it) and at the same time regard it as a representation of something other than itself (i.e., the room and its contents). Although the younger children obviously treat the model as an object, they have difficulty simultaneously thinking of it as a representation of the room. In other words, they have difficulty realizing *that* the model is a symbol or understanding *what* it represents.

According to the *dual representation hypothesis* (DeLoache, 1987, 1991, 1995), the salience and attractiveness of the model as an object makes it difficult for 2½-year-olds to simultaneously think of it as a representation of the room. Several counterintuitive predictions follow. One is that making the model more salient as an object should make it more difficult for 3-year-olds to think of it as a representation of the room. Playing with the model as a toy may increase children's tendency to treat it as an object and decrease the likelihood of their detecting the model-room relation. In one study (DeLoache, 1995), the salience of the model as an object was increased simply by allowing children to play with it for 5 to 10 minutes before the standard model task. As predicted by the dual representation hypothesis, the 3-year-olds who participated in this study performed significantly worse than children their same age who did not have the extra experience with the model. Thus, manipulating and playing with a symbolic object diminished its symbolic status.

Another prediction that follows from the dual representation hypothesis is that decreasing the salience of the model as an object should make it easier for children to think of it as a representation of the room. The standard model task was altered by placing the model behind a plastic window (DeLoache, 1995). Neither the experimenter nor the child ever touched the model or its contents. Rather than hiding a miniature toy to indicate the hiding place, the experimenter simply pointed to the relevant hiding place in the model. As predicted, the children in the window condition performed significantly better than children their age typically do in the standard model task. Thus, decreasing the salience of the model as an object made it easier for our young subjects to think of it as a representation of the room. Keeping children from playing with the model *improved* their performance. (We know that performance in the standard model task is the same regardless of whether the experimenter points to the hiding place in the model or hides a miniature toy. Thus, the superior performance of the children in the window condition is not due to the manner in which the hiding place was indicated.)

The dual representation hypothesis was investigated further by examining young children's understanding of pictures (DeLoache, 1987; DeLoache & Burns, 1994). Although pictures are physical entities, they are very uninteresting as objects. Toddlers know to look at but not play with pictures. Thus, the dual representation hypothesis predicts that pictures should be relatively easy for young children to understand as representations. Hence, 2½-year-old children, an age group that typically fails the standard model task, should succeed in an object retrieval task in which information about the location of the toy is conveyed via a picture. This prediction is counterintuitive in light of extensive research that suggests that better cognitive performance is achieved with real objects than with pictures (e.g., Daehler, Lonardo, & Bukatko, 1979; DeLoache, 1986; Sigel, 1953; Sigel, Anderson, & Shapiro, 1966).

In a series of studies, the experimenter pointed to a picture of the hiding place and told the child that was where she was going to hide the toy in the room. In one study, the experimenter pointed to the hiding place on a wide-angle color photograph of the room. In another, we used four photographs of the individual hiding places, pointing to the appropriate one on each trial. In yet another study, we used a line drawing of the entire space. As predicted by the dual representation hypothesis, the 2½-year-olds who participated in these studies were very successful, regardless of the type of picture used. Thus, while children this age typically do not appreciate the relation between a scale model and the space it represents, they clearly understand the relation between a picture and what it represents. These results support the dual representation hypothesis: Young children understand pictures as representations because they do not have to think of them as objects and as representations at the same time. Pictures are not usually playthings.

In the most stringent test of the dual representation hypothesis to date, we sought to remove the need for children to think of the model as a representation of the room (DeLoache, 1993; DeLoache, Miller, Rosengren, & Bryant, 1993). To do this, we convinced a group of 2½-year-old children that we were shrinking the room. Our reasoning was that if the children believed that the model actually *was* the room after being shrunk, then they should be able to reason between the two spaces without thinking of the model as a representation of the room. Thus, no dual representation would be required.

We used a tentlike portable room (a 1.85 × 2.57 × 1.88 m structure constructed of opaque white fabric and a plastic pipe framework) and a scale model of that room, both of which have been used in numerous other model studies. During an orientation phase, the children were introduced to a troll doll, the "troll's room," and a "shrinking machine." The child was told that the machine could shrink toys and then make them big again. To demonstrate this, the experimenter placed the troll doll in front of the machine and turned it on. The child and experimenter waited in an adjacent room, listening to the "sounds the machine makes while its shrinking the troll." When they reentered the room, they found a much smaller troll in front of the machine. The experimenter then demonstrated how the machine could make the troll "get big again."

The experimental trials followed this orientation. On the first trial, the child watched as the experimenter hid the troll somewhere in the portable room. The experimenter told the child to remember where the troll was hiding so he or she could find it later. They then waited in the adjacent room while the machine shrank the troll's room. When the machine was done, the child discovered the model where the large room had been. She was encouraged to find the troll, which was, of course, hidden in the same place in the model that the experimenter hid the large troll in the room. After finding the troll, the child watched as the experimenter hid it in a different place in the model. They then waited in the adjacent room while the machine "made the room big again," after which the child searched for the large troll in the room. Subsequent trials alternated between the shrinking and enlarging events.

In order for this manipulation to work as expected, children had to believe that we were indeed shrinking and enlarging the same space. Based on the children's behavior, as well as independent ratings from two experimenters and the children's parents, we concluded that the children were convinced that our shrinking machine worked as advertised.

As predicted, the 2½-year-olds who participated in this study were quite successful at finding the toy in one of the spaces based on where they saw the other toy hidden in the other space (see Figure 4.4). They performed significantly better than children in two different control conditions using the same artificial room and model. The children did everything necessary to solve the standard model task; that is, they used their knowledge of the location of the toy to figure out where the second toy was hidden. The only difference is that in the shrinking room task, children did not have to think of the model as a representation of the room.

These studies demonstrate one factor that influences young children's appreciation of symbol-referent relations: salience of the symbol as an object. When a symbol is very salient as an object, it is difficult for young children to appreciate it as a representation of something else.

Experience. A second factor that influences children's appreciation of the relation between a symbol and its referent is the experience that they have with other symbols. We have proposed that insight into specific symbol-referent relations contributes to a child's *symbolic sensitivity* or basic readiness to appreciate that one object or event can stand for another (DeLoache & Marzolf, 1992; Marzolf & DeLoache, 1994). Thus, more experience with one kind of symbol makes a child more likely to detect other symbol-referent relations. However, it is important to note that this experience involves using the object as a symbol. Experience *playing* with the object is not helpful.

A series of easy-to-hard transfer studies illustrates this point (DeLoache, 1991; Marzolf & DeLoache, 1994). In these studies, children were first given

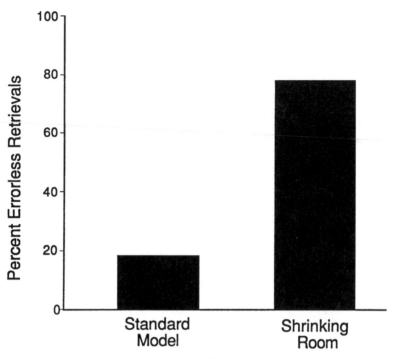

FIGURE 4.4
PERFORMANCE IN THE STANDARD MODEL TASK VERSUS THE
SHRINKING ROOM VERSION OF THE TASK

an object- retrieval task that involved a symbolic relation that children their age typically understand. On the following day, the same children were given a task involving a relation that children their age typically do not appreciate. Our rationale was that insight into the easy relation on the first day would help children appreciate the difficult relation on the second day. This hypothesis was supported in all of the transfer studies that we have conducted to date. In one study, for example, 2½-year-old children who first experienced an easy picture task subsequently succeeded on the standard model task, a task that children their age typically fail. Thus, insight into the picture-room relation helped children notice the model-room relation.

The transfer effects in these studies are quite robust. Transfer has occurred within and between symbol types (as in the picture-to-model transfer study described above). In some of the studies, the easy task was conducted in one space and the difficult task was conducted in a different space, demonstrating transfer across contexts. Finally, we have reported transfer effects for both 2½- and 3-year-old children. Thus, we believe that previous experience with symbol-referent relations is an important factor determining whether children subsequently detect more difficult relations.

Understanding that a symbol and its referent are related, however, is often not enough to allow use of a symbol; the child must still know *how* to use the information. In the model tasks described so far, for example, the child has to map the relation between the miniature toy and its hiding place in the model to the room in order to infer the location of the large toy. In other words, the children must know how the information in the model specifies the location of the toy in the room. The 3-year-olds in our model task are very capable of mapping this relatively simple information. Would they be able to map more complex relational information in this task?

To investigate this issue, we have conducted a number of model studies in which we used four identical white boxes as hiding places (Marzolf, 1994, 1995). In most of these studies, the boxes were located directly on top of or immediately next to distinctive landmarks (i.e., items of furniture). To succeed at this task, children have to encode the hiding relation between the toy and the box as well as the relation between the box and a landmark, and map this entire set of relations from the model to the room. Thus, this seemingly trivial manipulation increases the complexity of the information that children have to map.

Three-year-old children, who would succeed in the standard model task, were surprisingly unsuccessful at locating the large toy in the room (43%). They always looked in a box, but did not know which one was correct. Interestingly, the same children were very good at retrieving the miniature toy they had seen hidden in one of the boxes in the model (77%). This indicates that they did encode and remember the entire set of relations, but failed to map them across the spaces. Thus, these 3-year-old children are clearly limited in their ability to map a set of relations between a symbol and its referent in this task. These results demonstrate that even when a child appreciates *that* something is a symbol and knows *what* the symbol represents, understanding *how* to map information between the two may still be quite difficult.

Dolls

Another case in which the dual representation hypothesis leads to a counterintuitive prediction concerns young children's use of a doll as a symbol for themselves. Adults generally assume that a doll is such an obvious representation for a person that even very young children would appreciate the relation between themselves and a doll. This assumption is bolstered by the fact that very young children's doll play is meaningful. Children often act out realistic and plausible scenarios in which dolls are made to behave sensibly.

The assumption that children readily understand dolls as symbols for themselves underlies the extensive use of dolls in the forensic arena. Clinicians, social workers, and police often use anatomically explicit dolls to interview children who are suspected victims of abuse (Boat & Everson, 1988). The claim is that dolls should be particularly useful with very young children whose verbal skills may not be adequate to describe their experience (Yates & Terr, 1988).

In fact, dolls are not a transparent symbol to very young children. A study by DeLoache and Marzolf (1995) explored 2½- to 4-year-olds' ability to recount their experiences with a male experimenter in a lab setting. The children were asked to tell about and show on a doll where the experimenter had touched them during a "Simon Says" game. Results indicated that the children provided just as much information verbally as they did using the dolls.

A second study (DeLoache, Anderson, & Smith, 1995) further investigated young children's ability to use a doll as a self-symbol. In an attempt to have a better analog of a real abuse situation, children were questioned about an event in their everyday lives in which someone had done something to them that they did not like and about which they became emotionally upset. Preschool teachers provided crucial assistance in this study; they recorded every incident in which a child became upset because of something another child had done to him or her. The children were then questioned about the incident. All children heard the same questions, but the interviewer asked half of the children to use a doll to answer the questions. The results were the same as in the earlier lab study: Using the dolls did not confer an advantage. The children provided the same amount of information when they were simply questioned as they did when they were also asked to use the dolls to demonstrate what had happened to them.

These two studies are consistent with our laboratory research on scale models and with the dual representation hypothesis: One reason that the presence of the dolls failed to enhance the children's memory reports could be that they did not fully appreciate that the doll was supposed to represent themselves or they were not sure how to map between themselves and the doll.

In a recent series of studies (Smith, 1995), we investigated in more detail young children's use of a doll as a self-symbol. In this research, an even simpler task was used. We asked children to place a sticker on a doll in the location analogous to where the experimenter had just placed a sticker on the child. This task had no memory requirement, as the sticker on the child remained in view while he or she placed the smaller sticker on the doll. Nevertheless, the children in this study correctly placed the stickers only 52% of the time. Even in this very simple task, young children had difficulty using the relation between themselves and a doll. These results provide a strong challenge to the common assumption that children can easily use a doll as a representation of themselves.

APPLICATION OF RESEARCH ON EARLY SYMBOLIC DEVELOPMENT TO EDUCATIONAL PRACTICE

In the final section, we consider the application of our theory to education. We have chosen as an example the use of *manipulatives* to teach arithmetic to young children. We believe, however, that the implications of our work would hold true for other domains, such as instruction in reading. Manipulatives are concrete objects, such as blocks and rods, that are designed to help children understand complex mathematical concepts. Many teachers believe that children learn more effectively when they can work through problems with concrete objects that they can hold and touch. The assumption has been that making problems tangible makes the mathematics concepts tractable (Kennedy & Tipps, 1994; Boling, 1991).

Unfortunately, research on the effectiveness of manipulatives has lagged far behind the enthusiasm for their use (Ball, 1992). Moreover, the studies that have been conducted have yielded mixed results (see Scott & Neufeld, 1976; Suydam & Higgins 1977). Put simply, current research does not support the unqualified and widespread belief in the power of manipulatives.

Why has research failed to confirm an advantage for manipulatives? We believe the central problem may stem from the assumption that manipulatives will help because they are *concrete* (e.g., Fennema, 1972). That is, teachers assume that because the manipulatives are solid objects, they reduce the cognitive effort that children must exert to understand the underlying concept (Scheer, 1985). In Ball's (1992) words, "Concrete is inherently good; 'abstract' is inherently not appropriate—at least at the beginning, at least for young learners" (p. 16). This assumption is derived in part from Piaget's theory. It has been argued that abstract, symbolic thought requires formal operations (Fennema, 1972). Manipulatives are assumed to make information accessible for the younger, concrete-operational child (Marzola, 1987; Williams & Kamii, 1986). Hence, the Piagetian-based assumption is that manipulatives provide an important bridge from the concrete to the abstract.

Our research and theoretical perspective lead us to a different conclusion: Concrete manipulatives may be quite difficult for young children to understand *as representations* of abstract mathematical concepts. That manipulatives invite play and exploration may cause children *not* to treat them as representations. We believe that concrete manipulatives are symbols, and that using a manipulative is thus similar to using our model. To succeed, children must realize that the manipulative, like the model, is not just an object, but also a symbol. Just as in our previous discussion of photographs and models, one cannot assume that children can simply "see through" the manipulative to what it represents. Making something concrete does not make its relation to a referent necessarily transparent or even clearer (see Fuson & Briars, 1990;

Gentner & Ratterman, 1991; Hiebert & Carpenter, 1990; Resnick & Omanson, 1984). In the remainder of this section, we discuss how our theoretical perspective leads to conclusions and suggestions about manipulatives that run counter to many commonly-held beliefs.

Understanding That Manipulatives Are Symbols

A brief review of some of the literature on children's use of manipulatives demonstrates clearly that children often have difficulty grasping that a concrete manipulative is intended to be a symbol. The results of several studies and anecdotes strongly suggest that children often have difficulty realizing that a manipulative is intended to represent something (Goswami, 1992). For example, Hughes (1986) asked 5- to 7-year-olds to use simple bricks to represent sums, such as 1 + 7 = 8. The children were told to use the bricks to show the experimenter what was written in the problem. Thus, children were asked to translate the abstract, symbolic representation of the written problem into the concrete representation of the bricks.

On average, children's performance was poor; most could not use the bricks to represent the written problems. More importantly, children's errors shed light on the source of the difficulty. Many of the children took the instructions literally; they used the blocks to *copy* the written problems. For example, some children arranged the bricks as shown in Figure 4.5. They did not understand that the bricks were intended to represent a mathematical concept; they did not comprehend *that* the bricks were symbols or *what* the bricks were intended to represent. Just as children in our model task sometimes fail to grasp the relation between the model and the room, the children in Hughes's study did not realize that the bricks were more than objects, that they provided an alternate format for representing the numbers.

Figuring out what a manipulative represents may be particularly difficult for young children because they may not understand the underlying concept (e.g., fractions, addition, multiplication, etc.). For example, if they do not yet understand fractions, then it may be quite difficult for them to use manipulatives to learn about fractions. In contrast, teachers understand the concepts so they can appreciate fully how the manipulative stands for those concepts. Ball (1992) provides an example of the difficulties children may encounter when they are asked to use a manipulative that is intended to represent a concept they have not yet grasped completely. The children (third-graders) were attempting to use fraction bars to figure out the concept of parts and wholes. The teacher asks, "Which is more—three-thirds or five-fifths?" A student moved two of the fraction bars and stated, "Five fifths is more . . . because there are more pieces" (p. 17). The child did not understand fractions and hence he was unable to use the fraction bars as a symbol. Instead, he resorted

Problem: Use small bricks to solve 1 + 7

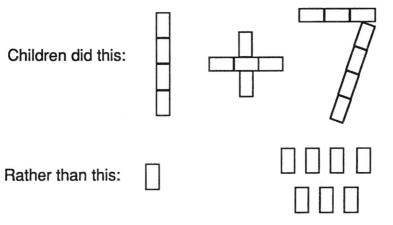

Children did this:

Rather than this:

FIGURE 4.5
CHILDREN'S USE OF BLOCKS TO REPRESENT "4 + 3 = 7"

Source: Adapted from Hughes, 1986

to what he did know: counting. This example demonstrates clearly that children's understanding of the relation between manipulatives and their intended referents may be quite different than what the teacher expected.

Are Interesting Manipulatives the Best Manipulatives?

A second implication of our theoretical perspective is that interesting or novel manipulatives may be *more* difficult to use as symbols. This runs counter to the common belief that exciting and engaging manipulatives are best for young children (DeLoache, Uttal, & Pierroutsakos, in press; Uttal, Scudder, & DeLoache, 1997).

Our studies have demonstrated that appreciating a symbol-referent relation requires that children treat the model (or any symbol) as more than an object; they must treat it as a representation of something else. To this end, highlighting the characteristics of the object as a thing in itself may undermine the goal of helping the child use the object as a representation of something else. Highly attractive educational symbols may focus children's attention on the symbol itself and away from where it needs to be—the *relation* of the symbol to what the child is supposed to learn.

Interestingly, the belief that manipulatives should be engaging and entertaining is not universal. In Japan, children begin first grade with a small set of manipulatives, including blocks and other shapes. They continue to use the same manipulative for multiple tasks throughout the lower elementary grades. These objects thus become highly familiar, leading the children to no longer view them as toys, freeing them to focus instead on what the manipulatives represent. Support for this claim comes from Sowells (1989) meta-analysis, which revealed that manipulatives were most effective when they were used consistently over extended periods of time.

In the United States, however, teachers place great emphasis on the use of a *variety* of objects in a variety of contexts. An unintended result of this practice may be that children attend to the objects rather than what the objects are intended to represent. Stevenson and Stigler (1992) have noted:

> Japanese teachers . . . use the items in the math set repeatedly throughout the elementary school years. . . . American teachers seek variety. They may use Popsicle sticks in one lesson, and marbles, Cheerios, M&M's, checkers, poker chips, or plastic animals in another. The American view is that objects should be varied in order to maintain children's interest. The Asian view is that using a variety of representational materials may confuse children, and thereby make it more difficult for them to use the objects for the representation and solution of mathematics problems. Multiplication is easier to understand when the same tiles are used as were used when the children learned to add. (pp. 186–187).

CONCLUSION

Our research and analysis indicate that no symbol, no matter how simple it appears to an adult, is necessarily transparent to young children. There is an interesting developmental story to be told even for children's understanding of highly iconic symbols, such as photographs and scale models. We hope our examples have illustrated why it is necessary to study and pay attention to this story.

Our results suggest a new perspective on the role of play in cognitive development. Rather than viewing play as universally positive, we see it as a two-edged sword. Play certainly is vital to cognitive development. However, just because children have played with an object does not mean that they have learned from the experience. In fact, as we have pointed out, play can sometimes be counterproductive when the object is intended to serve as a symbol.

REFERENCES

Ball, D. L. (1992). Magical hopes: Manipulative and the reform of math education. *American Educator, 16,* 14–18.

Boat, B. W., & Everson, M. D. (1988). Use of anatomical dolls among professionals in sexual abuse evaluations. *Child Abuse and Neglect, 12,* 171–179.

Boling, A. N. (1991). They don't like math? Well, let's do something! *Arithmetic Teacher, 38,* 17–19.

Daehler, M. W., Lonardo, R., & Bukatko, D. (1979). Matching and equivalence judgment in very young children. *Child Development, 50,* 170–179.

DeLoache, J. S. (1986). Memory in very young children: Exploitation of cues to the location of hidden objects. *Cognitive Development, 1,* 123–137.

DeLoache, J. S. (1987). Rapid change in the symbolic functioning of very young children. *Science, 238,* 1556–1557.

DeLoache, J. S. (1989). Young children's understanding of the correspondence between a scale model and a larger space. *Cognitive Development, 4,* 121–139.

DeLoache, J. S. (1991). Symbolic functioning in very young children: Understanding of pictures and models. *Child Development, 62,* 736–752.

DeLoache, J. S. (1993). *What do young children understand about symbolic relations?* Paper presented at the meeting of the Society for Research in Child Development, New Orleans.

DeLoache, J. S. (1995). Early symbol understanding and use. In D. Medin (Ed.), *The Psychology of learning and motivation* (Vol. 33), pp. 65–114. New York: Academic Press.

DeLoache, J. S., Anderson, K., & Smith, C. (1995). *Interviewing children about real-life events.* Paper presented at the meeting of the Society for Research in Child Development, Indianapolis.

DeLoache, J. S., & Burns, N. M. (1994). Early understanding of the representational function of pictures. *Cognition, 52,* 83–110.

DeLoache, J. S., Kolstad, D. V., & Anderson, K. N. (1991). Physical similarity and young children's understanding of scale models. *Child Development, 62,* 111–126.

DeLoache, J. S., & Marzolf, D. P. (1992). When a picture is not worth a thousand words: Young children's understanding of pictures and models. *Cognitive Development, 7,* 317–329.

DeLoache, J. S., & Marzolf, D. P. (1995) The use of dolls to interview young children: Issues of symbolic representation. *Journal of Experimental Child Psychology, 60,* 155–173.

DeLoache, J. S., Miller, K. F., Rosengren, K. S., & Bryant, N. (1993). *Symbolic development in young children: Honey, I shrunk the troll.* Paper presented at the meeting of the Psychonomic Society, Washington, DC.

DeLoache, J. S., Strauss, M. S., & Maynard, J. (1979). Picture perception in infancy. *Infant Behavior and Development, 2*, 77–89.

DeLoache, J. S., Uttal, D. H., Pierroutsakos, S. L., Rosengren, K. (1993). *Do infants grasp the representational nature of photographs?* Unpublished manuscript, University of Illinois at Urbana-Champaign.

DeLoache, J. S., Uttal, D. H., & Pierroutsakos, S. L. (in press). The development of early symbolization: Educational implications. *Learning and Instruction: The Journal of the European Association on Learning and Instruction.*

Dow, G. A., & Pick, H. L. (1992). Young children's use of models and photographs as spatial representations. *Cognitive Development, 7*, 351–363.

Fennema, E. H. (1972). Models and mathematics. *Arithmetic Teacher, 19*, 635–649.

Fuson K. C., & Briars, D. J. (1990). Using a base-ten blocks learning/teaching approach for first and second grade place-value and multidigit addition and subtraction. *Journal for Research in Mathematics Education, 21*, 180–206.

Gentner, D., & Ratterman, M. J. (1991). Language and the career of similarity. In S. A. Gelman & J. P. Byrnes (Eds.), *Perspectives on thought and language: Interrelations in development.* London: Cambridge University Press.

Goswami, U. (1992). *Analogical reasoning in children.* East Sussex, England: Lawrence Erlbaum.

Hiebert, J., & Carpenter, T. P. (1990). Learning and teaching with understanding. In D. A. Grouws (Ed.), *Handbook of research on mathematics teaching and learning* (pp. 65–97). New York: Macmillan.

Hughes, M. (1986). *Children and number: Difficulties in learning mathematics.* Oxford: Basil Blackwell.

Kennedy, L. M., & Tipps, S. (Eds.). (1994). *Guiding children's learning of mathematics.* Belmont, CA: Wadsworth.

Marzola, E. S. (1987). Using manipulatives in math instruction. *Reading, Writing, and Learning Disabilities, 3*, 9–20.

Marzolf, D. P. (1994). *Remembering and mapping relations in a symbolic task.* Paper presented at the International Conference for Infant Studies, Paris.

Marzolf, D. P. (1995). *Spatial correspondence and scale models: Understanding and mapping symbol-referent relations.* Paper presented at the meeting of the Society for Research in Child Development, Indianapolis, IN.

Marzolf, D. P., & DeLoache, J. S. (1994). Transfer in young children's understanding of spatial representations. *Child Development, 64*, 1–15.

Murphy, C. M. (1978). Pointing in the context of shared activity. *Child Development, 49*, 371–380.

Ninio, A., & Bruner, J. (1978). The achievement and antecedents of labeling. *Journal of Child Language, 5*, 1–15.

Resnick L. B., & Omanson S. F. (1987). Learning to understand arithmetic. In R. Glaser (Ed.), *Advances in Instructional Psychology* (Vol. 3, pp. 41–96). Hillsdale, NJ: Lawrence Erlbaum.

Scheer, J.K. (1985). Manipulatives make math meaningful for middle schoolers. *Child Education, 62,* 115–121.

Scott L. F., & Neufeld, H. (1976). Concrete instruction in elementary school mathematics: Pictorial versus manipulative. *School Science and Mathematics, 76,* 68–72.

Sigel, I. E. (1953). Developmental trends in the abstraction ability of children. *Child Development, 24,* 131–144.

Sigel, I. E., Anderson, L. M., & Shapiro, H. (1966). Categorization behavior of lower and middle class Negro preschool children: Differences in dealing with representations of familiar objects. *Journal of Negro Education, 35,* 218–229.

Smith, C. M. (1995). *Young children's use of dolls as self symbols.* Paper presented at the meeting of the Society for Research in Child Development, Indianapolis, IN.

Sowell E.J. (1989). Effects of manipulating materials in mathematics instruction. *Journal for Research in Mathematics Education, 20,* 498–505.

Stevenson, H. W., & Stigler, J. W. (1992). *The learning gap: Why our schools are failing and what we can learn from Japanese and Chinese education.* New York: Summit Books.

Suydam, M. N. & Higgins, J. L. (1977). *Activity-based learning in elementary school mathematics: Recommendations from research.* Columbus, OH: Center for Science, Mathematics and Environmental Education. (ERIC Document Reproduction Service No. ED-144–840)

Troseth, G. L., & DeLoache, J. S. (1996). Very young children's understanding of a video representation. Paper presented at the annual meetings of the Midwestern Psychological Association, Chicago (May, 1996).

Uttal, D. H., Scudder, K. V., & DeLoache, J. S. (1997). Manipulatives as symbols: A new perspective on the use of concrete objects to teach mathematics. *Journal of Applied Developmental Psychology, 18,* 37–54.

Williams C. K., & Kamii, C. How do children learn by handling objects? *Young Children, 42,* 23–26.

Yates, A., & Terr, L. (1988). Anatomically correct dolls: Should they be used as a basis for expert testimony? *Journal of the American Academy of Child and Adolescent Psychiatry, 27,* 254–257.

Chapter 5

The Development of Pretense and Narrative in Early Childhood

Robert D. Kavanaugh and Susan Engel

The early childhood years mark the beginning of an understanding of imagination, drama, and narrative. Young children's participation in this fictive world is all the more remarkable if we bear in mind the starting point only a few years earlier. During the first year, and for a good part of the second, infants often comprehend their surroundings by acting on them, by exploring—quite literally—the people and objects in their environment. Within the first few months of birth, infants learn how to manipulate familiar objects, such as mobiles hanging over a crib, to produce the perceptual and auditory consequences they desire (Rovee-Collier, 1987). As early as 4 months infants understand that objects continue to exist even when they disappear momentarily from view (Baillargeon & DeVos, 1991). At roughly 9 months they show an understanding of purposeful, goal-directed actions by using one object (e.g., a cloth) to obtain another (e.g., an attractive toy) that lies beyond reach (Willatts, 1989). By their first birthday, infants not only produce a number of self-initiated, purposeful actions, they also demonstrate the ability to *reproduce* novel actions that adults make, such as touching a toy with their forehead, as long as a week after watching adults carry out such actions (Meltzoff, 1988). Infants' competency in manipulating and exploring objects continues to grow during the first half of the second year when they become relentless explorers of virtually every object in their environment, often to the dismay of their beleaguered parents.

While there can be little doubt about the competence of young infants, there are also clear limitations on what infants know. Before 15- to 18-months of age, infants attend primarily to people, objects, and events in their immediate environment. They are preoccupied, as many observers have noted, with the here-and-now. Furthermore, there is a strikingly literal quality to virtually everything they do. During the first year, infants may manipulate and explore objects endlessly, but they are not likely to use objects in symbolic fashion, that is, to allow one object represent another. For example, both 12- and 24-month-olds enjoy exploring the physical properties of household utensils, by manipulating and banging together objects such as pots, pans, and spoons. But only the 24-month-old is apt to place a pot on her head and pretend that it is a hat, or to simulate the movements of a racing car by shouting "broom, broom" as she pushes the spoon across the floor.

At first, these symbolic behaviors appear only as brief and isolated actions in the play of young children. Nonetheless, they represent a clearly demarcated entry point into a new and different way of knowing. The child who can permit one object from her immediate surroundings (e.g., a spoon) to represent another (e.g., a car) that is not actually present is no longer limited to what Piaget called a sensorimotor (physical) understanding of the world. This child can go beyond the here-and-now to comprehend events that are represented in mind. Within a few short months this "symbolic child" will talk about the past, make reference to the future, engage in pretend play, and begin to construct narrative fragments that tell brief "stories" about salient life events.

In this chapter, we explore the emergence of two distinct elements of symbolic thought in young children—pretend play and narrative. Our principal aim is to provide an overview of the growing literature on pretense and narrative, and to show the conceptual relationship between these two related expressions of symbolic thought. We argue that the relationship between pretense and narrative has important implications for an understanding of the nonliteral, fictive world that emerges during early childhood.

PRETENSE

Piaget's (1946/1962) seminal work *Play, Dreams and Imitation in Childhood* launched the developmental study of pretense. Replete with intriguing observations of the pretend play of Piaget's own children, this book offered a compelling theoretical explanation of pretense, and also served as the inspiration for a series of influential studies of pretend play in 12- to 30-month old children. Below we summarize the results of this substantial body of work, beginning with a brief conceptual overview of pretense.

What Is Pretense?

Pretense is a construct used to indicate that an organism (human or animal) is acting in a simulative, nonliteral, or "as if" modality (Fein, 1981). Pretense behavior takes many different forms. A mother is acting in an as-if modality when she simulates "pouring" imaginary tea into an empty cup. Similarly, an actor playing the part of Hamlet is engaged in simulative behavior when he acts as if he were the prince of Denmark.

Researchers have developed specific criteria to identify pretense behavior in young children (cf., Fein, 1981; Nicolich, 1977), but we generally recognize it quite easily. Most people would safely assume that a 2-year-old child is pretending when she lifts an empty tea cup to her mouth, makes exaggerated drinking noises, and then smiles knowingly at her mother. The child's behavior signals her appreciation of simulation, of nonliteral versus literal actions. She is acting as if the empty cup contained tea. So too would we label as pretense the play of two preschool children, one of whom wears a hat and describes herself as "bus driver," while the other sits dutifully behind the "driver" and refers to herself as the "sitter."

Although pretense is often used to refer to the simulated actions that individuals *produce*, such as sipping imaginary tea from an empty cup, it can also refer to the ability to *comprehend* the nonliteral actions of others. Comprehension is a crucial component of pretense, particularly joint or shared pretense. For instance, in our first example above, the mother must correctly identify the child's behavior as nonliteral if she wishes to continue with the theme of a make-believe tea party. Obviously, failures to comprehend the pretense overtures of a play partner will either disrupt or terminate shared pretend play.

Solitary Pretend Play

Beginning early in the second year, children produce pretend actions with familiar objects often while playing alone. Piaget's (1946/1962) observation of his 15-month-old daughter, Jacqueline, provides a clear example of the type of pretending that emerges during solitary play:

> J. saw a cloth whose fringed edges vaguely recalled those of a pillow; she seized it, held a fold of it in her right hand, sucked the thumb of the same hand, and lay down on her side, laughing hard. She kept her eyes open, but blinked them from time to time as if she were alluding to closed eyes. (p. 96)

Recognizing the interpretative nature of his observations, Piaget was careful to draw attention to several features of Jacqueline's behavior that helped to determine that she was actually pretending. He noted that the sleeping sequence she enacted took place outside of her normal bedtime routine, and that Jacqueline incorporated several actions, such as laughing and blinking, which suggested a simulated or nonliteral quality to her behavior.

Although Piaget's observations were limited to his own three children, subsequent researchers have corroborated his findings in a number of large-scale studies. These investigations have shown that pretense originates with self-representation, such as Jacqueline's simulation that she was asleep, but that shortly thereafter children begin to incorporate people and toy objects (e.g., dolls, animals) into their pretend play (Fein & Apfel, 1979; Nicolich, 1977). For example, children may use a spoon to "feed" make-believe cereal to a doll or to a play partner. Once children have the capacity to represent the behavior of others in pretend play, they tend to build more complex scenarios involving self and object in the same sequence (Nicolich, 1977; Wolf, 1982). For example, a 24-month-old might "feed" herself and a doll during the course of a make-believe tea party. At a slightly older age, children are likely to make replica objects act as agents who carry out their own pretend actions (Fenson, 1984; Wolf, Rygh, & Altshuler, 1984). This is a far more sophisticated form of pretense that involves ascribing actions, feelings, and even thoughts to inanimate objects, for example, making a doll go to sleep because "she's tired," or making a toy animal say "ouch, too hot" as it steps into a make-believe bathtub (Wolf et al., 1984).

Social Pretend Play

As our brief review suggests, Piaget established a research tradition that produced a rich account of the developmental changes in children's pretend play. While subsequent researchers refined and improved his methods, there can be little doubt about the debt owed to Piaget, whose theoretical writings continue to promote lively debates about the cognitive-social underpinnings of pretense. One issue of particular interest is the consequence of Piaget's intense focus on the cognitive bases of pretense to the near exclusion of the social context—the interactions with parents and peers—in which pretend play occurs. Although Piaget acknowledged that higher levels of pretense often involved collaborative interactions between the child and others (e.g., parents/peers), both he and his immediate followers focused primarily on pretense as it emerged during solitary play (Fein, 1981).

Recently, a number of investigators, some inspired by Piaget's contemporary, Lev Vygotsky, have begun to examine more closely the social context of pretend play. Vygotsky was a Russian psychologist whose postrevolutionary writings resolutely embraced the notion that *inter*personal experience is the guiding force that shapes *intra*personal development (Wertsch, 1985). Vygotsky's theory suggests, for example, that the play of parents or older children has a formative influence on the way in which young children organizes, interpret, and understand their own play.

Pretend play with adults. Several different investigators have compared children's spontaneous pretend play under two conditions: when the child's mother is present but otherwise occupied, and when the mother is fully available as a play partner (O'Connell & Bretherton, 1984; Slade, 1987; Fiese, 1990). One consistent finding from this literature is that the mother's active involvement generally improves the child's pretend play. For example, children who were approximately 2 years old demonstrated an increase in the duration of pretend play, greater diversity in pretend episodes, and a longer time spent in preparing or planning pretend episodes when the mother was available as a play partner (O'Connell & Bretherton, 1984; Slade, 1987).

Several researchers have documented what mothers actually do to enhance pretend play. In the course of spontaneous play with 18- to 30-month-olds, mothers make direct suggestions for pretense as well as demonstrating pretend sequences that the child then mimics, either partially or completely (O'Connell & Bretherton, 1984; Kavanaugh & Harris, 1991). Mothers are also effective in shaping and sustaining pretense by responding to ambiguous prompts from the child with nonliteral words and actions that help to create make-believe episodes (Kavanaugh, Whittington, & Cerbone, 1983). Finally, some researchers found that mothers actively structured pretend play by arranging situations in which such play could take place and by providing appropriate props, such as dolls, dishes, bottles, and the like (Miller & Garvey, 1984).

Pretend play with peers. Children's pretend play with peers has a distinctly different character from their pretend play with adults. Mothers often use props and toys to stimulate pretend sequences by encouraging their child to carry out particular nonliteral actions. By contrast, play with peers often involves jointly produced scenarios rich with pretend roles and psychological states (Dunn & Dale, 1984).

Children engage in social pretend play with siblings and peers at a surprisingly early age. For instance, Dunn and Dale (1984) reported selected examples of one form of social pretend play, known as role play, among 2-year-olds. Role play is a sophisticated form of social pretend play in which children simulate the attitudes and behavior of another person. The following example of role play involves a 2-year-old child (Richard) and his older sister:

RICHARD: *Train coming now*
SISTER: *Choo choo. I wonder when they're going to come. Do you know?*
RICHARD: *Yes*
SISTER: *There's one going this way and one going that way.*
RICHARD: *Go London.*
SISTER: *Look Richard. Got a little tunnel (of cushions).*
RICHARD: *(drives tractor into tunnel) Rrrrrrrrrrrrrrr...... Broom, broom. Engine broke down.*

SISTER: *Richard, can you get some more petrol. The train's got stuck. Go and get some more petrol.*
RICHARD: *(puts "petrol" in). Sssssssssssss.*
SISTER: *Not here it keeps leaking. Try it here near my finger. 'Cos you're the petrol man.*
RICHARD: *No, I run out. . . . I'm a driver.*

(Dunn & Dale, 1984, p. 141)

What is particularly striking about this example is that 2-year-old Richard not only assumes a role assigned to him ("petrol man") and then dutifully carries out his responsibilities, but that he also negotiates for a different and presumably more interesting role ("driver").

Although the above example is quite provocative, normative data suggest that less than 33% of 2-year-olds engage in collaborative role play (Dunn & Dale, 1984). Furthermore, other investigators report that collaborative role play emerges toward the middle of the third year, somewhere around 30 months (Howes, Unger, & Seidner, 1989), and still others believe that clear instances of role play do not emerge until the fourth year (Miller & Garvey, 1984). One potential resolution of these differences, consistent with Vygotsky's position, is that social pretend play in young children is dependent on a positive emotional relationship between the play partners (Dunn, 1991). In support of this claim, Dunn and her colleagues observed that in two separate family studies social pretend play was closely related to independent measures of the quality of affection between the siblings (Dunn, 1991).

Social Pretend Play and Mental Representation

Social pretend play, particularly role play, encourages children to imagine the world from someone else's point of view. When you assume a role with the gusto of a young pretender, that is, when you eagerly become petrol man or driver, you appreciate temporarily a perspective that is not your own. Because appreciating someone else's viewpoint is a major accomplishment of adult life, we might wonder whether the role play among 2- and 3-year-olds is a precursor to higher levels of thought.

One of the principal achievements of the preschool years is the ability to understand that mental states, such as one's thoughts and beliefs, govern much of human behavior. We act in certain way because of what we think or believe. Beginning somewhere around age 3 children come to appreciate that people's beliefs guide their actions. Later in the preschool period children develop an even more complex understanding of mental representation. They understand that people act on their beliefs even if those beliefs are false or mistaken. For example, consider the response of a 5-year-old confronted with the following problem: An experimenter shows the child a box of M&Ms and asks what is inside. When the bemused child replies, "M&Ms," the researcher opens up the box and reveals that a pencil is inside. Next the experimenter asks the child what her friend, who is waiting outside the room, will think is in the box when she sees it for the first time. The 5-year-old answers correctly by indicating that her friend will expect to find M&Ms in the box. But this is not a foregone conclusion. Up until age 4 or 5, most children insist that the friend will expect the box to contain a pencil. That is, young preschoolers do not realize that the friend's response will be guided by her mistaken belief rather than the actual state of affairs. But by the close of the preschool period children recognize that people act on mental representations, even if those representations do not portray reality correctly (Moses & Chandler, 1992; Russell, 1992).

Recently, several independent investigations have suggested a provocative link between role play and mental representation (Youngblade & Dunn; Taylor, Gerow, & Carlson, 1993). Youngblade and Dunn (1995) conducted a brief longitudinal study with children who were nearly 3 years old when they were first observed at home engaged in pretend play with mothers and siblings. These pretend play episodes were scrutinized carefully for instances of role play in which children assumed the kind of make-believe roles (e.g., driver, petrol man) that we described earlier. Approximately 6 months later these same children were assessed on measures of false belief, similar to the M&M task described above. The results revealed that children who frequently enacted make-believe roles at approximately age 3 were more likely to pass tests of false belief administered 6 months later. Equally important was the specific nature of these findings, that is, other measures of pretend play, such as how often children pretended or how many different make-believe themes they enacted, did *not* have any bearing on success on the false belief tasks. Although it is important to bear in mind that these correlational data do not permit direct conclusions about cause and effect, Youngblade and Dunn's findings were corroborated by Taylor et al. (1993), who also found a specific link between role play and mental representation. In this study, $3^1/_2$-to-$4^1/_2$-year-olds were assessed on two measures: role play as judged by the presence of an imaginary companion or the impersonation of imaginary characters, and success on a series of tasks that measured false beliefs and other forms of mental representation. The results revealed a positive relationship between role play and performance on the tests of mental representation. Even with verbal ability controlled, the children who scored highly on role play scores were more likely to succeed on the false belief and representational tasks.

These recent findings attach special significance to social pretend play, and particularly to role play, as a vehicle for developing an awareness of the workings of other people's minds. In the context of a safe and supportive environment, role play allows children to explore new identities and to extrapolate what others think and feel. It is perhaps not surprising, then, that later in development the experienced role player easily imagines the thoughts and beliefs of others, even when those whose beliefs are objectively mistaken. From this perspective, role play is far more than a series of brief and playful interactions between two willing compatriots. Rather, it is the stuff that mature thoughts are made of.

Understanding Pretense

Social pretend play provides crucial information about how interactions with a more mature play partner guide and support the development of pretense in young children, particularly those under the age of 3 years. At the same time research on this topic raises questions about what toddlers actually understand about the pretend overtures of another person. It is possible, for example, that young children participate in joint pretend scenarios without fully comprehending the nonliteral intentions of the play partner. They are able to respond appropriately because of the careful structure provided by more mature play partners, including props, verbal cues, and pretend demonstrations.

Such an interpretation is strengthened by one of the few studies to investigate young children's pretense comprehension during social pretend play. (DeLoache & Plaetzer, 1985). After first confirming that 15- to 30-month-olds produced higher levels of pretense when playing with their mothers than when playing alone, DeLoache and Plaetzer reported that roughly 25% of the children appeared to misunderstand their mothers' make-believe intentions. The protocol from one 30-month-old is instructive. During a make-believe tea-party, this child dropped a sponge and knocked over a cup causing his mother to remark, "Oh oh, you spilled your tea. You better wipe it up." The child responded by picking up the sponge, looking around carefully, and asking, "where," as though he were searching for real rather than pretend tea (DeLoache & Plaetzer, 1985).

To provide a more direct assessment of what children understand about the pretend play of others, Harris and Kavanaugh (1993) conducted a series of studies in which young children watched an adult experimenter carry out unexpected pretend actions, such as "squeezing" imaginary toothpaste onto the tail of a toy monkey, or "pouring" make-believe tea onto the floor. By approximately age 2½, children were able to describe the consequences of these imaginary actions (e.g., referring to the monkey as "messy" and the floor as "wet") and to carry out remedial pretend actions (e.g., "clean" the monkey and "wipe" the floor). Subsequent research has demonstrated that young children's pretense comprehension skills extend even further to include an understanding of the causal link between successive pretend actions, such as "pouring" make-believe milk into a bowl and then "emptying" the contents of the bowl onto a surface. Older 2-year-olds who viewed such actions correctly described the surface as "milky" (Harris, Kavanaugh, & Meredith, 1994).

Although it has received less attention than the ability to produce pretend actions, pretense comprehension, or the ability to understand someone else's make-believe intentions, is the foundation for truly interactive social pretend play. To participate fully in pretend play with another, not only must children initiate make-believe scenarios they must also respond appropriately to the imaginary stipulations of their play partner. It appears that by age 2½ children have the ability to understand the make-believe sequences of others and to become full partners in the enriching enterprise of shared pretend play.

NARRATIVE

As the world of drama and imagination unfolds for the child, it begins to involve a related but different form of playful interactions, first with parents and later with peers. These interactions center around brief but coherent stories, initially constructed by someone else, that organize and structure the child's actions. Consider the following interchange between a mother and her 2-year-old who are playing with two small action figures, Lantern Man and Spider Man.

> As the child begins to move the figures about, her mother supplies a thematic narration, saying, "Oh look, Lantern Man is chasing Spider Man. Oh no, he is pushing him down. Spider Man says, 'Help, Lantern Man is grabbing me.' Look, Spider Man is getting away."

In this vignette, the mother's narration elaborates on the joint play and provides a thematic structure that gives meaning and coherence to what the child is doing. Furthermore, it is likely that episodes such as these underlie the acquisition of the child's own storytelling abilities. Long before children can construct their own narratives, they are engaged in playful interactions with others that foreshadow the stories they will tell in the preschool years and beyond (Engel, 1995).

What Is Narrative?

Narrative is one of the essential modes of communication through which people express their thoughts and feelings. Just as children learn about the physical world through logical problem solving, they learn about the social-emotional world—the world of people—through narrative (Bruner,

1986). The story form is particularly well suited to explore people's actions and experiences, and to unveil their desires and motives.

Although there is no universally agreed upon definition, the various descriptions of narrative share a few essential characteristics. Narratives are verbal or written accounts of experience that center around a particular theme. The theme of a narrative may or may not describe something that has actually happened, but it always conveys something meaningful about the events (Snow, 1990). Narratives have characters, or actors, and a point of view, often communicating the subjective experience of one or more actors, or the narrator (Bruner & Lucariello, 1989). Finally, narratives are indifferent to facts. We judge a story by its internal cohesion and structure rather than its correspondence to a real event (Bruner, 1986).

The past 10 years have witnessed a surge of interest in the origins and psychological functions of narrative. A substantial body of work suggests that narrative plays a crucial role in allowing children to make sense of the world around them, in deepening their self-knowledge, and in helping them to understand the values and mores of their culture (Brice Heath, 1983; Feldman, 1989; Stern, 1989). Narratives also allow children to express their innermost thoughts and feelings, and permit them to communicate to others who they are (Engel, 1995; Miller & Sperry, 1988).

Emergence of Narrative

When compared to other linguistic accomplishments, true narratives are a relatively late developmental achievement. Research on narrative discourse, for example, often begins with children who are in their third, fourth, or fifth year (Ninio, 1988). However, other forms of narrative are present much earlier, emerging from conversations in which parents remark on imagined or nonpresent events (Engel, 1995; Ninio, 1988). Consequently, researchers interested in the fledgling signs of narrative focus on the brief story fragments that young children produce.

Two crucial experiences seem to underlie the child's ability to construct narratives (Engel, 1995): One is conversations between parents and children about child-salient life events, particularly discussions of shared activities that have occurred in the recent past. The other is the type of parental discourse that occurs when parents and toddlers engage in joint pretend play. For clarity, we explore each of these issues separately, but in reality they are interrelated events in the lives of many children.

Memory and Narrative

Conversations between parents and young children about events in the recent past become common during the second year. As studies of language acquisition have shown, parents not only talk about the here-and-now with their youngest language users, they also talk about objects and events that are not in the immediate environment—people and toys not present, or activities that happened a few hours or days before (Sachs, 1983). Beginning around 1½ to 2 years, at a time when some children may be using only single words, parents tell stories about past events and encourage their children to participate in those stories by embellishing and elaborating on the child's contribution (DeLoache, 1983; Engel, Kyratzis, & Lucariello, 1984; Horn-Ratner, 1980). The following conversation between a mother and her 18-month-old child illustrates this process of "co-constructing" a brief narrative:

MOTHER: *Look at the pretty lights on the tree. Daddy put those lights on didn't he?*
CHILD: *Lights.*
MOTHER: *Yes, the lights are pretty. Daddy climbed up on a ladder, didn't he? Dan helped Daddy with the lights, right? And we watched from the window.*

Through repeated conversations such as these children learn that there is a special kind of language use that is a very effective vehicle for describing shared memories. Longitudinal research has shown that initially parents provide highly structured conversations, similar to the one above, but that children assume a more active role in recounting past experiences as they master the conventions of story telling (Snow, 1990).

Development of storytelling. Somewhere around 18 months, at a time when children are beginning to engage in active pretense play, they also begin to use language to refer to past events. At first, as in the example above, children are likely to repeat a word from a parent's description of a shared recent experience. Although this may appear to be a minor contribution to the overall narrative, it is important to recognize that at this very early age the child is participating actively in storytelling. Within a short period of time, children are likely to begin adding novel information to their parents' stories (Eisenberg, 1985). For example, if a mother is recalling a trip that she and her child took to the zoo, the child may name an animal that they saw there. Although the child contributes only one word to the zoo story, she inserts it at the proper moment in the story and remains within the boundaries of her mother's narrative framework. Over time, children gradually assume a more active role in the process of "co-constructing" stories with parents and other familiar caregivers. Not only do they insert appropriate words and phrases into adult's stories, but they also offer their own descriptions of events, both real and imagined.

Research on narrative suggests that by age 3 most children are able storytellers (Engel, 1995). Preschool children spontaneously describe events in terms of space and time—something happened somewhere, and then something else happened (Schank, 1990; Nelson & Gruendel, 1979). Gradually, their stories include such sophisticated narrative characteristics as dramatic tension, or a problem and the resolution of that problem. As they reach ages 5 and 6, children are likely to communicate clearly about the perspective from which a story is told, and what the principal characters think and feel. They are also likely to include explicit comments on the meaning or moral of a story they have created.

Individual differences in storytelling. Not all children tell stories about personal experiences in the same way. Research on the development of narrative has identified two kinds of young storytellers for whom the form and function of storytelling differ. Some children seem to view talk about the past as an intrinsically interesting form of interaction with adults or peers. They tell long detailed stories with frequent reference to past events. Other children seem only to refer to the past as a way of clarifying something in the present. They refer to the past infrequently and their stories are brief and sparse (Engel, 1995).

This difference in narrative style emerges first among young children (2-year-olds) but has also been found among preschoolers. We do not yet know if it lasts into middle childhood, nor do we know if it is related to other individual differences in play and language acquisition. However, at least one investigator has offered the intriguing suggestion that differences in narrative style may be linked to the ease with which children attain literacy in school (Wells, 1986). Other investigators who have studied children's play patterns have identified two types of children, one they call dramatists and the other modelers (Wolf & Gardner, 1979). Dramatists tend to use toys and play opportunities to interact with others and to explore interpersonal dynamics; modelers tend to focus on the intrinsic qualities of objects and to use toys to make patterns, build shapes, and so forth. Although it has not been demonstrated empirically, it is possible that young children who tell long detailed stories about past events, what we might call reminiscers, are also likely to be dramatists who explore interpersonal relationships in their play with others. By the same token, children who tell brief stories that refer sparingly to past events are more likely to be modelers whose play is focused primarily on what can be done with objects.

It is clear that the complex relationship between language development, play, and narrative is a very fruitful area of research. We expect that future studies in this area will show how cultural and individual differences affect symbolic functioning across these three domains, and will begin to specify the complex interrelationship among these domains throughout development.

Pretense and Narrative

Long before children are able to construct their own real or imagined stories independently, they are able to create make-believe scenarios that an adult play partner can shape into a brief narrative. For example, consider the remarks of a father while playing with his 2½-year-old. During the course of their play, the child picked up a wooden spoon and "stirred" the contents of an empty bowl. As he did this, the father said "Oh, you're baking a cake, are you? Are you going to have a party? With cake? And balloons? That'll be a great cake."

What this example demonstrates is that young children's pretend play contains an implicit narrative structure that a parent can make salient to the child. When parents narrate the child's pretend gestures, as in the above example, they confer structure and meaning on the child's nonliteral actions, and in so doing highlight the narrative features implicit in the child's actions. In addition, by enacting make-believe sequences young children develop some facility with the components of narrative structure, much as they first experience grammatical structure through their nonverbal play routines (Bruner, 1975).

Pretend play with parents is rewarding and productive, but as children develop they are more likely to coordinate their imaginary play with siblings and friends who share similar interests (Rubin, 1980). Play narratives constructed with peers offer young children the opportunity to assume different roles and to express feelings, intentions, and even personalities that are not their own . For example, consider the play of two preschool age girls acting out a mother and child scenario, using dolls as props.

CHILD 1 (MOTHER'S VOICE): *Now Cindy, I told you not to go into the woods alone.*

CHILD 2 (BABY'S VOICE): *But Mommy Mommy, I'm hungry. I want toast!*

CHILD 1 (MOTHER'S VOICE): *No. You frightened me very badly. Now I have to punish you. Go take a nap!*

In this play episode, the narration describes an event and expresses the ideas and experiences of two interconnected characters, a mother and daughter. The children use play narration to consolidate and express their knowledge of social roles.

At other times children use play narratives to learn more about themselves and their play partners. In the following example, while planning a game, two boys explore the thoughts and feelings of their invented characters. They appear less concerned with conventional social roles, and more interested in the individual feelings and characteristics of their protagonists with whom they identify strongly.

CHILD 1: *OK, I'll be invisible man. And whenever I need to save someone I'm gonna turn invisible. And my enemies wont be able to see me, but everyone else will.*

CHILD 2: *Yeah, and I'll be boomerang man. And if you are in trouble I can send my boomerang to hit the bad guy. But you like me. You like me!*

CHILD 1: *Yeah, but I don't know who you are. You come from another planet, so I don't know you.*

In these fairly sophisticated play narratives, children exhibit both an understanding and a continued exploration of what people feel and think. These intricate constructions are an outgrowth of the early pretend play and reminiscing that toddlers engage in, both with parents and each other.

In sum, we argue that play narratives offer several distinct opportunities for young children to learn about intrapersonal feelings and interpersonal relationships. First, by responding to and collaborating with peers, preschool children learn what others want and need to hear from a story. Second, by attending to the interest, questions, and criticisms of their play partner's narratives, preschoolers learn something about the accepted canons of their culture. Third, by exploring the intentions and experiences of the characters they invent, preschoolers learn about their own thoughts and feelings as well as the thoughts and feelings of others.

EDUCATIONAL IMPLICATIONS

An understanding of pretense and narrative typically begins early in life. By the beginning of the third year, many children show an appreciation for some of the critical elements of drama and fiction. For example, they realize that pretend episodes do not convey real-world truths but are comprised of the make-believe happenings of an imaginary world. If asked about the consequences of tipping an empty cup over the head of a toy animal, most toddlers do not respond with a literal account of what happened but rather with an accurate description of the pretend outcome. Furthermore, toddlers engage willingly in pretend play with others where they often demonstrate a capacity for rich and complex make-believe episodes.

What are the consequences of make-believe play? First, we should note that contrary to older reports in the clinical literature, children who engage frequently and robustly in pretend play, including those with imaginary companions, are not likely to experience social-emotional problems. For example, recent studies of preschoolers with imaginary friends reveal that these children are more sociable and have more real world friends than children without imaginary companions (Taylor, Cartwright, & Carlson, 1993). Second, it appears that social pretend play, and in particular role play, may actually bear a positive relationship to children's cognitive development. Recent research has shown that involvement in role play before age 3 is positively correlated with later success on tasks of mental representation (Youngblade & Dunn, 1995).

At the same time that pretense play is unfolding during the second and third year, most toddlers are beginning to attend to their parents' stories about past experiences. These brief but thematic stories provide one of two developmental prerequisites to mature narrative ability. By listening to and participating in stories about their past, young children master some of the basic structures of narrative discourse. At the same time that they are "co-constructing" their past experiences, young children are also learning about narrative through social pretend play. The narrative features of their pretend play may be most salient when articulated by a parent in the ways we have suggested.

Several researchers have pointed to interesting and important individual differences in children's narrative style that appear for the first time during the third year. Some children construct sparse stories primarily confined to the present while others create long and detailed stories with frequent reference to past events. Although these individual differences are not fully accounted for, one plausible suggestion is that differences in children's narrative style may be linked to differences in parental styles of play and storytelling (Engel, 1995; Wells, 1986). A common finding in this literature is that parents who engage in a wealth and diversity of joint play and narrative construction are likely to have school-aged children who feel able and interested in storytelling, including such mature forms of narrative activity as writing (Engel, 1995).

What do the findings on pretend play and narrative mean for the educator of young children? It is by now a cliché to assert that play is the young child's work, but if we pause to unpack this statement we can find several suggestions for educators that are well grounded in basic research.

First, we believe that pretend play, particularly social pretend play, should be valued and encouraged. Although it may not be possible to induce social pretend play, we know that it flourishes when the partners have close emotional ties and when one of the partners is somewhat older and more mature than the other. This situation is particularly likely to promote role play, a form of pretense that appears to have important consequences for the cognitive-social development of the young child. Moreover, there is no obvious downside to social pretend play, including "play" with imaginary partners. Worries about emotional difficulties arising from children's overly active imaginations do not appear to be justified by the contemporary literature on fantasy and imagination (Singer & Singer, 1990).

Second, we believe that research on narrative suggests that not only should parents encourage opportunities for storytelling in young children, but that they should collaborate in these activities as well. Furthermore, this proscription would seem to apply to daycare workers, preschool teachers and other adults who have extensive contact with young children. Adults promote skills essential to the development of an understanding of self and others when they provide young children with ample time for storytelling, and with opportunities for pretense play that encourages story construction. But it is not sufficient simply to provide children time and space for pretend play and storytelling. Young children also need flexible, responsive, and interactive partners to guide them toward mature forms of narrative construction. To wit, partners who both elicit and elaborate on the details of children's stories, as well as partners who expose children to a rich and varied array of narrative forms through conversation, stories, poems, word play, and dramatic play. In short, it is essential to provide young children with an environment that is dense with narrative activity.

CONCLUSION

We conclude where we began by noting the importance of pretense and narrative in the lives of young children. At a very early age, children understand and participate in make-believe enterprises that provide a foundation for entrance into the nonliteral world of drama and fiction. It is a world rich with opportunity for discoveries about how others think and feel, and a world that allows the child to explore her own literary constructions. And though it remains speculative at the psychological level, children's early experience with make-believe may dispose them toward a general appreciation of the arts in adulthood. Several recent philosophical analyses stress the continuity between the child's participation in make-believe and the adult's response to works of art (Currie, 1990; Walton, 1990). Currie (1990) notes that the author of a work of fiction invites the reader to engage in a game of make-believe that is constrained by a set of "fictional truths" generated by the text. Similarly, Walton (1990) observes that a painting serves as an elaborate prop in which viewers imagine themselves at the scene which the artist has created. These observations highlight one additional feature of the role of make-believe in the lives of young children. Early participation in pretense and narrative is neither truncated nor short lived. Children continue to use the capacity for make-believe throughout the childhood years and even into adulthood.

REFERENCES

Baillargeon, R., & DeVos, J. (1991). Object permanence in young infants: Further evidence. *Child Development, 62,* 1127–1146.

Brice Heath, S. (1983). *Ways with words*. Cambridge: Cambridge University Press.

Bruner, J. (1975). The ontogenesis of speech acts. *Journal of Child Language, 2*, 1–19.

Bruner, J. (1986). *Actual minds, possible worlds*. Cambridge, MA: Harvard University Press.

Bruner, J., & Lucariello, J. (1989). Monologue as narrative recreation of the world. In K. Nelson (Ed.), *Narratives from the crib*. Cambridge, MA: Harvard University Press.

Currie, G. (1990). *The nature of fiction*. Cambridge: Cambridge University Press.

DeLoache, J. S., & Plaetzer, B. (April, 1985). *Tea for two: Joint mother-child symbolic play*. Paper presented at the meetings of the Society for Research in Child Development, Toronto.

DeLoache, J. (April, 1983). *Joint picture book reading as memory training for toddlers*. Paper presented at the meetings of the Society for Research in Child Development, Detroit, Michigan.

Dunn, J., & Dale, N. (1984). I a Daddy: 2-year-olds' collaboration in joint pretend with sibling and with mother. In I. Bretherton (Ed.), *Symbolic play: The development of social understanding*. New York: Academic Press.

Dunn, J. (1991). Understanding others: Evidence from naturalistic studies of children. In A. Whiten (Ed.), *Natural theories of mind: Evolution, development and simulation of everyday mindreading*. Oxford: Blackwell.

Eisenberg, A. (1985). Learning to describe past experiences in conversation. *Discourse Processes, 8*, 177–204.

Engel, S. (1995). *The stories children tell: Making sense of the narratives of childhood*. New York: Freeman.

Engel, S., Kyratzis A., & Lucariello, J. (May, 1984). Early past and future talk in a social interactive context. In K. Nelson (Chair), *Memory development and the development of memory talk*. Symposium presented at the meetings of the International Conference on Infant Studies, New York.

Fein, G. G. (1981). Pretend play: An integrative review. *Child Development, 52*, 1095–1118.

Fein, G. G., & Apfel, N. (1979). Some preliminary observations on knowing and pretending. In M. Smith & M. B. Franklin (Eds.), *Symbolic functioning in childhood*. Hillsdale, NJ: Lawrence Erlbaum.

Feldman, C. (1989). Monologue as problem solving narrative. In K. Nelson (Ed.), *Narratives from the crib*. Cambridge MA: Harvard University Press.

Fenson, L. (1984). Developmental trends for action and speech in pretend play. In I. Bretherton (Ed.), *Symbolic play: The development of social understanding*. New York: Academic Press.

Fiese, B. H. (1990). Playful relationships: A contextual analysis of mother-child interaction. *Child Development, 61,* 1648–1656.

Harris, P. L., & Kavanaugh, R. D. (1993). Young children's understanding of pretense. *Monographs of the Society for Research in Child Development, 58* (Serial No. 231).

Harris, P. L., Kavanaugh, R. D., & Meredith, M. (1994). Young children's comprehension of pretend episodes. The integration of successive actions. *Child Development, 65,* 16–30.

Horn Ratner, H. (1980). The role of social context in memory development. In M. Perlmutter (Ed.), *Children's memory: New directions for child development* (Vol. 10). San Francisco: Jossey-Bass.

Howes, C., Unger, O., & Seidner, L. B. (1989). Social pretend play in toddlers: Parallels with social play and with solitary play. *Child Development, 60,* 77–84.

Kavanaugh, R. D., & Harris, P. L. (1991, September). *Comprehension and production of pretend language by 2-year-olds.* Paper presented at the annual meeting of the developmental section, British Psychological Society, Cambridge.

Kavanaugh, R. D. , Whittington, S., & Cerbone, M. J. (1983). Mothers' use of fantasy in speech to young children. *Journal of Child Language, 10,* 45–55.

Meltzoff, A. N. (1988). Infant imitation after a 1-week delay: Long term memory for novel and multiple stimuli. *Developmental Psychology, 24,* 470–476.

Miller, P., & Garvey, C. (1984). Mother-baby role play: Its origins in social support. In I. Bretherton (Ed.), *Symbolic play: The development of social understanding.* New York: Academic Press.

Miller, P. J., & Sperry, L. L. (1988). Early talk about the past: The origins of conversational stories of personal experience. *Journal of Child Language, 15,* 293–316.

Moses, L. J., & Chandler, M. J. (1992). Traveler's guide to children's theories of mind. *Psychological Inquiry, 3,* 286–301.

Nelson, K., & Gruendel, J (1979). At morning its lunchtime: A scriptal view of children's dialogues. *Discourse Processes, 2,* 73–94.

Nicolich, L. (1977). Beyond sensorimotor intelligence: Assessment of symbolic maturity through analysis of pretend play. *Merrill-Palmer Quarterly, 23,* 89–99.

Ninio, A. (1988). The roots of narrative: Discussing recent events with very young children. *Discourse Processes, 10,* 35–52.

O'Connell, B., & Bretherton, I. (1984). Toddler's play, alone and with mother: The role of maternal guidance. In I. Bretherton (Ed.), *Symbolic play: The development of social understanding.* New York: Academic Press.

Piaget, J. (1962). *Play, dreams and imitation in childhood.* New York: Norton. (Original publication, 1946)

Rovee-Collier, C. K. (1987). Learning and memory in infancy. In J. D. Osofsky (Ed.), *Handbook of infant development* (2nd ed.). New York: Wiley.

Rubin, Z. (1980). *Children's friendships.* Cambridge, MA: Harvard University Press.

Russell, J. (1992). The theory theory: So good they named it twice. *Cognitive Development, 7,* 485–519.

Sachs, J. (1983). Talking about the there and then. In K. Nelson (Ed.), *Children's language* (Vol. IV). Hillsdale, NJ: Lawrence Erlbaum.

Schank, R. (1991). *Tell me a story.* New York: Scribner.

Singer, D. G., & Singer, J. L. (1990). *The house of make-believe.* Cambridge, MA: Harvard University Press.

Slade, A. (1987). A longitudinal study of maternal involvement and symbolic play during the toddler period. *Child Development, 58,* 367–385.

Snow, C. (1990). Building memories: The ontogeny of autobiography. In C. Cicchetti & M. Beeghly (Eds.), *The self in transition: Infancy to childhood.*

Stern, D. (1989). Crib monologues from a psychoanalytic perspective. In K. Nelson (Ed.), *Narratives from the crib.* Cambridge, MA: Harvard University Press.

Taylor, M., Cartwright, B. S., & Carlson, S. M. (1993). A developmental investigation of children's imaginary companions. *Developmental Psychology, 29,* 276–285.

Taylor, M., Gerow, L. E., & Carlson, S. M. (1993, March). The relation between individual in fantasy and theory of mind. In J. Wooley (Chair), *Pretense, imagination, and the child's theory of mind.* Symposium presented at the meetings of the Society for Research in Child Development, New Orleans.

Walton, K. L. (1990). *Mimesis as make-believe.* Cambridge, MA: Harvard University Press.

Wells, G. (1986). *The meaning makers.* London: Heinemann.

Willats, P. (1989). Development of problem solving in infancy. In A. Slater & G. Bremner (Eds.), *Infant development.* Hillsdale, NJ: Lawrence Erlbaum.

Wolf, D. (1982). Understanding others: A longitudinal case study of the concept of independent agency. In G. Forman (Ed.), *Action and thought: From sensorimotor schemes to symbol use.* New York: Academic Press.

Wolf, D., & Gardner, H. (1979). Style and sequence in early symbolic play. In N. Smith and M. Franklin (Eds.), *Symbolic functioning in childhood.* Hillsdale, NJ: Lawrence Erlbaum.

Wolf, D., Rygh, J., & Altshuler, J. (1984). Agency and experience: Actions and states in play narratives. In I. Bretherton, *Symbolic play: The development of social understanding.* New York: Academic Press.

Youngblade, L. M., & Dunn, J. (1995). Individual differences in children's play with mother and sibling: Links to relationships and understanding of other people's feelings and beliefs. *Child Development, 66,* 1472–1492.

Chapter 6

Play as an Opportunity for Literacy

Kathleen Roskos and Susan B. Neuman

Play has been an object of study by early childhood researchers for nearly a hundred years, its processes and products the investigatory focus of thousands of studies (Bergen, 1988). However, it is only within the last 15 years or so that play's role in young children's literacy learning has become a serious topic of inquiry, stimulated partially by an expanded view of literacy as a social and cultural phenomenon that occurs long before children participate in formal schooling. Described as 'emergent literacy,' a growing body of descriptive work shows young children as active constructors of literacy knowledge through their interactions in everyday activity, not the least of which is play (Christie, 1991; Jacob, 1984; Teale & Sulzby, 1986; Neuman & Roskos, 1992, 1993, 1997). Attention to connections between play and literacy also reflects a logical extension of the enduring search for play's utility, more recently directed to its cognitive benefits (Sutton-Smith, 1995). The idea that children learn useful things as a result of their play is deeply held among scholars and educators and thus holds promise for literacy as for other areas of development, for example, social skills.

In this chapter we examine play as an opportunity for literacy activity in children's early years. We use the word *opportunity* in the active sense to refer both to the availability of play in children's lives and to how settings are organized structurally and normatively to press for literacy activity in play. To begin we briefly overview literacy-play connections in two domains: (1) the psychological, which focuses on relationships between pretense and literacy-related discourse that occur in play texts, and (2) the ecological, which explores the forces of environmental press on children's literacy behavior in the play context. Teasing out the practical implications of this work, we describe how it might be applied to the creation of literacy-enriched play opportunities for young children, particularly in educational settings. In closing we point to possibilities for further research that may enlarge our understanding of play's literacy potential, but we also highlight issues that surround the literacy-in-play line of inquiry that require thoughtful consideration by scholars and educators alike.

CONNECTIONS BETWEEN PLAY AND LITERACY

Let's Pretend: Story Sense and Language Use

While there is considerable distance between children's spontaneous bids to spin pretend play scenarios and their efforts to read or write real storybooks, research suggests that these outwardly dissimilar acts may actually involve similar mental processes (Pellegrini, 1985). Pretending, like reading or writing, depends on abilities to comprehend and use language in ways independent of the immediate situation, as when 5-year-old Claudia informs her peer, "Pretend one of the babies got sick, OK? . . . The baby has to stay in the hospital for 2 days." Several studies have demonstrated the significance of opportunity to engage in symbolic transformations and pretend play talk for literacy development (see Pellegrini & Galda, 1993, for a review). Longitudinal research, for example, shows that 3-year-olds' symbolic transformations in play predicted their writing status at age 5 and that their oral language use in pretend play episodes predicted their reading achievement (Dickinson & Moreton, 1991; Galda, Pellegrini, & Cox, 1989). To change the 'here and now,' 'you and me,' 'this and that,' demands explicit and elaborated language for pretending to even occur—and it is the opportunity to use language in these ways that may have important consequences for literacy development.

Pretending also calls on children's narrative competence and thinking if they are to join in symbolic play episodes with their peers. Pretend sequences can be quite storylike, including characters, settings, and plot plans, for instance, averting threat or treating-healing, that lead to rousing and sustained bouts of play, seen clearly when Emily and friends seek to save Baby Shamu after a dangerous slip on the ice (Roskos, 1990).

S: *(To Emily) Would you come with us? Let's go to Sea World.*
E:*Sea World! Let's watch Shamu! I'm the mom. (All three children run to one end of the room and sit down next to one another. They gaze towards the other end of the room.)*
S: *Oh! I see Shamu.*
E: *It's starting (presumbably the show).*
A. J.: *Yeah!*
E: *There's a little fish. There's a big mom.*

S: *There's a daddy.*
E: *Look! He fell on the ice. Look at 'em. Mommy and Daddy are fell! Oh-h-
  h-h!*
S: *Oh-h-h-hh. Baby Shamu slipped. Let's go see 'em. (The three run to the
  other end of the room.)*
S: *(Patting a pretend Baby Shamu) Oh-h-h-h! I know you're all right. (All
  make stroking motions on a pretend Baby Shamu.)*
E: *Look! All better now. (She pretends to lift Baby Shamu back into the water;
  the boys assist. They then run to the other side of the room.)*

A number of researchers have observed structural parallels between these pretend play stories and narrative competence, suggesting that through pretense children develop the building blocks of story (Guttmann & Fredericksen, 1985; Sachs, Goldman, & Chaille, 1984; Wolf & Pusch, 1985). For example, in their investigation of pretend play productions using a story grammar analysis, Eckler and Weininger (1989) observed a precise structural correspondence between Rummelhart's story grammar scheme (1977) and pretend play behavior in children 4 through 8 years of age (p. 740), which led them to suggest that skill in one may affect skill in the other. Using language to create new possibilities in their play, to go beyond the mundanities of the here and now, engages children in the composing of texts—a metalinguistic act equally essential for literacy as a means of exploring and inventing new worlds (Hall & Robinson, 1995).

Play Places, Literacy Roles, Routines, and Resources

Toys, props, friends, time, and a place to play—the 'stuff' of play activity—contribute mightily to the creation of the play context and what it affords young children. Together these represent the 'environmental press' or those physical and social forces that shape and hone individual behavior in a particular direction. More extensively than most, the ecological psychologists have studied environment-behavior relationships as they pertain to children in their natural environments, observing the coercivity of settings on children's activity (Gump, 1989). Rosenthal (1973), for example, examined children's attention spans by observing what attracted and held them at a play setting in preschool. In this case, the block play proved to be a setting with high attraction (visited by many children), but only of moderate holding power (keeping them there) whereas art and role play had both strong appeal and high holding power. Subsequent analyses suggested at least two reasons why these settings 'held' children to a greater degree than others: The role play offered a variety of actions and the art activity provided concrete point outs of progress—factors that tethered the children's attention to the setting's activity system.

Drawing on the ecological perspective, several researchers have examined the power of environmental variables on children's literacy activity in play, observing the influence of literacy objects, literacy-explicit settings (e.g., post office), and adult involvement on children's literacy behavior and knowledge in the play situation (see Christie, 1991, for a collection of studies). The working hypothesis, here, is that literacy-enriched settings create opportunities for children to behave as if writers and readers, thus allowing them to rehearse literacy roles and routines that are beyond them in any real sense. In the Vygotskian framework, how play as an activity setting is constituted creates a zone of proximal development where literacy interactions with objects and peers may assist children in using related processes and skills that advance their individual literacy development (Forman & McPhail, 1993). Our research, for example, shows how well-crafted play centers that incorporate literacy roles, objects, and routines within children's cultural repertoires provide important opportunities for them to practice and discover the functions and features of written language. Children afforded these play opportunities in their daycare and preschool environments made significant gains in terms of print knowledge (Neuman & Roskos, 1992). These effects appear further enhanced when adults sensitively intervene in children's play to guide, model, and extend literacy interactions as a natural part of the unfolding play activity (Christie & Enz, 1992; Morrow, 1991; Vukelich, 1991a). Put plainly, play enviroments rich in literacy resources, including people, push children to reveal what they know about writing and reading and pull at their literacy development in seemingly beneficial ways.

CREATING OPPORTUNITIES FOR LITERACY IN PLAY

Looking at the play-literacy research from both sides, the potential of play for literacy has made considerable strides in the span of 15 years: Play provides an attractive arena for children's early explorations of the tools, scripts, and roles associated with literacy in their culture, and it stimulates the use of language in ways that apply to literate behavior, such as the use of metalinguistic verbs and narrative skills. How might educators apply this knowledge to the design and facilitation of play as it transpires in the daily activity of child care and early childhood education?

Recognizing the tremendous diversity and uncertainty in early education work, we offer below a set of guidelines that orient individuals to literacy in play practices. Certainly not a prescription for practice, our intention is to provide a frame of reference within which professional judgment and decision making can function comfortably.

Organizing Play Areas

A well-developed body of play research shows that the amount and variety of play materials, and the amount of space and its organization affect the play behavior of young children (Phyfe-Perkins, 1980). Applied to environmental studies of literacy in play, this work has yielded several set-up strategies that guide the preparation of physical space for children's print encounters in play activity.

Organization begins with definition. As research on children's environments indicates, boundaries between play areas that are clearly visible to children help them to focus their play and sustain it (Ramsey & Reid, 1988). Establishing boundaries between play settings is often accomplished by using physical cues, for example, furniture, plants, and hangings, to indicate where one kind of interactive space ends and another begins. But symbolic cues, such as printed signs, inventories, labels, and directions, can also be employed to inform and guide young children's behavior in the play environment. In fact, we are reminded of this every now and then by the children themselves, who create signs identifying special play areas and post warnings for unwanted intruders, like Steven's "Sta outta hr."

Another set-up strategy involves adapting play settings typically found in early childhood environments for literacy activity rather than introducing novel play settings for the sake of literacy. The familiar and well-worn housekeeping and block settings, for example, offer exciting, new opportunities for literacy activity if amply stocked with appropriate literacy tools and objects. Housekeeping, for example, can be expanded to include children's cookbooks for browsing, notepads for writing, grocery packages for reading, and recipe cards or coupons for sharing. Other settings commonly found in the children's broader community may also offer considerable literacy potential and can be easily replicated in the play environment, for instance, the library or post office.

A third strategy is the incorporation of literacy objects and tools that are authentic, appropriate, and useful for children's play purposes in different play settings. The value of object-familiarity and prior experience is well documented in play research, which indicates that pretense is facilitated by prototypical objects and settings (Fein, 1975). Children's familiarity with objects and their functions allows them to use what they know, to demonstrate their competence, and to invent new behavioral combinations. Stocking play settings with literacy objects and tools relevant to the setting and within children's knowledge repertoires supports their literacy-related activity in the flow of play. Our recent work with a library play setting comes to mind. It resembled a real library with books, pamphlets, magazines, and comfortable places to sit and read. On the walls, posters related to children's literature and authors and art selections were displayed. On low shelves, labelled baskets for storing writing supplies and props, such as puppets, could be found. The setting even had rules made up by the children—such as one 3-year old's contribution: "Don't never spit on books." Set apart from noisier play areas, it was a quiet, intellectual place frequently visited by the children and rich with literacy activity for their enjoyment and pleasure.

Applying these set-up strategies to the play environment for purposes of literacy enrichment has important consequences for the quality of children's literacy activity in play since well-defined and familiar settings provisioned with authentic literacy artifacts have been shown to increase children's literacy interactions and knowledge (Morrow, 1990; Neuman & Roskos, 1992, 1993). It follows, then, that literacy opportunities in the course of daily play may be significant for children's literacy development, given the power of practice in learning, and that play environments should afford young children such opportunities, albeit sensitive to local and cultural factors.

Serving as Social Resources

While play is certainly the business of children, part of its richness is also in the hands of caring adults, who arrange for play and periodically assist in its development. Adults' presence and participation can lead to higher levels of play and longer-lasting, more complex play episodes (Bruner, 1983; Sylva, Roy, & Painter, 1980). Although few studies have directly examined adults' facilitation of literacy in play, results generally concur with this broader observation and suggest at least two ways adults can support children's literacy discoveries in their play activity (Enz & Christie, 1993; Roskos & Neuman, 1993; Vukelich, 1991a).

Adults can demonstrate writing and reading for young children by guiding them in the use of various literacy materials, which children may choose (or not choose) to incorporate into their play. Anchored in a Vygotskian conception of knowledge acquisition, the adult communicates literacy information and shows how it may be used, thus leading the child to do as seen done, providing additional support as needed. Here, active participation in play per se is not the adult's goal, but rather the provision of a social context that enables children to use what they know flexibly and to invent new combinations of literacy behaviors in the course of their play. Indirectly, adults may perform literacy demonstrations, for example, writing a check in a bank dramatic play setting or reading a menu in a pretend restaurant, coinciding their behavior with the theme of children's play yet not entering the play itself (Vukelich, 1991b). Or, using an extending style of interaction (Schrader, 1994), the adult might pick up on children's literacy-related play ideas, moving them beyond their presumed meaning and introducing new elements related to that meaning. Watching children write pretend speeding tickets, for example, the adult might ask, Who's that ticket for? What does it say? and suggest, You need to sign it. In either case, the adult's stance is essentially nonparticipatory, remaining on the edge of children's play, not entering its flow, while supplying literacy hints or cues that children may choose to acknowledge or not. Even this modest level of adult involvement, however, has been found to positively impact children's engagement with literacy during play both in terms of the frequency of writing and reading behaviors as well as the variety of literacy acts (Morrow & Rand, 1991; Vukelich, 1991b).

To promote literacy, adults can also enter into children's play, relying on familiar forms of participation found effective in other literacy-oriented settings, such as storybook reading, as ways to become actively involved. Just as they lovingly accept children's approximations of storybook texts, they can appreciate and applaud children's efforts to use writing and reading in their play; they can play with children as they use literacy to construct a meaningful play scenario; and they can show children how to play new literacy roles and explore unfamiliar routines. In short, they can use a repertoire of literacy-assisting roles to interrelate with children's play activity and move it toward greater complexity. What seems key is adopting a flexible stance toward children's literacy-in-play interactions, knowing when and how to participate so as to contribute to children's emerging literacy interests, skills, and needs while respecting their play intentions (Roskos & Neuman, 1993b). As an example, we recall a rather remarkable scene in day care, where the children had turned the book corner into a recording studio. At first looking on, a teacher was eventually drawn into their play, given the role of tape recorder, listening to and playing back their silly songs. To sustain the fun, she asked the children to write down their songs so as to remember them, which they eagerly proceeded to do with many of these scribbly compositions finding their way home to be sung again. While we do know some about developing a participatory stance toward children's play through professional development and parent involvement programs, we still don't know enough about how to genuinely deepen adults' understandings of play, emergent literacy, and their integration in the play context—a matter we take up a bit later in this chapter.

Encouraging Peer Interactions

Of course, one of the richest resources available to children in their literacy-related play is one another. While young children's literacy learning is more likely to profit from adult assistance, research also cites the benefits of peer interactions in literacy-enriched play environments (Neuman & Roskos, 1991, 1997). Conversations that occur throughout the play convey children's interpretations of the functions and features of written language, as they attempt to extend their knowledge with help from their peers. Busy writing notes to their friends, for example, Dana reminds Hillary that "We hafta sign our names"—an important bit of literacy information in the routine of letter writing. In this respect, as noted by Cook-Gumperz and Gumperz (1976), the context of the play situation seemed to encourage language and literacy-related talk. Although research tells us little about the significance of such exchanges for literacy development, studies of peer interaction do suggest features that seem to foster conversation and the circulation of literacy information in the course of play activity.

Joint play, for example, requires children to work together, actively negotiating meaning so as to create a play scenario. To maintain intersubjectivity as they collaborate, children practice making their intentions known and understanding the intentions of others, thus plying their skill at communicating, planning, and negotiating (Göncü, 1993). In solving problems that inevitably arise when playing together they test their solutions, share expertise, and assist one another's performance. Playing post office, for example, Matthew asks his friend, "Hey man, could you get me an enn . . . , an ennnn . . . An envelope?" Joey replies, "Yup, and make it a big one." Giving and receiving information in the context of these activities allows children to meaningfully apply and extend what they know about literacy, thus practicing not only what written language is for, but also how it works.

Noteworthy as well in joint play is that children often reverse the role of the more capable peer, or teacher according to the purpose of the play. We found that sometimes a child teacher might assume the role of guiding and correcting, while the other children go about performing a literacy task; at other times, however, these roles will reverse, with the teacher initiating a bid for assistance. Due to children's varying experience in literacy, the actual definition of what constitutes the more capable peer can change often according to the particular demonstrations and routines required in the play experience. Consequently, in the play context children are likely to play many parts and thus exercise a broad repertoire of literacy strategies and skills. Making provision for social play and collaborative problem solving, therefore, creates a wide range of possibilities for literacy activity that may potentially engage children in processes of meaning construction tied to their actual use.

A second and closely related feature of social play activity is the composition of play groups. Acknowledging friendships and clustering the range of ability levels in a play group has been found to facilitate negotiations and cooperation necessary for the accomplishment of joint play (Howe, Moller, & Chambers, 1994). Yet there is some recent evidence that more expert play partners can facilitate the play pretense in low-play peers and not at their own expense (Fryer & Fein, 1995). Demonstrating how to pretend, they teach their less-skilled peers how to think symbolically with a greater range of information available in their environment. Literacy is likely no exception here. Examining critical features of literacy in practice, for example, we observed the importance of feedback from peers in the context of literacy-related play activity (Neuman & Roskos, 1997). Consider Kara and Lisa as they play in the post office as Kara tells Lisa, "If you want something, you have to give us money." She replies, "OK," and begins to write on the money, to which Kara swiftly responds, "Lisa, you don't write on money." Coming in many forms—correcting, modeling, demonstrating, instructing—feedback such as this was frequent and immediate, providing important information that allowed children to adjust and adapt their actions to meet the demands of the situation. This suggests the significance of relative expertise in literacy matters among peers and the potential benefit of mixed ability groups that are afforded sufficient opportunity to play together in literacy-enriched play settings.

Informing Families

The incorporation of writing and reading in children's play at home and in their neighborhoods is probably not new. Quite on their own and in the absence of any adult guidance or direction, children engage in actual and pretend reading activities, practice skills, and develop social behaviors as they explore roles for literacy in their personal lives. What is new is a growing recognition of how worthwhile this might be for enculturating children into a community of literacy practitioners. The wellspring of young children's playful writing and reading is the family and the social processes embedded in their relationships, activities, and settings of daily life. Out of these arise literacy models, resources, routines, and scripts that contribute to the depth and complexity of social play and exploration. Aware of their critical roles in children's early literacy development, parents and other caregivers can inspire playful literacy activity by demonstrating literate behavior and by guiding young children's participation in literacy play. Neuman and Gallagher (1994) cite three interactional techniques as particularly important at an early age: labeling, scaffolding, and responding contingently to children's language and literacy initiatives.

In the context of daily family activity, parents should give meaning to objects and events in the environment by naming them, thus aiding children's ability to make sense of the world around them and to organize experience. In constructing meaning with language, children learn what is important about a specific thing or act, such as writing a grocery list, and what may be ignored. For example, picking up the telephone book and saying, "Oh, remember that delicious pizza we had last week?" and "Let's find the number and order it again," helps children recall familiar labels or concepts and offers opportunities to expand their experience. Exchanges like these that naturally occur around basic literacy tools, routines, and functions help children to construct literacy knowledge and use it in meaningful ways.

Parents and caregivers can also structure young children's involvement in learning situations by working together with them. Engaging in joint activity, adults can use scaffolding behaviors to focus children's attention, demonstrate actions, and assist performance in order to ensure children's success (Wood, Bruner, & Ross, 1976). The popular bedtime story routine provides a case in point. Children love to participate in this activity, but are not yet ready to take on all of its aspects by themselves. Parents help by catching children's interest, then reading together, and finally encouraging them to perform certain tasks, such as page turning and pointing to words. As studies of parent-child interaction during storybook reading show, establishing a scaffolding dialogue that maintains children's involvement in the overall process and purpose of the activity in a well-managed way enables them to gain both skill and vision about literacy and its functions (Heath, 1984; Whitehurst et al., 1988). The vividness and richness of these experiences in turn provide children with valuable knowledge for the creation of play scenarios with literacy elements and for active participation in dramatic discourse they engender (Bruner, 1984).

Thirdly, it is important for parents to respond sensitively to their children's literacy attempts and discoveries, including providing access to literacy materials. Considerable research indicates the power of adult contingency behaviors for children's language and learning with even modest changes in mothers' responsivity found to signficiantly impact children's verbal capacity and cognition (Goodnow, 1985; Schaefer, 1991; Neuman & Gallagher, 1994). In play activity, parents can supply the tools of literacy within children's reach (paper, markers, pencils, lots of books and magazines), affirm children's effort ("My goodness. You're a quick writer"), acknowledge requests (Sara asks, "Know what my letter says?" and Mom responds, "No, Won't you tell me?"), and extend children's pretend play ("OK, I'll be the customer. You take my order. Do you have a pad and paper to write it down? I hope you have delicious desserts"). Some research suggests that parents' facilitation of their children's developing literacy in these ways not only enhances the play, but also their own sense of efficacy as parents (Roskos & Neuman, 1993a). Taking children's scribble writing and pretend reading seriously, parents show their children that their ideas are important. They also discover how capable their young children are, which affirms their own effectiveness as their child's first teacher.

RESEARCH DIRECTIONS AND EMERGING ISSUES

In its brief history the play-literacy line of inquiry has broadened understanding of play contexts as opportunities for literacy experiences in the everyday lives of young children. Whether playing around with language and thinking or exploring what literacy and its tools can do, play is an appropriate place and time in young children's search for meaning about written language. Yet, although play and emergent literacy studies have provided insightful descriptions of literacy behaviors in play, the functional significance of language and literacy interactions in this context for children's literacy development and learning remains open to question. Still to be addressed is the issue of equifinality, which Christie (1991) urged some time ago. What is the efficacy of play for developing young children's literacy knowledge and competence? How does it stack up against storybook reading, television viewing, and just plain watching what others do? What does it do or not do for individual children? Further research around this point seems critical, since we may intrude too far where we need not in our effort to support literacy development in the early years.

Also needed is basic research that examines in detail changes over time in individual children's literacy behavior in play situations. Unlike the storybook reading context, which has been linked to the origins and development of emergent literacy through social interactive processes and individual actions (Bus & van IJzendoorn, 1993; Sulzby, 1985), analyses of how maturing children use their self-regulatory abilities to become active learners of literacy in play situations are lacking. Our recent work moves in this direction in an attempt to understand the kinds of literacy knowledge children bring to their play efforts and the strategic behaviors they employ to solve problems in this context, although we are far from understanding what these might mean for literacy acquisition and instruction (Neuman & Roskos, 1997). Relatedly, while there is research evidence that literacy-enriched play settings support children's participation in literacy events and their comprehension of literacy as representational activity, process analyses of the influences of peer interaction during play on literacy engagement and knowledge construction are few. Studies that investigate the dynamics in groups of children that construct shared knowledge claims about literacy and negotiate differences in order to achieve a course of action in the flow of play would be helpful, since fine-grained analyses of collaborative processes might reveal the benefits of the play situation for literacy learning. This also shifts analysis from a focus on individual endeavors to processes of participation, thus broadening the lens to include sociocultural contexts in which the cognitive processes of emerging literacy are embedded.

A third research direction concerns adult facilitation of literacy in the play situation. Recent strategy research from the Vygotskian view provides insights into the cognitive skills that foster literacy acquisition and how, in general, these psychological tools may be passed from adult to child (Rogoff, 1990). While substantial research has produced evidence of the origins of emergent literacy in the linguistic and nonlinguistic interactions between adult and child in the storybook reading context, we know far less about this cognitive enterprise in play situations that involve literacy. Micro-process level studies of adult-child interaction in literacy play are rare, although the few conducted suggest that literacy-enriched play contexts appear to evoke familiar forms of adult tutorial behavior found effective in other settings (Roskos & Neuman, 1993b). But we do not know enough about efficacious joint participation structures that might assist children in their developing conceptions of literacy in this situation, much less how to help parents and teachers develop their knowledge, skill, and a host of personal qualities that also matter if they are to facilitate literacy in play with confidence and sensitivity.

In closing we are heartened by the progress made toward understanding play-literacy connections in such a short span of time, for it reveals clearly young children's interest in and knowledge of literacy as well as play's power for creating literacy learning opportunities. Such progress, however, does not come without problems and before ending we urge caution in two areas. One of these has to do with the infusion of literacy materials into the play environment. Here we stress deliberateness over littering and encourage the creation of places for play with print that are familiar, culturally sensitive, conservative in terms of supplies, and thematically integrated. The other concerns design of the indoor play environment, particularly in educational settings. In this regard we urge the incorporation of literacy into play areas where it makes sense and fits, not tailoring the play environment specifically to suit literacy or a case of the tail wagging the dog. As Brian Sutton-Smith reminds us, play is quite complex and when linked to emergent literacy, quite the more so—which continues to challenge our efforts to understand and unravel the essential meanings that bring the crucial relationship between the two into sharp focus.

REFERENCES

Bergen D. (1988). *Play as a medium for learning and development: A handbook for theory and practice.* Portsmouth, NH: Heinemann Educational Books.

Bruner, J. (1983). Play, thought and language. *Peabody Journal of Education, 60,* 687–708.

Bruner, J. (1984). Language, mind and reading. In H. Goelman, A. Oberg, & F. Smith (Eds.), *Awakening to literacy* (pp. 193–200). Portsmouth, NH: Heinemann Educational Press.

Bus, A., & van IJzendoorn, M. (1995). Mothers reading to their 3-year-olds: The role of mother-child attachment security in becoming literate. *Reading Research Quarterly, 30,* 998–1015.

Christie, J. F. (1991). *Play and early literacy development.* Albany: State University of New York Press.

Christie, J. F., & Enz, B. J. (1992). The effects of literacy play interventions on preschoolers' play patterns and literacy development. *Early Education and Development, 3,* 205–220.

Cook-Gumperz, J., & Gumperz, J. (1976). *Paper on language and context* (Working Paper No. 46). Los Angeles: Language Behavior Research Laboratory.

Dickinson, D., & Moreton, J. (1991, April). *Predicting specific kindergarten literacy skills from three-year-olds' preschool experiences.* Paper presented at the biennial meeting of the Society for Research in Child Development, Seattle.

Eckler, J. A., & Weininger, O. (1989). Structural parallels between pretend play and narratives. *Developmental Psychology, 25,* 736–743.

Enz, B. J., & Christie, J. (1993). *Teacher play interaction styles and their impact on children's oral language and literacy play.* Paper presented at the annual meeting of the National Reading Conference, Charleston.

Fein, G. (1975). A transformational analysis of pretending. *Developmental Psychology, 11,* 291–296.

Forman, E., & McPhail, J. (1993). Vygotskian perspective on children's collaborative problem-solving activities. In E. Forman, N. Minick, & C. A. Stone (Eds.), *Contexts for learning* (pp. 213–229). New York: Oxford University Press.

Fryer, M. G., & Fein, G. (1995, April). *Social pretend play in young children: Partner effects.* Paper presented at the annual meeting of the American Educational Research Association, San Francisco.

Galda, L., Pellegrini, A., & Cox, S. (1989). Preschoolers' emergent literacy: A short-term longitudinal study. *Research in the Teaching of English, 23,* 292–310.

Goncu, A. (1993). Development of intersubjectivity in the dyadic play of preschoolers. *Early Childhood Research Quarterly, 8,* 99–116.

Goodnow, J. (1985). Change and variation in ideas about childhood and parenting. In I. E. Siegel (Ed.), *Parental belief systems: The psychological consequences for children* (pp. 235–270). Hillsdale, NJ: Lawrence Erlbaum.

Gump, P. (1989). Ecological psychology and issues of play. In M. Bloch & A. Pellegrini (Eds.), *The ecological context of children's play* (pp. 35–56). Norwood, NJ: Ablex.

Guttman, M., & Fredericksen, C. H. (1985). Preschool children's narratives: Linking story comprehension, production and play discourse. In L. Galda & A. Pellegrini (Eds.), *Play, language and stories: The development of children's literate behavior* (pp. 99–128). Norwood, NJ: Ablex.

Hall, N., & Robinson, A. (1995). *Exploring writing and play in the early years*. London: David Fulton.

Heath, S. (1984). The achievement of preschool literacy for mother and child. In H. Goelman, A. Oberg, & F. Smith (Eds.), *Awakening to literacy* (pp. 51–72). Portsmouth, NH: Heinemann Educational Press.

Howe, N., Moller, L., & Chambers, B. (1994). Dramatic play in day care: What happens when doctors, cooks, bakers and pharmacists invade the classroom? In H. Goelman & E. Jacobs (Eds.), *Children's play in child care settings* (pp. 102–118). Albany: State University of New York Press.

Jacob, E. (1984). Learning literacy through play: Puerto Rican kindergarten children. In H. Goelman, A. Oberg, & F. Smith (Eds.), *Awakening to literacy* (pp. 73–86). Portsmouth, NH: Heinemann Educational Press.

Morrow, L. M. (1990). Preparing the classroom environment to promote literacy during play. *Early Childhood Research Quarterly, 5*, 537–554.

Morrow, L. M. (1991). Relationships between adult modeling, classroom design characteristics, and children's literacy behaviors. In J. Zutell & S. McCormick (Eds.), *Learner factors/teacher factors: Issues in literacy research and instruction* (pp. 127–140). Chicago: National Reading Conference.

Morrow, L. M., & Rand, M. (1991). Preparing the classroom environment to promote literacy during play. In J. Christie (Ed.), *Play and early literacy development* (pp. 141–165). Albany: State University of New York Press.

Neuman, S. B., & Gallagher, P. (1994). Joining together in literacy learning: Teenage mothers and children, *Reading Research Quarterly, 29*, 382–401.

Neuman, S. B., & Roskos, K. (1991). Peers as literacy informants: A description of children's literacy conversations in play. *Early Childhood Research Quarterly, 6*, 233–248.

Neuman, S. B., & Roskos, K. (1992). Literacy objects as cultural tools: Effects on children's literacy behaviors in play. *Reading Research Quarterly, 27*, 202–225.

Neuman, S. B., & Roskos, K. (1993). Access to print for children of poverty: Differential effects of adult mediation and literacy-enriched play settings on environmental and functional print tasks. *American Educational Research Journal, 30*, 95–122.

Neuman, S. B., & Roskos, K. (1997). Literacy knowledge in practice: Contexts of participation for young writers and readers. *Reading Research Quarterly, 32*(1), 10–33..

Pellegrini, A. D., & Galda, L. (1993). Ten years after: A reexamination of symbolic play and literacy research. *Reading Research Quarterly, 28*, 162–177.

Phyfe-Perkins, E. (1980), Children's behavior in preschool settings—A review of research concerning the influence of the physical environment. In L. Katz (Ed.), *Current topics in early childhood education* (pp. 91–124). Norwood, NJ: Ablex.

Ramsey, P., & Reid, R. (1988). Designing play environments for preschool and kindergarten children. In D. Bergen (Ed.), *Play as a medium for learning and development: A handbook for theory and practice* (pp. 213–240). Portsmouth, NH: Heinemann Educational Books.

Rogoff, B. (1990). *Apprenticeship in thinking.* New York: Oxford University Press.

Rosenthal, B. L. (1973). An ecological study of free play in the nursery school. Doctoral dissertation, Wayne State University, Detroit. *Dissertation Abstract International, 34,* 4004A.

Roskos, K. (1990). A taxonomic view of pretend play among four-and five-year old children. *Early Childhood Research Quarterly, 5,* 495–572.

Roskos, K., & Neuman, S. (1993a). Enhancing HeadStart parents' conceptions of literacy development and their confidence as literacy teachers: A study of parental involvement. *Early Child Development and Care, 89,* 57–73.

Roskos, K., & Neuman, S. (1993b). Descriptive observations of adults' facilitation of literacy in young children's play. *Early Childhood Research Quarterly, 8,* 77–98.

Rummelhart, D. (1977). Understanding and summarizing brief stories. In D. Laberge & S. J. Samuels (Eds.), *Basic processes in reading: Perception and comprehension* (pp. 265–303). Hillsdale, NJ: Lawrence Erlbaum.

Sachs, J., Goldman, J., & Chaille, C. (1985). Narratives in preschoolers' sociodramatic play. In L. Galda & A. Pellegrini (Eds.), *Play, language and stories: The development of children's literate behavior* (pp. 45–62). Norwood, NJ: Ablex.

Schaefer, E. (1991). Goal for parent and future parent education: Research on parental beliefs and behavior. *Elementary School Journal, 91,* 239–247.

Schrader, C. (1991). Symbolic play: A source of meaningful engagements with writing and reading. In J. Christie (Ed.), *Play and early literacy development* (pp. 189–214). Albany: State University of New York Press.

Sulzby, E. (1985). Children's emergent reading of favorite storybooks: A developmental study. *Reading Research Quarterly, 20,* 458–481.

Sylva, K., Roy, C., & Painter, M. (1980). *Childwatching at play group and nursery school.* London: Grant McIntire.

Sutton-Smith, B. (1995). Conclusion: the persuasive rhetorics of play. In A. D. Pellegrini (Ed.), *The future of play theory* (pp. 275–296). Albany: State University of New York Press.

Teale, W., & Sulzby, E. (1986). *Emergent literacy: writing and reading.* Norwood, NJ: Ablex.

Vukelich, C. (1991a). *Learning about the functions of writing: The effects of three play settings on children's interventions and development of knowledge about writing.* Paper presented at the annual meeting of the National Reading Conference, Palm Springs, CA.

Vukelich, C. (1991b). Materials and modeling: Promoting literacy during play. In J. Christie (Ed.), *Play and early literacy development* (pp. 215–232). Albany: State University of New York Press.

Whitehurst, G., Falco, F., Lonigan, C., Fischel, J., DeBaryshe, B., Valdez-Menchacha, M., & Caulfield, M. (1988). Accelerating language development through picture book reading. *Developmental Psychology, 24,* 552–559.

Wolf, D., & Pusch, J. (1985). The origins of autonomous text in play boundaries. In L. Galda & A. Pellegrini (Eds.), *Play, language and stories: The development of children's literate behavior* (pp. 63–78). Norwood, NJ: Ablex.

Wood, D., Bruner, J., & Ross, G. (1976). The role of tutoring in problem-solving, *Journal of Child Psychology and Psychiatry. 17,* 89–100.

Chapter 7

Play and Social Competence

Gary L. Creasey, Patricia A. Jarvis,
and Laura E. Berk

Tony is a 4-year-old attending a local preschool. Although he would like to play with the other children, he seems to have a difficult time getting peers to play with him. Many times, Tony can be seen attempting to "force" his way into ongoing play activities. For example, one day, as his peers were playing "dress up," he grabbed a police officer hat from another child. On the rare occasions when he and another child get involved in play, the other peer quickly breaks off the activity or an altercation develops over the use of play materials.

The preschool teacher notes that Tony has gradually become more withdrawn, often preferring to play alone. For example, during one free play period, when the other children were engaged in "Creatures from Outer Space," Tony scribbled on paper, randomly kicked blocks, and rolled around on the floor. Tony's father remarked to the teacher one day that the other children seemed to be close friends with one another, much to the exclusion of his son.

As professionals who work with young children, how concerned should we be with Tony's apparent lack of social skills? The most casual examination of the empirical literature would suggest that we should be quite concerned. A large number of studies indicate that children who lack social skills are at increased risk for serious adjustment problems during later childhood, adolescence, and adult life when contrasted with children who interact effectively and are well liked by peers, teachers, and other members of the child's social network (Coie & Dodge, 1988; Kupersmidt & Coie, 1990; Ladd, 1990; Morison & Masten, 1991; Ollendick, Weist, Borden, & Greene, 1992; Parker

& Asher, 1987). Consequently, uncovering factors that reflect and promote the socially skilled behaviors of some children and underlie the ineptness of others is important from both a theoretical and practical standpoint. This chapter addresses the role of play in the early development of socially competent behavior.

We begin by defining social competence and presenting evidence that children's play with objects, parents, and peers provides an important window on this construct. Children who display positive affect; cooperative, friendly social behavior; and a high level of pretense during play interactions are also well liked and have an easy time making friends. Indeed, some investigators assert that the quality of children's play with agemates is not just a reflection of social competence, but a central component of it (Howes & Stewart, 1987). This view gives new meaning to the plight of the child who tearfully cries, "Nobody likes me . . . nobody *ever* wants to play with me."

Although it is widely held that play *reflects* social competence, a second, stronger view of the role of play in development is that it *promotes* social competence (Haight & Miller, 1993; Parke, MacDonald, Beitel, & Bhavnagri, 1988; Vygotsky, 1934/1987). In this chapter, we review research indicating that certain forms of play during the preschool years have important implications for the development and refinement of social information processing, empathy, emotion regulation, conflict management, perspective taking, and skilled social interaction. Our discussion highlights two sets of findings that support this conclusion: play training studies and systematic observation of children's naturalistic play behaviors as predictors of short- and long-term markers of social competence.

Our discussion concludes with future directions and practical implications. We point out the limitations of available research, suggest new avenues of investigation, and consider how parents and early childhood educators can enhance play opportunities to promote the development of socially competent behavior.

DEFINITIONS OF SOCIAL COMPETENCE

If parents and teachers were asked to define social competence, their responses would probably include such behavioral and cognitive descriptors as "gets along well with other children," "a social butterfly," "liked by everyone," and "can really read social situations." Indeed, many researchers have measured this construct using these and other similar descriptors. For example, investigators who examine the development of peer social competence often assess whether or not the child is liked or disliked by peers (Coie, Dodge, & Copotelli, 1982), the extent to which other children like or dislike playing with the child (Connolly & Doyle, 1984), or how the child processes social information (Dodge, 1980). Although these descriptors are important from an assessment standpoint, they do not provide us with a working definition of social competence. Fortunately, definitions abound, for example, "aspects of social behavior that are important with respect to preventing physical illness or psychopathology in children and adults" (Putallaz & Gottman, 1983, p. 7), "able to make use of environmental and personal resources to achieve a good developmental outcome" (Waters & Sroufe, 1983, p. 81), and "the ability to initiate interaction, to respond contingently to the social gestures of others, and to refrain form the overt expression of negative behaviors that would inhibit reciprocal interaction" (Lieberman, 1977, p. 1279). The diversity of definitions leads the optimist to conclude that social competence is an unusually broad and encompassing construct, the pessimist to argue that it is vague, fragmented, and poorly defined.

Dodge, Pettit, McClasky, and Brown (1986) point out that definitions of social competence vary widely because they are guided by a multiplicity of theoretical orientations. Some stress the child's behavior, others the child's cognitive or affective capacities, still others the child's perceptions of other people, and yet another group the relation of social skills to psychological risk. As Dodge et al. (1986) assert, each of these definitions is correct to some degree, and scientific inquiry should not be as concerned with finding the perfect definition as with understanding how each of these facets of social functioning work together. On the basis of an integration of diverse definitions, we can conclude that socially competent children exhibit a positive demeanor around or toward others, have accurate social information processing abilities, and display social behaviors that lead them to be well liked by others. These competencies can be assessed through direct behavioral observation or through polling important people in the preschooler's social network, such as parents, peers, and teachers. Furthermore, individual differences in such assessments should predict both current and future psychological functioning.

THEORIES OF SOCIAL COMPETENCE I: THE INFLUENCE OF FAMILIAL AND EXTRAFAMILIAL SYSTEMS

Theories of how children develop social competence are as numerous as previously mentioned definitions, and each has merit in terms of empirical research. For many years, the quality of infant-caregiver attachment has been thought to serve as the foundation for social competence (Bowlby, 1969; Erikson, 1950; Mahler, Pine, & Bergman, 1975). Secure emotional relationships with caregivers were theorized to predict the child's active exploration of social environments, shape expectancies and perceptions of future interactions, encourage appropriate affect during social transgressions, and predict successful integration into the peer group (Bowlby, 1969; Sroufe & Waters, 1977; Bretherton, 1985). A number of empirical studies support these assertions. Compared to secure infant-caregiver attachment, insecure attachment classifications been found to forecast greater dependence (Matas, Arend, & Sroufe, 1978), less curiosity (Arend, Gove, & Sroufe, 1979), less positive affect during social interactions (Waters, Wippman, & Sroufe, 1979), and less optimal relationships with peers during the preschool and school years (e.g., Lieberman, 1977; Suess, Grossmann, & Sroufe, 1992; Parke & Waters, 1989).

Although early emotional relationships with caregivers may be important for later social competence, the continuity is far from perfect (e.g., Thompson, 1993). In addition, some studies have not confirmed the association (Fagot & Kavanaugh, 1990; Howes, Matheson, & Hamilton, 1994). These mixed outcomes suggest that other variables play an important role in predicting social competence. For example, social learning theorists argue that social competence may develop through ongoing (not just early) interactions with important figures in the young child's social network, such as parents and siblings (Bandura, 1977; Grusec, 1988). Proponents of this view assert that such interactions afford the child the opportunity to observe, incorporate, practice, and refine social skills, such as give and take, conflict management, and exchange of positive affect. Then the child introduces these competencies into emerging social relationships (Asher, Renshaw, & Hymel, 1982; MacDonald & Parke, 1984). In sum, a young child with a history of positive interactions within the family system might transfer these features to the peer system. Successful interaction with peers, in turn, leads to further refinement of social skills as well as unique opportunities for new social learning.

While positive interactions with family members may bolster children's social competencies in the peer group (Bhavnargi & Parke, 1991; MacDonald & Parke, 1984), it is widely recognized that caregivers can also engage in proactive efforts to facilitate social competence and peer acceptance in young children (Ladd, 1992; Parke, et al., 1988). For example, besides serving as "models" for and providing opportunities to practice appropriate social behavior, parents can influence the child's social competence by arranging contacts with peers and regulating the child's choices of friends (Ladd & Golter, 1988; Lieberman, 1977). Beyond directly organizing the child's social environment, parents can also "coach" young children in how to appropriately interact with peers as well as other important members of the child's developing social network, such as caregivers and teachers.

Today, researchers who study the relative importance of infant-caregiver attachment and ongoing parent-child interactions in predicting preschoolers' social competence agree on several points. First, there is growing consensus that several factors *working in conjunction* (warm, responsive early emotional ties, parental modeling and direct teaching of effective social behavior) facilitate the development of social competence during the preschool years (cf. Parke & Ladd, 1992). Second, competent relationships within the family system often predict competent relationships within the peer system and vice versa (Hartup & Rubin, 1986). Third, integration into the peer group during the preschool years leads to an expansion of effective social skills.

Finally, other routes to child social competence than secure emotional attachments and positive interactions within the family system exist. For example, Howes et al. (1994) found that preschoolers' social competence in peer groups was more closely associated with quality of attachment to teachers than mothers. In addition, Howes and colleagues (Howes & Stewart, 1987; Howes & Matheson, 1992) report that children enrolled in low-quality day care centers demonstrate more problems with social competence than do children attending high-quality centers after family characteristics (such as stress and parenting styles) are controlled. Thus, researchers have progressed from an "it's all in the family" orientation to a philosophy emphasizing that extrafamilial influences on children's social competence can support, compensate for, or even undermine the influence of the family context.

THEORIES OF SOCIAL COMPETENCE II: CHILDREN'S PLAY

Although theory and research supporting the view that secure emotional ties to parents and positive extrafamilial relationships with adults facilitate social competence, other theoretical perspectives stipulate that children's play may make an important contribution in conjunction with these influences. Furthermore, some theorists emphasize that certain aspects of children's play exert vital, independent effects on social competence. One perspective—Piaget's cognitive-developmental theory—highlights the facilitating role of peer arguments and disagreements on social-cognitive capacities widely recognized as important for skilled social interaction. Two additional approaches—psychoanalytic theory and Vygotsky's sociocultural theory—underscore the unique, facilitating role of make-believe play on social competence. Finally, ethological theory stresses that some features of children's playful interaction are rooted in our evolutionary past and serve the adaptive function of promoting harmonious, socially skilled peer interaction.

Jean Piaget's Cognitive-Developmental Theory

Jean Piaget (1945/1951) defined play as the exercise of already acquired schemes just for the pleasure of doing so. Consequently, he regarded play as placing its heaviest accent on assimilation and as having little to do with expansion of the child's repertoire of responses to the environment, including the social environment. Many investigators believe Piaget underestimated the power of play in children's development (Rubin, Fein, & Vandenberg, 1983). Nevertheless, his emphasis on play as pleasurable practice of schemes grants it a role in refining and polishing the interactive skills the child has acquired in nonplay contexts. For example, the reciprocal give and take of caregiver-infant exchanges may be consolidated through playful interactive games, such as peekaboo. Furthermore, effective strategies for communicating with others, once represented in the fantasy role play of the preschool years, can be strengthened through exercise of these symbolic schemes.

As Rubin (1980) points out, for Piaget, peer interaction within play contexts (rather than play itself) is vital for social-cognitive development. According to Piaget, arguments and disagreements with agemates jar children into noticing that people can hold perspectives different from their own and that intentions rather than objective consequences underlie behavior and are the appropriate basis for judging people's actions (Piaget, 1923/1926). Once children engage in social play, it creates circumstances in which play partners express conflicting viewpoints. Consequently, play provides children with interactive opportunities that are crucial for the development of social competence.

Psychoanalytic Theory

Sigmund Freud (1959) suggested that play was wish fulfillment and allowed children to act out uncertainties, anxieties, and wished for outcomes and therefore to master traumatic events. Erik Erikson (1950) accepted and expanded this view by underscoring the connection of make-believe play to the wider society. According to Erikson, make-believe is a central means through which children find out about themselves and their social world. It permits preschoolers to try out new skills with little risk of criticism and failure and creates a small social organization of children who must cooperate to achieve common goals. In addition, play provides children with important insights into the link between self and culturally prescribed roles. Through observing, emulating, and playing the roles of important adult figures, children integrate accepted social norms into their personalities. In these ways, play plays promotes mature, socially competent behavior.

Vygotsky's Sociocultural Theory

In accord with his emphasis on social experience and language as vital forces in development, Vygotsky (1966; 1930–35/1978) also highlighted representational play—the make-believe that blossoms during the preschool years—as a vital context for the acquisition of new cognitive and social competencies. According to Vygotsky, make-believe requires children to (1) generate an imaginary situation, and (2) follow a set of rules to act out the play scene. These two attributes of play provide the key to its role in development.

First, in creating an imaginary situation, children learn to act not just in response to external stimuli but also in accord with internal ideas. As preschoolers use objects in unconventional ways and pretend to be what they are not in real life, they sever thinking from the surrounding world. "[I]n play, things lose their determining force. The child sees one thing but acts differently in relation to what he sees. Thus, a condition is reached in which the child begins to act independently of what he sees" (Vygotsky, 1930–35/1978, p. 96). By detaching meaning from objects and behavior, make-believe helps teach children to think before they act and to choose deliberately from alternative courses of action.

Second, Vygotsky pointed out that although the pretense of preschoolers appears free and spontaneous to an outside observer, dramatic play constantly demands that children act against their immediate impulses because they must subject themselves to the rules of the make-believe context. Even the simplest imaginative situations created by very young children proceed in accord with social rules. For example, a child pretending to go to sleep follows the rules of bedtime behavior. Another child, imagining himself to be a father and a doll to be a child, conforms to the rules of parental behavior. By enacting rules in make-believe, children come to better understand social norms and expectations and strive to behave in ways that uphold them (Berk, 1994).

Finally, Vygotsky's sociocultural theory regards all higher mental functions, including imaginative play, as originating in children's social experiences with more competent members of their culture. Recent Vygotskian-based research reveals that in Western industrialized societies, make-believe first appears between caregivers and young children, who learn to pretend under the supportive guidance of experts (El'konin, 1966; Garvey, 1990; Haight & Miller, 1993; Smolucha, 1992). From these interactions, children acquire the communicative conventions, social skills, and representational capacities that permit them to carry out make-believe independent of adults—both by themselves and with agemates. In sum, Vygotsky's theory regards adult-child play as essential for scaffolding children's pretense and make-believe and, in turn, as a vital source of socially skilled behavior.

Ethological Theory

Many theories allow that play is adaptive from an evolutionary perspective (Piaget, 1970; Sutton-Smith, 1976; Vandenberg, 1981). According to

Sutton-Smith (1976), we create a storehouse of prototypes and associations from our play experiences that we draw on when the environment presents challenges. Similarly, Vandenberg (1981) suggests that play provides behavioral diversity that is crucial for the long-term survival of our species. Observations by ethologists have shown that many aspects of children's social play resemble those of our primate ancestors and are adaptive for survival.

For example, the normative situation for young primates is much rough-and-tumble peer play with reversal of dominant and submissive roles (Biben & Suomi, 1993). When peers are unavailable, adult-infant rough-and-tumble play provides younger members of the species with the important cognitive and physical experiences of being dominant that enhance assertiveness and self-confidence in later social interactions. Similarly, in human adult-child play, adults give children an extra edge by not using their full strength in a wrestling match or by letting the child have an extra turn at a game. These adult compromises serve to help the child gain experience with dominance and success, improve self-confidence, and insure that the child will seek such social interactions in the future (Biben & Suomi, 1993).

In sum, each of the theoretical positions discussed supports the idea that play and social competence are interrelated. However, each perspective highlights different pathways to this conclusion. Piaget's cognitive-developmental theory emphasizes the facilitating role of peer conflict on social-cognitive capacities widely recognized as important for skilled social interaction. The psychoanalytic approach and Vygotsky's sociocultural theory emphasize the unique, facilitating role of make-believe play on social competence. Finally, ethological theory stresses that some features of children's playful interaction are rooted in our evolutionary past and serve the adaptive function of promoting nonaggressive, socially skilled interactions.

PLAY AS A REFLECTION OF FACTORS UNDERLYING SOCIAL COMPETENCE

In this section, we discuss how children's play with objects, parents, and peers is an important marker of social competence. Because early emotional relationships with parents are thought to be one of the first signs of child social competence (Waters & Sroufe, 1983), we present research that compares the play behaviors of infants and toddlers identified as securely or insecurely attached to their caregivers. However, child play is more than just an uncovering of social competencies. Because of the repeated finding that the quality of children's play is related to parental support of play behaviors and play settings (Slade, 1987a), we also explore the possibility that child play is a reflection of an effective caregiving environment. In addition, during the preschool years, peers become an integral part of the child's broadening social network. Thus, we conclude this section with a discussion of why social competence is crucial for the initiation and maintenance of play interchanges between peers.

Play as a Reflection of Emotional Attachments to Caregivers

Attachment theorists predict that infants who have established secure emotional ties with caregivers will develop more sophisticated play capacities because such children will more readily explore novel environments, make friends, and be more receptive as play partners than children who have relationship difficulties with caregivers. This premise has been supported by empirical studies indicating that attachment security during infancy predicts exploration and symbolic play during toddlerhood (Belsky, Garduque, & Hrncir, 1984; Matas et al., 1978), more positive affect during play sequences (Main, 1983; Waters et al., 1979), and greater peer acceptance during the preschool years (Jacobson & Wille, 1986; Waters et al., 1979). As noted earlier, these investigations do not establish the pre-eminence of attachment in effective social development. Nevertheless, the weight of the evidence suggests that a secure attachment relationship is an important precursor of capacities manifested during play that are central ingredients of socially competent behavior.

Play as a Reflection of Effective Child Rearing

In addition to secure emotional relationships, several aspects of effective child rearing—ongoing parental interaction, parental structuring of children's environments, and direct teaching and encouragement—can promote preschoolers' social competence with peers. For example, research repeatedly shows that infants and preschoolers play in a more sophisticated manner—that is, display more symbolic play acts, more elaborate make-believe themes, and less mature, functional play with objects—when playing with parents than when playing alone (Dunn & Wooding, 1977; Fiese, 1990; Haight & Miller, 1992, 1993; O'Connell & Bretherton, 1984; O'Reilly & Bornstein, 1993; Slade, 1987a; Tamis-LeMonda & Bornstein, 1991; Zukow, 1986). These findings indicate that parents support and mentor the development of play through modeling, bolstering social-linguistic skills, suggesting novel ways to play with toys, and encouraging sophisticated pretend over functional play.

Until young children can gather with peers on their own, parents also act as social planners and "booking agents," scheduling play activities at home, taking children to community settings such as the library or pool, and enrolling them in preschool and other organized activities that offer contact with peers (Berk, 1994; Bhavnagri & Parke, 1991). Parents who frequently arrange informal peer-play activities tend to have preschoolers with larger peer networks and who display more prosocial behavior with agemates. In fostering peer play, parents show children how to initiate their own peer contacts and encourage them to be good "hosts" who are concerned about their playmates' needs (Ladd & Hart, 1992).

In Vygotskian (1930–35/1978) terms, parents play a vital role in assisting children in broadening their zones of proximal development in the social domain. If such mentoring is unavailable, then children's play development might be hindered. This idea may explain why early research found that family social class was positively related to the development of associative, cooperative, and sociodramatic play (Rosen, 1974; Rubin, Maioni, & Hornung, 1976). As Smilansky (1968) proposed, a stressful or nonstimulating environment may fail to provide the verbal, cognitive, and social skill mentoring needed to engage in advanced play. This premise was recently supported by Howes and Stewart (1987), who reported that children from nurturant and supportive families were more likely to demonstrate competent play with parents and objects than were children who came from overly restrictive or stressed families. Howes and Stewart also showed that the contribution of adult mentoring to socially competent play extends beyond the family to the quality of child care. Their findings indicate that a major symptom of a low-quality child care center is a paucity of rich, complex play interactions between preschoolers and their teachers.

Play as a Reflection of Effective Peer Relations

Play reflects social competence in the peer group during the preschool years. For example, successful peer play often requires such advanced social skills as verbal recruitment of play partners (e.g., "Come on, let's play Star Trek"), joining a group through polite, friendly proactive methods (e.g., "Can I play, too?"), and monitoring the responses of other children (Howes, 1985, 1987). In addition, play becomes more collaborative over the preschool years as peers become more adept at negotiating play themes, a capacity that rests on the child's ability to read the verbal and nonverbal cues of others (Göncü, 1993).

A large body of research suggests that children who are popular and well liked by peers engage in more symbolic solitary play as opposed to functional play, more collaborative sociodramatic play (e.g., Connolly & Doyle, 1984; Rubin & Maioni, 1975; Rubin, 1982), and more emotionally charged play with both peers and parents (MacDonald & Parke, 1984; MacDonald, 1987). In addition, Connolly and Doyle (1984) found that children who were better liked and more skilled in peer interactions engaged in high levels of fantasy play independent of the child's sex and intellectual ability.

Besides sociodramatic play, rough and tumble play reflects children's social competence. Although both unpopular and popular children engage in rough and tumble play in equal amounts (Coie & Kupersmidt, 1983), the quality of such play depends on the child's sociometric status. For example, Pellegrini (1988) found that over time, popular children's rough and tumble play often turned into more constructive forms of play, whereas unpopular children's rough and tumble tended to escalate into aggressive behavior. Additional evidence indicates that most children are quite adept at recognizing the difference between aggression and "playful wrestling." Conversely, rejected children, due to their difficulties in reading social cues accurately, are likely to misread the intentions of others and interpret certain benign play behaviors as threatening or hostile (Costabile, Smith, Matgheson, Aston, Hunter, & Boulton, 1991; Pellegrini, 1988; Smith & Boulton, 1990).

In summary, empirical evidence suggests that child play is indeed a window on general social competence. The quality of child play has been consistently linked to early infant-caregiver attachment formations, quality of the childrearing environment, and social competence within the peer group. Further, the relationship between quality of play and peer social competence is so strong that several major research groups now view the quality of peer play, from an assessment standpoint, as one major index of general social competence (Howes, 1987).

PLAY AS A FACILITATOR OF SOCIAL COMPETENCE

Although preschoolers who have competent relationships with parents and peers tend to "play well," play should not be viewed as a mere consequence of social competence or a simple unveiling of a child's social capacities. Play, as we previously indicated, can promote social competence through the development and refinement of such skills as sharing, cooperation, perspective taking, affect regulation, and pretend imagery (e.g., Bruner, 1972; 1973; Smilansky, 1968; Garvey, 1990; Gottman & Parker, 1986; Singer, 1973; Singer & Singer, 1990). These capacities are widely assumed to be elements of general social competence and friendship formation. In addition, play is a context in which children can practice new skills and behaviors within safe confines in which they are free to make, and rectify, miscues and mistakes (Sutton-Smith 1966; 1976). Finally, play may support the flexibility of children's social skills as they become more adept at smoothly shifting among forms of play behaviors—for example, from solitary fantasy to sociodramatic play and back again (DiLalla & Watson, 1988).

The research literature on play supports its potential to affect social competence. During the first few years, play becomes increasingly social. Until age 3, parents are the play partners of choice (Dunn & Dale, 1984; Haight & Miller, 1993; Miller & Garvey, 1984). Although young children's developing social competence undoubtedly influences adults' attraction to them as play partners (Slade 1987b), early social play is thought to have rich consequences in its own right as parents model social skills, encourage sophisticated social behaviors, and provide affective stimulation (Bruner, 1978).

Even some fortuitous aspects of parent-child play may equip children with skills that foster socially competent behavior. For example, research in a variety of cultures—Australia, Israel, India, Italy, Japan, and the United States—indicates that compared to mothers, fathers engage in more exciting, highly physical bouncing and lifting games with infants and toddlers (Lamb, 1987; Roopnarine, Talukder, Jain, Joshi, & Srivastave, 1990). Employed mothers, compared to their unemployed counterparts, also engage in more novel, playful stimulation of babies (Cox, Owen, Lewis, & Henderson, 1989). The unpredictability and element of surprise in such play may help prepare children for the social and emotional give and take required for successful participation in early interaction with peers, which is considerably less synchronous than adult-child communication (Parke et al., 1988).

Around age 2, peers become new and exciting play partners within the child's life. However, social play with peers is not simply an extension of play with parents. It has unique features. For example, the play between preschoolers of the same age is more evenly matched because of similarities in cognitive and social skills. Consequently, peer play more often leads to truly collaborative activities (cf. Garvey, 1990; Göncü, 1993; Howes, 1985). In addition, play between children often contains novel elements almost never observed in adult-child play. For example, Rubenstein and Howes (1976) noted that young children like to engage in such activities as repeatedly jumping off stairs or walking around with pots on their heads as hats. Researchers have also documented that with age, children begin to model the play behaviors of peers more often than those of parents, perhaps because peer behaviors are more unusual and experimental (Eckerman, Whatley, & Kutz, 1975; Rubenstein & Howes, 1976). Finally, around age 2½, children begin to incorporate fantasy into their social play, increasingly acting out real-life social roles, such as mothers and fathers, doctors and nurses, and astronauts (O'Connell & Bretherton, 1984; Howes, 1985). Such social pretend play, as opposed to social nonpretend, requires greater affect regulation and contains more reciprocal interchanges, bids to influence the behavior of others, and overt communication of planned behaviors (e.g., "I'm going to make the monster disappear with my magic wand!") (Connolly, Doyle, & Resnick, 1988; McLoyd, Warren, & Thomas, 1984). These capacities are often associated with general social competence.

Whereas descriptive and correlational research supports the view that effective peer play is an extension as well as elaboration of early parental play and that both may facilitate social competence, the research summarized so far does not tell us conclusively whether play, in and of itself, has special developmental significance. Does play foster skills that are essential ingredients of social competence? Two types of research have addressed this cause-and-effect issue.

Play Training Studies

One approach, the play training method, involves systematically coaching children to engage in greater amounts of pretend or sociodramatic play (e.g., Connolly, 1980; Saltz, Dixon, & Johnson, 1977; Smilansky, 1968, Smith & Syddall, 1978; Rosen, 1974). Manipulation of play behaviors can then be associated with future measures of social skills to determine whether or not increases in play behaviors contribute to social competence. In studies of this kind, concerted attempts to encourage social pretend (e.g., taking field trips to grocery stores followed by suggestions to reenact these experiences) led to increases in children's sociodramatic play with peers (Smilansky, 1968). In addition, children coached in fantasy play showed improvements in perspective taking, social problem solving, and group cooperation (Rosen, 1974; Saltz & Johnson, 1974; Smith & Syddall, 1978).

At first glance, these results suggest that play has unmitigated positive consequences for young children's social competence. However, a number of issues should be weighed carefully before accepting this conclusion. First, the evidence as a whole indicates that play tutoring is more beneficial for "high-risk" children—those from lower social-class families or who show low levels of fantasy or sociodramatic play to begin with. Similar research on "low risk," middle-class children shows no effects of play training on future social competence (e.g., Connolly, 1980). In addition, it remains unclear whether gains in social competence are the result of increased use of skills learned in the play setting or sustained interactions with competent adults during the training experience (Rubin et al., 1983). Finally, we must ask whether increases in certain facets of social competence, such as sharing or symbolic play bouts after play training procedures, actually leads to more global indicators of social competence, such as improved peer acceptance.

Short- and Long-Term Outcomes of Naturally Occurring Play

The role of play in developing social competence has been studied in a second way—through naturalistic observation of the quality of children's everyday play behaviors. In a majority of these studies, the manner in which children play—either alone or in conjunction with others—is used as a predictor of both short-term indicators (e.g., cooperation, sharing, and perspective taking) and long-term indicators (peer acceptance and parental and teacher reports) of social competence. Both play with parents and play with peers have been examined.

Play with parents. Theory and research on early parent-child play support its contribution to socially skilled behavior. The way parents play with their infants is related to the development of secure attachment (Ainsworth, Blehar, Waters, &Wall, 1978; Belsky, Rovine, & Taylor, 1984). For example, Kisler, Bates, Maslin, and Bayles (1986) observed mother-infant interactions at 6 months during "normal" play interaction and in interaction in which mothers were instructed to behave in an unresponsive or "low-key" manner. Mothers who were more entertaining and engaging during play had infants who were more likely to be rated as securely attached at 13 months. In addition, infants later rated as securely attached were more active in attempts to maintain interactions and more distressed during episodes in which mothers were instructed to deviate from "normal" play bouts.

These findings suggest that besides caregiving activities (such as feeding and bath time), parent-infant play is a vital context for promoting the responsive and reciprocal interactions important for secure attachment relationships. Indeed, in the play arena, members of the dyad may get to know one another especially well, since social exchanges are highly frequent, permitting social expectations and patterns of behavior to be easily established (Stern, 1985) . For example, during playful parent-infant exchanges, "mismatches" between infant characteristics (e.g., activity level, response to stimulation) and parent characteristics (e.g., stimulation, affect displays) may be particularly important in encouraging the baby of an uninvolved parent to begin responding angrily and demandingly to evoke greater attention. Conversely, infants of an overinvolved parent may receive a great deal of practice in withdrawal during overstimulating play (cf. Belsky et al., 1984b; Isabella, 1993).

Beyond studying the impact of parent-infant play on attachment, researchers have also examined whether such play assists children in successful peer group entry. As noted earlier, Parke et al. (1989) argue that parent-child physical play, in particular, may bridge the gap between parent-child and child-peer social contexts because of the wide range of emotional and social behaviors exhibited during such play bouts. Unfortunately, concurrent associations between parent-child physical play and peer social competence do not permit determination of whether such play is antecedent or consequent to children's social competence (MacDonald, 1987). However, a recent longitudinal study strongly suggests that certain aspects of parent-child physical play do forecast later indices of social competence.

Barth and Parke (1993) assessed physical play in 45 families shortly before children entered kindergarten and in two more sessions after school entry. In addition, teachers were asked to provide measures of classroom behavior, and children completed assessments of loneliness and feelings about school. Results suggested that children who engaged in dyadic play interactions rated as "resistant child-highly controlling parent" were more likely to be dependent, feel lonely, and express hostility toward others over the course of the school year. The authors speculated that highly dependent children with overly controlling parents may have difficulty initiating and organizing effective interaction in new settings. This, in turn, may lead to hostility or rejection within the peer group. In addition, Barth and Parke found that the ability of parents and children to sustain physical play predicted low dependency and hostility and good relations with others during kindergarten. Since maintenance of physical play is thought to be a function of both the parent's and child's ability to monitor and adjust behavior in relation to the partner's affective and behavioral cues (e.g., Parke et al., 1989), breakdowns in such communication may explain why some children failed to readily integrate into peer networks at school. Indeed, research has shown that parent-child synchrony during play interactions is a better predictor of later peer acceptance than the sheer quantity of parent-child physical or pretend play (Lindsey, Smith, & Benedict, 1995).

Play with peers. Bakeman and Brownlee (1980) conducted one of the first studies to suggest that children's everyday play may have important implications for social development. Preschoolers aged 32 to 42 months were carefully observed while playing alone, near others in a parallel fashion, or in social or group play. Findings revealed that the best predictor of children's transition to sophisticated group play was parallel play, in which children play along side other children in a similar fashion. Although children's social skills were not assessed, we can assume that if such skills are the sole facilitator of more complex, interactive play, then children would move smoothly from just about any form of play activity to more sophisticated social play. Yet in this study, only parallel play—not just any form of play—predicted the transition to social play. Hence, engaging in certain play forms, such as parallel play, seems to serve as an important bridge between solitary and joint, cooperative behavior.

Observing a sample of kindergartners and first graders, Doyle, Doehring, Tessier, de Lorimer, and Shapiro (1992) examined behavioral predictors of children's nonpretend and pretend play as well as the social consequences of such play. In general, children arrived at social pretend play through three routes: negotiation of pretend play plans (e.g., "Hey, the Ninja Turtle just bashed you!"), spontaneous pretend acts by one member of the dyad, or a merger of children's solitary pretend activities. Negotiation of pretend play plans, often viewed as a social skill necessary to "start up" social play (e.g., Howes, 1985), was actually found to be more important in sustaining sociodramatic play than initiating it. What assisted preschoolers in "starting up" fresh bouts of sociodramatic play? Nonpretend activities rarely predicted complex social pretend play among peers. Instead, other forms of pretend (i.e., solitary pretend play; spontaneous pretend play acts by one member of a peer dyad) were significant antecedents of such social play. Extending the findings of Bakeman and Brownlee (1980), these investigators assert that certain forms of play—notably solitary pretend—serve as an important bridge, or stepping stone, from solitary to cooperative social activities.

Additional studies suggest that social play with peers may have important developmental significance. For example, Howes and Matheson (1992) examined the relationship of various forms of toddler play to social competence at 30 to 35 and 44 to 60 months. Findings indicated that children who engaged in more complex play (e.g., complementary play with peers, such as peekaboo and chase) at earlier developmental periods were rated as more sociable and cooperative and less aggressive and withdrawn during the preschool years than children who frequently engaged in simpler play forms (e.g., parallel) during toddlerhood. Such findings, at first glance, seem to suggest that play may have important consequences for the development of social skills. However, the authors speculated that socially competent toddlers in all likelihood play in more complex ways when engaged in social play with peers. Therefore, the competing hypothesis—that early complex play may reflect rather than foster social competent behavior—cannot be entirely dismissed.

Nevertheless, there is reason to believe that early social play also assists children in developing social skills. When asked to describe the basis of their friendships, "we like to play" is a rationale that young children frequently provide. In one study of friendship development, Gottman (1983) observed unacquainted preschoolers and school-aged children for a period of several weeks and carefully documented which children became friends and which children "did not hit it off." Child play served several important functions. First, children playing together were frequently observed asking each other about the play materials and activities (e.g., "How do you make this work?" Reply: "You gotta push this button first") as well as requesting information not central to the play theme ("Why is the sky blue?"). In addition, children discussed important personal issues (e.g., "My mommy and daddy don't like one another."). Since seeking support for both informational and emotional reasons is widely viewed as an adaptive coping strategy that reduces the negative impact of stress on psychological adjustment (e.g., Carver, Schier, & Weintraub, 1989), one important function of social play among peers is that it may serve as a vital context for social support.

Gottman (1983) also reported that as children's play became more complex, it also became "riskier" and occasionally led to conflict. Children had to find ways to de-escalate their negative feelings, resolve their disagreements, and reframe their play. Elaborate social play appeared to provide an important context for the development of conflict management skills. This opportunity is unlikely to be present in activities not as conducive to conflict resolution, such as building block structures side by side or watching television together.

Finally, children whose play was synchronous, who were more successful at managing conflict, and who participated in more information exchange and self-disclosure were more likely to become friends than were dyads who did not did display these behaviors. Although a child's ongoing social skills undoubtedly contribute to these behaviors, it seems clear that young children who do not know one another eventually become friends *by way* of playing together.

In summary, research strongly suggests that play may serve as an important facilitator of social competence. Within the context of play interactions, parents and infants may develop the synchronous interchanges that are necessary for the development of healthy attachment relationships. As the child matures and develops, parent-child play may serve as an important context for the development and refinement of social skills that are necessary for initiating peer interactions. Finally, child-peer play may be an important context for the development of conflict management skills, intimacy, and role-taking opportunities. In addition, play with peers may offer a safe haven, free from adult constraints, in which children can readily share information and concerns. The findings just reviewed underscore the plight of the rejected child. Because children consistently indicate that they do not like to play with rejected peers (e.g., Coie et al., 1982), these disliked children miss out on the unique developmental opportunities of the play context. These missed opportunities, in turn, may further contribute to the rejected child's social ineptness.

FUTURE DIRECTIONS FOR RESEARCH AND IMPLICATIONS FOR PRACTICE

Throughout this chapter, we have considered theory and research indicating that play during early childhood reflects as well as promotes social competence. Although longitudinal work offers the tantalizing suggestion that quality of play with parents and peers predicts later competencies (e.g., Barth & Parke, 1993; Gottman, 1983), it is still unclear whether such play contributes *uniquely* to later social skills and adjustment. A conclusive answer to this question is hampered by the fact that researchers rarely measure social competence and play behaviors concurrently over time. Such studies would permit a critical test of the power of play to affect development by permitting investigation of relationships between child play and later social competencies while controlling for initial social competence.

However, simply recommending more longitudinal work does not address another important issue. Assuming there are predictive relations between child play and social competence, what are *the ingredients of play* that afford unique developmental advantages? For example, even casual observations of preschoolers reveal that children engage in many behaviors during play sessions—pretense, support seeking, metacommunication, and affect exchange, to name just a few. We cannot conclusively tell which feature, or which combination of features, is responsible for sparking emerging social competencies.

With these caveats in mind, we offer several joint recommendations for practice and future research. First, given the repeated finding that play becomes more sophisticated when children interact with parents and peers and that few children turn down invitations to engage in social play, promoting interactive play is one obvious application. Parents can be educated about the importance of early adult-child play, how to structure play settings and materials effectively for children of different ages, and how to scaffold play behaviors in ways that encourage children to acquire new skills. Adult intervention that recognizes children's current level of cognitive competence and builds on it is most successful in involving children. Lucariello (1987) reported that when 24- to 29-month-olds were familiar with a play theme suggested by their mother, both partners displayed advanced levels of imaginative activity and constructed the scenario together. When the theme was unfamiliar, the mother took almost total responsibility for pretense, and children's participation was greatly reduced.

Although "more is better" may seem like an obvious recommendation, on the basis of parent-child play research (e.g., Slade, 1987b; Belsky et al., 1984b; Isabella, 1993), parents also need to be sensitive to emotional and behavioral cues from children during play sessions and avoid overstimulation and excessive directiveness. The power of adult-child play to foster development is undermined by communication that is too overpowering or one sided. For example, Fiese (1990) found that maternal questioning, instructing, and instrusiveness (initiating a new activity unrelated to the child's current pattern of play) led to immature, simple exploratory play in young children. In contrast, turn taking and joint involvement in a shared activity resulted in high levels of pretense. In addition, parent play behaviors should form a "good match" with the child's temperament and socioemotional functioning.

Besides additional studies of the impact of parental encouragement of play, contextual factors that facilitate or undermine parental efforts need to be examined. Although a growing body of research suggests that parental psychological health, personality style, occupational status, marital satisfaction, and social support influence child-rearing practices, there is a dearth of work examining the influence of these variables on parent-child play behaviors. Such research is important, given the finding that family stress is linked to deficits in children's play (Creasey & Jarvis, 1994; Howes & Stewart, 1987).

Although parent-child play has been granted considerable research attention, a search of the literature revealed no studies of the developmental significance of teachers' participation in young children's play. Yet growing evidence on the role of adult-child play suggests that it is vital for teachers to engage in play with young children. Even after play with peers is well underway, teachers (like parents) need to create play opportunities and guide children toward effective relations with agemates. Yet observational evidence indicates that teachers mediate children's play only when intense disagreements arise that threaten classroom order or safety. When teachers do step in, they almost always use directive strategies, in which they tell children what to do or say (e.g., "Ask Daniel if you can have the fire truck next") or solve the problem for them (e.g., "Jessica was playing with that toy first, so you can have a turn after her") (File, 1993, p. 352). Efforts by teachers to tailor their guidance to children's current capacities and use techniques that help children regulate their own behavior need to be tried and evaluated. To implement intervention in this way, teachers must acquire detailed knowledge of individual children's social skills—the type of information they usually gather only for the cognitive domain. When intervening, they need to use a range of teaching strategies because (like cognitive development) the support that is appropriate for scaffolding social development varies from child to child and changes with age.

When teachers are confronted with a child who displays poor social skills, play training can be considered as one among several avenues of intervention, keeping in mind that experts still do not know which components of interactive play foster social competence. Furthermore, simply encouraging social behavior and positive affect in the context of play is unlikely, by itself, to improve social competence. Children who are disliked by peers often have seriously troubled home lives and great difficulty processing social information accurately (Dodge, 1980; Patterson, DeBaryshe, & Ramsey, 1989). Consequently, efforts to help them need to be multidimensional and extend well beyond sociodramatic play training.

In conclusion, the first author of this chapter once asked a highly regarded clinical psychologist what she believed to be the most important predictor of adjustment across the life span. She responded, "Being accepted by others"—an answer consonant with the repeated finding that social competence is a major predictor of future adjustment and life satisfaction. When we consider the strength of this association, uncovering those factors that reflect and promote social competence becomes a pressing concern. In this chapter, we have seen how child play serves as an important marker and facilitator of social competence. Extending this line of research makes sense because the desire to be social and the tendency for children to engage in play are powerful predictors of successful development. Indeed, close observation of the friendly rough and tumble or the rich, multifaceted joint pretense of preschoolers serves as an important reminder that play and social competence are not trendy research arenas. To the contrary, both phenomena, independently and in concert, increase children's chances of successfully adapting to the demands of an ever changing physical and social world.

REFERENCES

Ainsworth, M., Blehar, M., Waters, E., & Wall, S. (1978). *A psychological study of the strange situation.* Hillsdale, NJ: Lawrence Erlbaum.

Arend, R., Gove, F., & Sroufe, L. (1979). Continuity of individual adaptation from infancy to kindergarten: A predictive study of ego-resiliency and curiosity in preschoolers. *Child Development, 50,* 950–959.

Asher, S., Renshaw, P., & Hymel, S. (1982). Peer relations and the development of social skills. In S. Moore & C. Cooper (Eds.), *The young child* (Vol. 3). Washington, D.C.: National Association for the Education of Young Children.

Bakeman, R., & Brownlee, J. (1980). The strategic use of parallel play: A sequential analysis. *Child Development, 51,* 873–878.

Bandura, A. (1977). *Social learning theory.* Englewood Cliffs, NJ: Prentice Hall.

Barth, J., & Parke, R. (1993). Parent-child relationship influences on children's transition to school. *Merrill-Palmer Quarterly, 39,* 173–195.

Belsky, J., Garduque, L., & Hrncir, E. (1984). Assessing performance, competence, and executive capacity in infant play: Relations to home environment and security of attachment. *Developmental Psychology, 20,* 406–417.

Belsky, J., Rovine, M., & Taylor, D. (1984). The Pennsylvania Infant and Family Development Project, III: The origins of individual differences in infant-mother attachment: Maternal and infant contributions. *Child Development, 55,* 718–728.

Berk, L. E. (1994). Vygotsky's theory: The importance of make-believe play. *Young Children, 50* (1), 30–39.

Bhavnargi, N., & Parke, R. (1991). Parents as facilitators of preschool peer relationships: Effects of age of child and sex of parent. *Journal of Social and Personal Relationships, 8,* 423–440,

Biben, M., & Suomi, S. J. (1993). Lessons from primate play. In K. MacDonald (Ed.), *Parent-Child Play: Descriptions and Implications*. Albany: State University of New York Press.

Bowlby, J. (1969). *Attachment and loss: Vol. 1. Attachment*. New York: Basic Books.

Bretherton, I. (1985). Attachment theory: Retrospect and prospect. In I. Bretherton and E. Waters (Eds.), Growing points of attachment theory and research. *Monographs of the Society for Research in Child Development, 50* (1–2, Serial No. 209).

Bruner, J. (1972). The nature and uses of immaturity. *American Psychologist, 27*, 687–708.

Bruner, J. (1973). Organization of early skilled action. *Child Development, 44*, 1–11.

Bruner, J. (1978). How to do things with words. In J. Bruner & A. Garton (Eds.), *Human growth and development*. Oxford: Oxford University Press.

Carver, C., Scheier, M., & Weintraub, J. (1989). Assessing coping strategies: A theoretically based approach. *Journal of Personality and Social Psychology, 56*, 267–283.

Coie, J., & Dodge, K. (1988). Multiple sources of data on social behavior and social status in the school: A cross-age comparison. *Child Development, 59*, 815–829.

Coie, J., & Kupersmidt, J. (1983). A behavioral analysis of emerging social status in boys' groups. *Child Development, 54*, 1400–1416.

Coie, J., Dodge, K., & Copotelli, H. (1982). Dimensions and types of social status: Across-age perspective. *Developmental Psychology, 18*, 557–570.

Connolly, J. (1980). *The relationship between social pretend play and social competence in children: Correlational and experimental studies*. Unpublished doctoral dissertation. Concordia University. Montreal QC, Canada.

Connolly, J., & Doyle, A. (1984). Relation of social fantasy play to social competence in preschoolers. *Developmental Psychology, 20*, 797–806.

Connolly, J., Doyle, A., Resnick, E. (1988). Social pretend play and social interaction in preschoolers. *Journal of Applied Developmental Psychology, 9*, 301–314.

Costabile, A., Smith, P. K., Matgheson, L., Aston, J., Hunter, T., & Boulton, M. (1991). Cross-national comparison of how children distinguish serious and playful fighting. *Developmental Psychology, 27*, 881–887.

Cox, M. J., Owen, M., Lewis, J. M., & Henderson, V. K. (1989). Marriage, adult adjustment, and early parenting. *Child Development, 60*, 1015–1024.

Creasey, G., & Jarvis, P. (1994). Relationships between parenting stress and developmental functioning among 2-year-olds. *Infant Behavior and Development, 17*, 423–429.

DiLalla, L., & Watson, M. (1988). Differentiation of fantasy and reality: Preschoolers' reactions to interruptions in their play. *Developmental Psychology, 24,* 286–291.

Dodge, K. (1980). Social cognition and children's aggressive behavior. *Child Development, 51,* 162–170.

Dodge, K., Pettit, G., McClasky, C., & Brown, M. (1986). Social competence in children. *Monographs of the Society for Research in Child Development, 51* (2, Serial No. 213).

Doyle, A., Doehring, P., Tessier, O., de Lorimier, S., & Shapiro, S. (1992). Transitions in children's play: A sequential analysis of states preceding and following social pretense. *Developmental Psychology, 28,* 137–144.

Dunn, J., & Dale, N. (1984). I a daddy: 2-year-olds' collaboration in joint pretend with sibling and with mother. In I. Bretherton (Ed.), *Symbolic play* (pp. 131–158). New York: Academic Press.

Dunn, J., & Wooding, C. (1977). Play in the home and its implications for learning. In B. Tizard & D. Harvey (Eds.), *Biology of play* (pp. 45–58). London: Heinemann.

Eckerman, C., Whatley, J., & Kutz, S. (1975). Growth of social play with peers during the second year of life. *Developmental Psychology, 11,* 42–49.

El'konin, D. (1966). Symbolics and its functions in the play of children. *Soviet Education, 8,* 35–41.

Erikson, E. (1950). *Childhood and Society.* New York: Norton.

Fagot, B. I., & Kavanaugh, K. (1990). The prediction oif antisocial behavior from avoidant attachment classifications. *Child Development, 61,* 864–873.

Fiese, B. (1990). Playful relationships: A contextual analysis of mother-toddler interaction and symbolic play. *Child Development, 61,* 1648–1656.

File, N. (1993). The teacher as guide of children's competence with peers. *Child & Youth Care Forum, 22,* 351–360.

Freud, S. (1959). Creative writers and daydreaming. In J. Strackey (Ed.), *The standard edition of the complete psychological works of Sigmund Freud (Vol. IX).* London: Hogarth.

Garvey, C. (1990). *Play.* Cambridge, MA: Harvard University Press.

G-nc-, A. (1993). Development of intersubjectivity in the dyadic play of preschoolers. *Early Childhood Research Quarterly, 8,* 99–116.

Gottman, J. (1983). How children make friends. *Monographs of the Society for Research in Child Development, 48,* (3, Serial No. 201).

Gottman, J., & Parker, J. (1986). *Conversations of friends: Speculations on affective development*. Cambridge: Cambridge University Press.

Grusec, J. E. (1988). *Social development: History, theory, and research*. New York: Springer-Verlag.

Haight, W. L., & Miller, P. J. (1993). *Pretending at home: Early development in a sociocultural context*. Albany: State University of New York Press.

Haight, W., & Miller, P. (1992). The development of everyday pretend play: A longitudinal study of mothers' participation. *Merrill-Palmer Quarterly, 38*, 331–349.

Hartup, W., & Rubin, Z. (1986). *Relationships and development*. Hillsdale, NJ: Lawrence Erlbaum.

Howes, C. (1985). Sharing fantasy: Social pretend play in toddlers. *Child Development, 56*, 1253–1258.

Howes, C. (1987). Social competence with peers in young children: Developmental sequences. *Developmental Review, 7*, 252–272.

Howes, C., & Matheson, C. (1992). Sequences in the development of competent play with peers: Social and social pretend play. *Developmental Psychology, 28*, 961–974.

Howes, C., & Stewart, P. (1987). Child's play with adults, toys, and peers: An examination of family and child-care influences. *Developmental Psychology, 23*, 77–84.

Howes, C., Matheson, C., & Hamilton, C. (1994). Maternal, teacher, and child care history correlates of children's relationships with peers. *Child Development, 65*, 264–273.

Isabella, R. (1993). Origins of attachment: Maternal interactive behavior across the first year. *Child Development, 64*, 605–621.

Jacobson, J., & Wille, D. (1986). The influence of attachment pattern on developmental changes in peer interaction form the toddler to the preschool period. *Child Development, 57*, 338–347.

Kisler, L., Bates, J., Maslin, C., & Bayles, K. (1986). Mother-infant play at six months as a predictor of attachment security at thirteen months. *Journal of the American Academy of Child Psychiatry, 25*, 68–75.

Kupersmidt, J., & Coie, J. (1990). Preadolescent peer status, aggression, and school adjustment as predictors of externalizing problems in adolescence. *Child Development, 61*, 1350–1362.

Ladd, G. (1990). Having friends, keeping friends, making friends, and being liked by peers in the classroom: Predictors of children's early school adjustment? *Child Development, 61*, 1081–1100.

Ladd, G. (1992). Themes and theories: Perspectives on processes in family-peer relationships. In R. Parke & G. Ladd (Eds.), *Family-peer relationships: Modes of linkage* (pp. 3–34). Hillsdale, NJ: Lawrence Erlbaum.

Ladd, G., & Golter, B. (1988). Parents' management of preschoolers' peer relations: Is it related to children's social competence? *Developmental Psychology, 24,* 109–117.

Ladd, G. W., & Hart, C. H. (1992). Creating informal play opportunities: Are parents' and and preschoolers' initiations related to children's competence with peers? *Developmental Psychology, 28,* 1179–1187.

Lamb, M. E. (1987). *The father's role: Cross-cultural perspectives.* Hillsdale, NJ: Erlbaum.

Lieberman, A. (1977). Preschoolers' competence with a peer: Relations with attachment and peer experience. *Child Development, 48,* 1277–1287.

Lindsey, E., Smith, T., & Benedict, K. (1995, March). *Father-child play and children's peer relations.* Paper presented at the Biennial Meeting of the Society for Research in Child Development, Indianapolis, IN.

Lucariello, J. (1987). Spinning fantasy: Themes, structure, and the knowledge base. *Child Development, 58,* 434–442.

MacDonald, K. (1987). Parent-child physical play with rejected, neglected, and popular boys. *Developmental Psychology, 23,* 705–711.

MacDonald, K., & Parke, R. (1984). Bridging the gap: Parent-child play interaction and peer interactive competence. *Child Development, 55,* 1265–1277.

Mahler, M., Pine, F., & Bergman, A. (1975). *The psychological birth of the human infant.* New York: Basic Books.

Main, M. (1983). Exploration, play, and cognitive functioning related to infant-mother attachment. *Infant Behavior and Development, 6,* 167–174.

Matas, L., Arend, R., & Sroufe, L. (1978). Continuity of adaptation in the second year: The relationship between quality of attachment and later competence. *Child Development, 49,* 547–556.

McLoyd, V., Warren, D., & Thomas, E. (1984). Anticipatory and fantastic role enactment in preschool triads. *Developmental Psychology, 20,* 807–814.

Miller, P., & Garvey, C. (1984). Mother-baby role play: Its origins in social support. In I. Bretherton (Ed.), *Symbolic play* (pp. 101–130). New York: Academic Press.

Morison, R., & Masten, A. S. (1991). Peer reputation in middle childhood as a predictor of adaptation in adolescence: A seven-year follow-up. *Child Development, 62,* 991–1007.

O'Connell, B., & Bretherton, I. (1984). Toddlers' play alone and with mother: The role of maternal guidance. In I. Bretherton (Ed.), *Symbolic Play* (pp. 337–368). New York: Academic Press.

O'Reilly, A. W., & Bornstein, M. H. (1993). Caregiver-child interaction in play. In M. H. Bornstein & A. W. O'Reilly (Eds.), *New directions for child development* (No. 59, pp. 55–66). San Francisco: Jossey-Bass.

Ollendick, T. H., Weist, M. D., Borden, M. C., & Greene, R. W. (1992). Sociometric status and academic, behavioral, and psychological adjustment: A five-year longitudinal study. *Journal of Consulting and Clinical Psychology, 60*, 80–87.

Parke, K., & Waters, E. (1989). Security of attachment and preschool friendships. *Child Development, 60*, 1076–1081.

Parke, R., & Ladd, G. (1992). *Family peer relationships: Modes of linkage*. Hillsdale, NJ: Lawrence Erlbaum.

Parke, R., MacDonald, K., Beitel, K., & Bhavnargi, N. (1988). The role of family in the development of peer relationships. In R. Peters & J. McMahon (Eds.), *Social learning systems approaches to marriage and family* (pp. 17–44). New York: Brunner/Mazel.

Parker, J. G., & Asher, S. R. (1987). Peer relations and later personal adjustment: Are low-accepted children at risk? *Psychological Bulletin, 102*, 357–389.

Patterson, G. R., DeBaryshe, B. D., & Ramsey, E. (1989). A developmental perspective on antisocial behavior. *American Psychologist, 44*, 329–335.

Pelligrini, A. (1988). Elementary-school children's rough-and-tumble play and social competence. *Developmental Psychology, 24*, 802–806.

Piaget, J. (1926). *The language and thought of the child*. New York: Harcourt, Brace, & World. (Original work published 1923)

Piaget, J. (1951). *Play, dreams, and imitation in childhood*. New York: Norton. (Original work published 1945)

Piaget, J. (1970). Piaget's theory. In P. Mussen (Ed.), *Carmichaels' manual of child psychology* (Vol. 1). New York: Wiley.

Putallaz, M., & Gottman, J. (1983). Social relationship problems in children: An approach to intervention. In B. Lahey & A. Kazdin (Eds.), *Advances in clinical child psychology* (Vol. 6, pp. 1–25). New York: Plenum.

Roopnarine, J. L., Talukder, E., Jain, D., Joshi, P., & Srivastave, P. (1990). Characteristics of holding, patterns of play, and social behaviors between parents and infants in New Delhi, India. *Developmental Psychology, 26*, 667–673.

Rosen, C. (1974). The effects of sociodramtic play on problem-solving behavior among culturally disadvantaged preschool children. *Child Development, 45*, 920–927.

Rubenstein, J., & Howes, C. (1976). The effects of peers on toddler interaction with mothers and toys. *Child Development, 47,* 597–605.

Rubin, K. (1980). Fantasy play: Its role in the development of social skills and social cognition. In K. Rubin (Ed.), *New Directions for Child Development,* San Francisco: Jossey-Bass.

Rubin, K. (1982). Nonsocial play in preschoolers: Necessary evil? *Child Development, 53,* 651–657.

Rubin, K., & Maioni, T. (1975). Play preference and its relationship to egocentrism, popularity, and classification skills in preschoolers. *Merrill-Palmer Quarterly, 21,* 171–179.

Rubin, K., Fein, G., & Vandenberg, B. (1983). *Play.* In P. Mussen (Series Ed.) & E. Hetherington (Vol. Ed.), *Handbook of child psychology: Vol. 4. Socialization, personality, and social development* (4th ed., pp. 693–774). New York: Wiley.

Rubin, K., Maioni, T., & Hornung, M. (1976). Free play behaviors in middle- and lower-class preschoolers: Parten and Piaget revisited. *Child Development, 47,* 414–419.

Saltz, E., Dixon, D., & Johnson, J. (1977). Training disadvantaged preschoolers on various fantasy activities: Effects on cognitive functioning and impulse control. *Child Development, 48,* 367–380.

Saltz, E., & Johnson, J. (1974). Training for thematic-fantasy play in culturally disadvantaged children: Preliminary results. *Journal of Educational Psychology, 66,* 623–630.

Singer, D., & Singer, J. (1990). *The house of make-believe: Children's play and the developing imagination.* Cambridge, MA: Harvard University Press.

Singer, J. (1973). *The child's world of make-believe: Experimental studies of imaginative play.* New York: Academic Press.

Slade, A. (1987a). A longitudinal study of maternal involvement and symbolic play during the toddler period. *Child Development, 58,* 367–375.

Slade, A. (1987b). Quality of attachment and early symbolic play. *Developmental Psychology, 23,* 78–85.

Smilansky, S. (1968). *The effects of sociodramatic play on disadvantaged children: Preschool children.* New York: Wiley.

Smith, P. K., & Boulton, M. (1990). Rough-and-tumble play, aggression and dominance: Perception and behavior in children's encounters. *Human Development, 33,* 271–282.

Smith, P., & Syddall, S. (1978). Play and non-play tutoring in preschool children: Is it play or tutoring that matters? *British Journal of Educational Psychology, 48,* 315–325.

Smolucha, F. (1992). Social origins of private speech in pretend play. In R. M. Diaz & L. E. Berk (Eds.), *Private speech: From social interaction to self-regulation* (pp. 123–141). Hillsdale, NJ: Lawrence Erlbaum.

Sroufe, L.A., and Waters, E. (1977). Attachment as an organization construct. *Child Development, 48,* 1184–1199.

Stern, D. N. (1985). *The interpersonal world of the infant: A view from psychoanalysis and developmental psychology.* New York: Basic Books.

Suess, G. J., Grossmann, K. E., & Sroufe, L. A. (1992). Effects of infant attachment to mother and father on quality of adaptation in preschool: From dyadic to individual organisation of self. *International Journal of Behavioral Development, 15,* 43–65.

Sutton-Smith, B. (1966). Piaget on play: A critique. *Psychological Review, 73,* 104–110.

Sutton-Smith, B. (1976). Current research and theory on play, games, and sports. In T. Craig (Ed.), *The humanistic and mental health aspects of sports, exercise and recreation.* Chicago: American Medical Association.

Tamis-LeMonda, C., & Bornstein, M. (1991). Individual variation, correspondence, stability, and change in mother and toddler play. *Infant Behavior and Development, 14,* 143–162.

Thompson, R. (1993). Socioemotional development: Enduring issues and new challenges. *Developmental Review, 13,* 372–402.

Vandenberg, B. (1981). Play: Dominant issues and new perspectives. *Human Development, 24,* 357–365.

Vygotsky, L. (1978). The role of play in development. In M. Cole, V. John-Steiner, S. Scribner, & E. Souberman (Eds.), *Mind in society* (pp. 92–104). Cambridge, MA: Harvard University Press.

Vygotsky, L. S. (1966). Play and its role in the mental development of the child. *Soviet Psychology, 12*(6), 62–76.

Vygotsky, L. S. (1978). *Mind in society: The development of higher mental processes* (M. Cole, V. John-Steiner, S. Scribner, & E. Souberman, Eds. & Trans.). Cambridge, MA: Harvard University Press. (Original works published 1930, 1933, 1935)

Vygotsky, L. S. (1987). Thinking and speech. In R. Rieber, A. S. Carton (Eds.), & N. Minick (Trans.), *The collected works of L. S. Vygotsky: Vol. 1. Problems of general psychology* (pp. 37–285). New York: Plenum. (Original work published 1934)

Waters, E., & Sroufe, L. (1983). Social competence as a developmental construct. *Developmental Review, 3,* 79–97.

Waters, E., Wippman, J., & Sroufe, L. (1979). Attachment, positive affect, and competence in the peer group: Two studies in construct validation. *Child Development, 50*, 821–829.

Zukow, P. (1986). The relationship between interaction with caregiver and the emergence of play activities during the one-word period. *British Journal of Developmental Psychology, 4*, 223–234.

Chapter 8

Social and Nonsocial Play in Childhood: An Individual Differences Perspective

Kenneth H. Rubin and Robert J. Coplan

The goal of this chapter is to explore the causes, correlates, and consequences of individual differences in young children's social play. To the extent that social play appears to be clearly definable, our goal-oriented task seemed quite straightforward. Yet, as is the case with most every psychological phenomenon, social play is a complex entity that carries with it a variety of psychological meanings. And, *nonsocial* play is even more complex and multidimensional. As such, what started out as a less than daunting task has turned out to be one accompanied by a great many conceptual twists-and-turns replete with smoke-and-mirrors.

To begin with, young children's play behaviors vary along a number of important dimensions (see Rubin, Fein, & Vandenberg, 1983, for an extensive review). For example, following a neo-Piagetian line of thought, one can consider sensorimotor play, pretense, and games-with-rules (Piaget, 1962). But each of these forms of play takes place within a particular social context. And the psychological "meanings" and significance of these "cognitive" forms of play vary when they are frequently produced by a child who is alone or by one who is interacting with playmates. Thus, a guiding theme of this chapter is that the content of children's ludic activity must be considered within the given social context. For example, pretense produced frequently *on one's own,* in the presence of a play group must assuredly carry with it a very different psychological meaning than pretense produced frequently while interacting *cooperatively* with social partners. And likewise, observations of classroom produced *solitary*-pretense carry with them different developmental messages than solitary-constructive activities. These variations in the social contexts within which play activities are generated represent the substance of this chapter.

HISTORICAL ROOTS

Traditionally, researchers have sought to understand young children's play by referring to its *structural components* ("How is the child playing?"; "What is the child doing?"). These structural components are observed in a variety of *social participation* contexts ("With whom is the child playing?").

Structural Components of Play

The structural approach to the understanding and classification of children's play behaviors is drawn largely from Piaget's *Play, Dreams, and Imitation in Childhood* (1962). In this volume, Piaget outlined a classification system for the development of children's games. He distinguished three main types of ludic activities characterizing children's games—namely, practice games, symbolic games, and games-with-rules. As well, he suggested that constructive games constituted "the transition from all three to adapted behaviors" (p. 110).

These categories were subsequently elaborated upon by Smilansky (1968, p .5). She suggested that the child moves naturally from one "stage" of play to the next "in keeping with his biological development." The stages Smilansky described included:

1. *Functional activities* in which the same movements are repeated with or without objects. Functional play involves no purpose to construct anything; instead, children repeat actions, imitate themselves, try new actions and then imitate them, and so on. The child appears to gain pleasure from the performance of the behavior itself. Piaget (1962) referred to this type of activity, which develops during infancy, as sensorimotor play.
2. *Constructive activities* involve the building or creation of something. Play is sustained by constructive goals. From the sporadic handling of sand or blocks during functional play, the young preschooler engaging in constructive play moves to building something from these materials that will remain even after he/she has finished playing.
3. *Dramatic play*, in which there is some involvement of non-literality-symbolic transformation and the production of decontextualized behaviors. Pretend play allows the child to be many things at once; children can be themselves, actors, observers, and participators in a symbolic exercise.
4. *Games-with-rules*, in which there is spontaneous acceptance of a division of labor, prearranged rules, and the adjustment to these rules. Although rarely evident during the preschool and kindergarten years, this is one ludic activity that accompanies us into our adult lives.

According to Smilansky (1968), these four types of play developed in a relatively fixed sequence, with functional play appearing first in infancy, and games-with-rules last at about 6 or 7 years of age. Moving from functional play, to exploration, and finally to constructive and dramatic play, may allow the young child an opportunity to answer a series of important questions about objects. That is, opportunities to manipulate objects, in a functional-sensori-motor fashion, and to explore these objects, may serve to answer the question "What do these things do?" (Hutt, 1970). Once the object-derived question has been answered, the child may pose the self-derived question, "What can *I* do with these things?". The answers come in the forms of constructive and dramatic activities.

Social Participation

Each structural form of play occurs within given social participation contexts. Parten (1932) described several categories of children's social participation. The original focus was not on how children played, but whether they engaged others in the activities. Today, after only some minor modifications, social participation categories include:

1. *Unoccupied behavior* is observed when a child demonstrates a marked absence of focus or intent. Generally there are two types of unoccupied behaviors: (a) the child may stare blankly into space; or (b) she/he may wander aimlessly.
2. *Onlooker behavior* occurs when the child watches the activities of others but does not attempt to enter into an activity. Parten found that unoccupied and onlooker behaviors tend to decrease with child age.
3. *Solitary play* is said to occur when the child plays apart from the other children at a distance greater than three feet, or with her/his back to other children. The child is usually playing with toys that are different from those other children are using, and she or he is centered on his/her own activity, paying little or no attention to others in the area.
4. *Parallel play* involves the child playing independently; however the activity often, though not necessarily, brings him/her within three feet of other children. The child plays *beside,* or in the company of other children, but does *not* play with his/her companions. Parallel play represents the most common form young children's social interactions (Rubin, Maioni, & Hornung, 1976; Rubin, Watson & Jambor, 1978).
5. *Group play* consists of the child playing with others and there being a common goal or purpose to the social activity. Whatever the activity, the goals are definitely group-centered.

Parten (1932) found that the older the child, the more she/he played in the more highly integrated groups. Thus, with increasing age, children play in both cognitively and socially more mature fashions.

Almost twenty years ago, researchers began to merge or integrate the Piagetian structural components of play with Parten's social participation categories. It was argued that a complete understanding of children's play activities must consider the interaction of play *content* with play *context* (Rubin et al., 1976; Rubin et al., 1978). Thus, in order to understand individual differences in children's social participation, it became necessary to consider what children were doing, or how they were playing. These questions led to the development of the *Play Observation Scale.*

THE PLAY OBSERVATION SCALE (POS)

The Play Observation Scale (POS, Rubin, 1989) is an observational taxonomy designed to assess the structural components of children's play *nested* within social participatory categories. Accordingly, the POS employs a time sampling methodology within which 10-second segments are coded for both social participation (e.g., solitary, parallel, group) and the cognitive quality of children's play (e.g., functional-sensorimotor, constructive, dramatic). Several additional free play behaviors are also assessed, including instances of unoccupied behavior, onlooking, exploration, peer conversation, anxious behaviors, hovering, transitional behavior, rough-and-tumble play, and aggression. The POS taxonomy is illustrated in Table 8.1.

The POS provides a complete picture of children's free play activities. Its use in our laboratory, and in many others, has allowed for a clearer understanding, not only of children's play behavior, but also of social participation. In our own research, for example, we have found various mixes of play and social participation to convey meanings of *adaptation*, while others represent markers of maladjustment or incompetence. In the following sections, we examine the various "meanings" of the social and nonsocial play behaviors captured in the POS.

THE DEVELOPMENTAL COURSE
OF SOCIAL PARTICIPATION

Infancy and Toddlerhood

The origins of social participation can be traced back to early infancy. Although we may not expect young infants to display much peer interaction,

TABLE 8.1

BEHAVIORAL CATEGORIES ON THE PLAY OBSERVATION SCALE

			Time Sample				
	1	*2*	*3*	*4*	*5*	*6*	
Transitional							
Unoccupied							
Onlooker							
Solitary:							
Constructive							
Exploratory							
Functional							
Dramatic							
Games							
Parallel:							
Constructive							
Exploratory							
Functional							
Dramatic							
Games							
Group:							
Constructive							
Exploratory							
Functional							
Dramatic							
Games							
Peer Conversation:							
Double Coded Behaviors:							
Anxious behaviors							
Hovering							
Aggression							
Rough-and-Tumble							

given their obvious motoric, cognitive, and verbal limitations, some researchers have reported that infants demonstrate social interest (i.e. smiling, vocalizing, and reaching) toward peers during the first half year of life.

As infants near their first birthday, clear manifestations of social interest in peers are evidenced. In the company of agemates, infants will watch, vocalize, reach toward, and smile at each other (Maudry & Nekula, 1939;

Hay, Pederson, & Nash, 1982; Vandell, Wilson, & Buchanan, 1980). During the second year of life, toddlers begin to display more advanced social interchanges in terms of complimentarity, reciprocity, and coordination (e.g., Baudonniere, Garcia-Werebe, Michel, & Liegeois, 1989; Eckerman & Stein, 1982; Ross, Lollis, & Elliot, 1982). By the third year, there is marked increase in prosocial behaviors such as helping and sharing (Radke-Yarrow, Zahn-Waxler, & Chapman, 1983).

The Preschool Period

Parten (1932) concluded that the 3-year-old preschooler was characterized as a solitary or parallel player, while the 5-year-old was described as spending the most time in socially interactive (associative or cooperative) play. A closer examination of the literature reveals a more complex set of conclusions (e.g., Barnes, 1971; Rubin et al., 1976; Rubin et al., 1978).

During the preschool period, social play becomes more prominent, there is a substantial increase in the frequency of social contacts, and these social episodes become longer, more elaborated, and more varied (Blurton-Jones, 1972; Eckerman, Whatley, & Kutz, 1975; Holmberg, 1980; Rubin et al., 1978). As well, preschoolers tend to play with a wider range of playmates than do toddlers (e.g., Howes, 1983). However, even at 5 years, children spend less of their free play in classroom settings interacting with others than being alone or near others.

Moreover, the major developmental changes in the play of preschoolers concern the *cognitive* maturity of their solitary, parallel, and group interactive activities (e.g., Rubin, et al, 1978). For example, while solitary-sensorimotor behaviors become increasing rare over the preschool years, the frequency of solitary-constructive and exploratory activities remains roughly the same. Furthermore, it is *sociodramatic* play and games-with-rules that evidence the most significant increase in social activities.

The Functional Significance of Sociodramatic Play

With age, children's social activities increasingly incorporate pretense themes. Nonliteral behaviors with shared meaning represent complex cognitive coordinations and constructions. Moreover, it has been argued that one of the essential "tasks" of early childhood is to master the means to share and coordinate decontextualized and substitutive activities (e.g., Göncü, 1989).

Howes (1992) has proposed three essential functions of sociodramatic play. First, it creates a context for mastering the communicating of meaning. Second, sociodramatic play provides opportunities for children to learn to control and compromise; these opportunities arise during discussions and negotiations concerning pretend roles and scripts and the rules guiding the pretend episodes. Thus, during middle childhood, pretend play allows children to reveal to peers, their secrets, emotions, ambitions, and intentions (Rubin & Coplan, 1994). Third, social pretense allows for a "safe" context in which children can explore and discuss issues of intimacy and trust. Thus, for younger children, social pretense provides children with opportunities for developing communication skills. Consequently, it is no wonder that sociodramatic play is considered a "marker" of social competence in early and middle childhood (e.g., Howes, 1988, 1992).

THE DEVELOPMENTAL SIGNIFICANCE
OF SOCIAL INTERACTION

To fully understand the developmental significance of social play in childhood, it is important to consider the functional significance of peer interaction. For the young child, the peer group provides an important and unique context for the acquisition and implementation of social skills. Theorists have been positing the developmental significance of peer interaction for over 50 years.

Piaget (e.g., 1926, 1932) suggested, for example, that peer interaction provided children with an important and unique learning environment. In particular, exposure to instances of interpersonal differences of opinion and thought, and opportunities for discussion and negotiation about these differences, were viewed as aiding children in the acquisition and development of sensitive perspective-taking skills in interpersonal relationships.

Mead (1934) echoed Piaget's emphasis on the importance of the development of perspective-taking through peer interaction. In addition, Mead stressed the importance of peer interaction in the development of the self-system. Thus, exchanges among peers, in the contexts of cooperation, competition, conflict, and friendly discussion, allowed the child to gain an understanding of the self as both subject and object.

Sullivan (1953) proposed that the experience of peer relationships is essential for the child's development of the concepts of mutual respect, equality, and reciprocity. Moreover, Sullivan emphasized the importance of "chumships," or special relationships, for the emergence of these concepts. Thus, equality, mutuality, and reciprocity were acquired *between* special friends, and then these concepts were thought to be extended to other relationships.

It is now widely accepted that children who consistently experience an impoverished quality of peer interaction during the early and middle childhood years may be "at risk" for later problems in adolescence and adulthood. These problems include school dropout, delinquency, aggression, depression, low self-esteem, and loneliness (see Kupersmidt, Coie, & Dodge, 1990; Parker, Rubin, DeRosiers, & Price, 1995, for reviews).

Although, as we indicated above, children generally become more sociable with increasing age, there exist marked individual differences in the degree to which children are socially initiative. And sociability appears to be generally stable across time (Bronson, 1985; Kagan & Moss, 1962). Ostensibly, sociable children avail themselves of opportunities to interact with peers; as such, they should be less likely to develop problems of social and emotional maladjustment than their less sociable counterparts who, for whatever reason, preclude themselves from the positive "outcomes" associated with peer interaction. This proposition has been examined in recent research concerning the frequent demonstration of *nonsocial* activity during play.

NON-SOCIAL PLAY IN CHILDHOOD: A CLOSER LOOK

If social interaction or social participation is advantageous for children, it would make some initial sense to believe that the *lack* of social interaction should prove disadvantageous. Recently, this latter belief has become mainstream among those who have suggested that shy or socially withdrawn children are "at risk" for later social and emotional problems. But what precisely happens when children spend their time alone? Is it the case that the frequent display of nonsocial play in early childhood is "necessarily evil?" (Rubin, 1982). It is now rather clear that the answer is, "No". Nonsocial play is a complex and multidimensional construct. Various subtypes of nonsocial behaviors appear to have different underlying psychological mechanisms. In a series of recent studies, we have explored and investigated the different "meanings" of behavioral solitude. Our findings are described below.

The Multiple Forms of Nonsocial Play Behaviors

Martha is a four-year-old child attending a local preschool. Often, during free play time, she can be seen alone, drawing on a pad of paper with some colored markers. She is engrossed in her work, and pays little attention to the activities around her. On many occasions, she will spent the entire free play session painting, drawing, or building something in the sandbox.

Jeff is also 4-years-old and is in Martha's preschool class. Like Martha, Jeff spends most of his time alone; but instead of constructive activity, he is frequently off to the side of the room, intently watching other children play. He can often be seen biting his fingernails or pulling anxiously on his clothes or hair. Sometimes, Jeff will start to cry and ask to see his mother. And, every once in a while, Jeff will inch up close to where other children are playing, hovering on the edge of the social scene; he almost invariably stops when he gets within a few feet of his potential playmates, and makes no attempt to join in, waiting motionless. Usually, after a few minutes, he will wander off aimlessly.

Sean is a 4-year-old classmate of Jeff and Martha. He moves quickly and impulsively from one activity to another. When he is playing by himself, he often makes a lot of noises and sound effects. One of his favorite games involves throwing two woodblocks against the wall, and he always giggles when they crash to the ground. Sean frequently tries to join others in play, but his entries are usually rough and brusk. More often than not, his social overtures are rejected by his peers.

The children described above provide prototypical examples of different forms of nonsocial behaviors. In the following section, we discuss the results from a series of recent studies in which we have begun to explore and examine the theoretical amd empirical heterogeniety of young children's *nonsocial* play.

Solitary-passive behavior. Solitary-passive behavior includes the quiescent exploration of objects and/or constructive activity while playing alone. In *early childhood*, such behavior is reinforced positively by teachers, parents, and peers, and its display is associated with competent problem solving as well as peer acceptance (Rubin, 1982). Children who frequently engage in solitary-passive play (e.g., doing puzzles or artwork; or reading) appear to be object-oriented rather than people-oriented. These children excel at object-oriented tasks (e.g., ticket-sorting, toy clean-up), are more task persistent, and have a higher attention span (Coplan, 1995). On the other hand, they perform poorly during people-oriented social tasks (e.g., "show and tell" during small group time) (Coplan & Rubin, 1993). Generally, solitary-passive play among preschoolers is not associated with indices of maladaptation (Coplan, Rubin, Fox, Calkins, & Stewart, 1994).

Recently, researchers have attempted to provide an etiological explanation for children's frequent production of soiltary-passive play. One possibility mentioned is that the children who engage in high frequencies of solitary-passive play are relatively *disinterested* in social engagement and they have low approach and low avoidance motivations (Asendorpf, 1991; Rubin & Asendorpf, 1993). To the extent that such an explanation would not be suggestive of high-risk status for "solitary-passive" children, it is not surprising that Rubin and colleagues (Rubin, Coplan, Fox, & Calkins, 1995) recently reported that nonsociable, but emotionally regulated, children were more likely to display solitary-passive behavior, when engaged in solitary activities, as compared to any other form of nonsocial behavior. Thus, despite being a form of nonsocial play, solitary-passive behavior does not appear to be a risk factor for concurrent maladaptation. As such, one would not wish to consider providing such "withdrawn" children with ameliorative or intervention experiences directed to changing their social orientations.

Solitary-active behavior. Solitary-active behavior, when produced in a social group, is characterized by repeated sensorimotor actions with or without objects and/or by solitary dramatizing. It is important to distinguish solitary-dramatic play *in the presence of peers* from (1) dramatic *play when the child is alone,* and from (2) *sociodramatic* play in the presence of peers. The former is quite normal for young children, and the latter, as discussed previously, is a marker of social competence (e.g., Howes, 1992).

Solitary-active play is a very infrequent but highly salient form of nonsocial play. This extremely low frequency of occurrence makes it very difficult to study without the use of extensive observational periods. The cluster of behaviors comprising solitary-active play, however, has been associated with indices of (a) impulsivity among preschoolers (Coplan et al., 1994; Rubin, 1982), (b) peer rejection from as early as the preschool years, and (c) externalizing problems (in particular aggressiveness) and immaturity throughout the childhood years (Rubin, 1982; Rubin & Mills, 1988). Recently, Coplan (1995) found that the display of solitary-active behavior in the preschool was significantly and positively correlated with teacher ratings of children's externalizing problems. Thus, solitary-active behavior, although nonsocial in nature, appears to be associated with *externalizing,* as opposed to internalizing problems, in childhood. Rubin, LeMare, and Lollis (1990) have suggested that although some children may voluntarily withdraw *from* peer interaction, others may, in fact, be actively isolated *by* the peer group. This may be the case for those children who engage in a high frequency of solitary-active behaviors. Ameliorative action would thus be appropriate when it is noted that children's activties are dominated by solitary-active play.

Reticent behavior. The third cluster of solitary behaviors, which we label reticence, may be identified by the frequent production of prolonged watching of other children without accompanying play (onlooking), or being unoccupied (Asendorpf, 1991; Coplan et al., 1994). Reticent behavior is believed to reflect social fear and anxiety in a social context. From a motivational perspective, it appears to indicate an approach-avoidance conflict (Asendorpf, 1990). Thus, reticent children may be desirous of peer entry (high *approach* motivation), but this motivation is simultaneously inhibited by social fear and anxiety (high *avoidance* motivation).

Reticent behaviors, among preschoolers, have been associated empirically with the overt demonstration of anxiety (automanipulatives [e.g., digit sucking, hair pulling], crying), hovering near others during free play, and maternal ratings of shyness (Coplan & Rubin, 1993; Coplan et al., 1994). It is highly stable across situations. For example, children who are reticent during free play, also display high frequencies of onlooking and unoccupied behaviors during situations requiring task completion or self-presentation (Coplan & Rubin, 1993; Coplan et al., 1994). As well, there is a higher incidence of internalizing problems reported for children who exhibit a high frequency of reticent behavior both in the laboratory (Coplan & Rubin, 1993) and in preschool (Coplan, 1995) free play settings. Again, because of the potential risk status associated with behavioral reticence, it would behoove psychologists, educators, and caregivers to provide some form of intervention for extemely reticent young children. A description of intervention procedures can be found in Rubin, Hymel, Mills, and Rose-Krasnor (1991) and Schneider, Rubin, and Ledingham (1985).

Although reticence and passive-solitude appear to reflect distinct subtypes of social withdrawal among preschoolers, there is some preliminary evidence suggesting that during the *mid-childhood years*, these two forms of nonsocial behaviors become increasingly associated (Asendorpf, 1991). For one, the frequent display of reticent *and/or* passive-solitude becomes increasingly (with age) viewed by the child's community of peers as deviant from social behavioral norms (Younger & Daniels, 1992). Thus, the psychological meaning of passive-solitude appears to change, reflecting psychological uncertainly, negative self-appraisals, and insecurity in one's relationships. Indeed, passive solitude has been found to be correlated with internalizing problems and peer rejection during the mid-years of childhood (Rubin et al., 1989; Rubin & Mills, 1988).

In summary, it seems clear that different forms of social and nonsocial play have different psychological "meanings." Moreover, individual differences in these various forms of social and nonsocial play are fairly stable, and predict widely variant maladaptive and adaptive outcomes. In the following section, we explore the origins of individual differences in social play.

ORIGINS OF INDIVIDUAL DIFFERENCES IN SOCIAL PLAY

Few researchers have directly examined the origins of social play behaviors in children. Many researchers, however, have investigated theoretically related and relevant variables. An examination of the literature pertaining to the development of sociability, social competence, and shyness/social withdrawal, allows an initial picture to be drawn of those factors that may influence individual differences in children's social and nonsocial play.

Genetic Factors

There is growing evidence that shyness and sociability are influenced by genetic factors. The heritability of social play is evidenced through an examination of twin studies. For example, during the first year of life, identical twins are more similar than fraternal twins in their frequency of social smiling and their fear of strangers (Freedman, 1974). These differences in sociability are still apparent when pairs of fraternal and identical twins are retested at 18 and 24 months of age (Matheny, 1983). Plomin and Daniels (1986) reviewed 18 twin studies and reported that, particularly among younger children, shyness was more highly associated in monozygotic twins than in dizygotic twins. Moreover, Scarr (1968) reported that a genetic effect on sociability can still be seen in children 6 to 10 years of age.

Temperament and Physiology

Researchers have also attempted to establish a biological link with social play through studies of child temperament and physiology. Kagan (e.g., 1989; Kagan, Reznick, & Gibbons, 1989; Kagan, Reznick & Snidman, 1988), for example, has distinguished between *inhibited* and *uninhibited* children. The former group can be characterized as being quiet, vigilant, and restrained while they experience *novel* situations. The latter group, alternatively, reacts with spontaneity, as if they do not distinguish between novel and familiar situations.

Inhibited children, compared to their uninhibited counterparts, have higher and more stable heart rates, larger pupil diameters, greater motor tension, and higher levels of morning cortisol (Garcia-Coll, Kagan, & Reznick, 1984; Kagan, Reznick, & Snidman, 1987, 1988). These data are viewed as supporting the notion that inhibited children have a biologically predispositioned low threshold for arousal in the face of novelty.

Inhibited 2-year-olds are more likely, then their uninhibited counterparts, to engage in *reticent* behavior in a free play setting with peers at age 4 years (Calkins, Fox, Rubin, & Coplan, 1995). Thus, there is some indirect evidence to suggest that temperament and physiology are important factors in the development of social play.

Additional evidence for a biological explanation for individual differences in nonsocial and social play may be drawn from the research of Fox and colleagues. Fox (e.g., Fox & Calkins, 1993) has argued that physiological indices of emotional regulation are important components of social withdrawal and inhibition. These physiological indices include patterns of hemispheric imbalance (as measured by EEG activation) and vagal tone (a measure of parasympathetic control over heart rate). For example, in a short-term longitudinal study of infants at 4, 9, and 14 months, Calkins, Fox, and Marshall (in press) found that infants' tendencies toward negative reactivity at 4 months were related to greater right frontal EEG activation at 9 months and inhibited behavior at 14 months. As well, Fox, Rubin, Calkins, Marshall,

Coplan, Porges, and Long (1995) found that preschool children who were more socially competent and sociable during free play and other socially oriented episodes exhibited greater *left* frontal activation. Preschoolers who displayed more withdrawn and wary behaviors during free play sessions exhibited greater *right* frontal activation. Fox argued that frontal activity asymmetry may be a marker for certain temperamental dispositions, including shyness/social withdrawal.

In another recent study, it was discovered that indices of emotion regulation interacted with the frequency of observed social play to predict adaptive and maladaptive "outcomes" in early childhood (Rubin, Coplan, Fox, & Calkins, 1995). In this study, preschoolers were first observed and subsequently identified as engaging in extremely high or extremely low frequencies of social play. These children were also classified as being emotionally regulated or dysregulated. Emotionally *dysregulated* children were those who had been rated as temperamentally high in negative emotionality (e.g., "cries easily") and difficulty to soothe. Emotionally *regulated* children did not exhibit negative emotionality and were easy to soothe.

The socially *noninteractive and dysregulated* children were observed to display anxiety and social fear during peer play, and were rated as having more internalizing problems than were comparison groups of *socially noninteractive* and *well-regulated* children or *average* children. Thus, outcomes associated with nonsocial activities varied as a function of the children's ability to regulate their emotions—a temperamental trait linked to biological underpinnings.

Among *highly social* children, those who were also emotionally *dysregulated* had more externalizing problems than their *well-regulated and socially interactive* peers or *average* counterparts. Thus, it would appear as if highly sociable children are not immune to the development of psychological maadaptation. Hostility and aggression appear to be concomitants of high sociability *and* emotional dysregulation (see Figure 8.1).

Parenting Beliefs and Behaviors

Another potential influence on children's social play are their parents. In this regard, researchers have focused on the constructs of parenting style or discipline techniques and the quality of the parent-child attachment relationship.

Generally, *authoritative* parents (high in control and high in warmth) are likely to raise well-adjusted children who are socially responsible and competent, friendly, and cooperative with peers (Baumrind, 1967, 1971). Moreover, this parenting style has been found to correlate contemporaneously and predictively with measures of moral reasoning, self-esteem, and prosocial

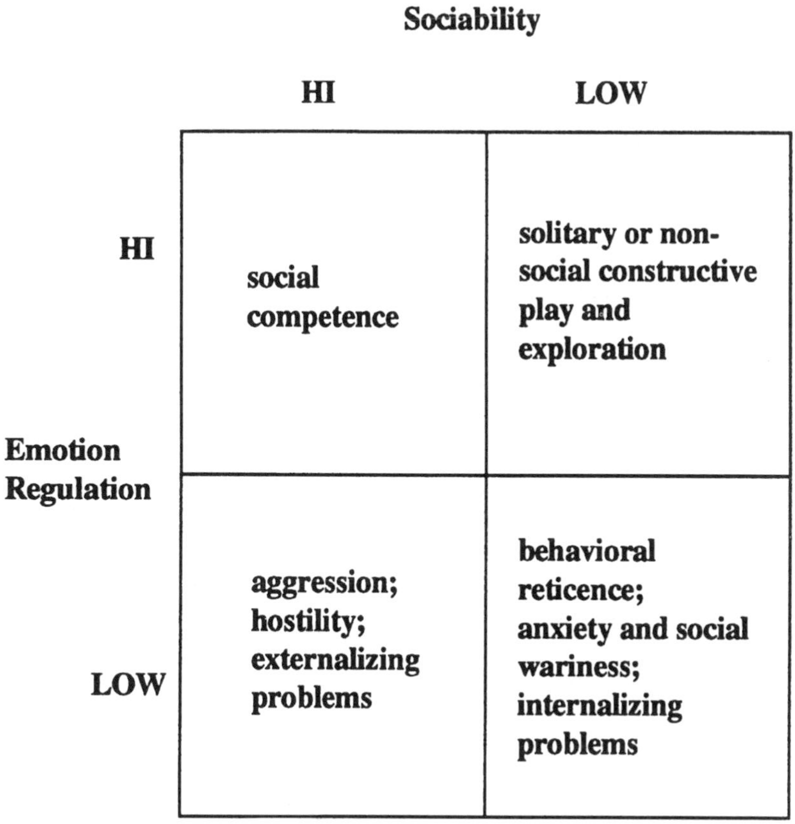

Sociability

	HI	LOW
HI	social competence	solitary or non-social constructive play and exploration
LOW	aggression; hostility; externalizing problems	behavioral reticence; anxiety and social wariness; internalizing problems

*(Left axis label: **Emotion Regulation**)*

FIGURE 8.1
THE INTERACTION BETWEEN SOCIABILITY AND EMOTION REGULATION

behavior in children (e.g., Hoffman, 1970; Roopnairine, 1987; Yarrow, Waxler, & Scott, 1971). In contrast, parents who provide insufficient or imbalanced responsiveness and control (authoritatian, permissive, or uninvolved) are likely to have children who are socially incompetent, aggressive, and/or socially withdrawn (Baumrind, 1967, 1971, 1991; Dishion, 1991, Lamborn et al., 1991).

There is also some evidence to suggest that parents of socially withdrawn children are more overprotective, overcontrolling, and more likely to attribute their children's withdrawal to internal, dispositional sources than are parents of nonwithdrawn children. That is, they explain their children's behaviors by referring to trait-like, biological, or genetic factors ("She was born that way"). Parents of withdrawn children are also less spontaneous, playful, and affectively positive than parents of more sociable children (see Rubin, Stewart, and Chen, 1995, for a recent review of the literature pertaining to parental correlates of social withdrawal).

Parent-Child Attachment Relationships

Many researchers have explored the role that the parent-child attachment relationship may play in children's social development. Again, there is evidence for a relation between security of attachment and the demonstration of social and nonsocial play.

Precursors to social competence and social play are predicted by the parent-child attachment relationship in infancy. For example, securely attached infants are more able than their insecurely attached counterparts to produce numerous, acceptable, and flexible solutions to hypothetical social dilemmas (Arend, Gove, & Sroufe, 1979). As well, secure attachment status in infancy has been found to predict, at 4 years of age, more elaborate and flexible play styles, and more positive social engagement than insecure attachment relationships (e.g., Sroufe, 1983). And, securely attached 4-year-olds are more likely to engage peers in social play than their insecurely attached agemates (Booth, Rose-Krasnor, McKinnon, & Rubin, 1994). In the following section, we elaborate on the importance of the parent-child attachment relationship insofar as the development of children's social and nonsocial play is concerned.

DEVELOPMENTAL MODELS OF SOCIAL AND NONSOCIAL PLAY

Rubin and colleagues (e.g., Rubin, LeMare, & Lollis, 1990; Rubin, Stewart, & Coplan, 1995) have described a number of pathways in which the *interplay* between physiology and the environmental result in the development of social competence and peer acceptance. They argue that the quality of children's peer relationships is a function of social competence, which in turn is a function of the developmental interplay between intra-individual, inter-individual, and macro-systemic forces.

A Developmental Pathway to Social Play

In the most positive of the developmental pathway models described by Rubin and colleagues (e.g., Rubin, Lemare et al., 1990; Rubin, Stewart et al., 1995), an easy-tempered child is born into a family in which there are sensitive and responsive parents, and a general lack of major stresses or crises. These starting points are viewed as providing an essential base for the establishment of a secure parent-child attachment relationship (Rubin & Lollis, 1988). A secure attachment relationship is caused and maintained, in part, by parents who are sensitive, responsive, and "in tune" with the child's behaviors (Isabella & Belsky, 1991; Spieker & Booth, 1988). In turn, secure primary relationships are hypothesized to predict the development of social and emotional adaptation (Sroufe, 1983).

Within the context of a secure relationship, the child comes to believe that parents are available to serve his or her needs. This allows the child to feel secure, confident, and self-assured when introduced to novel settings. Moreover, the *internal working model* of "felt security" fosters the child's active exploration of the social environment (Sroufe, 1983). In turn, exploration of the social environment allows the child to address a number of significant "other-directed" questions such as "What are the properties of this other person?", "What is she/he like?", and "What can and does she/he do?". Once these exploratory questions are answered, the child can begin to address "self-directed" questions such as "What can I do with this person?". Thus, felt security may have a central role in the enhancement of social exploration, and exploration results in peer play (Rubin, Fein, & Vandenberg, 1983).

A DEVELOPMENTAL PATHWAY TO NONSOCIAL BEHAVIOR.

Rubin and colleagues (e.g., Rubin, Lemare et al., 1990; Rubin, Stewart et al., 1995) have also described a pathway to the frequent production of *nonsocial* behavior. Most families experience, from time to time, stress, crises, and day-to-day hassles. There is growing evidence that environmental conditions can influence the quality of the parent-child relationship and the social emotional well-being of children. For example, factors such as poverty, unemployment, and inadequate housing can produce a generalized maladaptive response set in parents that leads to the neglect or overdirection of the child (Crnic & Greenberg, 1990; Patterson, 1983; Wahler & Dumas, 1987).

Rubin, Lemare, and Lollis (1990) note the developmental prognoses for infants who are biologically predispositioned to have a low threshold for arousal when confronted with social (or nonsocial) stimulation and novelty (see Kagan, Snidman, & Reznick, 1987; Miyake, Chen, & Campos, 1985), and who are born into stressful family circumstances. First, they argue that the baby's biologically driven "difficult" characteristics, even when experienced in the best of environmental circumstances, will make him or her extremely difficult to soothe and comfort. Indeed, parents, especially those under stress, may find such infantile responses of hyperarousal extremely aversive (Kagan, Reznick, & Garcia-Coll, 1984). Rubin and colleagues posit that parents who are experiencing stressful family conditions may react to their infant's wariness with insensitivity, and/or nonresponsivity (e.g., Engfer & Gavranidou, 1987).

The result of dispositional infant inhibition that is responded to with parental insensitivity or overcontrol, is the development of an insecure anxious-resistant ("C"-type) attachment relationship (Sroufe, 1983) and an internal working model of "felt insecurity." Rubin, Lemare, and Lollis (1990) note that insecure, inhibited children will fail to explore novel settings and unfamiliar others. As indicated previously, exploration is an important precursor to peer play (Rubin, Fein, & Vandenberg, 1983). Consequently, failure to explore the social milieu inhibits the experience of those forms of peer interaction that may be essential for the development of social competence. Thus, one can predict a developmental sequence in which an inhibited, fearful, insecure child withdraws from the social world of peers, fails to develop those skills derived from peer interaction, and, because of this, becomes increasingly anxious and isolated from the peer group.

As noted earlier, with increasing age, social reticence or withdrawal becomes increasingly salient to the peer group (Younger & Boyko, 1987; Younger, Gentile, & Burgess, 1993). It is also the case that perceived deviation from age normative social behavior is associated with the establishment of negative peer reputations and peer rejection. Thus, in their developmental model, Rubin et al. (1990) speculate that by the mid-years of childhood, the withdrawn, wary, insecure, socially incompetent child will become rejected by his or her peers.

DEVELOPMENTAL OUTCOMES OF
SOCIAL AND NONSOCIAL PLAY

What empirical evidence is there for the developmental model proposed by Rubin and colleagues (e.g., Rubin et al., 1989; Rubin, Lamre, & Lollis, 1990; Rubin, Stewart, & Caplan, 1995)? And what "outcomes" are associated with the frequent display of social withdrawal in childhood?

In actuality, there have been few follow-forward longitudinal studies of the developmental course of children's nonsocial play. We will focus our attention on results from the Waterloo Longitudinal Project (WLP), initiated originally in 1980 to examine the stability and predictive "outcomes" of childhood nonsocial play (e.g., Rubin, 1982, 1985; Rubin, Hymel, & Mills, 1989; Rubin, Hymel et al., 1991; Rubin, Chen, & Hymel, 1993; Rubin, Chen, McDougall, Bowker, & McKinnon, 1995).

To begin with, results from the WLP have indicated that social withdrawal is relatively stable from preschool through to adolescence (e.g., Rubin, 1993; Rubin & Both, 1989). Furthermore, during middle childhood, social withdrawal becomes associated with peer rejection (Rubin, Hymel et al., 1989; Rubin, Lemare, & Lollis, 1990). As well, social withdrawal is concurrently and predictively associated with selected deficiencies in children's interpersonal problem solving. For example, withdrawn children are unassertive, and submissive in their social problem-solving styles (Rubin, & Rose-Krasnor, 1992); they become increasingly less initiative in social interactions, and increasingly less assertive and successful in solving their interpersonal dilemmas with increasing age (Stewart & Rubin, 1993). Moreover, withdrawn children come to interpret social failure as caused by internal, stable causes (Rubin & Krasnor, 1986). As such, the child may be drawn into a vicious cycle whereby initially fearful, nonsociable youngster comes to believe that his/her social failures are dispositionally based, and these beliefs are strengthened by the increasing failure of his/her social initiatives. Ultimately, in response, the child will likely withdraw further from the peer milieu.

Having noted that interpersonal failure, peer rejection, and social anxiety are experiences characteristic of withdrawn children, it is not surprising to find that by middle childhood, social withdrawal becomes increasingly associated with negative self-perceptions of social competence and self-esteem (e.g., Rubin, 1985; Rubin & Mills, 1988). By late childhood, socially withdrawn children are not only more negative in their self-appraisals of social competence, but also express greater loneliness and depression than their more sociable agemates (Hymel, Rubin, Rowden, & LeMare, 1990; Rubin , Hymel, & Chen, 1993; Rubin, Hymel et al., 1989).

Results from the WLP have yielded insight into the negative outcomes (in middle and later childhood, and adolescence) predicted from social withdrawal in early childhood. For example, a high frequency of nonsocial activities in kindergarten predicted feelings of depression and low self-worth, and teacher-rated anxiety at age 11 years. Similar predictive correlations were found for observed social withdrawal at age 7 years (Hymel et al., 1990; Rubin & Mills, 1988).

In a recent study (Rubin, Chen et al., 1995), a sample of children from the WLP was followed into high school, at age 14 years. Results indicated that social withdrawal at age 7 years significantly predicted internalizing, but not externalizing difficulties at adolescent age 14 years. Specifically, in this unselected sample of school attending children, social withdrawal in mid-childhood predicted negative self-regard, loneliness, and felt insecurity among peers and family in adolescence. Thus, it would appear as if the frequent production of nonsocial play during early and middle childhood brings with it several developmental "costs."

FUTURE DIRECTIONS

In this final section, we discuss some areas of future direction in the study of individual differences in young children's social and nonsocial play.

Sex Differences

Several researchers have reported that socially withdrawn boys, and not girls, carry with them a greater risk status. For example, Morison and Masten (1991) reported that withdrawn boys were more likely than girls to develop problems of low self-esteem in adolescence. And, Rubin, Chen, and Hymel (1993) found that extremely withdrawn 11-year-old boys, but not girls, were more lonely and more negative about their own social skills than their more sociable agemates. When these sex differences first appear, and what the ontogenetic causes of these differences are, represent significant questions for future study.

Culture and Nonsocial Play

The studies we have described thus far are specific to Western cultures. Yet, it is well known that the evaluation of social behavior is influenced by social conventions (Gresham, 1986). Thus, adults view children's behaviors as normal or not from the perspective of cultural norms and values.

In Western culture, passive, reticent behavior is viewed negatively by parents and peers alike. However, in China, children are encouraged to be dependent, cautious, self-restrained, and behaviorally inhibited (Ho, 1986). Such behaviors are considered indices of accomplishment, mastery, and maturity (Feng, 1962; King & Bond, 1985). Similarly, shy, reticent, and quiet children are described as well-behaved. Indeed, inhibited behavior is praised and encouraged (Ho, 1986) and is positively associated with competent prosocial behavior and with peer acceptance (Chen, Rubin, & Li, 1995; Chen, Rubin, & Sun, 1992). These latter results suggest strongly that the cultural milieu and societal values may encourage or inhibit, accept or reject demonstrations of highly sociable or highly unsociable children. We argue that the definitions of normalcy and psychological adaptation described in the vast majority of textbooks fail to be sensitive to cultural variability. Thus, culture-specific meanings of given social behaviors are required; and research providing such meanings is necessary.

Conclusions

We began this chapter by describing the development of social and nonsocial forms of play in childhood. We argued for the need to pay heed to subtle differences in play while children were active on their own or with others. Subsequently, we centered on those children who participate infrequently in peer interaction; a developmental model was proposed to account for the etiology, the concomitants, and consequences of nonsocial play in childhood. The bottom line is that we have identified a group of children for whom a life course, *in Western societies*, may be markedly negative. These are children who do not often play socially with peers and who come by their nonsocial activity as a result of an intermix of biological and socialization factors. For the readers of this volume, our presentation is likely to be viewed as markedly different from the other contributions focused primarily on children's play. Our message is a rather simple one. Play carries with it different meanings depending on the social and cultural contexts within which it is displayed. And some forms of social play make contributions to psychological adjustment, whereas others represent deterrents to adjustment. These are strong statements that bear further substantiation in future research efforts.

ACKNOWLEDGMENT

Preparation of this chapter was aided by an Ontario Mental Health Foundation Senior Research Fellowship to author Rubin and a Social Sciences and Humanities Research Council of Canada Doctoral Fellowship to author Coplan.

REFERENCES

Arend, R., Grove, F., & Sroufe, L.A. (1979). Continuity of individual adaptation from infancy to kindergarten: A predictive study of ego-resiliency and curiosity in preschoolers. *Child Development, 50*, 950–959.

Asendorpf, J. (1990). Beyond social withdrawal: Shyness, unsociability and peer avoidance. *Human Development, 33*, 250–259.

Asendorpf, J. (1991). Development of inhibited children's coping with unfamiliarity. *Child Development, 62*, 1460–1474.

Barnes, K. E. (1971). Preschool play norms: A replication. *Developmental Psychology, 5*, 99–103.

Baudonniere, P., Garcia-Werebé, M., Michel, J., & Liegois, J. (1989). Development of communicative competencies in early childhood: A model and results. In B. H. Schneider, G. Attili, J. Nadel, & R. P. Weissberg (Eds.), *Social competence in developmental perspective*. Boston: Kluwer Academic Publishers.

Baumrind, D. (1967). Child care patterns anteceding three patterns of preschool behavior. *Genetic Psychology Monographs, 75*, 43–88.

Baumrind, D. (1971). Current patterns of parental authority. *Developmental Psychology Monographs, 4* (No. 1, Pt. 2).

Baumrind, D. (1991). To nurture nature. *Behavioral and Brain Sciences, 14*, 386.

Booth, C.L., Rose-Krasnor, L., McKinnon, J., & Rubin, K. H. (1994). Predicting social adjustment in middle childhood: The role of preschool attachment security and maternal style. *Social Development, 3*, 189–204.

Blurton-Jones, N. (1972). Categories of child-child interaction. In N. Blurton-Jones (Ed.), *Ethological studies of child behavior* (pp. 97–127). Cambridge: Cambridge University Press.

Bronson, W. C. (1985). Growth and organization of behavior over the second year of life. *Developmental Psychology, 21*, 108–117

Calkins, S. D., Fox, N. A., & Marshall, T. (in press). Behavioral and physiological antecedents of inhibition in infancy. *Child Development.*

Calkins, S. D., Fox, N. A., Rubin, K. H., & Coplan, R.J. (1995). *Longitudinal outcomes of behavioral inhibition: Implications for behavior in a peer setting.* Unpublished manuscript.

Chen, X., & Rubin, K. H. (1992). Correlates of peer acceptance in a Chinese sample of six-year-olds. *International Journal of Behavioral Development, 15*(2), 259–273.

Chen, X., Rubin, K. H., & Li, Z. (1995). Social functioning and adjustment in Chinese children: A longitudinal study. *Developmental Psychology, 31*, 531–539.

Chen, X., Rubin, K. H., & Sun, Y. (1992). Social reputation and peer relationships in Chinese and Canadian children: A cross-cultural study. *Child Development, 63*, 1336–1343.

Coplan, R. J. (1995, April). *Assessing multiple forms of nonsocial behaviors in a familiar setting: The development and validation of of the Preschool Play Behavior Scale.* Poster presented at the Biennial Meetings for the Society for Research in Child Development, Indianapolis.

Coplan, R. J., & Rubin, K. H. (1993, July). *Multiple forms of social withdrawal in young children: Reticence and solitary-passive behaviors.* Paper presented at the Biennial Meetings of the International Society for the Study of Behavioural Development. Recife, Brazil.

Coplan, R. J., Rubin, K. H., Fox, N. A., Calkiins, S. D., & Stewart, S. L. (1994). Being alone, playing alone, and acting alone: Distinguishing among reticence, and passive- and active-solitude in young children. *Child Development, 65*, 129–138.

Crnic, K., & Greenberg, M. T. (1990). Minor parenting stresses with young children. *Child Development, 61*, 1628–1637.

Dishion, T. J. (1990). The family ecology of boys' peer relations in middle childhood. *Child Development, 61*, 874–892.

Eckerman, C. O., & Stein, M. R. (1982). The toddler's emerging interactive skills. In K. H. Rubin & H. S. Ross (Eds.), *Peer relations and social skills in chidhood* (pp. 41–72). New York: Springer-Verlag.

Eckerman, C. O., Whatley, J. L., & Kutz, S. L. (1975). Growth of social play with peers during the second year of life. *Developmental Psychology, 11*, 32–49.

Engfer, A., & Gavranidou, M. (1987). Antecedents and consequences of matertal sensitivity: A longitudinal study. In H. Rauh & H. Steinhauser (Eds.), *Psychobiology and early development* (pp. 71–99). North Holland: Elsevier.

Feng, Y. L. (1962). *The spirit of Chinese philosophy* (E. R. Hughes, Trans.). London: Routledge, & Kegan Paul.

Fox, N. A., & Calkins, S. D. (1993). Pathways to aggression and social withdrawal: Interactions among temperament, attachment, and regulation. In K. H. Rubin & J. Asendorpf (Eds.), *Social withdrawal, inhibition, and shyness in childhood* (pp. 81–100). Hillsdale, NJ: Lawrence Erlbaum.

Fox., N. A., Rubin, K. H., Calkins, S. D., Marshall, T. R., Coplan, R. J., Porges, S. W., & Long, J. M. (1995). Frontal activation assymmetry and social competence at four years of age: Left frontal hyper and hypo activation as correlates of social behavior in preschool children. *Child Development, 66*, 1770–1784.

Freedman, D. G. (1974). *Human infancy: An evolutionary perspective*. Hillsdale, NJ: Lawrence Erlbaum.

Garcia-Coll, C., Kagan, J., & Reznick, J. S. (1984). Behavioral inhibition in young children. *Child Development, 55*, 1005–1019.

Goncu, A. (1989). Models and features of pretense. *Developmental Review, 9*, 341–344.

Gresham, F. M. (1986). Coneptual issues in the assessment of social competence in children. In M. P. Strain, M. J. Guralnick, & H. M. Walker (Eds.), *Children's social behavior: Development, assessment, and modification* (pp. 143–179). New York: Academic Press.

Hartup, W. W. (1983). Peer relations. In P. H. Mussen (Series Ed.), *Handbook of child psychology: Vol 4. Socialization, personality and social development* (pp. 103–196). New York: Wiley.

Hay, D. F., Peterson, J., & Nash, A. (1982). Dyadic interaction in the first year of life. In K. H. Rubin & H. S. Ross (Eds.), *Peer relations and social skills in childhood* (pp. 11–40). New York: Springer-Verlag.

Ho., D. Y. F. (1986). Chinese patterns of socialization: A critical review. In M. H. Bond (Ed.), *The psychology of Chinese people*. New York: Oxford University Press.

Hoffman, M. L. (1970). Moral development. In P. H. Mussen (Ed.), *Handbook of child psychology (Vol. 2)*. New York: Wiley.

Holmberg, M. C. (1980). The development of social exchange patterns from 12 to 42 months. *Child Development, 51*, 618–626.

Howes, C. (1983). Patterns of friendship. *Child Development, 54*, 1041–1053.

Howes, C. (1988). Peer interaction in young children. *Monographs for the Society for Research in Child Development, 53* (No. 217).

Howes, C. (1992). *The collaborative construction of pretend*. Albany: State University of New York Press.

Hutt, C. (1970). Specific and diverse exploration. In H. Reese & L. Lipsett (Eds.), *Advances in child development and behavior*. New York: Academic Press.

Isabella, R.A., & Belsky, J. (1991). Interaction synchrony and the origins of infant-mother attachment: A replication study. *Child Development, 62*, 373–384.

Kagan J. (1989). Temperamental contributions to social behavior. *American Psychologist, 44*(4), 668–674.

Kagan, J., & Moss, H. A. (1962). *Birth to maturity: A study in psychosocial development*. New York: Wiley.

Kagan, J., Reznick, J. S., Clark, C., Snidman, N., & Garcia-Coll, C. (1984). Behavioral inhibition to the unfamiliar. *Child Development, 55*, 2212–2225.

Kagan J., Reznick, J. S., & Gibbons, J. (1989). Inhibited and uninhibited types of children. *Child Development, 60*, 838–845.

Kagan J., Reznick, J. S., & Snidman, N. (1987). The physiology and psychology of behavioral inhibition in children. *Child Development, 58*, 1459–1473.

Kagan J., Reznick, J. S., & Snidman, N. (1988). Biological basis of childhood shyness. *Science, 240*, 167–171.

King, A. Y. C., & Bond, M. H (1985). The Confucian paradigm of man: A sociological view. In W. S. Teng & D. Y. H. Wu (Eds.), *Chinese culture and mental health*. New York: Academic Press.

Kupersmidt, J. B., Coie, J. D., & Dodge, K. A. (1990). The role of poor peer relationships in the development of disorder. In S. R. Asher & J. D. Coie (Eds.), *Peer rejection in childhood* (pp. 274–308). New York: Cambridge University Press.

Lamborn, S. D., Mounts, N. S., Steinberg, L., & Dornbusch, S. M. (1991). Patterns of competence and adjustment among adolescents from authoritative, authoritarian, indulgent and neglectful families. *Child Development, 62*, 1049–1065.

Matheny, A. P. (1983). A longitudinal twin study of the stability of components of the Bailey's Infant Behavior Record. *Child Development, 54*, 356–360.

Maudry, M., & Nekula, M. (1939). Social relations between children of the same age during the first two years of life. *Journal of Genetic Psychology, 54,* 193–215.

Miyake, K., Chen, C., & Campos, J. (1985). Infant temperament, mother's mode of interaction, and attachment in Japan: An interim report. In I. Bretherton & E. Waters (Eds.), Growing points of attachment theory and research. *Monographs of the Society for Research in Child Development, 50* (Serial No. 209), 276–297.

Mead, G. H. (1934). *Mind, self, and society.* Chicago: University of Chicago Press.

Morison, P., & Mastin, A. (1991). Peer reputation in middle childhood as a predictor of adaptation in adolescence: A seven-year follow-up. *Child Development, 62,* 991–1007.

Parker, J., Rubin, K. H., Price, J., & Desrosiers, M. (1995). Peer relationships and developmental psychopathology. In D. Cicchetti & D. Cohen (Eds.), *Developmental psychopathology: Risk, disorder, and adaptation, Vol. 2* (pp. 96–161). New York: Wiley.

Parten, M. B. (1932). Social participation among preschool children. *Journal of Abnormal Psychology, 27,* 243–269.

Patterson, G. R. (1983). Stress: A change agent for family process. In N. Garmezy & M. Rutter (Eds.), *Stress, coping, and development in children* (pp. 235–264). New York: McGraw-Hill.

Piaget, J. (1926). *The language and thought of the child.* London: Routledge & Kegan Paul.

Piaget, J. (1932). *The moral judgment of the child.* Glencoe, IL: Free Press.

Piaget, J. (1962). *Play, dreams, and imitation in childhood.* New York: Norton.

Plomin, R., & Daniels, D. (1986). Genetics and shyness. In W. H. Jones, J. M. Cheek, & S. R. Briggs (Eds.), *Shyness: Perspectives on research and treatment.* New York: Plenum.

Radke-Yarrow, M., Zahn-Waxler, C., & Chapman, M. (1983). Children's prosocial dispositions and behavior. In M. Hetherington (Ed.), *Handbook of child psychology: Vol. 3. Social development.* New York: Wiley.

Roopnairine, J. L (1987). Social interaction in the peer group: Relationship to perceptions of parenting and to children's interpersonal awareness and problem solving ability. *Journal of Applied Developmental Psychology, 8,* 351–362.

Ross, H. S., Lollis, S. P., & Elliot, C. (1982). Toddler-peer communication. In K. H. Rubin & H. S. Ross (Eds.), *Peer relationships and social skills in childhood* (pp. 73–98). New York: Springer-Verlag.

Rubin, K. H. (1982). Nonsocial play in preschoolers: Necessary evil? *Child Development, 53,* 651–657.

Rubin, K. H. (1985). Socially withdrawn children: An "at risk" population. In B. H. Schneider, K. H. Rubin, & J. E. Ledingham (Eds.), *Peer relations and social skills in childhood: Issues in assessment and training* (pp. 125–139). New York: Springer-Verlag.

Rubin, K. H. (1989). *The Play Observation Scale (POS)*. University of Waterloo.

Rubin, K. H. (1993). The Waterloo Longitudinal Project: Correlates and consequences of social withdrawal from childhood to adolescence. In K. H. Rubin & J. Asendorpf (Eds.), *Social withdrawal, inhibition, and shyness in childhood* (pp. 291–314). Hillsdale, NJ: Lawrence Erlbaum.

Rubin, K. H., & Asendorpf, J. (1993). *Social withdrawal, inhibition, and shyness in childhood*. Hillsdale, NJ: Lawrence Erlbaum.

Rubin, K. H., & Both, L. (1989). Iris pigmentation and sociability in childhood: A reexamination. *Developmental Psychology, 22,* 717–726.

Rubin, K. H., Chen, X., & Hymel, S. (1993). Socioemotional characteristics of withdrawn and aggressive children. *Merrill-Palmer Quarterly, 39,* 518–534.

Rubin, K. H., Chen, X., McDougal, P., Bowker, A., & McKinnon, J. (1995). The Waterloo Longitudinal Project: Predicting internalizing and externalizing problems in adolescence. *Development and Psychopathology, 7,* 751–764.

Rubin, K. H., & Coplan, R. J. (1992). Peer relationships in childhood. In M. Bornstein & M. Lamb (Eds.), *Developmental psychology: An advanced textbook.* Hillsdale, NJ: Lawrence Erlbaum.

Rubin, K. H., & Coplan, R. J. (1994). Play: Developmental stages, functions, and educational support. In F. Weinert (Section Editor), *International Encyclopedia of Education.* New York: Pergamon Press.

Rubin, K. H., Coplan, R. J., Fox, N. A., & Calkins, S. D. (1995). Emotionality, emotion regulation, and preschoolers' social adaptation. *Development and Psychopathology, 7,* 49–62.

Rubin, K. H., Fein, G., & Vandenberg, B. (1983). Play. In E. M. Hetherington (Ed.), *Handbook of child psychology: Vol 4. Socialization, personality, and social development.* New York: Wiley.

Rubin, K. H., Hymel, S., & Mills, R. S. L. (1989). Sociability and social withdrawal in childhood: Stability and outcomes. *Journal of Personality, 57,* 238–255.

Rubin, K. H., Hymel, S., Mills, R. S. L., & Rose-Krasnor, L. (1991). Conceptualizing different pathways to and from social isolation in childhood. In D. Cicchetti & S. Toth (Eds.), *The Rochester Symposium on Developmental Psychology, Vol. 2, Internalizing and externalizing expressions of dysfunction* (pp. 91–122). New York: Cambridge University Press.

Rubin, K. H., & Krasnor, L. (1986). Social cognitive and social behavioral perspectives on problem-solving. In M. Perlmutter (Ed.), *Minnesota Symposia on Child Psychology* (Vol. 18, pp. 1–68). Hillsdale, NJ: Lawrence Erlbaum.

Rubin, K. H., Lemare L. J., & Lollis, S. (1990). Social withdrawal in childhood: Developmental pathways to rejection. In S. R. Asher & J. D. Coie (Eds.), *Peer rejection in childhood* (pp. 217–249). New York: Cambridge University Press.

Rubin, K. H., & Lollis, S. (1988). Peer relationships, social skills, and infant attachment: A continuity model. In J. Belsky & T. Nezworski (Eds.), *Clinical implications of attachment* (pp. 219–252). Hillsdale, NJ: Lawrence Erlbaum.

Rubin, K. H., Maioni, T. L., & Hornung, M. (1976). Free play behaviors in middle and lower class preschoolers: Parten and Piaget revisited. *Child Development, 47,* 414–419.

Rubin, K. H., & Mills, R. S. L. (1988). The many faces of social isolation in childhood. *Journal of Consulting and Clinical Psychology, 6,* 916–924.

Rubin, K. H., & Rose-Krasnor, L. (1992). Interpersonal problem-solving and social competence in children. In V. B. van Hasselt and M. Hersen (Eds), *Handbook of social development: A lifespan perspective.* New York: Plenum.

Rubin, K. H., & Stewart, S. L. (1996). Social withdrawal. In E. Marsh & R. Barcley (Eds.), *Child psychopathology* (pp. 277–307). New York: Guilford.

Rubin, K. H., Stewart, S. L., & Chen, X. (1995). Parents of aggressive and withdrawn children. In M. Bornstein (Ed.), *Handbook of parenting* (Vol. 1, pp. 255–284). Hillsdale, NJ: Erlbaum.

Rubin, K. H., Stewart, S. L., & Coplan, R. J. (1995). Social withdrawal in childhood: Conceptual and empirical perspectives. In T. Ollendick and R. Prinz (Eds.), *Advances in clinical child psychology* (Vol. 17, pp. 157–196). New York: Plenum.

Rubin, K. H., Watson, K. S., & Jambor, T. W. (1978). Free-play behaviors in preschool and kindergarten children. *Child Development, 49,* 534–536.

Scarr, S. (1968). Environment bias in twin studies. *Eugenics Quarterly, 15,* 34–40.

Schneider, B. H., Rubin, K. H., & Ledingham, J. E. (1985). *Peer relations and social skills in childhood: Issues in assessment and training.* New York: Springer-Verlag.

Smilansky, S. (1968). *The effects of sociodramatic play on disadvantaged preschool children.* New York: Wiley.

Spieker, S. J., & Booth, C. L. (1988). Maternal antecedents of attachment quality. In J. Belsky & T. Nezworski (Eds.), *Clinical implications of attachment* (pp. 95–135). Hillsdale, NJ: Lawrence Erlbaum.

Sroufe, L. A. (1983). Infant-caregiver attachment and patterns of adaptation in preschool: The roots of maladaptation and competence. In M. Perlmutter (Ed.), *Minnesota Symposium in Child Psychology* (Vol. 16). Hillsdale, NJ: Lawrence Erlbaum.

Stewart, S. L., & Rubin, K. H. (1993, March). *The social problem solving skills of anxious-withdrawn children*. Poster presented at the Biennial Meeting of the Society for Reasearch in Child Development, New Orleans.

Sullivan, H. S. (1953). *The interpersonal theory of psychiatry*. New York: Norton.

Vandell, D. L., Wilson, K. S., & Buchanan, N. R. (1980). Peer interaction in the first year of life: An examination of its structure, content, and sensitivity to toys. *Child Development, 51*, 481–488.

Wahler, R. G., & Dumas, J. E., (1987). Family factors in childhood psychology: Toward a coercion-neglect model. In T. Jacob (Ed.), *Family interaction and psychopathology: Theories, methods, and findings* (pp. 581–627). New York: Plenum.

Yarrow, M. R., Waxler, C. Z., & Scott, P. M. (1971). Child effects on adult behavior. *Developmental Psychology, 5*, 300–311.

Younger, A. J., & Boyko, K. A. (1987). Aggression and withdrawal as social schemas underlying children's peer perceptions. *Child Development, 58*, 1094–1100.

Younger, A. J., & Daniels, T. M. (1992). Children's reasons for nominating their peers as passive withdrawn: Passive withdrawal versus active isolation? *Developmental Psychology, 28*, 955–960.

Younger, A. J., Gentile, C., & Burgess, K. (1993). Children's perceptions of social withdrawal: Changes across age. In K. H. Rubin & J. Asendorpf (Eds.), *Social withdrawal, inhibition, and shyness in childhood* (pp. 215–236). Hillsdale, NJ: Lawrence Erlbaum.

Chapter 9

Play in Special Populations

Fergus P. Hughes

Play is an essential ingredient in the lives of children. It is surprising, therefore, that so little is known about the play of children whose development is affected by physical, intellectual, social, or emotional conditions not experienced by an average child. This scarcity of information about the play of special populations can been attributed to two factors—a shortage of carefully designed research programs, and a difficulty in distinguishing between children's observed play behaviors in a specific environment and their inherent potential for play (Rubin, Fein, & Vandenberg, 1983).

Several factors contribute to the uneven quality of research on the play of the special child (Quinn & Rubin, 1984). First, play has often been defined too narrowly and observed in unduly restricted settings. As an example, much of the research on the play of children with cognitive delays consists of observations of solitary play with toys; such children have rarely been studied in situations that afforded opportunities for social play. Second, researchers have taken different philosophical directions, depending on the nature of the disability under study, and thus it is difficult to draw overall conclusions from their findings. Those who study physical disabilities are primarily from the professions of medicine and occupational therapy, and have examined the uses of play in physical therapy; professionals interested in intellectual impairments have looked at play as a tool for educational and intellectual enrichment; mental health professionals have explored the uses of play in clinical diagnosis and psychotherapy. Third, the research findings are sometimes ambiguous because the disabilities under investigation are not mutually exclusive. While children with multiple disabilities have been the subjects of much of the research, efforts have rarely been made to identify which disability, or combination of disabilities, might be responsible for observed play differences. Finally, even when children are diagnosed as having the same disability, they are as diverse a group as are children in the population at large. There is no reason to expect that all children will be equally affected by any particular disability.

Even when studies are well constructed, however, their findings may reveal little about the actual reasons for observed play differences. It is often concluded that children with disabilities have inherent play deficits when, in fact, the differences observed in play could as easily be explained by environmental variables. The play of any child can be influenced by factors in the physical environment, such as playground characteristics (Boyatzis, 1987) or the arrangement of space in a classroom (Bailey & Wolery, 1984; Hughes, 1995), and by features of the social environment, such as peer familiarity (Tessier, de Lorimier, & Doyle, 1993), age and/or gender of playmates (Lederberg, Chapin, Rosenblatt, & Vandell, 1986). Researchers must distinguish, therefore, between actual play behavior and potential for play. In the case of special populations, this distinction is critical, because their physical and/or social environments are often not conducive to the optimum display of their abilities. The lack of physical surroundings that facilitate play, the failure of adult supervisors to help them plan and carry out their play routines, and the unavailability of responsive playmates can all conspire to foster a false impression that children with disabilities suffer from basic play deficits. In fact, the observed play differences may be environmental in origin.

Despite the limitations of the research, however, there is a growing body of meaningful information about play in special populations. This chapter is an attempt to summarize some of that information and discuss its practical significance for adults who care for children. The characteristics that make children special are diverse, with some attributable to obvious biological factors, some to environmental conditions, and some to unknown causes (Bailey & Wolery, 1989). Much of what is included here pertains to children with specific sensory (e.g., blindness, deafness), intellectual (e.g., mental retardation, attention deficit disorder), or socioemotional impairments of various origins. Readers may question the inclusion of some of the groups discussed here, however, and wonder why being born prematurely or being a victim of physical or sexual abuse qualifies for inclusion in a "special population." The answer is that all of the children discussed in this chapter are challenged by a condition that interferes with the normal progress of their development. And, as is true of every child, all have a need to play.

PRETERM INFANTS

Because a person's age is calculated from the day of birth rather than from the day of conception, it is sometimes forgotten that a preterm infant has had less time to develop than a full-term infant of the same chronological age. It is for this reason that preterm babies typically lag behind full-term babies on measures of normal development, and this difference is also seen in their play.

A striking characteristic of preterm infants during their first year is that, compared to full-term infants, their play shows a lesser degree of exploratory competence (Sigman & Sena, 1993). One would expect 9-month-old infants to attend carefully to the properties of objects they manipulate, as opposed to indiscriminately incorporating them into repetitive action sequences, which is typical of 6- and 7-month-olds. By 9 months, the characteristics of the objects themselves should be as interesting as the actions that can be performed on them.

Preterm infants, however, are less likely than full-term infants of the same chronological age to explore new objects, to sustain attention to an object at hand, and to shift attention from one object to a new one (Morgan, Maslin-Cole, Biringin, & Harmon, 1991). They display less of what has been called "mastery behavior," which is the active manipulation of objects, the tendency to relate objects to one another, and the willingness to persist at tasks even if not immediately successful (Messer, McCarthy, McQuiston, MacTurk, Yarrow, & Vietze, 1986). Since mastery behavior and reaction to novelty are thought to be predictors of later intelligence (Fagan, Shepherd, & Knevel, 1991), there appears to be a connection between competence in object play and overall intellectual functioning. The issue for most preterm infants is one of delay, however. Most develop normally throughout their lives, and those who are free of serious medical complications display as high a degree of exploratory competence as do full-term infants when age is calculated not from birth but from gestation (Ruff, Lawson, Parinello, & Weissberg, 1990).

INFANTS EXPOSED PRENATALLY TO DRUGS

Another factor that places an increasing number of American infants at risk, and a possible cause of developmental delays, is the taking of illegal drugs by pregnant women. Drug abuse during pregnancy is almost certainly related to impaired fetal growth and behavioral abnormalities during infancy, but may be linked to developmental problems in toddlers as well, and to abnormalities in their play. This was the finding of a research group at the UCLA School of Medicine (Beckwith, Rodning, Phillipsen, Norris, & Howard, 1993), who compared the play of 31 two-year-olds in inner city Los Angeles who had PCP in their urine at birth, and often crack cocaine as well, with a comparison group matched for ethnicity and socioeconomic status and born drug-free in the same or nearby hospitals.

The children were observed at spontaneous play with age-appropriate toys (e.g., dolls, doll furniture, vehicles, a telephone, comb, brush, and mirror). The dependent measures were (1) *manipulative acts* (banging, mouthing, throwing objects, (2) *relational play* (stacking, placing one object inside another), (3) *functional acts* (brushing one's hair, driving the car into the garage), and (4) *symbolic acts* (letting a doll listen to the phone, pouring imaginary tea into a cup). Also observed was the children's ability to combine acts into sequences, as opposed to simply repeating the same act over and over again, which is a less mature behavior.

Toddlers exposed prenatally to drugs displayed more manipulative acts (e.g., banging, mouthing, throwing toys), were more likely to repeat the same acts rather than combining them into novel sequences, and tended to direct their activities toward themselves rather than toward others. Manipulative acts are thought to be less mature than symbolic ones, and play with a single theme is less mature than play in which themes are combined and integrated. In addition, make-believe acts directed toward the self are less mature than similar acts directed toward others (Fenson, 1986). The drug-exposed toddlers were less attentive than the drug-free children, less purposeful in selecting toys, and more likely to change abruptly from one activity to another.

Observations of the play of infants exposed prenatally to drugs suggest, as did the research on preterm infants, that factors that place a child "at risk" for normal development are reflected in distortions in play. In that sense, the play of very young children can reveal much about their developmental progress.

CHILDREN WITH VISUAL IMPAIRMENTS

The conclusions of a number of studies of the play of children with visual impairments (e.g., Singer & Streiner, 1966; Skellenger & Hill, 1994; Tait, 1973; Wills, 1972) indicates no evidence that a visual impairment results in a basic inability to play. Nevertheless, blind children differ in some ways from sighted children when they play, although the similarities far outweigh the differences. Blind children engage less often in imaginative fantasy play, and much of their play is more concrete, less varied, and less flexible than the play of sighted children (Singer & Streiner, 1966). They are more likely to simply manipulate objects in play, and less likely to let their imaginations take flight (Tait, 1973). The play differences between blind and sighted children are differences in amount rather than kind, however. Children who are blind do not appear to have a symbolic play deficit. In fact, they *can* engage in highly imaginative play, but tend to do so less often that do sighted children, perhaps because visual impairment can lead to a restricted interaction with the world. Visual impairment can make it difficult for children to orient themselves to space and time, and to separate reality from nonreality (Frost & Klein, 1979). Blind children may often face as an additional handicap the unfortunate stereotype that they are unable to, or simply do not want to, play as other children do, and this has been described as a secondary disability that can hinder the child's potential for independence (Missiuna & Pollock, 1991).

CHILDREN WITH DELAYED LANGUAGE

Human language and symbolic play both require the ability to use symbols—to let one thing represent another (McCune, 1986), leading some child development experts, most notably Piaget (1962), to suggest that language is an aspect of symbolic functioning that can be assessed through the observation of a child's make-believe play. Others argue that, while language and symbolic play are obviously related, the relationship is not as simple as implied by Piaget's view of symbolic play as "inner speech"; language and make-believe share common intellectual prerequisites, but each seems to rely on a variety of other abilities as well (McCune, 1986).

Perhaps suggestive of the relationship between the two, language and symbolic play assume parallel courses of development, in that both initially appear at the same time early in the second year, and the shift in symbolic play from an uncoordinated collection of activities to one that is coordinated and schematic parallels the transition at the end of the second year from one-word utterances to original two-word combinations in speech (Fenson, 1986). Furthermore, individual differences among children in their rates of language development seem to mirror individual differences in the development of symbolic play (Gould, 1986; Tamis-LeMonda & Bornstein, 1991, 1993; Shimada, Sano & Peng, 1979).

The language-symbolic play relationship raises questions about the make-believe play of children with linguistic impairments. Would children delayed in their language, even though free of other intellectual impairments, show symbolic play deficits as well? In fact, a number of researchers have reported a relationship between language deficits and deficits in symbolic play (Lombardino, Stein, Kricos, & Wolf, 1986; Terrell, Schwartz, Prelock, & Messick, 1984). This correlation does not unequivocally demonstrate, however, that children with delayed speech display basic deficits in overall symbolic functioning. In fact, in many of these studies the children actually did engage in make-believe play, although less often, and of a less mature variety, than do children whose speech is not delayed (Quinn & Rubin, 1984; Rubin, Fein, & Vandenberg, 1983). Since the ability to engage in make-believe acts was present, even if less frequently displayed and in a less sophisticated manner, there is no justification for concluding that children with speech delays experience an underlying symbolic deficit.

It would seem that the quantitative symbolic play differences found among children with delayed speech can best be explained by environmental variables. Clearly the relationship between language and symbolic play goes beyond a reliance on similar underlying mental abilities. Language can make it easier for children to engage in social varieties of make-believe, as in the case of complex forms of sociodramatic play (McCune, 1986; Quinn & Rubin, 1984). Children with delayed speech may find dramatic play more difficult to sustain than other children do, and because of their linguistic deficit, may retreat more readily into the less demanding world of solitary play.

CHILDREN WITH HEARING DIFFICULTIES

As was noted in the previous section, children whose speech is delayed often exhibit less mature forms of play during the early childhood years, particularly with regard to their interest in social forms of make-believe. A similar, and related, finding is that young children with hearing difficulties engage less often in sociodramatic play, and are less likely to make symbolic use of objects than are children of normal hearing ability (Esposito & Koorland, 1989; Higginbotham & Baker, 1981; Mann, 1984).

Again, however, it has not been demonstrated that such children have specific play deficits. It seems more likely that the play differences observed in comparisons of children with and without hearing impairments are differences in performance rather than potential. Depending on their surroundings and on cultural expectations, deaf children do not always display the behaviors they are truly capable of. Esposito and Koorland (1989) discovered, for example, that the play of the same children in integrated and in segregated settings was substantially different. Two children diagnosed as having severe hearing losses, were observed at play in their self-contained class for children with hearing impairments and in the regular daycare centers they also attended. The number of children in their play groups and the specific roles taken by the adult supervisors were the same in both environments. It was found that the play of both children in the integrated settings was more socially sophisticated. Parallel play was more often seen in the class for children with hearing impairments, while associative play was more typical in the daycare centers.

CHILDREN WITH COGNITIVE DELAYS

Up until the late 1960s, there existed an assumption that children with cognitive delays do not play, either because they do not want to or because they do not need to (McConkey, 1985). This belief has been changing gradually. It is interesting, however, that despite the realization among child development professionals that play is an essential ingredient in the lives of children, the play of the child with intellectual impairments has received relatively little attention. In part, this is because the emphasis of professionals who work with children with intellectual impairments has been on intellectual and educational enrichment; their efforts have been characterized by a remedial focus rather than an appreciation of basic patterns of child development as displayed by children in this special population (McConkey, 1985; Quinn & Rubin, 1984). In addition, the emphasis in the research has been on *differences* between populations, and researchers often failed to note that, the differences notwithstanding, children with cognitive delays do indeed play, as all children do.

Play with Objects

Researchers who have studied the uses of toys in free play by children with intellectual deficits have reported that such children seem to prefer structured materials, such as puzzles and jacks, while typical children of the same mental age prefer open-ended materials, such as art supplies that foster creativity (Horne & Philleo, 1942). In addition, children with intellectual impairments are less likely to combine objects appropriately in play (Tilton & Ottinger, 1964; Weiner & Weiner, 1974). Tilton and Ottinger (1964) discovered, for example, that children typically will bring objects together in play, as when they build with blocks, combine cups with saucers, or screw nuts on bolts; those with intellectual impairments, however, are less likely to do so, and instead engage in much nonspecific touching of their toys. Finally, children with Down syndrome appear to be less interested in toys in general, and, when presented with such materials, are more interested in visual exploration than in active manipulation (Sigman & Sena, 1993).

It is difficult to interpret the observed differences in the object play of these different groups of children because there are few studies, and because of methodological flaws that the older studies often contain. Accurate measures of group differences were difficult to obtain in the Horne and Philleo (1942), Tilton and Ottinger (1964) and Weiner and Weiner (1974) studies because there were no attempts to distinguish between exploratory behavior and play (Quinn & Rubin, 1984). Since the children were observed only in their first session with the toys, the greater amount of nonspecific touching by the group with cognitive delays may have indicated only that they were less familiar with the materials than is the typical child.

Symbolic Play

Symbolic play emerges during the second year of life, as children acquire the ability to represent the world mentally to themselves, and the normal pattern is of a gradual developmental progression into the world of make-believe. There are three main conclusions that can be drawn about the make-believe play of children with intellectual impairments. First, symbolic play has been observed consistently in these children, indicating that intellectual impairment in itself does not prevent children from engaging in imaginative acts of make-believe (Cunningham, Glenn, Wilkinson, & Sloper, 1985; Hellendoorn & Hoekman, 1992; Hill & McCune-Nicolich, 1981; Li, 1985; Wing, Gould, Yeates, & Brierly, 1977). Second, mental age is a better predictor of the onset of symbolic play than is chronological age; symbolic play typically appears later in children with cognitive delays than in those whose intellectual development is normal. For example, Wing, Gould, Yeates, and Brierly (1977) examined the symbolic play of 108 children with severe mental retardation ranging in age from 5 to 14 years. Symbolic play was found, but did not occur before the children had reached a mental age of 20 months, the age at which the typical child begins to become involved in make-believe. Third, symbolic play appears gradually rather than suddenly, and there are a series of stages through which children progress (Cunningham, Glenn, Wilkinson, & Sloper, 1985; Hill & McCune-Nicolich, 1981). While the stage progression seems to be identical in children at all levels of intellectual ability, those with intellectual deficits lag behind and are less likely to reach the most sophisticated levels.

Illustrating this last conclusion, Li (1985) compared the play of 25 children with mild mental retardation, aged 5 to 7 years, with a matched group of normal children. All were given a sand tray and a variety of miniature life toys, and told to "build something and tell a story about it." After 5 minutes, if a child had not yet begun to build, he or she would be asked "What are you making?."

Four levels of make-believe play were identified, with each representing refinements of and elaborations upon the preceding ones. The simplest was *object-related symbolic play*, in which children play out one pretend action sequence, either with themselves or with a one particular toy (e.g., "The soldier's shooting" or "It goes choo-choo"). Next came the level of *play with a scene*: the child decides in advance on an idea for the play and creates a scene around that idea (e.g., "This is a farm"). There followed the level of *play with a theme*, in which the play was characterized by a central pre-planned theme or action sequence; one child's theme was "making a city in winter," for example, and all of the play materials were then integrated into this theme. Finally, there was *play with a story*, which consisted of (1) imaginative play with (2) a sustained theme throughout, and (3) verbalization about the story.

Li (1985) discovered that most of the children with cognitive delays engaged in some forms of symbolic play, but that differences appeared in the levels of make-believe. For example, approximately half of the 5-year-olds whose developmental progression was normal were at the highest levels: themes and stories. None of the 5-year-olds with cognitive delays played at those levels. By contrast, only 15% of the 5-year-olds whose development was at the normal rate played at the first level, while 55% of the children with cognitive delays engaged in *object-related symbolic play*.

In conclusion, it seems that children of all intellectual levels engage in functional play with objects. In addition, make-believe play of one sort or another has been observed in children of all intellectual levels, although its onset may be delayed in the child whose overall intellectual development is delayed. Nevertheless, children with cognitive delays can play imaginatively as typical children do if groups are equated in terms of mental rather than chronological age.

ATTENTION DEFICIT HYPERACTIVITY DISORDER

As children mature, improvement can be expected in their span of attention, resistance to distraction, and ability to attend selectively to the world around them. However, some children—between 3 and 5% of the population—do not show developmental improvement in these areas. These children suffer from Attention Deficit Hyperactivity Disorder (ADHD), characterized by immature forms of inattention, impulsivity, and hyperactivity that first appear before the age of 7, are present for at least 6 months, and are not attributable to any known specific mental disorder or to mental retardation (American Psychiatric Association, 1987).

The presence of serious attentional problems has a significant impact on children's social environments in general, and on their play in particular. Preschoolers diagnosed as having ADHD are less sophisticated in peer play, and less attentive and cooperative during structured group activities (Alessandri, 1991). ADHD children are often rejected by their peers, perhaps because they display higher rates of inappropriate social behavior, including restlessness, impulsive acts, and critical and insulting comments to others (Barkley, Fischer, Edelbrock, & Smallish, 1990; Day, Steffy, & Cunningham, 1993). Observing the play of school-aged boys diagnosed as having ADHD, Day, Steffy, and Cunningham (1993) heard frequent unsolicited criticisms and derogatory comments (e.g., "You're not very good at math, are you?"). These boys had difficulty realizing that it is socially inappropriate to make continual assaults on another child's self-esteem.

On a positive note, however, the difficulties of children with ADHD seem to pertain to social interaction in general rather than to play in particular, and, as will be discussed in the concluding section of this chapter, there is encouraging evidence that social skills can be taught.

CHILDREN WITH AUTISM

Childhood autism, a neurologically based disability with multiple causes, affects 4 in every 10,000 children. It is characterized by significant impairments in reciprocal social interaction and in communication of both a verbal and a nonverbal type (American Psychiatric Association, 1987). Children with autism often display mental retardation as well, although many are of average intelligence or above. The common characteristic shared by all of them, however, regardless of intelligence, is a basic communication difficulty, a profound inability to understand and function within the normal social environment; the autistic child apparently fails to differentiate between the self and the external world (Atlas & Lapidus, 1987; Baron-Cohen, Leslie, & Frith, 1985; Kanner, 1971; Rutter, 1983).

Information about the play of children with autism is limited, but a number of patterns have appeared. First, in toy and object play, autistic children tend to engage in repetitive, stereotyped manipulation, and are less likely than normal children to explore the characteristics of objects, unless prompted to do so by adults, and to use them in representational ways (Kasari, Sigman, & Yirmiya, 1992; Tilton & Ottinger, 1964; Wing, Gould, Yeates, & Brierly, 1977; Wulff, 1985). Autistic children are also less likely to engage in complex toy play and less likely to use toys appropriately. It should be pointed out, however, that many autistic children do not engage in stereotyped, repetitive behaviors with toys, and so it would be unfair to conclude that such behaviors are inevitable symptoms of autism (Quinn & Rubin, 1984).

A more extensive area of research on the play of autistic children concerns the use of symbolic play, and the usual finding is that autistic children rarely engage in symbolic play (Atlas & Lapidus, 1987; Baron-Cohen, 1987; Baron-Cohen, Leslie, & Frith, 1985; Gould, 1986; Mundy, Sigman, Ungerer, & Sherman, 1987; Sigman & Sena, 1993). Even highly intelligent autistic children are unlikely to engage in symbolic play, whereas, as was pointed out in an earlier section, children with severe mental retardation will often do so (Hill & McCune-Nicolich, 1981)!

There are two prevailing explanations for the failure of autistic children to engage in make-believe. According to the *symbol deficit hypothesis*, autistic children lack basic representational skills, and this deficit explains both their social impairment and their failure to engage in symbolic play. Both symbolic play and social interaction require an ability to impute mental states to oneself and to other people—an ability described as a "theory of mind" (Baron-Cohen, 1987; Perner, Frith, Leslie, & Leekam, 1989; Wulff, 1985). For example, symbolic play requires children to represent to themselves the mental states of dolls, puppets, or characters whose roles they are playing.

The failure of children with autism to represent mental states of others to oneself is illustrated in a study by Baron-Cohen, Leslie, and Frith (1985), who compared the behavior of three groups of preschool children, one normal, one diagnosed as autistic, and one diagnosed as having Down syndrome. The children were shown two dolls, "Sally" and "Anne," as well as a basket for Sally and a box for Anne. Sally placed a marble in her basket, and then departed. Anne removed the marble from Sally's basket and placed it in *her* box. Then the children were asked three questions. First, "Where is the marble really?," the answer to which would indicate the child's understanding of reality. Second, "Where was the marble at the beginning?," which was designed to test their memory. Finally, "Where will Sally look for her marble?," a question designed to determine if the children realize that Sally has a belief system independent from their own. All three groups answered the first two questions correctly, but differences emerged in the answers to the third question. Neither the normal children nor the children with Down syndrome had difficulty realizing that Sally would *think* the marble was still in her basket, even though they knew that it was not. Four out of five of the autistic children failed the "belief" question, however; they indicated that Sally would look for the marble in the box, apparently failing to differentiate between their knowledge of the situation and that of the doll.

Some researchers do not believe, however, that autistic children lack a basic ability to symbolize. They prefer a *conative hypothesis*, interpreting the lack of make-believe among autistic children as primarily a motivational issue. This hypothesis is supported by the observation that autistic children often perform well when specific intellectual abilities are tested, even though they will not display these abilities spontaneously in natural settings. For example, autistic children who score as well on formal language tests as children with specific language disorders are still less likely to use language spontaneously in unstructured social situations (Bartak, Rutter, & Cox, 1975), and autistic children who score well on formal reading tests still display no spontaneous interest in reading for pleasure (Gould, 1986).

Illustrating the impact of motivational factors on the play deficits of autistic children, Lewis and Boucher (1988) examined the play of children with autism, children with mental retardation, and children whose developmental progression was normal under three conditions. In the *spontaneous* condition, a variety of toys were set out on the floor and the children were invited individually to play as they wished; in the *elicited* condition, children were handed toys and asked "Show me what you can do with these"; and in the *instructed* condition, children were given specific directions such as "Show me how the doll washes her/his hands." Lewis and Boucher(1988) reported no group differences in any of the three conditions. They interpreted their results as supportive of a motivational explanation for the lack of symbolic activity in autistic children, since adult questions or instructions elicited equal amounts of make- believe play in all three groups. The validity of these interpretations has been questioned by other researchers, however. Since differences did not occur in the spontaneous condition either, other researchers have argued that the task may not have been developmentally appropriate for the children (Sigman & Sena, 1993).

VICTIMS OF ABUSE

A number of researchers in recent years have examined the effects of maltreatment, whether physical, sexual, and/or emotional, on children's play. For example, Alessandri (1991) compared the play of 15 children in a preschool program (aged 4–5 years) who had a history of being abused with that of 15 matched (on gender, socioeconomic status, parents' age, ethnic background, parents' education, number of siblings, etc.) controls. The maltreated children had all experienced a documented occurrence of maltreatment (emotional abuse, physical abuse, sexual abuse, or neglect) within the previous 2 years. Ten of the fifteen had experienced more than one form of abuse, a not uncommon pattern. The children in both groups were observed at free play in a typical preschool classroom for a period of 6 weeks, with a total of 60 minutes of observation of each child.

Alessandri (1991) discovered that the abused children played in less mature ways, both socially and cognitively, than did the children in the control group, engaged in less play overall, involved themselves less often in group and parallel play, and used the play materials in less imaginative and more stereotyped ways. Their fantasy themes were more imitative and less creative. They repeatedly played out domestic scenes, for example, whereas the control group also played the roles of fantasy characters, such as monsters or superheroes.

Even though young victims of various forms of maltreatment are often grouped together for research purposes, some researchers have attempted to compare the play of the different abused groups. For example, Fagot, Hagan, Youngblade, and Potter (1989) observed the free play behavior of three groups of preschool children: sexually abused, physically abused, and those who were not abused. Consistent with other studies was the finding that the nonabused group played more than the other children, and spent less time passively doing nothing. They also reacted more positively to other children, spoke more to them, and engaged in a greater amount of associative play.

The differences between the victims of sexual abuse (SA) and the victims of physical abuse (PA) were quite interesting. The SA children were more passive than the control group, but they were not antisocial or negative. They didn't make trouble, and usually played quietly by themselves. By contrast, the PA group, although generally passive, engaged in quite a bit more aggression than the norm. They were disruptive, uncommunicative, and anti-social, offering clues that might lead a teacher to suspect there were problems in their lives that needed closer examination. The sexually abused children, however, did not call attention to themselves. Their play was certainly different from the norm, but this difference might not be noticed by someone who knew little about normal play and failed to realize that play can offer fascinating glimpses into a child's psychological world (Fagot, Hagan, Young-blade, & Potter, 1989).

An interesting line of research involving child victims of sexual abuse has been to observe their play with anatomically correct dolls. Since 1977, dolls with realistic-looking genitals have been used in interviews with children suspected of being abused, under the assumption that children will reveal in their play what they cannot reveal in words (August & Forman, 1989; Leventhal, Hamilton, Rekedal, Tibano-Micci, & Eyster, 1989). Actually, there have been very few scientific studies of differences in doll play between abuse victims and nonvictims, and the results obtained from the few existing studies have been contradictory. Some researchers found that sexually abused children play in more sexualized ways with anatomically correct dolls (August & Forman, 1989; Jampole & Weber, 1987). For example, August and Forman (1989) compared the play with anatomically correct dolls of 16 sexually-abused girls aged 5 to 8 years with 16 nonabused girls, and observed that abuse victims were more likely to attend to the sexual features of the dolls, touching their breasts or genitals, for example, or removing and examining their undergarments. Other researchers, however, reported that abused and nonabused children are equally likely to play in sexual ways with dolls (Cohn, 1991), indicating that it would be unwise at this time to draw conclusions about the link between doll play and child abuse.

CONCLUSIONS AND PRACTICAL IMPLICATIONS

As was mentioned at the beginning of this chapter, there is a fragmented quality to the research on the play of special populations of children. Not all groups have received equal attention from researchers, children with vastly different disabilities are often grouped under an umbrella category of "handi-capped," and multiple disabilities are often found within the same child. In addition, the research designs range from diaries to experimental designs, the sample sizes are often very small, and the findings often contradictory. It is difficult, therefore, to draw sweeping conclusions about the play of children with special needs. It can be concluded, however, that (1) *all* children play, regardless of their physical condition, level of intellectual functioning, emotional state, or environmental circumstance, and (2) children with disabilities play less effectively than those without them, since they are less likely to explore the physical environment, and/or to form mental representations of reality, and/or initiate and sustain social play.

Reasons for the differences in play have not been fully articulated. For some groups discussed in this chapter, including preterm infants and children with intellectual impairments, the issue is primarily one of delay. When compared to groups of normal children of the same gestational or mental age instead of the same chronological age, the play differences disappear. In general, developmental age seems to be a more appropriate predictor of the quality of play than does chronological age.

For other groups, such as children with physical disabilities and victims of child abuse, the issue seems to be one of opportunity. The observed play differences are most easily explained by circumstances in the physical and/or social environment that are not conducive to play, but might be made so with appropriate intervention. As an example, many of the physical restrictions on the play of blind children could be removed to allow the fullest expression of play. A number of suggestions for doing so were offered by Frost and Klein (1979). First, adults might help the children by *planning for play*, which includes informing them in advance of their available options in terms of play materials, equipment, activities, and playmates, and encouraging them to identify favorite activities and describe how they will use their upcoming play time. Second, adults should provide a *sensory-rich play environment*, with a variety of sensory cues. Tactile maps and audio cassette recorders with taped directions could be placed in strategic locations, and areas of the room, or outdoor playground, could be made distinctive through the use of texturing, such as different styles of carpeting or linoleum on the floor. Third, the supervising adult should *rehearse the uses of play materials* with the children. When children are given practice in the uses of play materials, they will become familiar enough to know them by their feel. Fourth, the adult supervisor should use *liberal amounts of reinforcement* to encourage play. Finally, after the play session the supervisor and child should reflect on the experience, in order to provide the *feedback and evaluation* that will encourage the children to follow through on their play plans.

Like the physical environment, the social environment can have a major influence on children's play. As an example of the impact of the social environment on the play of children with visual impairments, consider the findings of Skellenger and Hill (1994), who documented the value of teacher-child play experiences. Working with three children aged 5 to 7, a teacher modeled appropriate play activities, served as a play partner, and followed the child's lead in play. Over a period of 4 months, the sophistication of the children's play improved markedly.

Unfortunately, the social environment of children with disabilities is often not supportive of play for a number of reasons. First, adults may fail to recognize the value of play for young children with disabilities. As McConkey (1985) suggested more than a decade ago, a widely held belief is that children with disabilities do not play, and that play for such children is little more than a diversion. Second, children with disabilities may have limited social opportunities, and may associate primarily with children who have similar handicaps, despite the fact that researchers report that the play of "special" children is richer, more varied, and more sophisticated in an integrated social setting than in a segregated one (Esposito & Koorland, 1989; Kohl & Beckman, 1984). The most sophisticated play observed in children with disabilities occurs when their playmates are not disabled, are younger in chronological age, and are identical in developmental age (Bednersh & Peck, 1986). Third, early childhood special education programs put greater emphasis on teaching academic skills and less on free play than is found in mainstream early childhood programs. Since social interaction occurs more often during play than during preschool academic activities (Odom, Peterson, McConnell, & Ostrosky, 1990), it appears that children with disabilities may have fewer opportunities to socialize with peers.

It is increasingly evident that the play, and the overall development, of children with disabilities can be enhanced in the social environment of an integrated preschool. Indeed, since the early 1970s there has been a growing tendency among educators to argue for the full inclusion of children with disabilities in mainstream programs (Bricker, 1995), and, according to a recent survey of 900 preschool programs, three out of four included at least one child with a disability (Wolery et al., 1993).

There may be a danger, however, in assuming that the simple act of inclusion will automatically benefit children with disabilities. Even when such children are mainstreamed and encouraged to play freely with a variety of other children, they may lack the social skills to do so. Children with disabilities tend, for example, to be overly direct and disruptive when trying to enter a play group (Lieber, 1993), an approach that is also characteristic of unpopular children without disabilities. In addition, while the normal developmental pattern across the preschool years is that play becomes increasingly social in nature, with solitary play decreasing in frequency and cooperative play increasing, children with disabilities continue to engage in a greater than expected amount of solitary play (Beh-Pajooh, 1991; Gottlieb, Gottlieb, Berkell, & Levy, 1986). In general, positive social interaction is more likely to be seen among children without disabilities than among children who have them (Peck, Palyo, Bettencourt, & Cooke, 1988; Roberts, Pratt, & Leach, 1991), and there may be very little spontaneous interaction between the two groups (Beh-Pajooh, 1991). It seems that children with disabilities have difficulty initiating and sustaining social play, and, as a result, have difficulty with peer interactions in general (Roberts, Pratty, & Leach, 1991).

As Bricker (1995) persuasively argued, inclusion is not enough. Many "mainstreamed" children are not functionally involved in program activities to the full extent of their potential. Complete integration of children with disabilities requires (a) a strong commitment to inclusion on the part of parents, teachers, and administrators, (b) a staff that is knowledgeable about various disabilities and their effects on children, (c) access to consultants with expertise in working with children with special needs, (d) a safe, accessible physical environment with specialized equipment, and (e) a curriculum that emphasizes participation in relevant and meaningful activities and promotes social interaction among all of the children.

It is revealing that integration *can* have a positive effect on the play of young children with disabilities, and on their social competence (Jenkins, Odom, & Speltz, 1989; Pickett, Griffith, & Rogers-Adkinson, 1993), but for this to occur there must be teacher and staff intervention designed to facilitate cooperative play (Kugelmass, 1989; Odom & Brown, 1993). As an example, in one study the staff used peer modeling, puppets, role playing, and liberal reinforcement to teach children how to greet one another, ask appropriately, share, and initiate play. They also taught children the inappropriateness of behaviors such as acting too aggressively, as by grabbing toys away from others (Matson, Fee, Coe, & Smith, 1991).

Training special populations of children in the social skills necessary to initiate and sustain social play seems to increase peer responsiveness (Haring & Lovinger, 1989), the overall amount and sophistication of peer interaction (DeKlyen & Odom, 1988; Handlan & Bloom, 1993), and the amount of social play that is observed (Hundert & Houghton, 1992). In fact, when teachers are trained to promote peer interaction in preschool children, there is an increase in peer interaction not only among children with disabilities but among other children as well (Hundert & Hopkins, 1992). It should be pointed out, however, that generalization of these educational experiences from one situation to another has been difficult to obtain in the research (Hundert & Houghton, 1992; Lifter, Sulzer-Azaroff, Anderson, & Cowdery, 1993).

Structured approaches can do more than facilitate social play. The use of modeling and reinforcement by teachers can also encourage imaginative play, even in the case of children who are least likely to engage in acts of make-believe. In one recent study, autistic children who were taught to engage in dramatic play by the use of scripts and teacher prompts did, in fact, engage in more spontaneous theme-related social behavior (Goldstein & Cisar, 1992).

The necessity of staff intervention to facilitate the play of children with disabilities suggests that it is not enough to remove the physical or social barriers to play. Affirmative action is also needed. The special child may need special support and encouragement from adults in order to play to his or her maximum potential, similar, perhaps, to the support that all children need to play when they are very young. Mothers typically prompt their one-year-olds to engage in acts of make-believe, particularly when, early in the second year, the child is less likely to pretend spontaneously (Damast & Tamis-LeMonda, 1993; Tamis-LeMonda, Damast, & Bornstein, 1993). Mother may demonstrate an activity, such as pretending to talk on a toy telephone and then offering it to the child. As the child matures, however, parent-generated acts of make-believe decrease as they are replaced by spontaneous "child-generated" pretense (Tamis-LeMonda & Bornstein, 1991). Similarly, in parent-toddler social games, the parent provides the structure, or "scaffold," upon which the game is built, and as the child matures, the adult becomes less involved in the structuring process (Hodapp, 1984).

Perhaps the scaffolding necessary for play to occur in younger children must be provided for a longer period time when a child has a disability. And just as sensitive parents recognize the need to match their play to the child's level of sophistication, as parent-generated play is gradually replaced by that spontaneously generated by the developing child, caring adults must be attuned to the needs of the special child at play. Most importantly, they must recognize that children whose developmental paths differ from the norm derive the same benefits as do all children from this most natural of childhood activities.

REFERENCES

Alessandri, S. M. (1991). Play and social behavior in maltreated preschoolers. *Development and Psychopathology, 3*, 191–205.

American Psychiatric Association. (1987). *DSM-III-Revised.* Washington, DC: Author.

Atlas, J. A., & Lapidus, L. B. (1987). Patterns of symbolic expression in subgroups of the childhood psychoses. *Journal of Clinical Psychology, 43*, 177–188.

August, R. L., & Forman, B. D. (1989). A comparison of sexually abused and non-sexually abused children's responses to anatomically correct dolls. *Child Psychiatry and Human Development, 20*, 39–47.

Bailey, D., & Wolery, M. (1984). *Teaching infants and preschoolers with handicaps.* Columbus, OH: Merrill.

Bailey, D., & Wolery, M. (1989). *Assessing infants and preschoolers with handicaps.* Columbus, OH: Merrill.

Barkley, R. A., Fischer, M., Edelbrock, C. S., & Smallish, L. (1990). The adolescent outcome of hyperactive children diagnosed by research criteria: An eight-year follow-up study. *Journal of the American Academy of Child and Adolescent Psychiatry, 29*, 546–557.

Baron-Cohen, S. (1987). Autism and symbolic play. *British Journal of Developmental Psychology*, *5*, 139–148.

Bartak, L., Rutter, M., & Cox, A. (1975). A comparative study of infantile autism and specific developmental receptive language disorder: 1. The children. *British Journal of Psychiatry*, *126*, 127–145.

Beckwith, L., Rodning, C., Phillipsen, L., Norris, D., & Howard, J. (1993, March). *Spontaneous play in two-year-olds born to substance-abusing mothers.* Paper presented at the Biennial Conference of the Society for Research in Child Development, New Orleans.

Bednersh, F. & Peck, C. A. (1986). Assessing social environments: Effects of peer characteristics on the social behavior of children with severe handicaps. *Child Study Journal*, *16*, 315–329.

Beh-Pajooh, A. (1991). Social interactions among severely handicapped children, non-handicapped children and their mothers in an integrated playgroup. *Early Child Development and Care*, *74*, 83–94.

Boyatzis, C. J. (1987). The effects of traditional playground equipment on preschool children's dyadic play interaction. In G. A. Fine (Ed.), *Meaningful play, playful meaning* (pp. 101–109). Champaign, IL: Human Kinetics Publishers.

Cohn, D. (1991). Anatomical doll play of preschoolers referred for sexual abuse and those not referred. *Child Abuse and Neglect*, *15*, 455–466.

Cunningham, C. C., Glenn, S. M., Wilkinson, P., & Sloper, P. (1985). Mental ability, symbolic play, and receptive and expressive language of young children with Down's syndrome. *Journal of Child Psychology and Psychiatry*, *26*, 255–265.

Day, A. M. L., Steffy, R., & Cunningham, C. (1993, April). *Influence of Attention Deficit–Hyperactivity Disorder (ADHD) on social style with peers during cooperative play situations.* Paper presented at the biennial meeting of the Society for Research in Child Development, New Orleans.

DeKlyen, M., & Odom, S. L. (1988). Activity structure and social interactions with peers in developmentally integrated play groups. *Journal of Early Intervention*, *13*, 342–352.

Esposito, B. G., & Koorland, M.A. (1989). Play behavior of hearing impaired children: Integrated and segregated settings. *Exceptional Children*, *55*, 412–419.

Fagan, J. F. III, Shepherd, P. A., & Knevel, C. R. (1991, April). *Predictive validity of the Fagan Test of Infant Intelligence.* Paper presented at the biennial meeting of the Society for Research in Child Development, Seattle, WA.

Fagot, B. I., Hagan, R., Youngblade, L. M., & Potter, L. (1989). A comparison of the play behaviors of sexually abused, physically abused, and non-abused children. *Topics in Early Childhood Special Education*, *9*, 88–100.

Fenson, L. (1986). The developmental progression of play. In A. W. Gottfried & C. C. Brown (Eds.), *Play interactions: The contribution of play materials and parental involvement to children's development*. Lexington, MA: D. C. Heath.

Frost, J. L., & Klein, B. L. (1979). *Children's play and playgrounds*. Boston: Allyn and Bacon.

Goldstein, H., & Cisar, C. L. (1992). Promoting interaction during sociodramatic play: Teaching scripts to typical preschoolers and classmates with disabilities. *Journal of Applied Behavior Analysis. 25*, 265–280.

Gottlieb, B. W., Gottlieb, J., Berkell, D., & Levy, L. (1986). Sociometric status and solitary play of LD boys and girls. *Journal of Learning Disabilities, 19*, 619–622.

Gould, J. (1986). The Lowe and Costello Symbolic Play Test in socially impaired children. *Journal of Autism and Developmental Disorders, 16*, 199–213.

Handlan, S., & Bloom, L. A. (1993). The effect of educational curricula and modeling/coaching on the interactions of kindergarten children with their peers with autism. *Focus on Autistic Behavior, 8*, 1–11.

Haring, T. G., & Lovinger, L. (1989). Promoting social interaction through teaching generalized play initiation responses to preschool children with autism. *Journal of the the Association for Persons with Severe Handicaps, 14*, 58–67.

Hellendoorn, J., & Hoekman, J. (1992). Imaginative play in children with mental retardation. *Mental Retardation, 30*(5), 255–263.

Higginbotham, D. J. & Baker, B. M. (1981). Social participation and cognitive play differences in hearing-impaired and normally hearing preschoolers. *The Volta Review, 83*, 135–149.

Hill, P., & McCune-Nicolich, L. M. (1981). Pretend play and patterns of cognition in Down's syndrome children. *Child Development, 52*, 611–617.

Horne, E. M., & Philleo, C. F. (1942). A comparative study of the spontaneous play activities of normal and mentally defective children. *The Journal of Genetic Psychology, 61*, 32–36.

Hughes, F. P. (1995). *Children, play and development* (2nd ed.). Boston: Allyn & Bacon.,

Hundert, J., & Houghton, A. (1992). Promoting social interaction of children with disabilities in integrated preschools: A failure to generalize. *Exceptional Children, 58*, 311–320.

Hundert, J., & Hopkins, B. (1992). Training supervisors in a collaborative team approach to promote peer interaction of children with disabilities in integrated preschools. *Journal of Applied Behavior Analysis, 25*, 385–400.

Jampole, L., & & Weber, M.K. (1987). An assessment of the behavior of sexually abused victims with anatomically correct dolls. *Child Abuse and Neglect, 11,* 187–192.

Jenkins, J. R., Odom, S. L., & Speltz, M. L. (1989). Effects of social integration on preschool children with handicaps. *Exceptional Children, 55,* 420–428.

Kanner, L. (1971). Follow-up study of eleven autistic children originally reported in 1943. *Journal of Autism and Childhood Schizophrenia, 1,* 217–250.

Kasari, C., Sigman, M. D., & Yirmiya, N. (1992). *Focused and social attention in interactions with familiar and unfamiliar adults: A comparison of autistic, mentally retarded and normal children.* Unpublished manuscript, University of California, Los Angeles.

Kohl, F. L. & Beckman, P. J. (1984). A comparison of handicapped and non-handicapped preschoolers' interactions across classroom activities. *Journal of the Division for Early Childhood, 8,* 49–56.

Kugelmass, J. W. (1989). The "shared classroom": A case study of interactions between early childhood and special education staff and children. *Journal of Early Intervention, 13,* 36–44.

Lederberg, A. R., Chapin, S. L., Rosenblatt, V., & Vandell, V. L. (1986). Ethnic, gender, and age preferences among deaf and hearing peers. *Child Development, 57,* 375–386.

Leventhal, J. M., Hamilton, J., Rekedal, S., Tibano-Micci, A., & Eyster, C. (1989). Anatomically correct doll use in interviews of young children suspected of having been sexually abused. *Pediatrics, 84,* 900–906.

Lewis, V., & Boucher, L. (1988). Spontaneous, instructed, and elicited play in relatively able autistic children. *British Journal of Developmental Psychology, 6,* 325–339.

Li, A. K. F. (1985). Toward more elaborate pretend play. *Mental Retardation, 23,* 131–136.

Lieber, J. (1993). A comparison of social pretend play in young children with and without disabilities. *Early Education and Development, 4,* 148–161.

Lifter, K., Sulzer-Azaroff, B., Anderson, S. R., & Cowdery, G. E. (1993). Teaching play activities to preschool children with disabilities: The importance of developmental considerations. *Journal of Early Intervention, 17,* 139–159.

Lombardino, L. L., Stein, J. E., Kricos, P. B., & Wolf, M. A. (1986). Play diversity and structural relationships in the play and language of language-impaired and language-normal preschoolers: Preliminary data. *Journal of Communication Disorders, 19,* 475–489.

Mann, L. F. (1984). Play behaviors of deaf and hearing children. In D. S. Martin (Ed.), *International Symposium on Cognition, Education, and Deafness*, Washington, DC: Gallaudet College Press.

Matson, J. L., Fee, V. E., Coe, D. A., & Smith, D. (1991). A social skills program for developmentally delayed preschoolers. *Journal of Clinical Child Psychology, 20*, 428–433.

McConkey, R. (1985). Changing beliefs about play and handicapped children. *Early Child Development and Care, 19*, 79–94.

McCune, L. (1986). Play-language relationships: Implications for a theory of symbolic development. In A. W. Gottfried & C. C. Brown (Eds.), *Play interactions: The contribution of play materials and parental involvement to children's development*. Lexington, MA: D. C. Heath.

Messer, D. J., McCarthy, M. E., McQuiston, S., MacTurk, R. H., Yarrow, L. J., & Vietze, P. M. (1986). Relation between mastery behavior in infancy and competence in early childhood. *Developmental Psychology, 22*, 366–372.

Missiuna, C., & Pollock, N. (1991). Play deprivation in children with physical disabilities: The role of the occupational therapist in preventing secondary disability. *American Journal of Occupational Therapy, 45*, 882–888.

Morgan, G. A., Maslin-Cole, C. A., Biringin, Z., & Harmon, R. J. (1991). Play assessment of mastery motivation in infants and young children. In C. Schafer, K. Gitlin, & A. Sundgrund (Eds.), *Play diagnosis and assessment*. New York: Wiley.

Mundy, P., Sigman, M., Ungerer, J., & Sherman, T. (1987). Non-verbal communication and play correlates of language development in autistic children. *Journal of Autism and Developmental Disorders, 17*, 349–364.

Odom, S. L., Peterson, C., McConnell, S., & Ostrosky, M. (1990). Ecobehavioral analysis of early education/specialized classroom settings and peer social interaction. Special Issue: Organizing caregiving environments for young children with handicaps. *Education and Treatment of Children, 13*, 316–330.

Peck, C. A., Palyo, W. J., Bettencourt, B., & Cooke, T. P. (1988). An observational study of "partial integration" of handicapped students in a regular preschool. *Journal of Research and Development in Education, 21*, 1–4.

Perner, J., Frith, U., Leslie, A. M., & Leekam, S. R. (1989). Exploration of the autistic child's theory of mind: Knowledge, belief, and communication. *Child Development, 60*, 689–700.

Piaget, J. (1962). *Play, dreams, and imitation in childhood*. New York: Norton.

Pickett, P. L., Griffith, P. L., & Rogers-Adkinson, D. (1993). Integration of preschoolers with severe disabilities into daycare. *Early Education and Development, 4*, 54–58.

Quinn, J., & Rubin, K. (1984). The play of handicapped children. In T. D. Yawkey & A. Pellegrini (Eds.), *Child's play: Developmental and applied.* Hillsdale, NJ: Lawrence Erlbaum.

Roberts, C., Pratt, C., & Leach, D. (1991). Classroom and playground interaction of students with and without disabilities. *Exceptional Children, 57*, 212–224.

Rubin, K. H., Fein, G. C., & Vandenberg, B. (1983). Play. In P. H. Mussen (Ed.), *Handbook of child psychology* (4th ed.). New York: Wiley.

Ruff, H. A., Lawson, K. R., Parinello, R., & Weissberg, R. (1990). Long term stability of individual differences in sustained attention in the early years. *Child Development, 61*, 60–76.

Rutter, M. (1983). Cognitive deficits in the pathogenesis of autism. *Journal of Child Psychology and Psychiatry, 24*, 513–531.

Shimada, S., Sano, R., & Peng, F. C. C. (1979). A longitudinal study of symbolic play in the second year of life. *The Research Institute for the Education of Exceptional Children, Research Bulletin.* Tokyo: Gakugei University.

Sigman, M., & Sena, R. (1993). Pretend play in high risk and developmentally delayed children. In M. H. Bornstein & A. W. O'Reilly (Eds.), *The role of play in the development of thought* (pp. 29–42). San Francisco: Jossey-Bass.

Singer, J. L. & Streiner, B. F. (1966). Imaginative content in the dreams and fantasy play of blind and sighted children. *Perceptual and Motor Skills, 22*, 475–482.

Skellenger, A. C., & Hill, E. W. (1994). Effects of a shared teacher-child play intervention on the play skills of three young children who are blind. *Journal of Visual Impairment and Blindness, 88*(5), 433–445.

Tait, P. (1973). Behavior of young blind children in a controlled play setting. *Perception and Motor Skills, 34*, 963–969.

Tamis-LeMonda, C. S., & Bornstein, M. H. (1991). Individual variation, correspondence, stability, and change in mother and toddler play. *Infant Behavior and Development. 14*, 143–162.

Tamis-LeMonda, C. S., Damast, A. M., & Bornstein, M. H. (1993, March). *Individual differences in mother's play actions and beliefs: Correspondence to toddler play competence.* Paper presented at the Biennial Conference of the Society for Research in Child Development, New Orleans.

Terrell, B., Schwartz, R., Prelock, P., & Messick, C. (1984). Symbolic play in normal and language-impaired children. *Journal of Speech and Hearing Research, 27*, 424–429.

Tilton, J. R. & Ottinger, D. R. (1964). Comparisons of the toy play of and behavior of autistic, retarded, and normal children. *Psychological Reports, 15*, 967–975.

Tessier, O., de Lorimier, S., & Doyle, A. (1993, March). *The quality of social involvement in social play: The effects of mode of play, relationship, and age.* Paper presented at the Biennial Conference of the Society for Research in Child Development, New Orleans.

Weiner, E. A. & Weiner, E. J. (1974). Differentiation of retarded and normal children through toy-play analysis. *Multivariate Behavioral Research, 9,* 245–252.

Wills, D. M. (1972). Problems of play and mastery in the blind child. In E. P. Trapp & P. Himelstein (Eds.), *Readings on the exceptional child.* New York: Appleton-Century-Crofts.

Wing, L., Gould, J., Yeates, S. R., & Brierly, L. M. (1977). Symbolic play in severely mentally retarded and in autistic children. *Journal of Child Psychology and Psychiatry, 18,* 167–178.

Wolery, M., Holcombe-Ligon, A., Brookfield, J., Huffman, K., Schroeder, C., Martin, C., Venn, M., Werts, M., & Fleming, L. (1993). The extent and nature of preschool mainstreaming: A survey of general early educators. *Journal of Special Education, 27,* 222–234.

Wulff, S. B. (1985). The symbolic and object play of children with autism: A review. *Journal of Autism and Developmental Disorders, 15,* 139–148.

Chapter 10

The Cultural Contexts of Children's Play

Jaipaul L. Roopnarine, Jennifer Lasker,
Megan Sacks, and Marshall Stores

To write a chapter on the complex patterns of social and functional organization of behavior in any culture is a challenging and risky undertaking. The risk is often multiplied when one pursues the goal of providing a synopsis of the literature in a given area for wide-ranging cultures. As formidable a task as it may be, we will attempt to provide a glimpse of children's play across cultures. Decidedly, such an exercise would entail an examination of not only the content and nature of children's play in different settings but also beliefs about the value of play inherent in different cultures and the implications of play for formal/informal education during a child's formative years. Before we proceed, however, a few caveats are in order. Barring some lucid anthropological accounts, there are few detailed studies of children's wide-ranging play activities per se in diverse cultural settings. Needless to say, the play literature is built on data largely compiled on North American and European families and children; it is biased and may be limited in its generalizability especially when considering culture, gender, and social class issues (See Rubin, Fein & Vandenburg, 1983; Johnson, Christie & Yawkey, 1987; Hughes, 1994). In a similar vein, play theories that were substantiated on these data appear culturally myopic. To the extent that it is possible, we will weave culture-specific frameworks and practices into our discussions throughout the chapter. While we recognize that social class differences exist in children's modes of play, the limited data base on play and socioeconomic status (SES) differences across cultures will not be a major focus of our discussion.

In this chapter, we hope to achieve four goals:

1. Provide some arguments as to why we need to examine the cultural context of play in young children further
2. Discuss culture-specific propositions that may be useful in future explorations of children's play across cultures
3. Review studies on parent-child play and children's playful activities across select cultures
4. Delve into the implications of play for children's development across cultures

WHY CONSIDER PLAY IN DIVERSE CULTURES FURTHER?

The value of the cognitive and social attributes of young children's play is fairly well established (see Macdonald, 1993; Monaghan-Nurot, Scales, Van Hoorn, & Almy, 1987; Rubin et al., 1983). Furthermore, the role of play in the early childhood curriculum has received increasing attention over the last two decades (Johnson et al., 1987; Roopnarine, Johnson, & Hooper, 1994; Spodek & Saracho, 1990). It can safely be said, then, that play has become an integral part of the early childhood curriculum in the developed countries of the world and it is gradually being integrated into educational efforts in societies that have historically embraced a rigid academic curriculum for young children (e.g., Thailand, India, Taiwan). Why then focus on play and culture further?

There are at least three strong reasons to focus on the cultural underpinnings of young children's play. Foremost, teasing out intercultural and intracultural variations in children's play can help us to recognize the unique cultural properties that are reflected in children's activities. This, in turn, can provide requisite knowledge that can assist us in developing culturally relevant theories and curricular practices. Culturally contextualized curricula can enhance cultural pride and concurrently self-esteem. Native beliefs and practices should not be sacrificed in order to fit in "imported" educational philosophies or dominant culture views (e.g., Eurocentric) on the role of play in early learning. In the same vein, parental efforts to enhance the cognitive and social development of children through playful interactions should reflect a profound respect for socialization practices that are embedded within the sociocultural context. In some cultures, health and nutrition may be given greater priority over social and cognitive stimulation during the early childhood period. Second, the dramatic growth in interest in preschool education in diverse cultures around the world necessitates an understanding of how different cultures incorporate play as a central part of the curriculum.

An immediate challenge would entail blending cultural practices and parental psychology about the value of early preschool education into educational efforts. Third, the structural and social organization of families continue to change in important ways. While North Americans and Europeans opt for more egalitarian roles, there has been movement toward quasi-egalitarian roles in several other societies. In societies that have been governed by patriarchy and filial piety, women have entered the labor force in increasing numbers. This has led to interesting modifications in early caregiving responsibilities. The maternal/caregiving role once held predominantly by mothers and other adult women in the community has shifted to involve nonrelatives in a formalized setting. Multiple caregiving has taken on a new meaning and children's peer groups are sure to assume a burgeoning role in early childhood development.

THEORETICAL CONSIDERATIONS ABOUT PLAY ACROSS CULTURES

For some time now, ethnic scholars and cross-cultural researchers (for more recent views see Ogbu, 1981; Roopnarine & Carter, 1992; Soto & Negron, 1994) have questioned the wisdom of using the white social science play literature to measure childhood functioning in other subcultures and cultural settings; and traditional play paradigms and theories do not seem to be able to choreograph very well the play of children in other cultures. A prime example, is the face-to-face paradigm outlined by Tronick and his colleagues (Tronick, Beeghly, Fetters, & Weinberg, 1991). Simply put, not all cultures value face-to-face play and some rarely engage in such activities (see Martini & Kirkpatrick, 1992).

In a related manner, Western theories of play or the way they are utilized seem to imply a search for universals and orderliness among players. Following these theories researchers vigorously look for different modes of cognitive and social play patterns in terms of what Parten/Smilansky/Piaget proposed (e.g., Pan, 1994). There is also the argument that make-believe play may be absent from the activities of children in nonindustrialized societies (Ebbeck, 1973). This mind-set has led researchers to direct their energies toward the validation or refutation of the absence of make-believe play. The result is a flagrant disregard for modes of functioning among children and families that promote competence within specific sociocultural niches. These traditional approaches disregard acculturation and syncretism in pluralistic societies and/or cultural persistence of other patterns of behaviors that do not fit into existing paradigms (e.g., developmental milestones, status-leveling).

Theoretical considerations regularly presented on play (e.g., cognitive-developmental, psychoanalytic, arousal modulation) have ably discussed the value of play for learning and cognition. Most textbooks and articles on play have failed to provide a comprehensive theory of play that seriously incorporates the vast properties of culture. Even the Association for the Study of Play monograph series has failed to tackle this issue as it pertains to parent-child and child-child play. This is unfortunate given our earlier argument about the recognition of diversity in culturally continuous and discontinuous contexts (see Roopnarine, Johnson, & Hooper, 1994). Given the different make-up of societies around the globe (e.g., industrialized pluralistic, industrialized homogeneous, post-colonial, hunting-gathering, etc.) this would not be an easy task.

It is by some counts unfair to criticize existing modes of conducting business in this domain without providing some alternative suggestions. The work of Vygotsky (1978), Bruner (1972), Rogoff (1990), and others have been instrumental in guiding our understanding of how sociocultural interactions lend themselves to interpretations of development. It would be premature to attempt to outline a theory of culture and play here. Instead, we provide a list of possible considerations that may serve as a guide in future attempts to study play across cultures.

• Biosocial factors, both somatic and reproductive, influence parent-child participation (see Hewlett, 1992). The parent-child play literature is comprised primarily of mother-child play activities. Paternal investment in children, of which involvement is a component, goes beyond biological concerns. Presumably, male investment in children increases when there is paternity certainty. In societies where there is low paternal investment parent-child interactions will rest with the mother and boys more so than girls will mimic the activities of men through their association within predominantly male groups.
• Possible intersections among culture, social class, and gender must be considered in examining early childhood development.
• Differences also exist in the psychology of the importance of play whether it is in the peer group or parent-child system. Further, the possible links between peer group play and parent-child relationships may be more important for post-industrialized societies since the functions of the family have become "socially specialized" (Harkness & Super, 1992).
• Finally, in preindustrial societies education occurs in formal and informal settings. Because there are different patterns and settings for children's lives (see Whiting and Edwards's [1988] concept of "maintenance systems") some children must balance work and play activities. Theories of play must account for the myriad of ways in which play is used for learning social and

adaptive skills that are essential for successfully negotiating the demands of the individual's sociocultural world. The socioecological contexts that represent the work-play mixture is antithetical to most Western frameworks regarding children's play.

PARENT-CHILD PLAY

The short-term and long-term benefits of parent-child social activities and play for children's social and cognitive growth, learning cultural and social roles and rules, human adaptation, and social skills with peers have been thoroughly reviewed (Bruner, 1972; Parke & Ladd, 1992; Rubin et al., 1983; Sutton-Smith, 1993). Further, the critical role of parent-child activities in the remediation of social and cognitive deficits in disadvantaged groups of children has been duly noted (see Monighan-Nourot, Scales, Van Hoorn, & Almy, 1987; Powell, 1988; Segal, 1993). More specifically, adult-child play has been studied in the context of attachment relationships (see Lamb, 1985; Roopnarine, Hooper et al., 1993), the dynamic nature of parent-child games (see Macdonald, 1993), rough and stimulating play (see Roopnarine, Ahmeduzzaman, Hossain, & Riegraf, 1992), cultural variations in adult participation in parent-child play (see volume by Roopnarine, Johnson, & Hooper, 1994), adults' beliefs about the value of play for development (e.g., Pan, 1994), visual, auditory, and tactile stimulation (Stern, 1977; Roopnarine, Hooper et al., 1993), language development (Monighan-Nourot et al., 1987), successful peer group participation (see Parker & Asher, 1987), play participation and performance on standardized tests (see Johnson et al., 1987), among other issues.

For the purpose of this chapter, we focus on variations in parent-child play across cultures. This issue has continued to receive increasing attention in the anthropological, sociological, and psychological literature and emphasis has surrounded prevailing beliefs about the value of play, the nature of parent-child play, and societal and cultural beliefs about the socialization of children and parent-child play and social activities. In considering parent-child play across cultures, we center our discussion around three dimensions of play that have received a good deal of attention: parent-child games, rough-and-tumble play, and work/play and parent-child activities. We will skirt the literature on parent-child play on North-American and European children because it has been presented in several recent volumes (Johnson et al., 1987; Hughes, 1994; Macdonald, 1993; Monighan-Nourot et al., 1988); and because the studies conducted in these portions of the world rarely considered the cultural context of social or cognitive activities or the value placed on social versus technological intelligence. Arguably, this state of affairs is changing as the pluralistic nature of North American and some European countries (e.g., England and Holland) are increasingly being embraced by scholars and lay persons alike (see Gibson & Ogbu, 1991; Soto & Negron, 1994).

Before we proceed with our discussion, however, we need to acknowledge key concepts in the socialization of children and prevalent views about child development and childrearing across some cultures.

- Parent-child play and social activities occur more often in work-related settings in some societies (e.g., African, Asian, Latin American) than in others (e.g., the United States, Canada, Europe). It is, therefore, important to consider work/play connections in cross-cultural considerations of play (Bloch & Adler, 1994).
- Face-to-face play and parent-child games are more characteristic of white North American and European parents than in Polynesian and African parents (e.g., Gusii, Marquesan, Fias). Western paradigms of face-to-face interactions appear inapplicable to some other societies.
- Concepts of self-reliance and autonomy are socialized within different cultural dynamics. In North America and Europe, individual pursuits or goals are valued. By the same token, competition and assertive/aggressive play are encouraged. In other contexts, socialization occurs within a community of people ("The village raises the child," "Many laps to play on"). Group participation is valued and encouraged (e.g., Aka, Marquesan). There is a greater emphasis on social capital, and individual activity is seen as uncongenial. Concepts of autonomy and self-reliance are achieved but through a different set of parental demands (e.g., the continuum of interdependent to individualistic goals).
- In older societies (e.g., India, China, Japan, and a host of hunting-gathering societies) socialization is deeply embedded in filial piety. The sexual division of labor/play reflects historical injunctions. Moreover, play is tied to sociocultural rituals and rites of passage (e.g., in Africa, India). In the industrialized societies, egalitarian or quasi-egalitarian roles may warrant the equitable division of household labor and social participation with children. This, however, is hardly the case.
- Modes of parenting or parenting styles may lead to different outcomes in different cultures (equi-finality). For instance, a permissive parent-child orientation will lead to different outcomes in North America and Africa. Aka parents are quite permissive but raise instrumentally competent children. This is not so for white North American parents (see Hewlett, 1992).
- Beliefs about the value of play and concepts of child development vary across cultures. In North America and Europe, childrearing practices are driven by expert child development advice and adults actively engage children in play for desired cognitive and social outcomes. Play in other cul-

tures involve mimicking adult activities, and parents often follow their children's inclinations (e.g., India). Similarly, concepts of "developmental milestones" vary from culture to culture, and adults may prioritize socialization goals differently across cultures.

- In some societies, adult-child play may involve nonparental figures who serve as multiple caregivers (see Andaman Islanders). Thus, family social-organization (space, number of adult members, etc.) and structure may limit or enhance the availability of play partners and opportunities for adult-child interactions (see Whiting & Edwards, 1988).

Parent-Child Games

Beliefs about the role of games in different societies vary; but researchers have discerned their importance for the cultural transmission of basic childhood skills required for social interactions and participation in a given culture (Fogel, Nowak, & Karns, 1993). By guiding the child's participation in the game, the adult can regulate the assimilation of cultural skills eventuating in the organization of internal structures of the external sociocultural world (see Vygotsky, 1978). While such participation may be more regularized and highly structured in industrialized societies, it may range from informal participation (through singing and holding in the absence of face-to-face interaction) to more enmeshed participation of highly structured activities as in sociocultural rituals in developing societies (e.g., ceremonies that involve placing a *teka* on a baby's face to ward off evil spirits).

The North American literature is replete with examples of social and intellectual games parents play with young children (e.g., Peek-a-boo, Pat-a-Cake, This Little Piggy, Incy Wincy Spider, putting a puzzle together, board games, computer games, and so on). Variations of some of these games are also seen in a wide range of other cultures. For example, variations of Peek-a-boo are seen in South Africa (Uphi, Uphi), Japan (Inai inai ba!), Polynesian cultures, India, Malaysia, Russia, Brazil, and several other societies (Fernald & O'Neill, 1993). It is the manner in which parents play with children and the nature of the play that may be characteristically different across cultures, however. In one analysis of parent-child games in different regions of India (Roopnarine et al., 1994), it was found that parents used songs and touched children quite a bit during play (e.g., Chal, Chal Mate, Habba Bonthu Anthanthe, Kan Dol Dol). The songs were linguistically rich in their properties, and socially inviting . Other dimensions of touching, albeit of a more vigorous nature (clapping, rocking, swinging, tickling), were observed among Chinese, Filipino, and Mexican immigrant families in California (Van Hoorn, 1988). In societies where face-to-face interactions are not commonly displayed, parents are more likely to use songs and social actions, as is the case of the Gusii of Kenya (Dixon et al., 1981), Navajo (Fajardo & Freedman, 1981) or Igbo mothers (Nwokali, 1987), or the infant faces outward so that the back of its head is facing the adult's face as in cultures of the South Pacific (e.g., Fias and Marquesan) (see Sostek, Vietze, Kreiss, Van der Waals, & Rubinstein, 1981; Martini & Kirkpatrick, 1992).

Differences have been documented in the style in which parents engage in play with infants as well. Japanese mothers use their bodies to loom in and out and use their hands to tap the infant and to create visual displays (Fogel, Toda, & Kawai, 1988), while Bambara mothers from Kenya zero in on the postural definitions of the infant's body in motor games (Bril, Zack, & Nkounkon-Hombessa, 1989). Among Euro-Americans, the mother's body posture remains the same during play and is close to the infant's body (Fogel et al., 1988).

A final point about parent-infant games involves gender-differentiated activities with sons and daughters. In the North American studies mother-infant play has been observed to be more intellectual and conventional (e.g. pat-a-cake, peek-a-boo, putting a puzzle together) than father-infant play. Furthermore, fathers encourage boys to explore and play with objects while encouraging daughters to be more passive and to be near them during play (Lamb, 1978). These differences have not been consistently observed in other societies (see Sun & Roopnarine, 1996), but their existence should not be dismissed given the value placed on sons over daughters in more traditional societies.

Parent-Child Rough-and-Tumble Play

The immediate benefits of rough play has been debated for some time now (see Macdonald, 1993). Whether it is viewed as a biological adaptation (e.g. Panksepp, 1993) or as contributing to the development of father-child attachments (Lamb, 1985), it does not seem to be prevalent in the activities of parents and children in a number of societies. It appears to be more characteristic of the play of Euro-American fathers and children (Roopnarine et al., 1992) than of the parent-child play of East Indians (Roopnarine, Talukder, Jain, Joshi, & Srivastav, 1990), Aka Pygmies (Hewlett, 1987), Malaysians (Roopnarine, Lu, & Ahmeduzzaman, 1989), Taiwanese (Sun & Roopnarine, 1996), and families in some Caribbean societies (Roopnarine & Brown, 1997). Nor does it occur in high frequencies in Swedish (Lamb, Frodi, Hwang, Frodi, & Steinberg, 1982) and Israeli families (Sagi, Lamb, Shohan, Dvir, & Lewkowicz, 1985). In Italian families, other adult nonmaternal figures are the ones who engage in rough stimulating activities with young children (New & Benigni, 1987). In societies in which rough-and-tumble play is more characteristic of parent-child activities, fathers are more likely to engage in vigorous stimulating activities with sons than daughters (Lamb, 1977).

To reiterate: the context for parent-child play activities in some societies appear more sedate, involving more close physical contact and holding, as compared with the more vigorous stimulating play of white fathers in the United States.

The Work/Play Connection

Perhaps nowhere else in the world is the work/play connection more evident than in some African societies. While earlier accounts portrayed African children as aimless and passive, often imitating their parents, more recent descriptions have considered the expressiveness and contributions of play to personality (Bloch, 1994; Schwartzman & Barbera, 1977) and the socioecological context within which play occurs. The interrelationship of work and play has been couched within the framework of "directed activities" (mostly work) and "undirected social activities" (mainly play). The two are affected by parental beliefs about the value of work as opposed to play, the seasonal and economic variations on the demand for work efforts, responsibilities and expectations of individual members of the group/kinship network, and the social and structural organization of the group (Bloch & Adler, 1994; Harkness & Super, 1986; Whiting & Edwards, 1988).

Despite the maligned views of earlier writers, there was consensus that children mimicked adult roles that became integrated into their adult life (for example the Nigerian Igan, Kenyan Gikuyan). Children who accompany their parents to work in the field or to herd animals often express adult roles in make-believe play (see Bloch, 1994). Invariably play patterns reflect adult work activities: women dancing, adult jokes, the blacksmith's bold strokes, hunting play, weddings, and court meetings. As the following example from Bloch and Adler (1994) demonstrates, Senegalese children directly incorporate the roles of men and women into their play.

Small two- to four-year-old boys engaged in pretense that included some similar themes—cooking, child care, some agriculture, for example—but also included more pretense with vehicles or play construction. By five to six years, girls' play and play-work activities, where there was greater emphasis on playing at learning work, in the first author's opinion, continued; in addition, assigned or initiated activities that transformed the former "play/play-work" into nonplay or real work activities was also done. Boys, on the other hand, at five to six years, were no longer observed in pretend activities that had been observed earlier: carrying a baby on their back at age two years, helping others to cook with play materials, or even play with toy trucks that might be called pretense. They spent more time with other boys, frequently outside their village, exploring the countryside, climbing trees, swimming in nearby lakes, or playing sports games. After six years of age, even greater divergence in boys'–girls' activities were observed, with girls, by age seven, spending more and more time outside of school, helping with "women's work" activities, including agriculture, when possible; boys began to help more seriously with agricultural activities in family fields as well as small animal herding activities, work generally only assigned to seven- to twelve-year-old boys. (p. 168)

The involvement of children in adult games and mock fighting are also discussed elsewhere (see Sutton-Smith, 1976). The work/play interface will become clearer in the next section.

CHILDREN'S PLAY

In examining children's play across cultures, we must first consider the composition of children's groups—gender and age, the context within which play occurs (e.g., courtyard, playground, compound, field, work setting, beaches, classroom), as well as the prevalence of different modes of play and games. From the extant literature, we know that gender segregation appears endemic to most early childhood play groups across cultures. Maccoby (1988) has estimated that by age 4½ children are thrice as likely to play with same gender peers as opposite-gender peers and by age 6½ that possibility increases to 11 times among North American children. The robustness of same-gender play groups have been ascertained in Kowket and Kalblen (Harkness & Super, 1985), among the Nyansango, Ngeca, Rajputs, in Tarong, Taira, and Juxtlahucca (Whiting & Edwards, 1988) and among Lese and Efe groups in Zaire (Morelli, 1986). Relatedly, age segregation is more characteristic of postindustrialized societies at least in school settings (Roopnarine & Bright, 1993) but less so in neighborhood play groups (Ellis, Rogoff, & Cromer, 1981; Barker & Wright, 1955). Age-segregation is less pronounced among hunting-gathering societies since children interact and play with kinship members and cousins who are older or younger (Konner, 1975). Taken together, gender-segregation increases with age during the early childhood period across cultures and it appears that girls are introduced into work roles sooner than boys (Whiting & Edwards, 1988).

Another element of children's play encompasses where it occurs. As might be expected, this ranges considerably: from organized play groups in school yards and classrooms to courtyards, slums, beaches, and play spaces around dwellings. Following the conceptual framework of Whiting and

Edwards (1988) regarding the increasing competence of young children as they graduate from their parents' back and lap to the yard, and eventually to the wider world of community and school, it is possible to differentiate where boys and girls play. In postindustrialized societies, boys are more likely to play in streets and parks, girls in yards and in homes (Maccoby, 1988). In the six culture study, boys and older children had greater and wider access to the community than girls or younger children (Whiting & Edwards, 1988). What this means is that the farther away boys roam from the home/compound, the greater the likelihood that they will have opportunities to engage in undirected adult requested activities and gravitate to play. As some researchers have described, yards, streets, beaches, and fields all provide different opportunities for play (see Brodber, 1973, for a discussion of the yard as a context for human interactions in Caribbean societies, and Martini & Kirkpatrick, 1994, for play on the beach among Marquesan children). Undoubtedly, the latitude given to boys to wander farther away from home increases the breadth and variety of their play. The differential manner in which boys and girls explore and engage in play activities beyond the immediate home environment may influence their ability to interact with diverse groups of people, affect group membership and opportunities to fine-tune leadership and other personal skills (Lever, 1993; Munroe & Munroe, 1994; Whiting & Edwards, 1988).

In the rest of this section, we would like to focus on children's play in formal and informal settings starting with the traditional games children play before turning to a discussion of modern play forms and some factors that may affect play participation. The benefits children accrue from participation in make-believe, constructive, solitary, and cooperative modes of play have been addressed in some detail (Johnson et al., 1987), and in an earlier section we alluded to the manner in which young children may internalize sociocultural aspects of their environments through play. At this juncture, it is necessary to point out that observations of children's play across cultures have not been specific enough in some studies and were often couched within children's social activities or have been largely described through games inherent in a given culture. Thus, it will be difficult to describe play uniformly across cultures and we are not sure this should be the practice anyway.

Traditional Forms of Play

Initially obsessed with the play activities of "primitive" peoples, and the affirmation of the absence of play forms present in children in the Western world, anthropologists and psychologists have begun to pay greater attention to the meaning behind children's activities for functioning within culture. This latter emphasis has led to more accurate depictions of how children play in different socioecological contexts with a definite shift away from "deficit-structure" views.

The preservation of traditional play modes and games has become increasingly challenging and a few are at risk of disappearing in some cultures altogether (e.g., mud knifing among the Yu'Pik). Nevertheless, there is evidence to suggest that traditional modes of play and games are practiced to varying degrees in a number of cultures. Chinese children engage in games that have been preserved through several eras: lighting firecrackers during Chinese New Year, preparing lanterns for the Lantern Festival, kite flying on tomb-sweeping day, chopstick games, Chinese chess, cock kicking, Chinese yo-yo, and rope skipping (Pan, 1994). Similarly, in Japan, games that were recorded during the Edo period (1603–1867) are still seen today, for example, playing house and tag; play materials such as bamboo horses, kites, battledores, masks, toy drums, fireworks, and shell tops were also used in the Edo period during play (Takeuchi, 1994). In India, play is embedded in religious and nonreligious festivals and ceremonies that are centuries old (e.g., Holi, Diwali), and play objects that are made of wood and clay date back to 2,500 B.C. (Baig, 1979). Hunting, fighting, social, and athletic games, pastimes, and imitating elders have been passed on among the Native people of Australia (e.g., various string games), the Kumngo of central New Guinea, (e.g., Kiam tondip—making faces and grimaces), Native Indians in the United States, Scandinavians, Latin Americans, and among people in several other cultures (see volume by Sutton-Smith, 1976, for specific descriptions.

Play in Formal and Informal Settings

Researchers (Bloch & Adler, 1994; Bloch, 1988; Harkness & Super, 1986; Lancy, 1977; Munroe & Munroe, 1984; Negussie, 1989; Whiting & Edwards, 1988) have examined African children's play activities vis-à-vis work and the division of labor in nonschool settings and in the context of economic and political oppression (Hampton, 1989; Liddel & Kvalsig, 1991; Reynolds, 1989). The studies concerned with play in nonschool settings are quite instructive. Among Kpelle villagers of Sierra Leone it was determined that children engaged in Nee-pele or make-believe, Sua-Kpe-pele or hunting play, Pelle-seng or toys, Pele-Kee or games, Polo or storytelling; Mana-Pele or dancing, musical instrument play, and Kppa-kolo-pele or adult play (Lancy, 1977). Likewise, Bloch and Adler (1994) have provided elaborate descriptions of Senegalese children's play. Notably, children 2 to 4 engaged in a variety of fantasy play themes but along gender stereotypic lines; girls were more likely to engage in domestic cleaning, cooking, and child care. On the other hand, boys' fantasy play was more likely to reflect transportation and hunting themes. The divergence in activities became acerbated as children got older with girls' play themes representing the work activities of women.

In Chinese society Confucian ethics emphasized the value of play through the "polite arts." The polite arts referred to ceremonies, music, archery, charioteering, language characters, and arithmetic (Pan, 1994). Children enacted these art forms to learn social rules and adult customs. But throughout Chinese history play assumed an ancillary role to a more formalized educational curriculum. Nonetheless, as noted previously, Chinese children engage in a wide range of traditional games and cross-national comparisons of Taiwanese and U.S. children's cognitive and social modes of play were quite comparable. Mothers viewed play as cognitively enriching and often arranged constructive play activities for children (Pan, 1994).

Although play became increasingly recognized as an important ingredient in children's growth and development as views of children changed from the Archaic Age to the present, it was only recently that play received serious attention within Japanese society (Takeuchi, 1994). The process was aided by reform-minded educators and prominent Japanese scholars who argued that playing with bows and arrows, balls, dolls, tops, and flying kites were deeply enmeshed in childhood experiences (Takeuchi, 1994). Today, concerns have been raised about Japanese children's greater involvement in video games and the decrease in outdoor play. Children in the United States, United Kingdom, and France play outdoors more than Japanese children (see Sutton-Smith, 1976, for a more complete list of games). Traditional forms of play such as blindman's bluff, hide-and-seek, spinning a top, and playing house are rarely seen among Japanese children as they opt for more indoor play that include the use of ready-made toys and machines (Takeuchi, 1994). In a survey of boys' play preferences, it was reported that the preference of play activities was as follows: softball and baseball, video games, soccer, dodgeball, and tag and hide-and-seek (Takeuchi, 1994).

Unlike Japanese and Chinese societies, contemporary play patterns in the East Indian context are still strongly embedded in religious and nonreligious celebrations. During festivals such as *Diwali*, the festival of lights, and *Holi*, children engage in joyous activities with peers and adults. Diwali celebrations involve lighting oil containers and playing with fireworks. Holi allows children to sprinkle colors and water on their friends while in other celebrations children may enact the roles of important figures in Hindu philosophy. Additionally, throughout Indian history, songs, dance, mime, and puppetry have been used to convey tales about kings, queens, and courtiers (Baig, 1979). Most of the recent play studies on Indian children reflect intervention efforts geared at improving the cognitive and social skills of children. The results of these studies are mixed; some have shown gains in children's test scores after systematic play intervention, while others have failed to show any salutary effects (see Roopnarine, Hooper, et al., 1993, for an overview). This may be due in part to the fact that low-income Indian mothers do not fully realize the value of play for children's cognitive and social growth. Alternatively, within the Indian setting, childhood survival may be a more important goal for parents than teaching play skills to their children.

If we look at Indian society more carefully we find a large nonschool early childhood population. For these children, learning through play/work or sibling caregiving is not uncommon. Among non-schoolgoing children, craft work, animal husbandry, fieldwork, peddling, and other related activities may provide little room for children to engage in undirected play. Nevertheless, there are games and play activities that are common to school and non-schoolgoing children. Marble games, hide and seek, tag games, "police and thief," and pretend play have been catalogued in rural and urban Indian children (see Roopnarine, Johnson, & Hooper, 1994). In the more structured school environment, children engage in role playing and art activities that stress constructive play, storytelling, and the recitation of rhymes through puppetry, books, and flashcards. These activities employ indigenous play materials. The group and circle games (e.g., play in school or in surrounding spaces) require high levels of cooperation, imitation, and pretense (Muralidharan et al., 1981). Like the play activities of Indian parents and children, the games and social play activities of Indian children reflect a lot of holding and close physical contact (Roopnarine, Johnson, & Hooper, 1994).

In contrast to the competitive and individualized nature of social activities in the postindustrialized societies, children's play in some Polynesian cultures avoid distinct leaders, being singled out from the group, or extensive negotiations of rules and roles. Children prefer activities that do not require competition (Martini, 1994). In her careful observations, Martini (1994) calculated that young Marquesan children spent 35% of their time in group object-oriented play (e.g., groups of children rolling wheels down a ramp; gathering leaves at the same time), 24% of their time in mostly scripted fantasy play (e.g., fishing, hunting, preparing feasts), 9% consisted of fighting and negotiating (e.g., engaging in teasing and "status leveling" of someone claiming dominance), and 18% of the time sitting and talking (e.g., about ships coming in), 5% of the time in physical play (e.g., run up and down the boat ramp chasing waves), and occasionally in organized games. Marquesan children rarely, if ever, play alone and only 7% of their play was of a dyadic nature. Fully 93% of their play was of a cooperative nature reflecting cultural beliefs about group consensus.

THE CHANGING SOCIAL MILIEU
OF CHILDREN'S PLAY

As the world becomes more interconnected through travel and trade, agricultural lands and rain forests diminish (e.g., among the Aka, Efe, and

Yanomamo), industrial and residential buildings usurp space once allocated for play (e.g. Taiwan), technological gadgets replace traditional toys (e.g., the United States and Japan), and educational goals are better articulated in the developing countries, both the context for and the nature of young children's play across cultures have witnessed visible changes. By some accounts (e.g., Block & Adler, 1994) in African countries work and play may become more distinct as educational goals become more formalized. Consequently, children may have fewer opportunities to observe, learn, and modify their knowledge of their environment and roles within it in informal ways—mainly through work and play (Leacock, 1976). The implementation of "Western" preschool philosophies in countries such as Taiwan and Japan has led to a greater emphasis on constructive and symbolic play in educational settings. Recent analysis of Taiwanese children's play activities (e.g., Pan, 1994) suggests that preschool-age children show a preference for slides and swings and transportation toys over more traditional objects (e.g., kites, paper folding). In Japan, the rapid rise of video games (see Takeuchi, 1994) may lead to more indoor play and social activities. Today Japanese children are more likely to watch television, read comic books, and play with video games than they were just a decade ago.

In some cultures, the availability of play spaces is at a premium. As the rain forests disappear in Africa and South America, the habitat of the Aka, Efe, and other hunting-gathering societies are endangered and families and children are becoming increasingly displaced. The types of play materials available from the immediate environment have diminished and the types of activities they invite may be curtailed. But this phenomenon is not restricted to subsistence societies. In the industrialized world, play space in large cities has diminished (see Pan, 1994) and traditional games children used to play are giving way to play with modern technological instruments. The impact of modern play materials (video games, power-rangers) on children's imaginative and aggressive tendencies is largely unknown.

Tied to the above points, is the concept of exporting "Western" cultural ideals. This has influenced the distribution of certain manufactured toys worldwide. In the first author's travel through South Asia, South America, and the West Indies, it was not unusual to see billboards with advertisements of Barbie Dolls and other play materials that are culturally tied to the United States. The tragedy behind the preference for toys that are specifically tied to the cultural values of the postindustrialized societies is obvious. For one, the use of native toys and play practices are questioned and in some instances discarded. There is the perception that play objects imported from the industrialized world are superior. At a time when there is a resurgence of ethnic pride here and abroad, educators and early childhood professionals may need to analyze this issue more carefully.

IMPLICATIONS FOR EARLY CHILDHOOD DEVELOPMENT/SCHOOLING

Several authors (e.g. Whiting & Edwards, 1988; see also Hewlett, 1992) have made excursions into the parental psychology of having and rearing children, while others (e.g. LeVine, 1987) have pointed to the hierarchy of goals parents adopt for children. Clearly, parents in preindustrial societies place a premium on children's survival above all else (LeVine, 1987), whereas in postindustrialized societies parental goals fall in line with the demands of the technological and highly structured environment. Thus, making recommendations regarding the role of play for childhood growth and development across cultures is obviously challenging if one is sensitive to the varying needs of diverse cultures. Nor do we know that adults and children in other societies place great stock in play in the systematic way that we do in the postindustrialized societies. Play seems such an integral part of rituals, festivals, and sociocultural activities in some societies that individuals "just play," even though its adaptive roles are not etched into the psyche of the players. People play because others have done so for generations and it seems enjoyable. With these points in mind, we offer some words of caution in looking at play as a viable "educational tool" in a formalized way, and concurrently discuss some implications for early childhood education.

As noted before, efforts to introduce play in a formalized curriculum must contend with different aspects of the child's sociocultural environment, including but not limited to parental beliefs about socialization, economic and social resources, the cultural construction of the concept of development, and the educational goals of specific societies, whether the case is made for children in the postindustrialized or in the developing countries of the world. Play themes and materials should reflect the cultural niche with the goals of fostering cultural identity and human dignity. In this regard, early childhood educators must be cognizant of the need to include toys, props, and related materials that are culture-relevant or reflect a multicultural focus for children in pluralistic societies. Early childhood professionals too must display the cultural savvy that is required to work with diverse groups of children. A good working knowledge of child development and parent-child relations in cultural contexts as well as an examination of cultural stereotypes we harbor are absolutely necessary.

The different cultural learning styles and avenues for learning that have proven to be adaptive must be considered in introducing play as a part of the early childhood curriculum. For example, some children display cultural learning styles that are wholistic rather than analytical (e.g., Native Indian children), whereas critical thinking conveyed through verbal skills of analysis may collide with the belief structures of promoting good listening and paying deference to elders in some cultures (e.g., Mexican-American families; Delgado-Gaitan, 1994). The early childhood curriculum must introduce play themes and activities that incorporate cultural practices central to socialization that are inherent in different cultures. After all, the goal of any good early childhood program is to imbue children with the adaptive skills that equip them to be productive members of society later on.

Play intervention should embrace culture-specific and society-wide goals. Play intervention strategies developed in the United States and Europe may not be relevant for some children because quite often the early childhood curricula reflect play materials and activities relevant to white families, disregarding the diverse environments within which children live. Similarly, cognitive enrichment programs may not be quite applicable in countries that value "social" rather than "technological" intelligence (see Greenfield, 1994). Some cultures place a heavy investment on interdependence and group activities with little room for individualistic pursuits. Unfortunately, in some developing countries, the play intervention strategies imported from the post-industrialized world are adopted in a wholesale manner because of their perceived superior quality. That is, they must "be good" because they come from the "developed world." Exporting early childhood practices as if they are sacred may lead us to superimpose our value structures and ideologies in a manner that suggests that these are the panaceas for the developing world. Further, importing early childhood philosophies that are play based without considering why it would work and how it might fit into different cultures may be frustrating in that the yields may be minimal when some societies have other more pressing health and nutritional agendas. Are we overpromising others because we are operating from a context of advantage?

Nor should we treat cultural norms and practices as static. As individual societies move toward implementing society-wide early childhood education programs, we must be aware of the social and technological changes that affect parent-child and peer relationships. In some cases it may be necessary to encourage parents to use play to stimulate children's development and to modify parenting styles that are harsher. Research conducted in Sudan has shown the powerful effects of short-term early play stimulation on children's cognitive development and the feasibility of modifying maternal interaction styles (Grotberg, Bardin, & King, 1987; Grotberg & Bardin, 1989).

Finally, there should be concerted efforts to preserve traditional modes of play through formal and informal efforts; simultaneously the impact of violence, wars, and other societal inflictions on children's play must be brought to the forefront of the world community. Recent studies have demonstrated the impact of violence on children's well-being (Cairns & Dawes, 1996; Garbarino & Kostelny, 1996) and the aggressive nature of children's spontaneous narratives in a riot torn area (Farver & Frosch, 1996). It appears that boys are more susceptible to the effects of prolonged violence than girls, and older children are less susceptible to negative developmental outcomes of wars and violence than younger children (Garbarino & Kostelny, 1996).

AFTERTHOUGHTS

We did not realize how challenging it would be to write a chapter of this nature. If we have omitted vital aspects of play across cultures, it was not deliberate. Above all, we hoped to expose the reader to complex and often related factors that govern any examination of children's play across cultures. The need to further consider sociocultural issues and play across cultures is obvious. On the theoretical front, perhaps intellectual efforts should temper the search for "universals" and acknowledge that cultures do achieve certain childrearing and socialization goals through different time-tested macro- and micro-cultural practices. Additional energy directed toward unraveling the cultural complexities behind the meaning of play will certainly capitalize on the individual differences among us.

REFERENCES

Baig, T. A. (1979). *Our children*. New Delhi: The Statesman Press.

Barker, R. G. & Wright, H. G. (1955). *Midwest and its children*. Englewood Cliffs, NJ: Prentice-Hall.

Bloch, M. N. (1988). The effect of seasonal maternal employment on young Senegalese children's behavior. *Journal of Comparative Family Studies, 19*(3), 397–417.

Bloch, M. (1989). Young boys' and girls' play at home and in the community: A cultural-ecological framework. In M. N. Bloch & A. D. Pellegrini (Eds.), *The ecological context of children's play* (pp. 120–154). Norwood, NJ: Ablex.

Bloch, M., & Adler, L. (1994). African children's play and the emergence of the sexual division of labor. In J. Roopnarine, J. Johnson, & F. Hooper (Eds.), *Children's play in diverse cultures* (pp. 148–178). Albany: State University of New York Press.

Bril, B., Zack, M., & Nkounkou-Hombessa, E. (1989). Ethnotheories of education and development. A view from different cultures. *European Journal of Psychology of Education, 4*, 307–318.

Brodber, E. (1974). *The abondonment of children in Tamaica*. Institute for Social and Economic Research, University of the West Indies, Kingston, Jamaica.

Bruner, J. (1972). Nature and uses of immaturity. *American Psychologist, 27,* 687–708.

Cairns, E., & Dawes, A. (1996). Children: Ethnic and political violence—A commentary. *Child Development, 67,* 129–139.

Delgado-Gaitan, C. (1994) Socializing children in Mexican-American families: An intergenerational perspective. In P. Greenfield & R. Cocking (Ed.), *Cross-cultural roots of minority child development* (pp. 55–86). Hillsdale, NJ: Lawrence Erlbaum.

Dixon, S., LeVine, R. A., Richman, A., & Brazelton, T. B. (1984). Mother-child interaction around a teaching task: An African-American comparison. *Child Development, 55,* 1252–1264.

Dixon, S., Tronick, E., Keefer, C., & Brazelton, T. B. (1981). Mother-infant interaction among the Gusii of Kenya. In T. Field et al. (Eds.), *Culture and Early Interactions* (pp. 149–168) Hillsdale, NJ: Lawrence Erlbaum.

Easterbrooks, M. A., & Lamb, M. E. (1979). The relationship between quality of infant-mother attachment and infant competence in initial encounters with peers. *Child Development, 50,* 380–387.

Eastman, C. M. (1986). Nyimbo Za Watoto: The Swahili child's world view. *Ethos, 14,* 144–173.

Ebbeck, F. (1973). Learning from play in other cultures. In J. L. Frost (Ed.), *Revisiting early childhood education* (pp 321–326). New York: Holt, Rinehart, & Winston.

Ellis, S., Rogoff, B., & Cromer, C. (1981). Age segregation in children's social interaction. *Developmental Psychology, 17,* 399–407).

Fajardo, B., & Freedman, D. (1981). Maternal rhythmicity in three American cultures. In T. Field, A Sostek, P. Vietze, & P. H. Leiderman (Eds.), *Culture and early interactions.* Hillsdale, NJ: Lawrence Erlbaum.

Farver, J., & Frosch, D. (1996). L.A. stories: Aggression in preschoolers' spontaneous narratives after the riots of 1992. *Child Development, 67,* 19–32.

Fernald, A., & O'Neill, D. (1993). Peek-a-boo across cultures. In K. Macdonald (Ed.), *Parent-child play* (pp. 259–285). Albany: State University of New York Press

Fogel, A., Nwokah, E., & Karns, J. (1993). Parent-infant games as dynamic social systems. In K. Macdonald (Ed.), *Parent-child play* (pp. 43–70) Albany: State University of New York Press.

Fogel, A., Toda, S., & Kawai, M. (1988). Mother-infant face-to-face interaction in Japan and the United States: A laboratory comparison using 3-month-old infants. *Developmental Psychology, 24,* 398–406.

Garbarino, J., & Kostelny, K. (1996). The effects of political violence on Palestinian children's behavior problems: A risk accumulation model. *Child Development*, 67, 33–45.

Gibson, M., & Ogbu, J. (Eds.) (1991). *Minority status and schooling: A comparative study of immigrant and involuntary minorities.* New York: Garland.

Greenfield, P. (1994). Independence and interdependence as developmental scripts: Implications for theory, research and practice. In P. Greenfield & R. Cocking (Eds.), *Cross-cultural roots of minority child development* (pp. 1–37). Hillsdale, NJ: Lawrence Erlbaum.

Grotberg, E., Bardin, G., & King, A. (1987). Changing childrearing practices in Sudan: An early stimulation demonstration program. *Children Today, 16*, 26–29.

Grotberg, E., & Badrin, G. (1989). Shifting from traditional to modern child rearing practices in the Sudan. *Early Child Development and Care, 50*, 141–150.

Hampton, J. (1989). Play and development in Zimbabewan children. *Early Child Development and Care, 47*, 1–61.

Harkness, S., & Super, C. (1985). The cultural context of gender segregation in children's peer groups. *Child Development, 56*, 216–224.

Harkness, S., & Super, C. (1986). The cultural structuring of children's play in a rural African community. In K. Blanchard (Ed.), *The many faces of play* (pp. 96–103). Champaign, IL: Human Kinetics.

Hewlett, B. (1987). Patterns of parental holding among Aka Pygmies. In M. E. Lamb (Ed.), *The father's role: Cross-cultural perspective* (pp. 295–330). Hillsdale, NJ: Lawrence Erlbaum.

Hewlett, B. (1992). The parent-infant relationship and social-emotional development among Aka Pygmies. In J. Roopnarine & D. B. Carter (Eds.), *Parent-child socialization in diverse cultures* (pp. 223–243). Norwood, NJ: Ablex.

Hughes, F. (1994). *Children, play and development.* New York: Allyn & Bacon.

Jipson, J. (1991). Developmentally appropriate practice: Culture, curriculum, connections. *Early Education and Development, 2*, 120–136.

Johnson, J. E., Christie, J. F., & Yawkey, T. D. (1987). *Play and early childhood development.* Glenview, IL: Scott, Foresman & Company.

Kakar, S. (1978). *The inner world: A psycho-analytic study of childhood and society in India.* New Delhi: Oxford University Press.

Konner, M. (1975). Relations among infants and juveniles in comparative perspective. In M. Lewis & L. Rosenblum (Eds.), *Friendship and peer relations* (pp. 99–129). New York: Wiley.

Lamb, M. E. (1985). Observational studies of father-child relationships in humans. In D. Taub (Ed.), *Primate paternalism* (pp. 407–430). New York: Van Nostrand Reinhold.

Lamb, M., Frodi, A., Frodi, M., Hwang, C., & Steinberg, J. (1982). Characteristics of maternal and paternal behavior in traditional and non-traditional Swedish families. *International Journal of Behavioral Development, 5*, 450–458.

Lamb, M., Sternberg, K., Hwang, C., & Broberg, A. (Eds.). (1992). *Child care in context*. Hillsdale, NJ: Lawrence Erlbaum.

Lancy, D. (1977). The play behavior of Kpelle children during rapid cultural change. In D. F. Lancy and B. A. Tindall (Eds.), *The anthropological study of play: Problems and prospects* (pp. 72–79). West Point, NY: Leisure Press.

Leacock, E. (1976). At play in African villages. In J. S. Bruner, A. Jolly, & K. Sylva (Eds.), *Play: Its role in development and evolution* (pp. 466–473). New York: Basic Books.

Lever, J. (1993). Sex differences in the complexity of children's play and games. In R. Wozniak (Ed.), *Worlds of childhood*. New York: Harper/Collins.

LeVine, R. A. (1987). Human parental care: Universal goals, cultural strategies, individual behavior. In R. LeVine, P. Miller, & M. West (Eds.), *Parental behavior in diverse societies* (pp. 3–12). San Francisco: Jossey-Bass.

LeVine, R. A., & White, M. I. (1986). *Human conditions: The cultural basis of educational development*. New York: Routledge & Kegan Paul.

Liddell, C. (1988). The social interaction and activity patterns of children from two San groups living as refugees on a Namibian military base. *Journal of Cross-Cultural Psychology, 19*, 341–360.

Liddell, C., & Kruger, P. (1987). Patterns of activity and social behavior in a South African township nursery: Some effects of crowding. *Merrill-Palmer Quarterly, 33*, 206–228.

Liddell, C., & Kvalsvig, J. (1991). *Urbanicity as a predictor of children's social behavior and activity patterns: Black South African children in the year before school.* Unpublished manuscript.

Liddell, C., Kvalsvig, J., Strydom, N., Qotyana, P., & Shabalala, A. (undated). *An observational study of five-year-old Black South African children in the year before school*. Unpublished manuscript.

Lu, M. (1987). *Maternal and paternal assessments of their activities with their infants in Kuching, Malaysia*. Unpublished master's thesis, Syracuse University.

Maccoby, E. (1990). Gender and relationships. *American Psychologist, 45*, 513–520.

Macdonald, K. (Ed.). (1993). *Parent-child play*. Albany: State University of New York Press.

Martini, M. (1994). Peer interactions in Polynesia: A view from the Marquesas. In J. Roopnarine, J. Johnson, & F. Hooper (Eds.), *Children's play in diverse cultures* (pp. 73–103). Albany: State University of New York Press.

Martini, M., & Kirkpatrick, J. (1992). Parenting in Polynesia: A view from the Marquesas. In J. L. Roopnarine & B. Carter (Eds.), *Parent-child socialization in diverse cultures* (pp. 199–222). Norwood NJ: Ablex.

Monighan-Nourot, P., Scales, B., Van Hoorn, J., & Almy, M. (1988). *Looking at children's play: A bridge between theory and practice.* New York: Teachers College Press.

Morelli, G. A. (1986). *Social development of 1, 2, and 3 year old Efe and Lese children within the Ituri Forest of Northeastern Zaire: The relation amongst culture, setting, and development.* Ph.D. dissertation, University of Massachusetts, Amherst.

Munroe, R. H., & Munroe, R. L. (1984a). Infant experiences and childhood cognition: A longitudinal study among the Logoli of Kenya. *Ethos, 12,* 291–306.

Munroe, R. H., & Munroe, R. L. (1984b) Children's work in four cultures: Determinants and consequences. *American Anthropologist, 86,* 369–379.

Munroe, R. L., & Munroe, R. H. (1994). *Cross-cultural human development.* Prospect Heights, IL: Waveland Press.

Munroe, R. H., & Munroe, R. L., Michelson, C., Bolton, C., & Bolton, C. (1983). Time allocation in four societies. *Ethnology, 22,* 255–270.

Muralidharan, R., Khosla, R., Main, G., & Kaur, B. (1981). *Children's games.* New Delhi: Child Study Unit of National Council of Educational Research and Training.

Negussie, B. (1989). *Health, nutrition and informal education of preschool children in south-west Ethiopia.* Paper presented at the International Conference on Early Education and Development, Hong Kong.

New, R. & Benigni, L. (1987). Italian fathers and infants: Cultural constraints on paternal behavior. In M. E. Lamb (Eds.), *The father's role: Crosscultural perspectives* (pp. 139–167). Hillsdale: Lawerence Erlbaum.

Nwokah, E. (1987). Maidese versus motherese-is the language input of child and adult caregivers similar? *Language and Speech, 30,* 213–237.

Ogbu, J. (1981). Origins of human competence: A cultural-ecological perspective. *Child Development, 52,* 413–429.

Pan, W. H. L. (1994). Children's play in Taiwan. In J. Roopnarine, J. Johnson, & F. Hooper (Eds.), *Children's play in diverse cultures* (pp. 31–50). Albany: State University of New York Press.

Panksepp, J. (1993). Rough and tumble play: A fundamental brain process. In K. Macdonald (Ed.), *Parent-child play* (pp. 147–184). Albany: State University of New York Press.

Parke, R., & Ladd, G. (Eds.). (1992). *Family-peer relationships*. Hillsdale, NJ: Lawrence Erlbaum.

Parker, J. G., & Asher, S. R. (1987). Peer relations and later personal adjustment: Are low-accepted children at risk? *Psychological Bulletin, 102*, 357–359.

Powell, D. (Ed.). (1988). *Parent education as early childhood intervention: Emerging directions in theory, research, and practice*. Norwood, NJ: Ablex.

Ramsey, P. G. (1987). *Teaching and learning in a diverse world: Multicultural education for young children*. New York: Teachers College Press.

Ranter, N., & Bruner, J. S. (1978). Games, social exchange, and the acquisition of language. *Journal of Child Language, 5*, 391–402.

Reynolds, P. (1989). *Childhood in crossroads*. Cape Town: David Philip.

Richter, L. M., Grieve, K. W. E., & Austin D. (1988). Scaffolding by Bantu mothers during object play with their infants. *Early Child Development and Care, 34*, 63–75.

Rogoff, B. (1990). *Apprenticeship in thinking: Cognitive development in social context*. New York: Oxford University Press.

Roopnarine, J. L., Ahmeduzzaman, M., Hossain, Z., & Riegraf, N. B. (1992). Parent-infant rough play: Its cultural specificity. *Early Education and Development, 4*, 298–311.

Roopnarine, J. L., & Bright, J. (1993). The social individual model: Mixed-age socialization. In J. Roopnarine & J. Johnson (Eds.), *Approaches to early childhood education* (pp. 223–242). Columbus, OH: Merrill/Macmillan.

Roopnarine, J. L. & Brown, J. (Eds.) (1997). *Caribbean families: Diversity among ethnic groups*. Norwood NJ: Ablex.

Roopnarine, J. L. & Carter, B. (1992a). The cultural context of socialization: A much ignored issue. In J. Roopnarine & D. B. Carter (Eds.), *Parent-child socialization in diverse cultures* (pp. 245–251). Norwood, NJ: Ablex.

Roopnarine, J. L. & Carter, B. (Eds.). (1992b). *Parent-child socialization in diverse cultures*. Norwood, NJ: Ablex.

Roopnarine, J. L., Hooper, F. H., Ahmeduzzaman, M., & Pollack, B. (1993). Gentle play partners: Mother-child and father-child play in New Delhi, India, In K. Macdonald (Ed.), *Parents and children playing* (pp 287–304). Albany: State University of New York Press.

Roopnarine, J. Johnson, J. & Hooper, F. (Eds.) (1994). *Children's play in diverse cultures.* Albany: State University of New York Press.

Roopnarine, J. L., Lu, M. W., & Ahmeduzzaman, M. (1989). Parental reports of early patterns of caregiving, play, and discipline in India and Malaysia. *Early Child Development and Care, 50,* 109–120.

Roopnarine, J. L., Talukder, E., Jain, D., Josh P. & Srivastav, P. (1990). Characteristics of holding, patterns of play, and social behaviors between parents and infants in New Delhi, India. *Developmental Psychology, 26,* 667–673.

Rubin, K., Fein, G., & Vandenburg, B. (1983). Play. In P. H. Mussen (Ed.), *Handbook of child psychology: Vol. 4. Socialization, personality and social development* (pp. 393–474). New York: Wiley.

Sagi, A., Lamb, M., Shosham, R., Dvir, R., & Lewkowics, K. (1985). Parent-infant interaction in families on Israeli Kibbutzim. *International Journal of Behavioral Development, 8,* 273–284.

Saracho, O. N., & Spodek, B. (1990). Early childhood teacher preparation in cross-cultural perspective. In B. Spodek & O. Saracho (Eds.), *Early childhood teacher preparation* (pp. 103–117). New York: Teachers College Press.

Schwartzman, H. (1978). *Transformations: The anthropology of children's play.* New York: Plenum.

Schwartzman, H. (1986). A cross-cultural perspective on child-structure play activities and materials. In A. W. Gottfried and C. C. Brown (Eds.), *Play Interactions: The contributions of play materials and parental involvement to children's development.* Proceedings of the eleventh Johnson and Johnson pediatric round table (pp. 13–29). Lexington, MA: Lexington Books.

Schwartzman, H., & Barbera, L. (1977). Children's play in Africa and South America: A review of the ethnographic literature. In D. F. Lancy and B. A. Tindall (Eds.), *The anthropological study of play: Problems and prospects.* (pp. 11–21). Cornwall, NY: Leisure Press.

Segal, M. (1993). Classes for parents and young children: The Farnily Center Model. In J. L. Roopnarine & J. Johnson, J. (Eds.), *Approaches to early childhood education* (pp. 33–45). Columbus, OH: Merrill.

Slaughter, D., & Dombrowski, J. (1989). Cultural continuities and discontinuities: Impact on social and pretend play. In M. N. Block & A. D. Pellegrini (Eds.), *The ecological content of children's play* (pp. 282–310). Norwood, NJ: Ablex.

Sostek, A. M., Vietze, P., Zaslow, M., Kreiss, L., Van der Waals, F., & Rubenstein, D. (1981). Social context in caregiver-infant interaction. A film study of Fais and the United States. In T. Field, A. M. Sostek, P. Vietze, & P. H. Leiderman (Eds.), *Culture and early interactions* (pp. 21–37). Hillsdale, NJ: Lawrence Erlbaum.

Soto, L., & Negron, L. (1994). Mainland Puerto Rican children. In J. L. Roopnarine, J. Johnson, & F. Hooper (Eds.), *Children's play in diverse cultures* (pp. 104–122). Albany: State University of New York Press.

Spodek, B. & Saracho, O. (1990) (Eds.). *Early childhood teacher preparation.* New York: Teachers College Press.

Stern, D. (1974). Mother and infant play: The dyadic interaction involving facial, vocal, and gait behaviors. In M. Lewis & L. Rosenblum (Eds.), *The effect of the infant on its caregiver* (pp. 187–213). New York: Wiley.

Stern, D. (1977). *The first relationship.* Cambridge, MA: Harvard University Press.

Sun, L., & Roopnarine, J. (1996). Mother-infant and father-infant interaction and involvement in childcare and household labor among Taiwanese families. *Infant Behavior and Development, 19,* 121–129.

Sutton-Smith, B. (1976). (Ed.). *A children's game anthology.* New York: Arno Press.

Sutton-Smith, B. (1993). Dilemmas in adult play with children. In K. Macdonald (Ed.), *Parent-child play* (pp. 15–40). Albany: State University of New York Press

Swaminathan, M. (1985). *Who cares? A study of child care facilities for low-income working women in India.* Center for Women's Development Studies. New Delhi: Indraprastha Press.

Takeuchi, M. (1994) Children's play in Japan. In J. Roopnarine, J. Johnson, & F. Hooper (Eds.), *Children's play in diverse cultures* (pp. 51–72). Albany: State University of New York Press.

Tobin, J. J., Wu, D. Y., & Davidson, D. H. (1989). *Preschool in three cultures: Japan, China, and the United States.* New Haven, CT: Yale University Press.

Tronick, E., Beeghley, M., Fetters, L., & Weinberg, K. (1991). New methodologies for evaluating residual brain damage in infants exposed to drug abuse: Objective methods for describing movement, facial expressions, and communicative behaviors. NIDA Monograph Series, *"Methodological Controlled Studies on the Effects of Prenatal Exposure to Drug Abuse," 114,* 262–290.

Udwin, O., & Shmukler, D. (1981). The influence of sociocultural, economic, and home background factors on children's ability to engage in imaginative play. *Developmental Psychology. 17,* 66-72.

Van Hoorn, J. (1987). Games that babies and mothers play. In P. Monighan-Nourot, B. Scales, J. Van Hoorn, & M. Almy. *Looking at children's play: A bridge between theory and practice* (pp. 38–62). Teachers College Press.

Vygotsky, L. S. (1978). *Mind in society*. Cambridge, MA: Harvard University Press.

Whiting, B. B. (1980). Culture and social behavior. *Ethos, 2,* 95–116.

Whiting, B. B., & Edwards, C. P. (1988). *Children of different worlds*. Cambridge, MA: Harvard University Press.

Chapter 11

Play and the Assessment of Young Children

A. D. Pellegrini

Play and assessment are two terms currently being used with great frequency in early childhood education. Play, as we are often told, is very important in the lives of young children: Children must play if they are to remain and develop into healthy and socially competent individuals. To these ends, play is often presented as a counterweight to the excessive demands of less child-centered approaches to education. For example, it is advocated in the National Association for the Education of Young Children (NAEYC, 1992a,b) guidelines for developmentally appropriate practice for preschool and primary school children. Consequently, play has been "institutionalized" (Sutton-Smith, 1995) in preschools, children's museums, public parks, and in the home.

Assessment, too, is an ever present force in educational and child-care settings. Assessment typically involves the systematic documentation of children's progress through educational institutions. In the best cases, it is used to by teachers to help improve instruction. Simultaneously, assessment is also concerned with the impact of educational programs on children's learning and development. In the present age of accountability, funding agencies, whether they be politicians, taxpayers, or parents, rightly want documentation of the impact of programs on children's lives. Unlike play, however, assessment is seen as threatening the emotional well-being of children. Taking the NAEYC as a bellwether again, we find that "narrowly defined" cognitive skills and norm-referenced assessment are considered inappropriate practice (1992b).

Consequently, play and assessment, despite their co-occurrence in today's schools, make very strange bedfellows. At one level they seem very incompatible. Play is conceptualized as a child-defined activity where the "means" of an activity are more important than the "ends" of the activity (See

Rubin, Fein, & Vandenberg, 1983; Smith & Vollstedt, 1985). Assessment contexts, on the other hand, are typically defined by adults, rather than children, and are concerned with end products of an activity, whether they be children's projects or the children's ability to cooperate with peers.

Can these two seemingly opposite constructs be reconciled? In this chapter I will attempt to do so. First, I will briefly define what I mean by play and assessment. Next, I review some of the controversy surrounding the assessment of young children and the use of children's play as an assessment context. Third, I discuss one compelling theory of play that suggests play can be applied to assessing young children. Fourth, I provide some guidance in using play as a form of assessment. I conclude with a note of caution for the field.

DEFINING TERMS: PLAY AND ASSESSMENT

The definition of each of these frequently used terms is a reasonable starting point. Putting aside the debate over operational and formal definitions (Chalmers, 1980; Mathews & Mathews, 1982), clarity and consistency in the use of terms is crucial in any sort of communication, particularly a discussion involving such a "high stakes" issue as assessment. Consistency in the meaning assigned to words is needed where the same terms are used by different constituents. For example, some consider most forms of unstructured peer interaction "play," while others take a more measured approach, considering play only those behaviors meeting specific criteria. With assessment, clarity is important to the extent that all assessment should make very explicit what it is assessing, if for no other reason than to indicate the content and construct validity of the assessment. The importance of clarity and consistency of terms should be very clear when we consider the fact that assessment has an impact on the lives of children, their families, and their schools.

Play is a very difficult construct to define (Wilson, 1975). Many consider the task a nearly impossible one (Bekoff & Byers, 1981), while others, recognizing this difficulty, have presented very clear-cut criteria for defining play (Caro & Martin, 1985). Those most successful at the difficult task of defining have suggested that play be defined according to numerous criteria as no one set of behaviors or descriptors is sufficient (Martin & Caro, 1985). Most commonly, play is defined according to structural, functional, and dispositional criteria. As more thorough discussions are available elsewhere (Martin & Caro, 1985; Pellegrini & Boyd, 1993; Smith & Cowie, 1988), I will only present a brief definition of play.

Structural definitions include descriptions of specific behaviors that co-occur under the rubric of play. Those behaviors typically included in definitions of play are: positive affect, exaggerated movements and vocalizations, and reciprocal role taking. Functional dimensions of play are concerned with consequences of target behavior. Playful behaviors have "nonserious" consequences, that is, the outcome of a play behavior differences from its serious counterpart. For example, rough-and-tumble play and aggression are behaviorally similar in some ways. Rough-and-tumble play is play because its consequence is not serious: It does end in someone's getting hurt as is the case with aggression. When rough-and-tumble bouts end children continue to interact, often in cooperative games (Pellegrini, 1988). Rough behavior that is aggressive and not playful, on the other, results in one of the participants trying to leave the field of interaction.

Dispositional criteria, as they are labelled by Rubin and colleagues (Rubin et al., 1983), include flexibility (or negotiating and following self or group defined rules), positive affect, intrinsic (contrasted with extrinsic) motivation, nonliterality (or make-believe), attention to means (not ends), and "What can I do with it?" (compared to "What can it do?"). As we will discuss later, these dispositional criteria are particularly important in our discussion of assessment. Taken together, the paradigm case of play (Mathews & Mathews, 1982) for preschool children is social pretend. For this reason we will concentrate on social fantasy play in this chapter.

Assessment refers to the process of collecting information on children, typically through observations, tests, teacher checklists, and so on, in order to make inferences about their status, typically in school-related areas. It should be stressed that not all assessment involves testing; testing is merely one dimension of assessment. Commonly, assessment is used in early childhood education as a way to determine children's progress toward some developmental hallmark or, more insidiously, to determine school "readiness" (see Shephard & Graue, 1993, for a critique), academic tracking, or grade retention (see Meisels, Steele, & Quinn-O'Leering, 1993, for a critique). Besides these more questionable uses, assessment is sometimes used to gauge students' progress either normatively or in relation to some criterion. "High stakes" assessment refers to cases where assessment data are used for promotion from one grade to another or to place children in special programs, such as remedial classes. Also, assessment is used to gauge the impact of an educational program; for example, assessment techniques are used to determine the impact of Head Start on children's subsequent school status.

ISSUES IN ASSESSING YOUNG CHILDREN

Assessment of young children in school settings has a very stormy history, a history that continues into the present with little likelihood of immediate abeyance. The storminess derives primarily from the misuse of one specific form of assessment, tests, with young children. Tests typically have been limited to assessing restricted dimensions of children's cognitive status, and the scores are then used to make "high stakes" decisions, such as grade retention. An important part of the controversy is the argument that young children are not very good test-takers, resulting in test scores that are typically unreliable; thus, high-stakes decisions are made with very questionable data.

Young children are indeed not terribly good test-takers. As we have known for a number of years (see Messick, 1983, for a review), children's performance on tests varies considerably, depending upon a number of ecological factors; consequently, test-retest reliability coefficients of tests for young children are typically low, if they are reported at all. This problem of stability of scores reflects children's extreme susceptibility to external factors, such as race and gender of the tester, and test format issues, such as familiarity with props or use of separate answer sheets. A reason for this phenomenon may be that children are not very motivated to perform on a task that they probably see as uninteresting and associated with teacher-, parent-, and self-related anxiety. Given these problems with tests, it becomes very questionable (to put it mildly) when they are used in "high stakes" situations.

Tests, even when their technical properties are adequate, often assess a very limited universe of competence (Miller-Jones, 1989). Tests for young children have been and continue to be concerned primarily with their cognitive processing (often assessing only low-level processes) to the exclusion of the social-emotional aspects of children's lives (Zigler & Trickett, 1978). We have been aware of this limitation problem for a number of years.

In light of the these limitations and the terrible misuses of tests in the past, one is tempted to question the role of assessment (to be distinguished from tests) of young children. This is too simple a solution to a very complex problem. I do not advocated throwing out the baby (i.e., reasonable information gathered from different sorts of assessment procedures) with the bath water (i.e., inappropriate use of tests). Assessment of young children, when it is done in an appropriate way, can provide information that is very useful to caregivers, parents, and teachers. "Good" (read: valid) assessment for young children must overcome the limitations of more tradition forms of assessment, such as tests. A major problem seems to be children's lack of motivation to perform in a situation that is uninteresting and anxiety producing. In addition to this, we must begin to assess a wider variety of sophisticated social cognitive skills and strategies.

A particularly fruitful approach to assessing young children involves observing them as they interact with their peers in situations that are simultaneously motivating and demanding high levels of social cognitive processing (Pellegrini, 1992; Waters & Sroufe, 1983; Scarr, 1981). High levels of motivation are necessary if children are to sustain their attention and activity in the assessment context. The assessment context must also be demanding enough for children to have opportunities to exhibit their full range of competence. Observations of children's "play" seems to be a context that meets both these criteria.

PLAY AS A CONTEXT FOR ASSESSMENT

Children enjoy playing. The joy that they experience in play is evidenced by the hallmark of play, the "play face" or wide grin/smile. Indeed, most definitions of play, across many species, include play face as a basic play marker. The inherent joy of play is a signal that children are motivated to play. Simply put, children want to play because they enjoy it; they are, following some definitions of play, "intrinsically motivated" to engage in play (Rubin et al., 1983).

What does joy, smiling, and intrinsic motivation have to do with assessment? When individuals are happy and motivated to engage in activities such as play, they are often willing to expend considerable time and energy in the service of these acts. For example, when two children who are friends and who enjoy each other's company are interacting with each other, they are usually willing to compromise their possessions so as to sustain their interaction. Thus, unlike most testing situations, children see a value in play and are willing to spend considerable social and cognitive resources in it. With this as a basic proposition, the task for assessors is to derive meaningful observational measures of play that provide insight into children's social and cognitive status.

A reasonable starting place seems to be observations of children playing with peers. Play with peers, as Piaget (1970) observed, demands considerable social cognitive sophistication. Briefly, when children engage in most sorts of *social* play a number of very demanding social cognitive skills must be exercised in order for play to be maintained. If children do not use these skills, play will break down. Because breakdowns usually lead to children separating, they typically try their utmost to avoid them. Two examples of the skills necessary to sustain social play during the preschool period follow.

First and probably most basic, social play demands that children take each other's perspective. The reciprocal role-taking characteristic of social play certainly necessitates that children view events from different perspectives (Burns & Brainerd, 1979). Second, and relatedly, in order to communicate fantastic (and consequently very abstract) play themes and enactments, children must use a very sophisticated form of explicit oral language (Pellegrini & Galda, 1993). This form of language verbally encodes meaning, minimizing reliance on shared knowledge between players to convey meaning. Without such verbal explication, players do not understand the meaning of play overtures, and play is usually terminated (Garvey, 1984, 1990). Consequently, children draw upon a wide range of their social cognitive and linguistic resources in the service of sustaining social play simply because they enjoy it.

These dimensions of children's social play could easily be expanded into an observational instrument or teacher/parent checklist to indicate social cognitive competence. For example, we could consider the number of different roles a child enacts. Does the child and his/her playmate disagree? How do they resolve the disagreement? Regarding oral language, we could record the extent to which children explicitly define play roles and other transformations. Do they use conjunctions to weave play themes? Garvey (1990) has a whole array of language measures that we might consider. Our research suggests that children's use of these language forms in preschool are reliable predictors of more traditional forms of achievement (reading and writing) in primary school (Pellegrini, 1991, 1993).

By way of contrast, children probably exhibit low levels of competence, or at least inconsistent levels, on tests because they are not motivated to perform. This lack of motivation, or at least variable levels of motivation, is reflected in the low rates of test-retest reliability for most young children. Somehow, preschool kids do not seem to be concerned with the link (as tenuous as it may be) between test performance and increased earning power as adults!

VYGOTSKY'S THEORY AND ITS ROLE IN ASSESSMENT

Vygotsky's discussion of play, centered around the play of the preschool child, was concerned with symbolic play. A primary concern for Vygotsky (1967), as stated in the title of his article, "Play and Its Role in the Mental Development of the Child," was the role of symbolic play in children's subsequent development: Through symbolic play children come to organize meaning in language and thought (Fein, 1979).

Children are motivated to play, in this catharsis-like theory, because of their desire to fulfill unrealizable tendencies (Fein, 1979). A child may make a broom a horse because of her desire to own and ride a horse. Correspondingly, as children are realizing the unrealizable in play, they are also confronted with the desire to impose societal rules on their play. Thus, a dialectical tension exists between doing what brings pleasure and subordinating those same actions to rules that limit that pleasure. The quest for desire provides a

strong motivational component to act, while the omnipresence of rules introduces impulse control. Children's play actions come to be mediated by this
desire-rule tension. The ability to have one's actions guided by meaningful
rules, which first appears in symbolic play, is generalized to other aspects of
children's lives, primarily their language.

These two aspects of play (high motivation to satisfy desires and the
cognitive sophistication to subordinate these desires to rules) are crucial in the
discussion of play as a mode of assessment. For Vygosky, play created a "zone
of proximal development." In this zone, children exhibit higher levels of competence than when outside it. The more familiar rendering of the zone
involves children exhibiting higher levels of competence, compared to solitary or peer activities, when they interact with a more competent partner; the
more competent partner can guide children through an otherwise non-nego-
tiable terrain. Children use these skills with adults, or more competent agemates, before they are capable of using them alone. The zone of proximal
development was an important assessment/diagnostic construct because it
revealed children's optimum levels of competence, whereas more traditional
assessment contexts often inhibited exhibition of high levels of competence.

In play, the zone of proximal development operates in a fashion similar
to when children interact with more competent partners. Children, most
importantly, are motivated to engage in play because they derive pleasure
from it. Moreover, there are cognitive demands inherent in subordinating
these desires to rules. Thus, in play we have a wonderful mixture of children
being motivated and this motivation is directed toward highly sophisticated
goals. For this reason, Vygotsky believed, children tend to exhibit higher levels of competence in play than in more traditional assessment contexts.

USING PLAY AS AN ASSESSMENT CONTEXT

We can now agree, as good developmentalists, that play is a reasonable
context in which to assess children to the extent that it supports their exhibition of maximum competence. Given the abuses of other forms of assessment,
play seems like an almost "too good to be true" answer to the problem of
assessing young children. As noted above, we have a limited understanding of
the value of play. Thus, in using play to assess, as when we use other forms
of assessment, we should exercise caution and utilize a broad base of strategies.

I will discuss some basic principles that are helpful in designing assessment programs: developmental hallmarks and children's ecological sensitivity. My recommendations are however, limited to using direct observations of
children behaviors as a means of assessment. It is my opinion that direct

observations of play, while time consuming and expensive, are ultimately the best way to assess children. Other approaches, such as teacher and parent checklists and rating scales, are also available, though I will not discuss them here.

Developmental Hallmarks

A developmental perspective implies that individuals at certain periods of developmental are *qualitatively* different from individuals at other periods. Thus what we expect from a 2-year-old should be qualitatively different from what we expect from a 10-year-old. Differences in quantity, not quality, involve cases where the different groups are capable of the same task or concept, but there will be differences in the amount that each is capable of. For example, groups of children 2-year-olds and 10-year-olds can both walk, yet they probably differ in terms of speed and endurance. These are differences in quantity or degree. These two groups are also different in quality or kind. The younger children are not capable of making inferences about others' mental states, whereas the older group is. The needs and capabilities of each are different, and as developmentalists our teaching and assessment should examine hallmarks specific to the periods under consideration.

Bringing assessment into sharper focus, a developmental perspective dictates that we assess those hallmarks that are important for a specific developmental period. First, by way of negative example, we don't take a skill appropriate for older children, such as working alone on a writing task, and impose it on preschool children. While this task is appropriate for a third grader, it less appropriate for a preschooler, given their differences in information-processing capabilities (Bjorklund & Green, 1992).

Fortunately, we have some positive examples to guide our teaching and assessment. Waters and Sroufe (1983, p. 85) have targeted developmental hallmarks, with an eye on assessment issues, from infancy though the preschool period. Using the construct of social competence as a basis for assessment, they suggest the following salient issues for assessing young children. Thus, in assessing young children we should be concerned primarily with assessing salient points in their development. We should guard against exporting issues relevant to older children into younger periods. The basic idea is that children should be assessed on criteria appropriate for their age group, not on criteria for older children.

Ecological Sensitivity

This section is concerned primarily with the effects of contextual and venue variables on fantasy and the ways in which they affect issues related to assessment. In considering play, especially as an assessment context, it is impor-

TABLE 11.1
SALIENT ISSUES IN DEVELOPMENT

Age in Months	Issue
0–3	Physiological regulation
3–6	Tension management
6–12	Establishing attachment relationship
12–18	Exploration and mastery
18–30	Autonomy
30–54	Impulse management
	Sex role identification
	Peer relations

tant to recognize contextual factors that both elicit and inhibit play. Within classrooms there are numerous micro-level variables that affect children's exhibition of competence in fantasy play. I will discuss only a few, as they are reviewed thoroughly elsewhere (e.g., Rubin et al., 1983; Smith & Connolly, 1980).

First, the presence of adults and children affects the level of fantasy play. At a gross level, we know that for preschool children (that is, around 3 to 6 years of age) adult presence actually inhibits children's exhibition of fantasy and forms of oral language associated with fantasy (Pellegrini, 1984). Peer presence, on the other hand, facilitates fantasy (Pellegrini, 1984; Pellegrini & Perlmutter, 1989). These findings correspond to Piaget's (1970) discussions of the role of peer interaction, and the corresponding forms of reciprocal interaction, on development. At a more differentiated level, we find that not all peers are equal in their facilitation of fantasy. When children play with friends, compared to nonfriends, the duration of play is longer and level of play is higher (Howes, 1992).

Children's fantasy is also influenced by the props with which they are interacting. Generally, children's play tends to follow the themes suggested by play props, even though they are capable of transforming the meaning of props from the second year of life (Rubin et al., 1983). So children playing with doctor props are likely to enact doctor/patient themes. The sex role stereotypicality of the toys, however, will also influence the degree to which children participate in play themes. Generally, boys and girls exhibit the highest levels of competence in play with gender-consistent toys (Huston, 1983; Pellegrini & Perlmutter, 1989). Boys are more reluctant than girls to play with toys preferred by the opposite gender. Consequentially, if we want to maximize children's exhibition of competence in an assessment context, we should have them playing with toys preferred by their gender.

Regarding venue, I will discuss the relative merits of observing children in their "natural" habitats, for example, classrooms or homes, and in contrived settings such as experimental playrooms. The differences discussed here are often the differences between experimental and field approaches to child study. Contrived settings, like experimental playrooms, have the inherent benefits and costs of a controlled environment. This approach allows us to control and manipulate variables in the service of causal explanations. The costs are equally familiar. Like testing contexts, contrived settings often inhibit children's maximum exhibition of competence. Only after children become familiar with the playroom and the experimenter do they feel safe enough to exhibit high levels of competence. Habituation is accomplished, usually, by first having the experimenter spend prolonged periods of time in the children's classrooms. Next, children should be observed on more than one occassion, and then the data from those sessions should be aggregated across sessions.

If we opt for field study of children's play, we typically observe children in their classrooms, playgrounds, and homes. A short list of precautions is necessary in this sort of work. First and foremost, we must be aware that in such settings, unlike experimental settings, we are observing children where they choose to be observed and where they exhibit those competencies that they choose to exhibit. In short, in most classrooms, especially during free play periods, children *self-select* themselves into certain contexts. While in those contexts, they exhibit those skills and behaviors that they choose to exhibit; they usually do not have an adult trying to elicit specific skills and behaviors. With this in mind, we recognize that the play that children are exhibiting is indicative not only of their level of social cognitive sophistication, self-selection, and preferred mode of interaction but also of other contextual variables. For example, the toys and peers that children play with have important, interactive effects on the types of play they exhibit (Pellegrini & Perlmutter, 1989). Children's play, as noted above, is related to their playmates' status (e.g., friends compared to nonfriends) and to their preference for certain props, among other things.

We must come to terms with these multiple influences on children's play if we want to use play to assess children. This can be accomplished in at least two ways. First, we can sample children's play behaviors across a wide variety of play environments in their classrooms or home, aggregate those observations, and then make a general statement about their competence. This is a reasonable procedure for making inferences about competence in general as we are sampling across a wide array of contexts. Further, aggregate data, compared to data from disparate sources, are more stable (i.e., reliable) because measurement error is minimized.

Alternatively, we could observe children only when they are present in a specified play location, for example, in the dramatic play center. In this way we make limited, though more specific, inferences. In either case, we must accumulate a representative number of observations of individual children.

Regarding experimental or contrived analogues of "natural" settings, we recognize the effect of contextual variables and we design settings to elicit specific forms of play. In contrived settings, too, we must be concerned with adequate samples of behavior. To this end, it seems reasonable to observe children a number of times in each play context and then aggregate the multiple observations into one score. So, for example, if we are interested in the effect of play configurations PC1 and PC2 on children's pretend play, we would observe children twice in PC1 and twice in PC2; the scores for PC1 and PC2 would be the aggregate of each of the two observations in each setting. The idea behind this strategy is quite simple. Given the contrived nature of experiments, children need time to habituate to these settings. Multiple observations allow them to do this. Again, aggregate scores of multiple observations are more stable than single scores.

Critics of experimental approaches most often question the validity of results derived from contrived settings. The argument typically goes something like this: Results from experiments settings don't generalize to "real" settings, thus they lack external validity. Further, the experimental analogues often do not resemble the real worlds in which children live, thus they lack ecological validity. Bronfenbrenner (1979) suggests a solution to this conundrum by proposing that we design ecologically valid experiments. To accomplish this task, our experiments should resemble the world in which children interact both in terms of social and material configurations and in terms of expectations.

So, for example, if we wanted to determine the ways in which children played with specific toys, we would first observe children in classrooms to determine the toys that they played with and the social configurations in which the play was embedded. Let's say that children played primarily with blocks and dramatic props. The former context typically had dyads of boys in it, while the latter had dyads of boys and dyads of girls. In terms of expectations, children in our hypothetical classrooms were expected (required) by their teachers to play in a variety of centers in each week; if they didn't, teachers encouraged them to do so.

With this descriptive information in mind, we could design an ecologically valid experiment by observing the same or similar children that we observed in the classroom in male and female dyads interacting with blocks and dramatic props. That we manipulated their exposure to these contexts would not be inconsistent with their classroom expectations (see Pellegrini & Perlmutter, 1989) because the demand characteristics are the same in the experiment and in the classroom. The benefits of ecologically valid experiments are large in that they provide specific (cause-effect) information about children's play and environments that are meaningful to children. The costs of such experiments, too, are large. They require that naturalistic data be collected and then used to design experiments and multiple observations in each setting.

The influence of familiarity of props on play is related to the venue issue to some degree. When we assess children's play, especially in contrived settings, we typically give them a set of materials, or toys, to play with. An implicit assumption in this approach is that the toys will be equally meaningful to all children, and that variations in play will be indicative of variations in children's developmental competence.

This was the very assumption at work as researchers were studying the cognitive sophistication of children from different socioeconomic backgrounds (see Rubin et al., 1983). As good developmentalists, these researcher used play to uncover the deep secrets of children's cognitive developmental status. Middle-class and poor children were given toys to play with and inferences were made about their cognitive status relative to their social class. Interestingly, the toys that these children were typically given were more familiar to middle-class children than to lower-class children, thus suppressing the play level of the latter group relative to the former group. (See McLoyd, 1982, for an interesting discussion of reported SES differences in play.)

When children are presented with a set of toys that is unfamiliar to them, they do not initially play with it, they explore it. Recall that in my definition of play, I stressed that play was governed by the question: What can *I* do with it? Exploration, on the other hand, is guided by the question: What can *it* do? Before children can play with an object, they must explore it (Belsky & Most, 1981; Pellegrini & Boyd, 1993). The information that they gather from their exploration (e.g., its tall, cylindrical shape) is then used in play themes (e.g., it can be used as a tree). Thus, if children are given novel toys, they will explore them before they play with them. If we are making inferences about their cognitive status based on the sophistication of their play with those props, the unfamiliarity of the props is suppressing their competence. Repeated opportunities to play with the unfamiliar props should remediate the problem.

In short, we can make reliable and valid assessments of children's play in both natural and contrived settings. We must, however, recognize that children's play behaviors are extremely sensitive to contextual effects. To minimize children's reactivity to assessment, we must recognize potential ecological effects on behavior. Also, it is necessary to observe children on multiple occasions. In this way we maximize the possibility that the data we collect actually represent children's level of competence.

In the next section, I will briefly present two specific observational instruments that I have used in observing young children as forms of assessment.

TWO SPECIFIC OBSERVATION INSTRUMENTS

The use of any instrument, whether it be observational or psychometric, should be grounded in a specific question or theory (see Pellegrini, 1996). Measures are designed with those specific questions/theories in mind, and validity considerations are usually based on those questions/theories. In terms of assessment of educational programs, choice of an assessment measure should be guided by the specific theory of your program. Theory is usually operationalized in program goals and objectives. Thus, your measure should have indicators of your objectives. Then, you can either develop your own observational instrument or use one that has already been developed. In either case, the behaviors listed on the instrument should be indicators of skills/concepts that are relevant to your own program.

I will present two instruments. The first is the play matrix developed by Ken Rubin (Rubin, Maioni, & Hornung, 1976) and has been widely used by researchers and practitioners. For this reason, I will discuss it very briefly. Specific use of the matrix by educators for assessment has been discussed extensively in Pellegrini (1991). The matrix considers cognitive and social aspects of children's behavior simultaneously, as shown in Table 11.2.

Note first that the matrix considers the context in which play is observed. As mentioned above, factors such as playmates and props relate to levels of play exhibited. Second, the observer should chose a sampling intervals (e.g., observations every 30 seconds for separate children) and recording rules (e.g., instantaneous or 0/1) in advance (see Pellegrini, 1996). I recommend that teachers make a "ditto" master of this matrix and then make many copies. Separate sheets should be used for individual observations of each child. Teachers can observe individual children (following scan sample/instantaneous recording rules) in the class, once a week every 30 seconds. These sheets can then be kept in a file for each child, thus providing a powerful documentation of children's exhibition of competence across the school year.

TABLE 11.2
SOCIAL COGNITIVE PLAY MATRIX

Child's Name _____ Date _____ Location _____
Others Present _____

	Functional	*Constructive*	*Dramatic*	*Play*
Solitary				
Parallel				
Interactive				

The power of data derived from this matrix for use in assessment relates to the research done with it. Researchers have used this matrix for 20 years and have shown the ways in which specific play behaviors relate to other outcome measures. For example, preschool children engaging in solitary constructive play tend to do well in school; school activities also tend to be solitary constructive (Rubin et al., 1983). Further, children engaging in interactive dramatic play are facile at taking others' perspectives (Rubin et al., 1983). The reader interested in using this matrix for assessment is encouraged to see the Rubin et al. (1983) chapter for the many (contemporaneous and longitudinal) correlates of play behavior.

While the matrix is a powerful tool for assessing preschool children play in classrooms, its usefulness is more limited for observing outdoor play and the play of primary school children (see Pellegrini, 1995, for a discussion). To describe and assess children's outdoor behavior, I have developed, based on the work of Humphries and Smith (1987), an observational scheme for studying primary school children on the playground at recess (Pellegrini, 1995). The behaviors are summarized in Table 11.3. These behaviors can be sampled and recorded using the same rules as used with the matrix.

While there has been less empirical work with this observational model than with the play matrix, some consistent patterns relevant to assessment emerge. In our longitudinal work we found that kindergarteners' playground behavior predicted significantly more of the variance in first-grade achievement (on a standardized achievement test) than kindergarten test scores. For example, spending time in adult-directed behavior was a negative indicator of social competence, while object play was a positive predictor of first-grade achievement. In short, observations of play provide important insights into children's social cognitive status. It should also be noted, however, that kindergarten and first-grade test scores were significantly related. Conse-

TABLE 11.3
PLAYGROUND BEHAVIORS

Passive/Noninteractive
Passive/Interactive
Adult Directed
Adult Organized
Aggressive
Rought-and-Tumble Play
Vigorous Behavior
Games
Object Play
Role Play

quently, the "don't throw out the baby with the bath water" lesson invoked earlier. The more powerful forms of assessment use many different methods: tests, observations, and teacher/parent checklists.

As in all forms of assessment, issues of reliability and validity should be considered. While it is beyond the scope of this chapter to address these issues, we must note that they are primary considerations. Whether you design your own observational measure or use one already developed, keep these concerns in mind. Most importantly, when you are considering a measure, ask yourself what it is you want to know about children and then how will that information be used. These are basic construct validity questions that should be foregrounded. What's valid as an observational measure for one school may not be valid for another!

CONCLUSION

Assessment of young children is very tricky business. It's tricky because young children tend not be very motivated to exhibit high levels of competence in most assessment contexts. Variable motivation relates directly to variable performance in most of these situations. The end result is that many forms of assessment for young children are not reliable. The problem is compounded and moves into a very questionable area when these tests are used to make "high stakes" decisions, such as placement in special classes.

Both the knowledge gained from the assessment of children and the uses of that information have recently been considered an important part of construct validity (Messick, 1989; Moss, 1992), In schools we usually use an assessment procedure with some intent in mind. That intent should be made clear and the validity of the procedure should be related to its intended use. In light of this, many assessment procedures for young children used for high-stakes decisions would not be construct valid.

My own bias is to steer away from high stakes. When decisions must be made, we should utilize as many different forms of data as are available. An important component of any assessment context in school, especially those involving young children, should be behavioral observations. Observations of children in highly motivating and highly demanding contexts, such as pretend play for preschoolers, afford an excellent opportunity to gain insight into children competence. The benefits of this approach have been espoused throughout this chapter: Kids exhibit high levels of competence in a meaningful situation. These data should be used in conjunction with data from other sources, such as parents, teachers, and peers.

I was also careful not to "oversell" the value of play. The role of play in children's development in not well understood. We do not sure, for example, whether play is beneficial for children or whether it is merely an epiphenom-enon. If it is beneficial, we are not clear where the benefits lie: In long-term payoffs or in short-term payoffs. Thus, as in the use of other forms of assess-ment, we should exercise caution when using play as a mode of assessment. It should probably be used as part of a broad-based, multimethod approach. The behavioral observational approach in this chapter is valuable to use when children are in highly motivating and demanding situations.

There are also costs associated with the using direct observations of children's play as a form of assessment. Most of those costs are monetary. Simply put doing observations are expensive: Many qualified observers are needed to collect large quantities of data. Indeed, one of the benefits of tests vis-à-vis observations is economy: Tests are less expense to administer. We already know the unfortunate costs associated with reliance on tests.

Educators, politicians, and parents should commit to the costs associ-ated with this form of assessment, but not for use in "high stakes" areas. Assessment is a crucial part of teaching. We use it to gauge instruction, learn-ing, and development. If we think good assessment is expensive, consider the expense of the alternatives!

REFERENCES

Bekoff, M., & Byers, J. (1981). A critical reanalysis of the ontogeny and phylogeny of mammalian social and locomotor play: An ethological hornet's nest. In K. Immelmann, G. Barlow, L. Petrinovich, & M. Main (Eds.), *Behavioral devel-opment* (pp. 296–337). New York: Cambridge University Press.

Belsky, J., & Most, R. (1981). From exploration to play. *Developmental Psychology*, *17*, 630–639.

Bjorklund, D., & Green, B. (1992). The adaptive nature of cognitive immaturity. *American Psychologist, 47*, 46–54.

Bronfenbrenner, U. (1979). *The ecology of human development*. Cambridge, MA: Har-vard University Press.

Chalmers, N. (1980). The ontogeny of play in feral oliver baboons (*Papio anubis*). *Animal Behaviour, 28*, 570–585.

Christie, J., & Johnsen, E. P. (1983). The role of play in social intellectual develop-ment. *Review of Educational Research, 53*, 93–115.

Dansky, J., & Silverman, I. (1973). Effects of play on associative fluency of preschool-age children. *Developmental Psychology, 9*, 38–43.

Dansky, J., & Silverman, I. (1975). Play: A general facilitator of associative fluency. *Developmental Psychology, 11*, 104.

Fagen, R. (1981). *Animal play behavior.* New York: Oxford University Press.

Fagen, R. (1995). Animal play, games of angels, biology, and Brian. In A. D. Pellegrini (Ed.), *The future of play theory* (pp. 23–44). Albany: State University of New York Press.

Fein, G. (1979). Echoes from the nursery: Piaget, Vygotsky, and the relationship between language and play. In E. Winner and H. Gardner (Eds.), *Fact, fiction, and fantasy* (pp. 1–14). San Francisco: Jossey-Bass.

Fein, G. (1981). Pretend play: An integrative review. *Child Development, 52,* 1095–1118.

Galda, L. (1984). Narrative competence: Play, storytelling, and story comprehension. In A. D. Pellegrini and T. Yawkey (Eds.), *The development of oral and written language in social context* (pp. 105–118). Norwood, NJ: Ablex.

Garvey, C. (1990). *Play.* Cambridge, MA: Harvard University Press.

Haight, W., & Miller, P. (1993). *Pretending at home.* Albany: State University of New York Press.

Howes, C. (1992). *The collaborative construction of pretend.* Albany: State University of New York Press.

Humphries, A., & Smith, P.K. (1987). Rough-and-tumble play, friendship, and dominance in school children. *Child Development, 58,* 201–212.

Huston, A. (1983). Sex-typing. In WE. M. Hetherington (Ed.), *Manual of child psychology: Vol. 4* (pp. 387–468). New York: Wiley.

Martin, P., & Caro, T. (1985). On the functions of play and its role in behavioral development. In J. Rosenblatt, C. Beer, M. Bushnell, & P. Slater (Eds.), *Advances in the study of behavior* (Vol. 15, pp. 59–103). New York: Academic Press.

Mathews, W., & Mathews, R. (1982). Eliminating operational definitions: A paradigm case approach to the study of play. In D. Pepler and K. Rubin (Eds.), *The play of children: Current research and theory* (pp. 21–29). Basel, Switzerland: Karger.

McLoyd, V. (1982). Social class differences in social dramatic play: A critique. *Developmental review, 2,* 1–30.

Meisels, S., Stelle, D., & Quinn-Leering, K. (1993). Testing, tracking and retaining young children. In B. Spodek (Ed.), *Handbook of research on the education of young children* (pp. 279–292). New York: Macmillan.

Messick, S. (1983). Assessment of children. In W. Kessen (Ed.), *Handbook of child psychology* (Vol. 1, pp. 477–526). New York: Wiley.

Messick, S. (1989). Meaning and values in test validation. *Educational Researcher, 18*(2), 5–11.

Miller-Jones, D. (1989). Culture and testing. *American Psychologist, 44*, 360–366.

Moss, P. (1992). Shifting conceptions of validity in educational measurement: Implications for performance assessment. *Review of Educational Research, 62*, 229–258.

National Association for the Education of Young Children (1992a). *Developmentally appropriate practice in early childhood programs serving young preschoolers.* Washington, DC: Author.

National Association for the Education of Young Children (1992b). *Appropriate education in the primary grades.* Washington, DC: Author.

Pellegrini, A. D. (1984). The social cognitive ecology of preschool classrooms. *International Journal of Behavioural Development, 7*, 321–332.

Pellegrini, A.D. (1988). Elementary school children's rough-and-tumble play and social competence. *Developmental Psychology, 24*, 802–806.

Pellegrini, A. D. (1991). *Applied child study: A developmental approach* (2nd ed.). Hillsdale, NJ: Lawrence Erlbaum.

Pellegrini, A.D. (1992). Kindergarten children's social-cognitive status as a predictor of first grade success. *Early Childhood Research Quarterly, 7*, 564–577.

Pellegrini, A. D. (1995). *School recess and playground behavior.* Albany: State University of New York Press.

Pellegrini, A. D. (1996). *Observing children in their natural worlds: A primer in observational methods.* Hillsdale, NJ: Lawrence Erlbaum.

Pellegrini, A.D., & Boyd, B. (1993). The role of play in early childhood education: Issues in definition and function. In B. Spodek (Ed.), *Handbook of research on the education of young children* (pp. 105–121). New York: Macmillan.

Pellegrini, A.D., & Galda, L. (1993). Ten years after: A re-examination of symbolic play and literacy research. *Reading Research Quarterly, 28*, 163–175.

Pellegrini, A. D., & Perlmutter, J. (1989). Classroom contextual effects on children's play. *Developmental Psychology, 25*, 289–296.

Piaget, J. (1970). Piaget's theory. In P. Mussen (Ed.), *Manual of child psychology* (Vol. 1, pp. 703–732). New York: Wiley.

Rubin, K. H., Maioni, T., & Hornung, M. (1976). Free play behaviors in lower-class and middle-class preschoolers: Parten and Piaget revisited. *Child Development, 47*, 414–419.

Rubin, K., Fein, G., & Vandenberg, B. (1983). Play. In E. M. Hetherington (Ed.), *Handbook of child psychology* (Vol. 4, pp. 693–774). New York: Wiley.

Rushton, J., Brainerd, C., & Pressley, M. (1983). Behavioral development and construct validity: The principle of aggregation. *Psychological Bulletin, 94*, 18–38.

Scarr, S. (1981). Testing for children. *American Psychologist, 36*, 1159–1166.

Shepard, L., & Graue, M. E. (1993). The morass of school readiness: Research on test use and test validity. In B. Spodek (Ed.), *Handbook of research on the education of young children* (pp. 293–305). New York: Macmillan.

Simon, T., & Smith, P. K. (1983). The study of play and problem solving in preschool children. *British Journal of Developmental Psychology, 1*, 289–297.

Smith, P. K. (1982). Does play matter? Functional and evolutionary aspects of animal and human play. *The Behavioral and Brain Sciences, 5*, 139–184.

Smith, P. K. (1988). Children's play and its role in early development. The "play ethos." In A. D. Pellegrini (Ed.), *Psychological bases for early education* (pp. 207–226). Chichester, England: Wiley.

Smith, P. K., & Connolly, K. (1980). *The ecology of preschool behavior*. London: Cambridge University Press.

Smith, P. K., & Cowie, H. (1988). *Understanding children's development*. London: Blackwell.

Smith, P. K., & Dodsworth, C. (1978). Social class differences in the fantasy play of preschool children. *Journal of Genetic Psychology, 133*, 183–190.

Smith, P. K., & Vollstedt, R. (1985). On defining play. *Child Development, 56*, 1042–1050.

Smith, P. K., & Whitney, S. (1987). Play and associative fluency: Experimenter effects may be responsible for previous positive effects. *Developmental Psychology, 23*, 49–53.

Sutton-Smith, B. (1993). Does play prepare for the future? In J. Goldstein (Ed.), *Toys, play, and child development* (pp. 130–146). New York: Cambridge University Press.

Sutton-Smith, B. (1995). The persuasive rhetorics of play. In A. D. Pellegrini (Ed.), *The future of play theory* (pp. 275–296). Albany: State University of New York Press.

Sylva, K., Bruner, J., & Genova, P. (1976). The role of play in the problem solving behavior of children. In J. Bruner, A. Jolly, & K. Sylva (Eds.), *Play—Its role in development and evolution* (pp. 244–261). New York: Basic Books.

Vygotsky, L. (1967). Play and its role in the mental development of the child. *Soviet Psychology, 3*.

Vygotsky. L. (1978). *Mind in society*. Cambridge, MA: Harvard University Press.

Waters, E., & Sroufe, L. A. (1983). Social competence as a developmental construct. *Developmental Review, 3,* 79–97.

Wilson, E. O. (1975). *Sociobiology: The new synthesis.* Cambridge, MA: Belnap.

Zigler, E., & Trickett, P. (1978). I.Q., social competence, and evaluation of early child-hood intervention programs. *American Psychologist, 33,* 789–798.

Chapter 12

What Is Stylish about Play?

Olivia N. Saracho

Play is a form of social behavior; in play, children encounter social situations and learn to cooperate, help, share, and solve social problems. These social behaviors require children to think, consider the others' points of view, make moral judgments, develop social skills, and acquire conceptions of friendship.

The ability to understand and perceive what others are experiencing is an essential prerequisite for children's play. As children expand their perspective-taking skills, they are able to understand how others view them and respond to them (Small, 1990). Older preschoolers engage in more prosocial behavior and enhanced relationships with peers (Hart, DeWolf, Michele, & Burts, 1992). Children with more spontaneous prosocial behaviors are more sensitive to the others' needs (Iannoti, 1985), have a more positive effect (Lennon & Eisenberg, 1987), and are more independent (Eisenberg, Cameron, Tryon, & Dodez, 1981) than their peers. Social behaviors have also been explored in relation to independence (Lennon, & Eisenberg, 1987). Children are more self-confident when they are able to meet the others' needs and accordingly encounter situations with confidence and without requests and directions from others. Children to use their cognitive processes in functioning socially. This has been called social cognition (Rubin, 1980). Research in social cognition (e.g., Shantz, 1983) emphasizes the importance of cognitive structures for social behaviors. A basic assumption of social cognition is that children's perspective-taking skills modify their concepts of self and others (Shantz, 1983).

Play has been considered a major source for cognitive growth in young children (e.g., Piaget, 1962; Vygotsky, 1962). It facilitates young children's abstract thinking (Vygotsky, 1962). In pretend play there is a reduction of the time encompassing important incidents. As children act out a situation, they begin to understand it. It allows children to learn about, practice, and analyze event relations (Stambak, & Sinclair, 1993). Vygotsky views pretend play as reflecting the child's zone of proximal development.

Piaget's (1950) developmental framework views cognitive processes as a way to gain and organize information about the environment and about oneself in relation to one's environment. Corrigan (1987) used pretend play to assess the children's cognitive level in two different contexts and two actor-role tasks. The results provide a scalable developmental sequence of cognitive levels. The children's cognitive style becomes evident when they gather and organize information. The way children process information and respond to various situations identifies their cognitive style, which has elements of perceptual styles, personality, intelligence, and social behavior. These individualistic dispositions based on cognitive style influence the children's play.

COGNITIVE STYLE THEORY

Cognitive style theory indicates that individuals communicate and refine information in a variety of modes. It incorporates facets of perceptual styles, personality, intelligence, and social behavior. Cognitive styles are distinctive modes of functioning that are observed within an individual's perceptual and intellectual experiences. They describe stable attitudes, preferences, or habitual strategies in perceiving, remembering, thinking, and solving problems. The field dependence–independence (FDI) dimension is the cognitive style construct that has generated more research for cognitive functioning and social behaviors. It differentiates an individual's mode of functioning in a variety of situations. Field-dependent (FD) and field-independent (FI) persons differ in behavioral characteristics that identify their cognitive style and categorize them as a FD (global or undifferentiated) or FI (analytic or differentiated) person. FD and FI cognitive styles indicate distinctly different ways of processing information. FD individuals differ from FI ones in important cognitive and personal characteristics. Saracho and Spodek (1981) compared the cognitive style characteristics that describe FD and FI persons.

These attributes are pervasive and consistent, affecting several areas including the individuals' socialization. Witkin and Goodenough's (1981) most current form of FDI theory emphasizes the value-neutral quality of a particular cognitive style. FI children can solve problems that require structuring or reorganization of any information that is presented, while FD children have a social sensitivity that provides them with good interpersonal relations with others (Kogan, 1987).

TABLE 12.1
COMPARISON BETWEEN FIELD-DEPENDENT AND FIELD-INDEPENDENT INDIVIDUALS

Field-Dependent Individuals	*Field-Independent Individuals*
1. Rely on the surrounding perceptual field	1. Perceive objects as separate from the field
2. Experience their environment in a relatively global fashion by conforming to the effects of the prevailing field or context	2. Can abstract an item from the surrounding field and solve problems that are presented and reorganized in different contexts
3. Are dependent on authority	3. Experience an independence from authority which leads them to depend on their own standards and values
4. Search for facial cues in those around them as a source of information	4. Are oriented towards active striving
5. Are strongly interested in people	5. Appear to be cold and distant
6. Get closer to the person with whom they are interacting	6. Are socially detached but have analytic skills
7. Have a sensitivity to others which helps them to acquire social skills	7. Are insensitive to others, lacking social skills
8. Prefer occupations which require involvement with others	8. Prefer occupations that allow them to work by themselves

Source: Saracho & Spodek, 1981, p. 154.

Social Behaviors in FDI

The relationship between social behaviors and FDI has mostly been investigated with older children or adults. The results indicate that FD persons have a sensitive radar system attuned to social components in the social milieu and are more socially oriented than FI persons (Saracho, 1985).

Adults. Studies with adults show that FD persons are more aroused by and are more attentive to social stimulation (Fitzgibbons & Goldberger, 1971; Eagle, Goldberger, & Breitman, 1969; Fitzgibbons, Goldberger, & Eagle, 1965). They focus on the faces of others to gain their primary source of information in relation to their feelings and thoughts (e.g., Konstadt & Foreman, 1965; Ruble & Nakamura, 1972). FD persons concentrate more on verbal messages that have social content than do FI persons (e.g., Eagle, Fitzgibbons, & Goldberger, 1966; Fitzgibbons & Goldberger, 1971). In comparison, FI persons remember and select nonsocial stimuli (Goldberger & Bendich, 1972).

School-age Children. Studies that have used school-age children to explore the relationship between social behavior and FDI support the research results with adults. These studies showed that FD children looked at the investigator's face for information more than did FI children (Ruble & Nakamura, 1972; Konstadt & Forman, 1965) and they appeared to be more interpersonally dependent (Beller, 1958). They also were more sensitive to the adults' negative feedback (Konstadt & Forman, 1965) and tended to depend on more social cues in solving problems (Ruble & Nakamura, 1972) than did FI children. Nakamura and Finck (1980) examined the effectiveness of task and social behaviors of 9- to 12-year-olds and found that FI children were low-social but task-effective, whereas FD children were more socially oriented. Conclusively, field-dependence relates to social sensitivity, although it has not been resolved if the elementary-school FD children are more socially competent or effective (Kogan, 1987).

Preschool Children. The relationship between social behaviors and FDI with preschool children focus on their play to provide a natural environment (e.g., Beller, 1958; Coates, 1972; Coates, Lord, & Jakabovics, 1975; Halverson & Waldrop, 1976; Steele, 1981). The social elements of FDI are supported in these studies. Most of these studies show similar results as those studies conducted with adults and school-age children. These studies are discussed in detail in the following section.

PLAY AND COGNITIVE STYLE

Young children's play is a form of social behavior requiring them to react to a variety of circumstances. When children play, they encounter social situations; they learn to cooperate, help, share, and solve social problems in acceptable ways. In learning these social skills, children think about their social world, considering the other persons' point of view, making moral judgments, and acquiring conceptions of friendship (Saracho, 1987). According to Coates et al. (1975) and Steele (1981), preschool FD children spend more of their free time in social play than do their counterparts. FD preschool children engage in social play, whereas FI preschool children participate in solitary play. These studies suggest a relationship between play and cognitive style. Further support of this relationship can be found in investigations that explore children's stages of play.

Children's stages of social play have been categorized as unoccupied, solitary play, onlooker, parallel play, group activity, associative group play, and organized supplementary group play (Parten, 1932). Several investigators (e.g., Rubin, 1976; Rubin, Maioni, & Hornung, 1976; Rubin, Watson, & Jambor, 1978) show that children absorbed in parallel play may choose to have the company of other children next to them, while those who successfully reflect on their peers' points of view select to participate in associative or cooperative play (Rubin et al., 1976; Rubin, 1976). Such results indicate that young children's degree of sociability may be related to their degree of FDI. FD persons are more social, look for facial cues as a source of information from those around them, have an interest in people, and like to be physically close to those with whom they are communicating (Saracho & Spodek, 1981). Children who engage in parallel, cooperative, and associative play may exhibit attributes of a FD cognitive style. In contrast, children engaging in solitary play may possess a more FI cognitive style.

Attributes of FI persons can also be identified in the children's play. FI individuals are actively striving, are independent of authority, rely on their own standards and values, can solve difficult problems, are more cold, are socially detached, and have analytic skills (Saracho & Spodek, 1981). Solitary play has been found to be educative, goal-directed, independent, and task-oriented (Moore, Everston, & Brophy, 1974). Rubin et al.'s (1978) study indicates that young children who choose to play by themselves probably want to "get away from it all." Rubin's (1976) research supports this deduction by demonstrating that 3- and 4-year-olds prefer to be by themselves for constructive purposes. Rubin and Maioni (1975) and Rubin et al. (1976) conclude that young children use their cognitive skills in choosing their level of social participation. The results from the cited studies support the assumption that young children's cognitive style influences their sociability. Since FD children have a strong interest in people and are sensitive to their needs, their FD cognitive style promotes their social skills. Thus, FD children are probably the ones who choose parallel, cooperative, or associative play. In contrast, FI children are socially detached but possess analytic instead of social skills; therefore, they are probably the ones who choose solitary play.

Cognitive style characteristics suggest that solitary play corresponds to impersonal objects, whereas social play is associated with objects or events with a human referent. Several researchers (e.g., Coates et. al, 1975; Kogan, 1987; Saracho, 1985, 1989a, 1989b, 1989c, 1991a, 1991b, 1994; Steele, 1990) support the FDI theory of people versus object orientation in young children (Kogan, 1987). Cognitive play can be observed as children transform objects and roles in their play as they simultaneously become cognizant of the original identity and performance of the object.

These studies suggest a relationship between play and cognitive style. Saracho (1985, 1986a) identified similar characteristics in the children's play and their cognitive styles. Renninger and Sigel (1987) found that 3- and 4-year-old children use a stylistic style to select strategies and processes that cognitively organize and interpret tasks. Their cognitive organization designate the patterns they believe are appropriate or more interesting. Children continually use strategies that achieve a stylistic level to create an organizational pattern that is applied to some tasks. The children perform steady and intentional play behaviors. Coates et al. (1975) support these outcomes. They detected a relationship among the children's play choices, FDI, and sex. The results showed that FD children favor social play areas (e.g., doll and block corners); whereas FI children favor solitary play activities (e.g., playing with blocks, table tasks). Thus, social play is similar to a FD cognitive style, whereas solitary activity is comparable to a FI cognitive style regardless of the presence of others. FD children selected activities that involved social participation rather than solitary activities. FI children selected solitary activities such as working by themselves (Coates et al., 1975).

In identifying social behaviors in cognitive functioning, Steele (1981) explored the relationship between several play behaviors of young children and cognitive style. She found a relationship between play behaviors (pretend play and playfulness) and cognitive style for 5- and 6-year-olds. She also examined the children's acts of aggression during their play and found more acts of aggression in FD children and less in FI children. Young children's play behaviors seemed to be related to cognitive style.

A study investigating social orientation and FDI was conducted by Halverson and Waldrop (1976). These investigators examined the relationship of fast-moving, vigorous, highly active behavior to the development of cognitive and social behavior in young children. In this longitudinal study, the social behavior of young children was related to differences in cognitive style. A primary focus in Halverson and Waldrop's study was their belief that children's high levels of activity and impulsiveness would affect the development of cognitive and social behaviors. Thus, the children's high levels of vigorous and intense play activity may block their cognitive thinking and limit their ability to select alternatives in responding to new situations. In their study, these investigators classified social behaviors as highly active, vigorous, and impulsive. These social behaviors did not refer to a clinical syndrome of hyperactivity but to behaviors found to a greater or lesser degree in most children participating in free and unrestricted situations. Highly active behaviors were positively correlated with field independence. Those children who were highly active during play were also more FI, whereas those children who were less active during play were more FD. These results support Kagan's (1971) proposition that a child's tempo of play, as indexed by variations in play levels, has important consequences for young children's social and cognitive functioning. Therefore, when children engage in play experiences, they use their cognitive style to understand the socialization process.

The relationship between children's play and cognitive style was also found in a two-part study by Coates (1972). The first part with children whose ages range from 3 to 6 years indicated that girls were slightly more FI than boys. The second part showed a relationship between the girls' play preferences and their cognitive styles. Children had the freedom to select from three play options: block building, playing house, or other activities (e.g., painting, making collages, working with puzzles). Most FD girls chose to play house, though a few FD girls choose to work on other activities. In comparison, all of the FI girls selected activities other than house play. Coates's (1972) study showed a relationship between the play and cognitive style of 4- and 5-year-olds. She found that (1) most FD girls chose a social activity (such as playing house) that require them to cooperate with several children, and (2) most FI girls chose nonsocial activities that allow them to play by themselves, even though they periodically interacted with other children. These outcomes are similar to the studies with older children that found that persons with low analytic capacities were more socially oriented than persons with a high analytic abilities. Saracho (1995a) also found cognitive style differences. FI children engaged more in social play than did FD children, who are considered to be more warm, socially oriented, and nurturant than FI children. This suggests that the play behaviors could be interpreted in a two-dimensional manner as reflecting both field-independence cognitive style and social orientation. Further understanding of this phenomenon may be gained with further studies.

The relationship between play and cognitive style has been further explored in a series of studies conducted by Saracho (1987, 1989b, 1989c, 1990, 1991a, 1991b, 1992, 1994, 1995a, 1995b) with 3- to 5-year-old children. In three of her studies (Saracho, 1987, 1992, 1995b), FI children played more than FD ones. In addition, play behaviors (e.g., ability and creativity to communicate ideas, social levels of participation, capacity to lead in their play) differ between FD and FI children (Saracho, 1987, 1992). FI children demonstrated more play behaviors and played more frequently than did FD children. The ability and creativity to communicate ideas was the least observed play behavior in both FD and FI children, whereas cooperative play was the most observed behavior in both FD and FI children (Saracho, 1987).

Investigations that explored the preschool children's cognitive style and their play preferences for the different forms of play indicated that

1. FD children engaged more frequently than FI children in the different forms of play (e.g., physical, manipulative, block, dramatic) (Saracho, 1991a, 1991b, 1995a).
2. FI children chose physical and block play more often than did FD children (Saracho, 1990, 1991a, 1991b, 1994).
3. FI children chose manipulative play (Saracho, 1991a, 1991b, 1994), which had more significant effects than the other forms of play (Saracho, 1994).

4. FI children showed more play behaviors (e.g., ability and creativity to communicate ideas, social levels of participation, capacity to lead in their play) than did FD children, although the children's frequency of play did not show great differences (Saracho, 1992).

Social Factors in Children's Play and Cognitive Style

Social factors that are integrated in the children's cognitive style were identified in a play context. Saracho (1989c) highlighted the social relations and concrete objects in FD children's play, and the role-playing ideas and block-building activities in FI children's play. Saracho (1989b) noted that FD children engaged in more play activities with others and with concrete objects, whereas FI children felt they had to reorganize the environment. For instance, FD children played with others using the play equipment that was accessible to them, indicating FD characteristics. FD persons have an interest in their peers (Saracho & Spodek, 1981, 1986) and ordinarily learn precise and organized knowledge. On the other hand, FI children developed new ideas and introduced their own play activities. Even when FI children immersed themselves in social roles, they designed the various roles or defined the roles in detail, indicating FI characteristics. Corresponding to Saracho and Spodek's (1981, 1986) description of FI persons, they solve problems that are presented and rearranged in mixed contexts and are autonomous of authority. Nevertheless, some FI children exhibited several FD qualities (e.g., taking part in social roles, conversing with others in manipulative play). Inasmuch as social roles and conversing with others are FD qualities, two inconclusive points may have been overlooked: (1) manipulative and physical play may really be FI forms of play with FI activities, and (2) children's play behaviors and cognitive style may be more perplexing than researchers and educators have initially assumed.

Using a sizable sample, Saracho (1992) denoted play factors of FD and FI preschool children. She found that both FD and FI children communicated ideas in physical, manipulative, block, and dramatic play; and that FI children played more frequently in the block and physical forms of play.

Social Competence in Children's Play and Cognitive Style

Children's social competence in play is also related to their cognitive style. Saracho (1991a, 1991b) found a relationship of FDI and children's social competence. Saracho (1991a) examined young children's social competence and found that more FI children were more able to assume a social role and solve a social problem.

Saracho (1991a, 1991b) examined several social correlates of FD and FI kindergarten children. She found that teachers perceived (1) FI children to be more socially competent, and (2) FD pairs of children where one child was accepted and the other was rejected to be more socially competent. Those FD and FI children who were rejected by other children engaged more in social play. Other studies by Saracho (1980), Saracho and Dayton (1980), and Saracho and Spodek (1981) support these results. They examined the teachers' perceptions of their FD and FI children on academic achievement. Teachers underestimated FD children, but they overestimated FI children. The results on the social competence and academic achievement studies suggest that teachers assess FD and FI children the same way across the board. FD children in these classrooms may be more socially competent, but the teachers' perceptions may be the same with both academic or social competence. Teachers seem to perceive FI children as more competent regardless of the task they are examining, although FD children may be more socially competent. The children's selections of peers to play with can validate the teachers' perceptions of their classroom children, inasmuch as children may also be using the teachers' criteria in assessing their peers. FI children were more popular, participated more in social play, and initiated their own play activities more often than their FD peers (Saracho, 1991a). Both FD and FI children chose FI children more to be their playmates. Both the children's and teachers' assessments were the same (e.g., FI children were more socially competent), even though FI children are considered to be socially detached, cold, and distant; whereas FD children are considered to be sensitive to others and manifest social skills (Saracho & Spodek, 1981, 1986). FI children were chosen as playmates, whereas FD children mutually rejected each other as playmates. This study was conducted in public school settings that focused on academic achievement. FD and FI children probably perceived the requirements for success in these settings and used the FI characteristics as criteria in their assessments. This may have influenced their selection of FI playmates.

The FDI theory support these results. According to Saracho and Spodek (1981, 1986), FI individuals can solve problems encountered in a variety of contexts. The FDI dimension is bipolar with the analytic field approach on one extreme and the global field approach on the other extreme. These approaches reveal how persons solve problems or perceive activities. FDI also relates to reasoning ability and the individuals' ability to process information. The solution of problems requires persons to use analytic thinking, and FI persons are the ones who can analyze and solve problems with ease. Cognitive stylistic differences rely on the individual's unique traits (Saracho, 1987).

Although the results conflict in some of the studies, the possibility still exists that young children's play behaviors may relate to their cognitive style. If so, such relationship has profound consequences for research and education.

EDUCATIONAL IMPLICATIONS

An educational program for young children should consider children's play and their cognitive style. Young children's cognitive styles can be determined early in the school year. Teachers can match the curriculum and their instructional strategies to individual child's cognitive style. However, this approach limits their opportunity to do what comes "naturally." A more appropriate approach may be to develop children's cognitive flexibility (Saracho & Spodek, 1986). This would extend their repertoire beyond their dominant cognitive style (Saracho & Spodek, 1981).

Children's cognitive style can be identified. Teachers may use (1) Ramírez and Castañeda's (1974) field-sensitive instruments, (2) the Learning Style Inventory (Saracho, 1983), and/or (3) the Goodenough-Harris Drawing Test (Saracho, 1983, 1984b, 1986b, 1989a). These measures and a play scale can help teachers plan their play experiences. Play experiences that match the children's cognitive styles can be provided at the beginning of the school year to help children feel comfortable and secure in the classroom (Saracho & Spodek, 1981). Such play experiences can include dramatic play and other social activities for FD children, and manipulative play, block play, and other nonsocial activities for FI children.

After children feel secure, teachers can gradually encourage children to engage in play activities that differ from the children's dominant cognitive style, where some degree of "cognitive-style dissonance" occurs (Saracho & Spodek, 1981). For example, FI children can gradually engage in social activities such as working within a group on a social experience like dramatic play. These activities require young children to use their social sensitivity, a FD characteristic. In contrast, FD children can gradually engage in nonsocial activities where they utilize their analytic skills such as working independently to solve a problem in block or manipulative play.

Teachers can learn to understand the children's needs and strengths based on their cognitive style and play behaviors. Teachers can test their knowledge by observing children in different play situations and comparing these observations and inferences with those of other observers (Saracho & Spodek, 1981). Teachers can initiate this process by assessing the children's play and cognitive style. They can use the play scale to assess the children's play and use several classroom measures including the rod-and-frame test, the tilting room–tilting chair test, the Articulation of the Body-Concept Scale, different forms of the Embedded Figures Test, and the Goodenough-Harris Drawing Test (Saracho, 1983, 1984b, 1985, 1986b, 1989a) to assess their cognitive style.

The assessment of play and cognitive style can help teachers to offer appropriate educational programs that meet the needs of young children. Such educational programs can insure that different information-processing skills that are inherent among individual children and the children's play behaviors are considered. Children's cognitive styles and play behaviors must be reflected in their educational programs for effective learning. Therefore, teachers need to learn the cognitive style differences in young children and the relationship between cognitive style and play behaviors. This knowledge can help teachers design developmentally appropriate types of teaching and developmentally appropriate educational programs for young children.

RESEARCH IMPLICATIONS

The relationship between young children's play behaviors and cognitive style needs to continue to be explored to support the reliability and functions of this line of research. Studies, such as the ones that have been reviewed, can be entirely or partially replicated by augmenting the realm of subjects (e.g., children from various socioeconomic groups, ethnic groups, ages), early childhood settings (e.g., Head Start, child care, public school, nursery school), and forms of assessment of cognitive style and play.

Studies can encompass several forms of play (e.g., manipulative, block, physical, dramatic) and play behaviors. The children's participation in these forms of play can be assessed in several ways, such as the mean time spent in each form of play. Teachers can use a classroom assessment of cognitive style to relate the children's cognitive style to their play preferences in these forms of play. Saracho (1984a) proposes an observation scale that identifies the children's play behaviors (e.g., communication of ideas, levels of social behavior, and leadership roles), which can be measured in each form of play. Communication of ideas, solitary play, and leadership roles suggest field independence. Children's stability in these patterns of behavior within each form of play and across the different forms of play can be studied, although researchers should avoid generalizing selective views of the children's behavior. Their logical reasons for their play behaviors and selections of the different forms of play may not easily be observed. Children can be interviewed, further observations can be recorded, and other types of evidence may be gathered to examine how children respond to different situations during their play. The relationship between young children's play and cognitive style is supported in several studies. A longitudinal study is essential before generalizing about this relationship.

REFERENCES

Beller, E. K. (1958). A study of dependence and perceptual orientation. *American Psychologist, 13,* 347.

Bretherton, I. (1985). Attachment theory: Retrospect and prospect. In I. Bretherton & E. Waters (Eds.), Growing points of attachment theory and research. *Monographs of the Society for Research in Child Development, 50* (Nos. 1–2).

Coates, S. (1972). *Preschool Embedded Figures Test.* Palo Alto, CA: Consulting Psychologists Press.

Coates, S., Lord, M., & Jakabovics, E. (1975). Field dependence–independence, social-nonsocial play, and sex differences. *Perceptual and Motor Skills, 40,* 195–202.

Corrigan, R. (1987). A developmental sequence of actor-object pretend play in young children. *Merrill-Palmer Quarterly, 33,* 87–106.

Eagle, M., Fitzgibbons, D., & Goldberger, L. (1966). Field dependence and memory for relevant and irrelevant incidental stimuli. *Perceptual and Motor Skills, 23,* 1035–1038.

Eagle, M., Goldberger, L., & Breitman, M. (1969). Field dependence and memory for social vs. neutral and relevant vs. irrelevant incidental stimuli. *Perceptual and Motor Skills, 29,* 903–910.

Eisenberg, N., Cameron, E., Tryon, K., & Dodez, R. (1981). The structure and content of 2$^1/_2$, 5$^1/_2$, and 7$^1/_2$ year olds' concepts of themselves and other persons. *Child Development, 60,* 1218–1228.

Fitzgibbons, D., & Goldberger, L. (1971). Task and social orientation: A study of field dependence arousal and memory for incidental stimuli. *Perceptual and Motor Skills, 32,* 167–174.

Fitzgibbons, D., Goldberger, L., & Eagle, M. (1965). Field dependence and memory for incidental stimuli. *Perceptual and Motor Skills, 21,* 743–749.

Goldberger, L., & Bendich, S. (1972). Field-dependence and social responsiveness as determinants of spontaneously produced words. *Perceptual and Motor Skills, 34,* 883–886.

Halverson, C. F., & Waldrop, M. F. (1976). Relations between preschool activity and aspects of intellectual and social behavior at age 7$^1/_2$. *Developmental Psychology, 12,* 107–112.

Hart, C. H., DeWolf, D., Michele, C., & Burts, D. C. (1992). Linkages among preschoolers' playground behavior, outcome expectations, and parental disciplinary strategies. *Early Education and Development, 3,* 265–283.

Iannoti, R. (1985). Naturalist and structured assessments of prosocial behavior in preschool children: The influence of empathy and perspective taking. *Developmental Psychology, 14,* 119–124.

Kagan, J. (1971). *Change and continuity in infancy.* New York: Wiley.

Kogan, N. (1987). Some behavioral implications of cognitive styles in early childhood, *Early Child Development and Care, 29,* 595–598.

Konstadt, N., & Forman, E. (1965). Field dependence and external directedness. *Journal of Personality and Social Psychology, 1,* 490–493.

Lennon, R., & Eisenberg, N. (1987). Emotional displays associated with preschoolers' prosocial behavior. *Child Development, 58,* 992–1000.

Lillard, A. S. (1993). Pretend play skills and the child's theory of mind. *Child Development, 64,* 348–371.

Moore, N. V., Everston, C. M., & Brophy, J. E. (1974). Solitary play: Some functional reconsideration. *Developmental Psychology, 10*(6), 830–834.

Nakamura, C. Y., & Finck, D. N. (1980). Relative effectiveness of socially oriented and task oriented children and predictability of their behaviors. *Monographs of the Society for Research in Child Development, 45* (3–4, Serial No. 185).

Parten, M. B. (1932). Social participation among pre-school children. *Journal of Abnormal and Social Psychology, 27,* 243–269.

Piaget, J. (1950). *The psychology of intelligence.* New York: Harcourt, Brace.

Piaget, J. (1962). *Play, dreams, and imitation in childhood,* New York: International Press.

Radke-Yarrow, M., Zahn-Waxler, C., & Chapman, M. (1983). Children's prosocial dispositions. In P. Mussen (Ed.), *Handbook of child psychology: Vol. 4. Socialization, personality and social development.* New York: Wiley.

Ramírez, M., & Castañeda, A. (1974). *Cultural democracy, bicognitive development, and education.* New York: Academic Press.

Renninger, K. A., & Sigel, I. E. (1987). The development of cognitive organisation in young children: An exploratory study. *Early Child Development and Care, 29,* 133–161.

Rubin, K. H. (1976). Relation between social participation and role-taking skill in preschool children. *Psychological Reports, 39,* 823–826.

Rubin, K. H. (1980). Fantasy play: Its role in the development of social skills and social cognition. *New Directions for Child Development, 9,* 69–84.

Rubin, K. H., & Maioni, T. L. (1975). Play preference and its relationship to egocentricism, popularity and classification skills in preschoolers. *Merrill-Palmer Quarterly, 21,* 171–179.

Rubin, K. H., Maioni, T. L., & Hornung, M. (1976). Free-play behaviors in middle- and low-class preschoolers: Parten and Piaget revisited. *Child Development, 47,* 414–419.

Rubin, K. H., Watson, K. S., & Jambor, T. W. (1978). Free play behaviors in preschool and kindergarten children. *Child Development, 49,* 534–536.

Ruble, K. N., & Nakamura, C. Y. (1972). Task orientations versus social orientation in young children and their attention to relevant social cues. *Child Development, 43,* 471–480.

Saracho, O. N. (1980). The relationship between the teachers' cognitive style and their perceptions of their students' academic achievement. *Educational Research Quarterly, 5*(3), 40–49.

Saracho, O. N. (1983). Assessing cognitive style in young children. *Studies in Educational Evaluation, 8,* 229–236.

Saracho, O. N. (1984a). Construction and validation of the play rating scale. *Early Child Development and Care, 17,* 199–230.

Saracho, O. N. (1984b). The Goodenough-Harris Drawing Test as a measure of field-dependence-independence. *Perceptual and Motor Skills, 59,* 887–892.

Saracho, O. N. (1985). Young children's play behaviors and cognitive styles. *Early Child Development and Care, 21*(4), 1–18.

Saracho, O. N. (1986a). Play and young children's learning. In B. Spodek (Ed.), *Today's kindergarten: Exploring the knowledge base, expanding the curriculum* (pp. 91–109). New York: Teachers College Press.

Saracho, O. N. (1986b). Validation of two cognitive measures to assess field-dependence/independence. *Perceptual and Motor Skills, 63,* 255–263.

Saracho, O. N. (1987). Cognitive style characteristics as related to young children's play behaviors. *Early Child Development and Care, 28,* 163–179.

Saracho, O. N. (1989a). Cognitive style and the evaluation of young children's educational programs. *Early Child Development and Care, 51,* 13–28.

Saracho, O. N. (1989b). Cognitive style in the play of young children. *Early Child Development and Care, 51,* 65–76.

Saracho, O. N. (1989c). The factorial structure of three- to five-year-old children's social behavior: Cognitive style and play. *Journal of Research and Development in Education, 22*(4), 21–28.

Saracho, O. N. (1990). Preschool children's cognitive style and their social orientation. *Perceptual and Motor Skills, 70*(3), 915–921.

Saracho, O. N. (1991a). Cognitive style and social behavior in young Mexican American children. *International Journal of Early Childhood, 23*(2), 21–38.

Saracho, O. N. (1991b). Social correlates of cognitive style in young children. *Early Child Development and Care, 76,* 117–134.

Saracho, O. N. (1992). The relationship between preschool children's cognitive style and play: Implications for creativity. *The Creativity Research Journal, 5*(1), 35–47.

Saracho, O. N. (1994). Relationship of preschool children's cognitive style to their play preferences. *Early Child Development and Care, 97,* 21–33.

Saracho, O. N. (1995a). Preschool children's cognitive style and their selection of academic areas in their play. *Early Child Development and Care, 112,* 27–42.

Saracho, O. N. (1995b). Relationship between young children's cognitive style and their play. *Early Child Development and Care, 113,* 77–84.

Saracho, O. N., & Dayton, C. M. (1980). Relationship of teachers' cognitive styles to pupils' academic achievement gains. *Journal of Educational Psychology, 72,* 544–549.

Saracho, O. N., & Spodek, B. (1981). The teachers' cognitive styles and their educational implications. *Educational Forum, 45,* 153–159.

Saracho, O. N., & Spodek, B. (1986). Cognitive style and children's learning: Individual variations in cognitive processes. In L. G. Katz (Ed.), *Current topics in early childhood education* (Vol. VI). Norwood, NJ: Ablex.

Shantz, C. (1983). Social cognition. In P. Mussen (Ed.), *Handbook of child psychology: Vol. 3. Cognitive development.* New York: Wiley.

Small, M. (1990). *Cognitive development.* New York: Harcourt, Brace, Jovanovich.

Stambak, M., & Sinclair, H. (Eds.). (1993). *Pretend play among 3-year-olds.* Hillsdale, NJ: Lawrence Erlbaum.

Steele, C. (1981). Play variables as related to cognitive constructs in three- to six-year-olds. *Journal of Research and Development in Education, 14*(3), 58–72.

Steele, C. (1990). Cognitive style and the gifted young children. In O. N. Saracho, (Ed.), *Cognitive style and early education.* New York: Gordon & Breach.

Vygotsky, L. S. (1962). *Thought and language.* Cambridge, MA: MIT Press.

Witkin, H. A., & Goodenough, D. R. (1981). *Cognitive styles: Essence and origins.* New York: International Universities Press.

Chapter 13

Physical Environments and Children's Play

Joe L. Frost, Dongju Shin, and Paul J. Jacobs

The materials, equipment, and context for play (indoors or outdoors) influence children's play preferences and behaviors. Since play is universal among healthy children and influential in promoting cognitive, social, affective and physical development (Frost, 1992; Berk, 1994), it is essential that optimal play environments be provided. Indeed, the nature and extent of children's play depends heavily upon the potential of the physical environment to meet children's needs, attitudes, and interests (Barker & Wright, 1955; Kritchevsky, Prescott, & Walling, 1977). Understanding the dynamics of the physical and social aspects of the play environment is important because the environment signals to children what they can do, supports their natural play needs, and in large part encompasses the curriculum of early childhood education (Dempsey & Frost, 1993).

This chapter emphasizes a research base for understanding the effects of the physical environment on the play of children. The physical environment for play includes the space in which play occurs, the materials that are present in the space, and how the space and materials are arranged. Environmental factors that affect children's play are discussed, specifically the effects of specific types of play materials and equipment in indoor (classroom) and outdoor (playground) settings. Since television is a pervasive influence in children's lives and even considered an environmental threat, a discussion about the effects of television viewing on children's play is included. The last part of the chapter is devoted to guidelines for creating optimal play environments.

Indoor and outdoor play environments are discussed collectively throughout this chapter. Although outdoor play environments permit more active, physical play than indoor environments, the research from both environments have implications for the effective use of space to promote elaborate, complex play with materials and equipment. Because of concerns for children's safety, there is a growing trend in the United States to establish indoor playgrounds that feature much of the equipment traditionally found only out of doors. Consequently, the current trend is toward integration of indoor and outdoor play materials and experiences.

For clarification, indoor play space is defined as enclosed space void of natural elements such as dirt and grass. Outdoor play space refers to space that includes natural elements as well as constructed features. "Materials" refers to portable play materials or "loose parts" that may be moved and manipulated by children. "Equipment" refers to relatively static, heavy duty, fixed structures typically available in outdoor playgrounds that are relatively static features of the play environment.

HUMAN ECOLOGY AND THE PHYSICAL ENVIRONMENT

Much of the research conducted within naturalistic settings has focused on the transactional relationship between the physical environment and children's peer culture. The impact of the physical environment on children's individual and social development should not be underestimated (Moore, 1989) for it is one of the most profound aspects of children's play culture, especially affecting the quality of their play and peer interaction.

Many studies have drawn attention to the interactive relationship that exists between children and environmental factors (social and physical) that creates a tension between the child and the environment (Sameroff, 1975; Scarr & McCartney, 1988). Part of the tension is due to the dialectical nature of human development and the conflict inherent among the interactive systems within which development occurs (Riegel, 1975).

Human ecology theory (Bronfenbrenner, 1979; Buboltz, Eicher, & Sontag, 1979) addresses how individuals interact with their systemic environments. The environment is regarded here as a set of nested systems within which the child is a participant. Bronfenbrenner (1979, 1975) proposed that four primary environmental systems impact human development: the micro-, meso-, exo-, and macro-. The family is the most immediate system impacting the child at the micro-systemic level (Steinberg, Elmen, & Mounts, 1989; Ninio, 1990; Haskins, 1986; Hagekull & Bohlin, 1990; Kyrios & Prior, 1990). Meso-systemic influences include transactional relationships between the family and institutions such as school and church (Fishbein, 1984; Duyme, 1988; Crnic & Greenberg, 1990; Howes & Stewart, 1987). Exo-systemic influences include social networks and culture (Ogbu, 1990; Heath, 1990; Elder, Caspi, & Burton, 1988). At the macro-system level, cultural values, norms, public policy, and institutional patterns shape the development of the three other systems (Kemerer & Walsh, 1994; Vittachi, 1989).

Tension among all levels of the human ecological system promotes growth of the individual (Riegel, 1975). Human development is predicated on the conflict that arises between the individual and her environment (Reigel, 1975; Dixon & Lerner, 1992). At the most basic level, conflict is inner bio-logical and individual psychological (Steinberg, 1986; Scarr & McCartney, 1988; Bateson, 1987; Scarr, 1988; Anastasi, 1958; Plomin, McLearn, Peder-sen, Nesselroade, & Bergeman, 1988). In addition, the child experiences ten-sion from within the cultural-sociological dimension (Ogbu, 1990; Heath, 1990; Schludermann & Schludermann, 1983; Simmons, Burgeson, & Carl-ton-Ford, 1987). Finally, the child must relate to the outer-physical dimension of the ecology through exploration, manipulation, discovery, and interpreta-tion (Moore, 1990; Hurtwood, 1968).

Individuals create interpretations through their interactions with the physical and social environment (Bruner, 1990; Donaldson, 1978; Vygotsky, 1978, 1962). These contexts are composed of physical structures, objects, and tools. These physical features become artifacts imbued with meaning and sig-nificance to the individuals within a particular context and culture. The child internalizes the salient features of a context and the meaning implicit within the environment through social interaction (Donaldson, 1978), creating a "folk psychology" (Bruner, 1990) within contextually significant interaction with adults and other children through scaffolding (Vygotsky, 1978, 1962; Donaldson, 1978).

Many studies have focused on childhood as a unique culture distinct from adult culture imbued with its own meaning and politics (Corsaro, 1985; Reimer, 1993). Children's culture has especially been studied within the frame of peer relations and friendship (Corsaro, 1985; Rubin & Caplin, 1992; Hartup & Moore, 1990). However, more recent studies focus on how children create meaning within peer culture and the adults' role in facilitating chil-dren's culture (Jacobs, 1995).

Physical contexts facilitate and discourage the development of peer cul-ture. Unlike the classroom, the playground serves as a unique context for social development among peers, providing physical and social resources, and thus allowing children to meet, interact, and form relationships with peers (Ladd & Price, 1993). However, on the playground, students with disabilities interact and play less with their peers than do nondisabled children (Roberts, Pratt, & Leach, 1991) which may be a function of the way teacher's perceive their roles on the playground (Jacobs, 1995).

Because of the luxury of space, playgrounds can provide a more flexible environment for facilitating peer interaction (Hartup & Larsen, 1993; Olweus, 1993). This is true for conflict as well. Serbin, Marchessault, Mcaffer, Peters, and Schwartzman (1993) found that playground contexts are uniquely qualified for conducting behavioral observations related to assessing behavioral problems among peers who may be at risk for social rejection. The playground permits greater degrees of child freedom to selectively interact with peers. This is especially true with regard to gender segregation. Children's preferences for partners according to gender and ethnicity are pronounced on the playground due to the unconstrained context (Boulton & Smith, 1993).

Children's playground interactions with peers serve an important function in social development when behavior leads to positive evaluations by teachers and peers but children suffer when their behavior elicits adverse reactions by teachers and peers (Pettit & Harrist, 1993). This is perhaps more evident on the playground due to the greater range of self-initiating social engagements with peers prompting the use of social skills among a greater variety of peers.

Interestingly, much of the peer behavior in the free play context of the playground is attributed to parental discipline strategies affecting peer status and relations (Hart, DeWolf, & Burts, 1993). Children whose parents used inductive discipline strategies exhibit fewer disruptive playground behaviors (Hart, DeWolf, Wozniak, & Burts, 1992). Children of inductive mothers are more preferred by their peers. The implication is that the freedom and flexibility offered in the outdoor environment promotes a greater range of social behavior that may not otherwise present itself in the classroom.

CHILDREN'S CLASSIFICATION OF ACTIVITIES AND PLAY OBJECTS

Holmes's (1991) ethnographic study of children's play concluded that their activities were classified into specific categories based upon multiple criteria: solitary or collective building if there were materials such as blocks to build with; dolls (Barbie) or action figures (G.I. Joe), if the toys were brought from home and were male (action figures) or female (Barbie), thus involving animation of characters and the performance of scripts (TV).

Children classified toys based upon whether they were "used to it" and they "like playing with it" and if it were "something you play with" (Holmes, 1991). Toy classification was based on the properties and functions of the play object: riding toys, props for house, stuffed animals, puppets, and puzzles. Children categorized their play among several categories based upon the features or attributes of particular play activities: number of participants, types of play, territory, and materials used.

These cultural domains identified by the children included smaller categories possessing their own unique characteristics that the children used to describe play behavior. This study highlights the complexity of understanding children's play from outside children's culture and the problem of accurately categorizing children's play (Piaget, 1962; Smilansky, 1968).

GENDER DIFFERENCES IN THE PHYSICAL ENVIRONMENT

There is a growing body of evidence for gender differences in choice of play environments and activities. Boys prefer outdoor environments, and girls prefer indoor environments (Cunningham, Jones, & Taylor, 1994). Ethnohistoric reconstruction of gender-specific patterns of game participation in traditional Alaskan Tlingit culture concluded that women engage in fewer competitive games and activities than do men (Heine, 1991). It appears that a distinct cultural framework shapes gender behavior and choice of activities.

Early exposure to particular toys and equipment has a pronounced effect on differences in spatial abilities between boys and girls (Einon & Barber, 1994). Boys' preferences for larger outdoor spaces influence the development of spatial orientation. In addition, there are differences in the games and use of play space by boys and girls.

Borman, Laine, and Lowe (1993) analyzed children's essay writing about soccer, a game that is played in large outdoor spaces. There were distinct differences in writing about soccer between boys and girls, reflecting differing perceptions of the game of soccer and competition in general. Girls spent more time in housekeeping areas of indoor classrooms than boys (Weinberger & Starkey, 1994). This is especially true if the themes of the housekeeping area are traditional, for instance, homeliving, and not novel, for instance, camping (Howe, Moller, Chambers, & Petrakos, 1993).

In yet another ethnography of children's culture, playground chase games bridged the dichotomy between the classroom and the playground through writing events (Reimer, 1993). Boys and girls planned and executed playground chase games through writing in the classroom. These reading and writing activities in the form of secret notes and strategies also took place in the form of classroom chase games.

In studies of the pretend verbal play of 5–6-year-olds, Wall, Pickert, and Gibson (1988) found that only girls mentioned dolls, horses, and animals (easily animated objects) in their fantasy play. Boys referred most often to nonanimated objects, primarily blocks, in their fantasy play and did so more frequently than girls. Boys used objects such as frisbees and footballs only for their generally accepted purpose, but girls were not constrained by their accepted, functional use. In contrast, a study of game preferences among children over several generations showed a trend toward similarity of game preferences for both girls and boys (Mergen, 1991). In addition, the style of games (imaginary versus physical) has changed over generations.

CHARACTERISTICS OF
PHYSICAL PLAY ENVIRONMENTS

Numerous characteristics of physical play space affect children's play behaviors. Many of these should be considered when planning and administrating play environments within classroom and playground contexts. Characteristics with pronounced behavioral effects include physical contextual cues and props, space arrangement, and play materials. In addition, the types, complexity, and quantity of play materials and equipment affects children's behavior. Other pertinent influences are toy realism and children's preferences for indoor and outdoor activities. Further, television has profound effects on children's play themes, toy selections, and physical behavior.

Play Context and Props

Children's play is affected by the equipment and materials comprising learning centers or play centers in the classroom (Pellegrini, 1985). The research suggests that children take cues from the environment about appropriate behavior within a specific context (Donaldson, 1978).

Children engage in more constructive play in the blocks context and in more functional and dramatic play in the home living area (Pellegrini, 1985). In addition, boys are more likely to engage in dramatic play within the blocks context than the girls, and the girls were more likely to engage in dramatic play in the home living context than the boys. In general, though, blocks elicit more construction play and the dramatic home living context elicits more dramatic play. Overall, children take cues from play props to interpret the appropriate behavior within a particular context (Pellegrini, 1985; Donaldson, 1978).

While children take cues from the physical environment that play is an acceptable behavior, children also engage in nontyped play in areas such as eating areas. During snack time, children take food and use it for symbolic representation (Holmes, 1991). This suggests that children's play needs may take precedence over social protocol when potential play props are available and the activity is boring.

This type of transformative environmental play behavior was also observed by Guerra (1989), who found that children used lunch time as an opportunity for verbal swaggering (play in language, i.e. butthead, poop in pants, etc.). Topics of swaggering focused on bodies, food, monsters, violence, and vulgar language. Care should be exercised in using play categories for child assessment, for children's exhibition of particular play types (cognitive and social) may be a function of contextual variables that dictate how they play rather than indicating cognitive or social competence (Christie & Johnson, 1989). Practitioners and researchers should also be wary of observations that do not take into account children's use of language in context (Donaldson, 1978) and the prolonged engagement and persistent observations of the adult (Lincoln & Guba, 1985).

Spatial Density

Clearly, children's play is mediated by age, sex, and environmental cues. However, the amount of space allocated for children's play also affects children's behaviors. Contrasting indoor and outdoor environments, Weinberger and Starkey (1994) found that the predominant type of play exhibited by children depended largely on the size of the play area. Functional play occurred most frequently outside on the climbing equipment, while constructive play occurred mostly within the classroom block area and dramatic play occurred in the housekeeping center.

The interpersonal and physical dimensions of context interact to affect children's play behavior (Pellegrini & Perlmutter, 1989). Pellegrini and Perlmutter found that children engaged in more constructive and solitary play in the blocks and art areas. Dramatic and interactive play occurred primarily in the housekeeping area. The physical provisions within a micro-context such as learning or play centers do influence the facilitation of imaginative social play. The props that invite dramatic themes requiring two or more players may be different from blocks and art materials, which are easily used in solitary play .

Findings about the effect of density (crowding) on children's social interactions are equivocal. Some studies suggest that high levels of spatial density (i.e., decreasing the space available to a constant group size) and social density (i.e., increasing the number of children in a same size space) have negative effects on children. Other studies, however, show no effect for crowding and spatial density.

Children in crowded physical contexts engage in passive or noninvolvement behaviors, such as onlooking, standing around, and random and deviant behaviors (Preiser, 1972; Shapiro, 1975). However, other studies of the relationship between density and children's aggression found that increased density causes aggression (Ginsburg, 1975). Ginsburg (1975) found that elementary school boys engaged in more frequent yet shorter fights on a small playground, and that the fights generally involved more children than those occurring on a large playground. Both normal and brain-damaged children exhibited more aggression as group size increased, while autistic children showed withdrawal behaviors and negligible aggression with increase in group size (Hutt & Vaizey, 1966).

Several studies have found no effect of spatial or social density on children's aggression and play behaviors. A cross-cultural study of five preschools in the United States and the Netherlands with varying conditions of density reported that the Dutch children in the high-density conditions spent approximately twice as much time in positive social interaction as children in less crowded American schools (Fagot, 1977). Crowding in the classroom forced teachers to adopt different strategies from those they might choose in less crowded conditions, and the differing cultural context and long-term adjustment to crowded conditions seemed to outweigh the effect of differing densities.

A study of children in day care also found no significant effect of crowding when space was reduced from 46.1 square feet per child to 29.1 square feet (Campbell & Dill, 1985). However, one child in the study was profoundly and negatively affected by the diminished space. This may underscore the importance of considering the individual needs of children in group programs and drawing the attention of caregivers toward the interaction between the needs of individual children and the needs of the entire program.

One study suggested a positive effect of increased social density on children's play behavior. In a naturalistic kindergarten setting, Peck and Goldman (1978) found that the increased social density of a play area was related to increases in imaginative play and the sharing of common play themes with other children. The researchers concluded that more intense levels of exposure to many peers seemed to provide children with more opportunities to share ideas and play themes within the smaller context. This study also found that the social density of the area appeared to have little relationship to aggressive play and physical aggression.

Loo (1972) also found significantly less aggression, less social interaction, and more frequent interruption of activities when a group of 4- and 5-year-old children was confined to a small room than when the group was situated in a larger room. Loo's findings suggest the importance of considering social dimensions of a context in addition to the physical dimensions.

Collectively, the research demonstrates that variables of space and group size influence children's behavior. In general, more physical contact among children occurs in crowded conditions, and it can cause more frequent interruption of activities and aggressive behavior as well as less running and attentive behavior. With decrease in density, there may be more solitary play and running behavior and less aggression because of spaciousness and less physical interaction among children. The seeming contradictions in the studies do suggest a need to consider dimensions beyond physical space per child when evaluating the quality of a play space.

Smith and Connolly (1980) point out that methodological problems might account for some of the discrepancies among studies. In some investigations, the quantity of space and number of children were varied, while the amount of equipment remained constant, suggesting that differences in the amount of equipment per child may have affected the children's play. Also, the definition of aggression is different among studies. Some researchers distinguish between rough-and-tumble play and true aggression, while others lumped the two behaviors together.

Further, there may be a threshold effect of about 25 square feet of classroom space per child, beyond which aggressive behavior increases (Smith & Connolly, 1980). Some studies did not reduce available space sufficiently to test the effects of very limited density. Density level can affect teacher behavior and resulting classroom or playground organization, but well-trained and experienced teachers may develop special strategies for handling crowded conditions.

Finally, the studies of effects of density were conducted primarily in classrooms. Equivalent studies of playground density are limited in scope. Generally, child-care centers regulated by state government agencies have established space and supervision (child/adult) ratios that are implemented in both indoor and outdoor environments. Child/adult ratios established for indoor environments are also implemented in outdoor environments (Wallach & Afthinos, 1990) and space requirements are enforced.

However, national surveys show that preschool playgrounds are poorly equipped and hazardous (Wortham & Frost, 1990). Only a few state departments of education recommend or require space or child/adult supervision ratios for public school playgrounds (Wallach & Edelstein, 1991). Although public schools typically have access to considerable outdoor space, the playgrounds are antiquated, hazardous (Bruya & Langendorfer, 1988), poorly maintained, and improperly supervised. In common practice, 50 to 200 children are supervised on the playground by one to three adults.

Collectively, the studies show that density affects children's play and social behavior, both in the classroom and on the playground. The effects of crowding are mediated by the level of density, the type and nature of play materials and equipment, the organizational skills of the teacher, and the arrangement of space.

Spatial Arrangement and Use

The physical design and arrangement of space and furniture affect the behaviors of children in two major ways. First, the physical arrangement communicates a symbolic message to children about what is expected to happen in a particular place. What is expected to happen is related to what is in the space and how these things are arranged or organized. Second, there are functional consequences resulting from the arrangement of the furniture (Proshansky & Wolfe, 1975).

Space arrangement should facilitate both concentration and sociability, and allow a flow of movement around the room that does not conflict with ongoing activity. Educators often create well-defined activity centers on the assumption that physical clarity helps children understand spatial order, find equipment, and make choices (Minuchin & Shapiro, 1983).

The major reason for partitioning play space is to maximize the flexibility of available space and enhance the overall quality of play, since children have been found to play differently in different physical settings (Johnson, Christie, & Yawkey, 1987). Researchers of space arrangement conclude that partitioned areas with clear boundaries enhance the quality of children's play.

Partitioned classrooms, arranged in small activity areas, encourage children to engage in interaction with peers, dramatic play, exploratory behavior, and associative-cooperative behavior during free play. Partitions are especially effective in fostering constructive activity under conditions of high density, when distractions are most common. Large open spaces, on the other hand, suggest to children that large muscle activities are appropriate. Children in a large undivided room are often involved in noisy and boisterous activities, and more likely to be distracted from a particular activity by other children, other play materials, and other ongoing play activities (Field, 1980; Fitt, 1974; G. T. Moore, 1986; Rohe & Nuffer, 1977; Sheehan & Day, 1975). In other words, the more desirable social and cognitive types of play occur in the classroom with small partitioned areas.

Research suggests that partitioning a large, open room into smaller areas can have beneficial effects. Such arrangements tend to discourage large motor activity (running, chasing, and rough-and-tumble play) and encourage dramatic and constructive play as well as the use of materials in appropriate areas. However, one should be careful about where partitions or barriers are placed.

Kinsman and Berk (1979) found that opening up a classroom by removing a barrier between the housekeeping area and the block play area had beneficial effects on children's play. Removing the barrier resulted in less solitary play and more mixed-sex play, especially dramatic play, in the housekeeping area. Integration of play materials from the two areas also increased. These data suggest that openings should be left between complementary areas so that activities can cross over and become integrated with each other.

In a series of studies of the effects of environmental planning on children's play behaviors, Cunningham, Jones, and Taylor (1994) found that the distance, physical characteristics, and social characteristics of the play environment influence where children play as well as how they play. These variables were especially pronounced for gender and age differences. Children were restricted from roaming within their neighborhoods. Freedom to roam through the neighborhood depended on whether they were girls or whether they were young children. On the other hand, parents tended to allow boys in general to roam with greater freedom. Other studies have shown similar findings where parental concerns about the physical geography of the neighborhood determined children's freedom to play and roam (Moore, 1990).

Children appear to have strong preferences for types of play spaces, especially private or semi-private areas. Even children in poorly equipped school playgrounds in England preferred to play near walls, fences, edges, and trees rather than in the center of the playground (White, Hargraves, & Newbold, 1995). The activity that occurred in the center of the playground was facilitated primarily by adults promoting games. These studies suggest that children seek out places of seclusion and privacy as spaces to call their own away from invasion by others, which includes the freedom to roam and explore.

Numerous other studies have examined the effects of the quality of classroom environments on children's play behaviors. Classroom quality affects children's academic achievement (Bryant, Burchinal, Lau, & Sparling, 1994), language development (McCartney, 1984), and literacy (Miller, Fernie, & Kantor, 1992; Reimer, 1993).

In a study by Miller, Fernie, and Kantor (1992) the art table allowed children the freedom to create and control their own work where print was explored as an integral part of art and construction experiences. Children appeared to use open-ended art materials to create and assume control over their learning and skill development. They did note, however, that the block area differed dramatically from the art table in the nature of the subcontext and in the literacy constructed there. The blocks context was primarily a place for boys to enact peer culture dynamics. That is, they exercised issues of control and ownership, equity and hierarchy, friendship and inclusion, and power and leadership. Beyond these issues, however, the boys used scant literacy in the block corner.

The restrictions of the classroom environment may also have an interactive effect with outdoor play. Contrasting the effects of confinement to seat work and outdoor play, Pellegrini and Davis (1993) found that children were less attentive to seatwork as a function of time and that longer confinement in the classroom resulted in more exercise play for boys and more social sedentary behavior for girls.

Interestingly, the children engaging in less physical activity outside were more attentive when reentering the classroom than the children who had engaged in greater physical activity. This was particularly true for boys who used outside time for physically active social and nonsocial play. For girls, however, playground time provided opportunities for less active social interaction. Other studies have examined children's spatial understanding, orientation, and comprehension. When preschool children were asked to represent the room arrangement of their classroom, the children performed more accurately positioning classroom furniture within their own classroom (Liben, Moore, & Golbeck, 1982). Their performance was less accurate when they worked with a classroom model within their real classroom. They performed least well positioning equipment within their classroom model in an experimental room that was unlike their own classroom.

Herman, Shiraki, and Miller (1985) also found that older children perform better on location identification tasks of large environments than younger children. Boys were more accurate in identification tasks than girls. The findings imply that children pay close attention to salient cues from a familiar environment for orientation and spatial comprehension and their comprehension of their physical environment improves with age.

Specific features of children's outdoor play behavior should be considered since playgrounds are almost always much larger than classrooms. First, there is greatly enhanced opportunity for free exploration of the outdoor environment. Second, the playground is usually less structured than the classroom in physical layout and arrangement of significant play materials and equipment. Further, the extent to which outdoor settings are frequented and utilized seems to increase steadily with age, as reflected in the expanding territorial range of the child (Wohlwill & Heft, 1987). Consequently, the play behaviors observed in the outdoor environment differ from those seen indoors.

Differences in children's play, indoors as compared with outdoors, have been noted in several studies. Large motor movement is more common outdoors than indoors because outdoor play areas are usually larger than indoor settings, and equipment for large motor activity is more likely to be available, permitting room for extensive movement. On the other hand, constructive play occurs more often in indoor settings because of the greater supply of construction materials found in most preschool classrooms (Henniger, 1985; Roper & Hinde, 1978).

Dramatic play themes are also influenced by gender and age. Indoor environments encourage significantly more dramatic play for girls and younger children and constructive play for boys. Outdoor environments are an important stimulus for the dramatic play of boys and older children (Henniger, 1985; Sanders & Harper, 1976).

A qualitative study of children in a richly equipped playground (Shin, 1994; Shin & Frost, 1995) concluded that children spent more time engaging in dramatic play in outdoor settings regardless of their gender, and dramatic play themes are more diverse outdoors than indoors. The spaciousness of the outdoor setting and the freedom to engage in large muscle activities allowed children, especially boys, to play a large number of chase games and, in most instances, the chase games were transformed into dramatic play, related to the themes of "chasing bad guys" or "gunfighting with bad guys."

Also, the fantasy world expressed in the children's play was different qualitatively, depending on the aids that they received from materials and equipment (Shin, 1994). The relatively unconstrained environment provided by the outdoor setting and an abundance of natural and loose materials in the setting offered children opportunities to freely create and organize their fantasy world to meet their imaginative needs and interests.

With regard to social class differences in children's play behavior indoors and outdoors, working-class children are more than twice as likely as middle-class children to play outside, particularly with wheeled vehicles, while middle-class children are more likely to choose indoor activities such as paints and pattern-making (Tizard, Philps, & Plewis, 1976). Also, working-class children engage in more dramatic play and in longer play episodes in outdoor settings than in classrooms, and their play is more mature outside. In general, there appear to be social class differences in children's play interests and in the quality of their play in both indoor and outdoor environments.

Characteristics of Playground Environments

Given that children's play behaviors and opportunities for peer interaction are relatively unrestricted on the playground, special attention to the quality of the outdoor play environment is warranted. Research on outdoor play includes comparisons of types of play environments to determine their influence on play behavior.

Designating types of play environments is highly arbitrary and specific to a particular site and/or a specific study. No two playgrounds are identical. Indeed, most playgrounds, including those used as research sites, are poorly equipped and hazardous and fail to meet the minimum criteria established by the United States Consumer Product Safety Commission (Bruya & Langendorfer, 1988; Wortham & Frost, 1990). However, the characteristics of a given playground can, in a very general sense be deduced from a given name or designation, particularly by those who work extensively in the field of playground design. The designations (types) of playgrounds used in some research include traditional, designer or contemporary, adventure, and creative or adapted playground (Frost, 1979). Some researchers have compared studies of playground types, by name, leading to faulty conclusions. To date no studies have been conducted that replicate materials, equipment, space, zoning, and so on, of playgrounds. These variables, not the labels assigned to playgrounds, should be the focus of attention in interpreting research reports.

The traditional playground is a flat, barren area equipped with steel structures, such as swings, slides, seesaw, climbers, and merry-go-rounds, fixed in concrete and arranged in a row. The playgrounds at most American public schools are of this type. The equipment is designed for exercise play exclusively and is primarily single or limited function (Frost, 1979, 1992; Dempsey & Frost, 1993).

The designer or contemporary playground is typically designed by a professional architect or designer using wood, metal, and/or plastic manufactured equipment, with plastic, concrete, or wood timbers to retain safety surfacing. The emphasis is on modular, linked equipment with a variety of heights and a range of motor challenges in aesthetically pleasing arrangements (Frost, 1979, 1992; Hartle & Johnson, 1993).

The adventure playground is a highly informal playground within a fenced area, stocked with scrap building materials, tools, and provision for animals and cooking. This playground is characterized by children's construction using loose parts and scrap materials. The success of this environment requires the guidance of a skilled adult playleader (Frost, 1979, 1992; Dempsey & Frost, 1993; Hartle & Johnson, 1993).

The creative or adapted playground is a semiformal environment combining features of the other types to meet the needs of a specific community, child-care center, or school. This type, sometimes designed and built with community involvement, varies widely in equipment and design. A wide range of manufactured and handmade equipment and loose materials is adapted, depending on availability and the play needs of children (Frost, 1979, 1992; Hartle & Johnson, 1993).

Research on types of playgrounds shows that traditional playgrounds have low attendance rates compared with other types of playgrounds and do not foster high levels of social and cognitive play. Campbell and Frost (1985) examined the effects of two contrasting playgrounds (creative and traditional) on the play behaviors of second-grade children, using an adaptation of the Piaget-Smilansky cognitive play categories (e.g., functional, constructive, dramatic, and games-with-rules) and the Parten social play categories (e.g., solitary, parallel, associative, and cooperative).

The results showed that significantly more solitary and associative play occurred on the creative playground than on the traditional playground. There was significantly more parallel play on the traditional playground than on the creative one. However, cooperative play was the most frequently occurring type of social play on both playgrounds: 45.6% on the traditional and 50.2% on the creative one.

The availability and diversity of play materials clearly stimulated the occurrence of dramatic and construction play on the creative playground. The absence of materials specifically appropriate for construction and dramatic play on the traditional playground resulted in more functional play and games-with-rules. The most general, overriding conclusion is that type of play is influenced by the type of materials available.

Similar results were found for third-grade children observed on creative and traditional playgrounds (Strickland, 1979). The creative playground supported more complex social and cognitive play behaviors and was selected more often by children than the traditional playground. Significantly, more nonplay occurred on the traditional playground than on the creative playground.

In addition, there were frequent arguments among children on the traditional playground. For example, several children argued frequently about using the swings. Relatively few situations of this type were observed on the creative playground due to the abundance and nature of the equipment. Also, significantly more parallel play was observed on the traditional than on the creative playground, and significantly more group play occurred on the creative playground.

Comparing play activities at traditional, contemporary, and adventure playgrounds, Hayward, Rothenberg, and Beasley (1974) reported that children stayed the longest period of time on the adventure playground, the next longest at the contemporary playground, and the shortest on the traditional playground. The adventure playground, which offered a selection of loose parts, seemed to allow children to define their own activities and create structure and levels of complexity.

Brown and Burger (1984) compared six playgrounds rated on a 19-item scale divided into four categories: social/affective, cognitive, motor, and practical considerations. They compared those playgrounds rating higher on the scale (those of more contemporary design) with those rating lower on the scale (traditional playgrounds), but found no significant differences in the amounts of children's social, language, or motor behaviors.

A closer inspection of the two environments showed that both settings were similar in the predominance of fixed equipment, though the contemporary playground was more aesthetically pleasing. The results affirmed the importance of certain attributes of materials and equipment in the setting: complexity via multifunctional and linked climbers, zoning (e.g., cloistered sand play areas sheltered from traffic), and movement (wheeled toys), encapsulation or enclosure, and manipulability through such items as loose parts.

Hart and Sheehan (1986) expressed concern about playgrounds that are made attractive to adults (contemporary playgrounds), but actually hold no more creative play potential for children than traditional playgrounds. Forty preschool children were observed during their regular outdoor period and were alternated randomly between the two playground environments. Social play categories of Parten (1932) and cognitive play categories of Smilansky were used to code play behaviors.

The investigators found that children's play was more passive on the contemporary playground than on the traditional playground, and no differences were found in verbal interaction and cognitive play. Significantly greater incidents of unoccupied behaviors, solitary play, sitting behavior, and walking were observed on the contemporary site, The researchers concluded that any differences in play behaviors were due not to the type of playground, but rather to the type of equipment and physical arrangement, supporting the view that labeling playgrounds is highly arbitrary.

There are clearly characteristics essential to the development of effective outdoor play environments. The best playgrounds are developed on the basis of children's natural play needs, taking into account the play behavior engaged in at different developmental periods, including both social and cognitive forms of play. The evidence throughout this review supports attention to such variables as degree of theme specificity, challenge, novelty, complexity, and variety of materials and equipment. Although not widely researched, provision for construction, gardening, and nature areas also enhances the outdoor environment.

Play Materials

Children's use of equipment and materials is affected by cultural, contextual, and intrapersonal variables. In children's peer culture, objects and equipment assume symbolic significance for a core group within a larger peer culture (Kantor, Elgas, & Fernie, 1993). Toys and object use also have differential uses according to the age group using the equipment (Fishbein & Burklow, 1994). As children mature, their use of objects assumes more social connotations and less solitary physical/manipulation. Object play also assumes a subordinate role to verbal interactions vital to the development of peer culture.

Results of studies on the relationship between use of objects and the peer culture of play indicate that objects are used more frequently for social purposes than for thematic purposes. Certain objects and contexts determine the membership of peers in particular groupings, termed the "core" group (Corsaro, 1985; Elgas, Klein, Kantor, & Fernie, 1988).

In Elgas et al.'s study (1988), superhero capes were regularly and often used to permit or deny entry to the core group's play episode, and rhythm sticks were often used as social markers (objects possessed by group members) where possession was deemed important but other play use was not apparent. Rhythm sticks signaled membership in much the same way cars and clothing ascribe status levels in adult society. Collectively, these findings suggest that objects are not used only in simple ways by children in the peer culture. Instead, they fit in with and serve the needs and social dynamics of complex relationships within the peer culture.

Children's use of equipment and materials is also affected by emotional and social needs. In Northern Ireland, children have been documented using materials such as fire as a means of empowerment within a war-torn sociopolitical environment (McKee, 1993). The significance of their manipulation of such a potentially dangerous play material underscores children's needs to gain control over their physical and social context through risk-taking and manipulation of their physical environment. Few opportunities to engage in constructive free play could have detrimental social effects on children's development of prosocial behavior (Frost & Jacobs, 1995).

All forms of play are closely related to play materials and equipment. Most free play activity involves some kind of natural or synthetic material (Shin, 1994). The play materials act as a stimulus or resource for play with certain types of materials tending to elicit specific forms of play. Children are attracted to some materials more frequently than others and play with them for longer periods of time.

An assessment of the quality of play materials and equipment can be based on the level of complexity and variety provided, and the amount to do per child (Kritchevsky, Prescott, & Walling, 1977). Complexity is the extent to which a play unit has the potential for active manipulation and portability by children. The more complex the unit, the more choices there are for the child to make in the course of play, and the more potential there is for group play.

The number of different kinds of unit can be called the degree of variety. Wide variety invites children to make choices among many different kinds of activities, eliciting immediate interest from children who are ready to find something to do. The amount to do per child is a calculation of the number of play units per child. If children are expected to choose their own activities at their own pace, the number of play units needs to be greater than one per child.

Complexity of play materials affects exploration, curiosity, and play behavior of children. Some researchers have found that children prefer complex play materials over simple materials. In a study of three climbable, trestle-type structures of varying degrees of complexity, children moved to the more elaborate structure first and spent more time on it than on the more simple structures (Gramza, Corush, & Ellis, 1972). On playgrounds, complex superstructures are of great interest for children and are incorporated into their play at a very high rate. Superstructures, void of multiple and challenging components, have low incidence of use by children (Deacon, 1994; Moore, 1992), and preference for complex structures tends to decline with familiarity

(Sholtz & Ellis, 1975). This is particularly true on well-equipped playgrounds where a wide range of portable materials and fixed equipment are available for play (Frost, 1992).

For example, young children may prefer simple, natural materials such as sand and water over expensive, complex superstructures. Unfortunately, many adults refuse to make natural materials available because of concerns about cleanliness and maintenance. With regard to the relationship between complexity and peer interaction, less complex structures may encourage more peer interactions since there is less for children to do on an individual basis (Sholtz & Ellis, 1975). Children tend to prefer more complex play units. When play structures are complex, children may interact more often with the materials than with peers.

Novelty also affects children's play behavior. The introduction of a novel object stimulates children to get to know its properties, and exploring high-complex materials may require more time than do low-complex ones. The complexity of equipment can also be seen in the classroom. Computers have been an increasingly common piece of play equipment in classrooms (Escobedo, 1992).

Lancy (1991) introduced children to computer electronic construction set games that require mastery over performance. However, the children did not sustain interest in the games because of the time required to master the tools of the game. While the focus of the study was on children's use of software, the findings suggest that the flexibility or complexity of the equipment and materials in the physical environment could have a negative impact on children's attention and interest in the play equipment.

Children use computer graphics programs for transformation of objects for constructive purposes and transformation of objects for imaginary play (Escobedo, 1992). When given appropriate activities and equipment, children engage in a wide variety of play activities even when using the computer. Contrasted with the findings of Lancy (1991), the children in Escobedo's study (1992) may have been encouraged by performance motivation rather than mastery. That is, they may have interpreted the computer activity as a more playful activity than one requiring an "end product" of mastery.

The quantity of available play material influences the quality of children's play. The degree and quality of social interaction, cooperative play, and conflict vary with the amount of available materials. Increasing quantity of play materials per child results in more participation in play and less aggression. Reduction in play materials results in more positive social contacts among children as well as more aggression and stress behavior such as thumb sucking (Getz & Berndt, 1982; Smith & Connolly, 1976, 1980). When children are required to check their toys out one at a time, they are likely to engage in more cooperative behavior, dramatic play, and complex language interactions (Montes & Risley, 1975).

The same phenomenon has been observed on playgrounds. Johnson (1935) observed children's behaviors after varying the quantity of equipment on three preschool playgrounds. Equipment was added to one playground and taken away from two others. Children played more with materials on the more extensively equipped playground, engaged in more physical exercise, had fewer social contacts, and fewer undesirable behaviors such as teasing, crying, quarreling, and hitting. When the amount of equipment was reduced, there were more social contacts, more undesirable behaviors, and less exercise.

Collectively, the evidence indicates that environmental conditions may result in both advantages and disadvantages. Abundant equipment reduces conflict but also decreases social interaction and cooperative play. At the other extreme, limited equipment produces the reverse by potentially increasing conflict through increased social play. By manipulating the quantity and types of play materials, adults may encourage positive social interaction in children's play and discourage aggressive behavior. However, judgment must be exercised in determining the optimal quantity of play materials per child because of the dialectical tension between the number of play materials and number of children per play area.

Researchers have studied the effects of different types of play materials on the social and cognitive quality of children's play since the early 1930s. Early studies conclude, in general, that housekeeping toys, dolls, dress-up clothes, and vehicles are associated with high levels of group play and dramatic play. The use of art and construction materials and puzzles tends to be related to nonsocial, constructive play. Clay, play dough, sand, and water are most often associated with nonsocial and functional play. Blocks appear to be related to various types of social play as well as constructive and dramatic play.

Research conducted during the 1970s concludes that availability of art materials, sand, water, and puzzles may inhibit group and dramatic play (Rubin, 1977; Rubin & Seibel, 1979). Such materials appear to encourage nonsocial and constructive behaviors. Tizard, Philps, and Plewis (1976) found that the provision of art construction materials was negatively correlated to the amount of dramatic play.

However, in a more recent observational study, Shin (1994; Shin & Frost, 1995) found that, on playgrounds, sand was the most frequently used material for children's dramatic play enactment and this play was frequently cooperative (group) in nature. Children liked to play out the theme of making foods using sand as a basic material. The sand in a container or a plate could be various kinds of cakes, pie, pizza, scrambled eggs, poison, chicken noodle soup, and so forth. Also, the sand in a plastic bottle was imagined as various kinds of drink, honey, poison wine, as well as canned foods for camping.

Sometimes, children combined sand with water to make hot chocolate, coffee, and poison, mixed grass with sand to make vegetable cakes, and leaves or stones on a sand mound were used to make a birthday cake. The characteristics of sand as a manipulative, open-ended and multifunctional material, which took on whatever meaning and form the children imposed on it, had high appeal to the children and they used it frequently as a basic material for their dramatic play.

Realism and Structure of Play Materials

Realism and structure are related features of play materials. Realism refers to the degree to which a toy resembles its real-life counterpart. Structure refers to the extend to which toys have specific uses. High-realism toys are considered to be highly structured and to have very specific uses (Johnson, Christie, & Yawkey, 1987).

Many studies provide strong support for the notion of age-related increase in the capacity to substitute objects in dramatic play. In general, the younger the child, the more dependent he or she is on the similarities between the original objects and the signifying toy. The older the child, the more capable he is of overriding the conflicting cues provided by the objects with unambiguous functions.

When substitution symbols first emerge, children incorporate objects whose functions are ambiguous (e.g., blocks, cloth). Only later are objects with clear functions (e.g., cups, spoons) used as substitutes for different objects (Elder & Pederson, 1978; Golomb, 1977; Johnson, 1983; Nicolich, 1977; Ungerer, Zelazo, Kearsley, & O'Leary, 1981).

Research on the amount and variety of dramatic play as a function of the realistic structure level of play materials suggests that minimally structured materials can stimulate children's fantasy more than extremely realistic materials, and may elicit a significantly greater number of themes because children's responses would be less anchored to specific stimulus situations. However, there may be more manipulative play and exploration with high realism materials than with unstructured materials (McGhee, Ethridge, & Benz, 1984; Phillips, 1945; Pulaski, 1973).

Interestingly, some research promotes different perspectives about the relationship between children's dramatic play and the structure of play materials. According to McLoyd (1983), high-structure objects, compared to low-structure objects, elicited significantly more dramatic play in 3½-year-old triads. This finding did not support the prevailing claim that low-structure objects enhance dramatic play. McLoyd noted that the sample of low-income children in her study contrasted with a middle-class sample in other studies. This phenomenon can be explained by the results of studies which have reported that the dramatic play of low-income and working-class children relies heavily on replica objects, whereas middle-class children are more likely to pretend with low-structure objects or without concrete signifiers altogether (Smilansky, 1968; Smith & Dodsworth, 1978).

These studies demonstrate that the implicit level of structure in play objects influences dramatic play both quantitatively and qualitatively. However, children's range of social experiences may affect their preferences or need for degree of toy realism. It appears that unstructured materials influence a wide variety of dramatic play for most children, but the absence of theme connotation in materials may not stimulate dramatic play for all low-income children due to their lack of experiences with various kinds of play materials.

Consequently, individual needs and experiences should be taken into account when selecting play materials. The classroom or playground should be equipped with a range of structured and nonstructured materials. When allowed free play in a well-equipped setting, most children select materials appropriate to their needs and, with skillful teacher guidance, tend to widen their choice of play materials over time.

Television and Play Environments

While the research consistently shows the important effects of quality play environments on children's development, there are many environmental teratogens that pose deleterious consequences for children's play. One of the most pervasive teratogens is television. Although children may prefer outdoor play and other activities to television, they spend more time viewing television than in any other activity except sleep. Some children are watching as much as 1½ hours of television per day before their first birthday. However, the dominant types of programming that children watch are children-oriented shows, especially cartoons (Clements & Nastasi, 1993; Lyle & Hoffman, 1972; Singer & Singer, 1981).

Winn (1977) cautions that television is a "plug-in drug," inhibiting children's fantasy and creativity. Children who watch a great deal of television are less playful and imaginative than those who watch less television (Singer & Singer, 1976, 1986), and children who watch programs containing high levels of action and violence show an increase in aggressive behavior (Friedrich & Stein, 1973; Eron, 1982; Eron, Huesmann, Lefkowitz, & Walder, 1972; Singer & Singer, 1981).

Preschool children who watch Batman and Superman cartoons containing instances of physical violence and verbal aggression decline in rule obedience, persistence, and tolerance for delay when observed at play (Friedrich & Stein, 1973). Television viewing has lasting effects. Eron et al. (1972) examined the relationship between children's aggressive behavior and their television viewing habits over a 10-year period. They concluded that a young male adult's aggressiveness is related to his preference for violent television when he was 8 to 9 years old.

Research on the effects of television on the content of children's play shows that television is an important source of thematic content for play, stimulating a variety of scenarios (James & McCain, 1982). Preschool children, especially boys, emulate cartoon superheroes and action heroes from viewing television and frequently invoke themes of good guys versus bad guys.

In her naturalistic inquiry of 4-year-olds on a preschool playground, Shin (1994) found that the violent and fairy-tale world of mass media and entertainment, as well as commercials aired on television, played an important part in children's play lives, and viewing cartoon violence seemed to increase aggressive play behaviors. The television cartoons televised on Saturday morning (e.g., X-Men, Power Rangers) were influential on boys. Most of the cartoons were very violent, and the boys claimed that they were one of the cartoon characters (Superheroes) while imitating their aggressive behaviors. They knew all of the characters' names and how each was armed to kill the others.

Shin also found that the tendency of boys to watch more action-adventure and violent television programs and their prior experiences with war toys, provided in their own rooms by parents, stimulated boys to enact violent play themes related to the content of the programs. On the other hand, girls did not engage in violent symbolic play episodes influenced by television. Instead, they were influenced by fairy tales (e.g., Aladdin, Snow White, etc.) that are cinematized, videotaped, or introduced by books.

The cultural or social expectations of gender role behaviors and the low frequency of occurrence of violently aggressive females shown on television seemed to be related to this minimal effect of television violence on girls. However, both boys and girls were influenced by certain features of advertisements. In particular, commercial slogans, as well as unusual and humorous elements, seemed to impress them more than brand names and made the children incorporate elements of television commercials into their dramatic play.

Even though there are many negative effects of children's television viewing, some studies suggest that television may have some positive effect on cognitive skill development and interpersonal behavior (Eron, 1986; Friedrich & Stein, 1975). However, the effectiveness of educational television programs may be limited to lower-level skills such as numbering and alphabet naming, and benefits may only occur when viewing is mediated by participating, caring adults (Choat & Griffin, 1986; Sprigle, 1972).

Television is one of the major socializing agents in children's lives, influencing their play and socioemotional development. Children's engagement in violent themes should be sensibly and skillfully mediated by adults to ensure that prosocial play themes are the most prevalent themes. To minimize the negative effects of television viewing and to use television for enhancing and enriching children's lives, Honig (1983) suggests that parents and teachers act as gatekeepers to the television world, assisting children in making good program choices and determining the amount of time spent watching television programs. The content of programs should be discussed with adults before, during, and after viewing. Children should not be left to face media options without guidance.

GUIDELINES FOR DEVELOPING PHYSICAL PLAY ENVIRONMENTS

Indoor and outdoor physical environments for young children are affected by a multitude of variables, including density, space arrangement, nature of materials and equipment, and special features, all of which can be influenced by parents, educators, and designers. This final section revisits the major areas of research previously reviewed and suggests guidelines for practice based on the reviews and the experience of the writers. Conflicting conclusions from much of the available research leads the writers to use personal judgment and experience in sorting realism from speculation and in constructing recommendations for adults who work and play with children.

Physical Space

Crowding large numbers of children into small spaces, indoors or outdoors, should be avoided, particularly if play materials and equipment are limited. Conflicts may occur when children are crowded and play materials and equipment are limited. Even on playgrounds with considerable space, paucity of materials and equipment limits children's play options and leads to increased levels of aggression. This is particularly true when large numbers of children are supervised by few adults.

Ideally, the ratio of adults to children on the playground should be comparable to the recommended ratio for the classroom. Well-trained adults can adequately supervise more children than those who are not specifically trained in play and play safety. For safety reasons, at least two adults should be on the preschool playground with children to ensure that one adult would be present if another adult must leave the playground in an emergency.

Adults can minimize the effects of crowded conditions on children's behavior by adapting their own behaviors, modifying play schedules, and creating optimal play environments. Supervision of play (the authors prefer the term "playleadership") requires insight, skill, and involvement. Perhaps the most restricting factor in play supervision or playleadership is the failure to train adults for the role of working within a play environment.

In child-care centers, supervision is frequently left to untrained aides and few private or public school teachers receive any training for the role of playleader. Further, outdoor play time is commonly viewed, even by educators, as released time for teachers. As a result, neither children nor their playgrounds receive appropriate, constructive attention. Compensation for this condition should include college courses in theories of play and play environment design as well as annual in-service training for all those who supervise children at play.

Physical Space Arrangement

There should be well-organized classroom space arrangement, including partitioned activity areas, to help children understand spatial order, find equipment, make choices, and as a result, engage in appropriate prosocial behaviors. Activity areas should be clearly defined with recognizable boundaries. Incompatible activities should not be placed in close proximity to one another, and openings should be left between complementary areas. One neglected factor in play is the need for children to take materials where they need to use them. With careful consideration by the caregiver, children may have flexibility with the number of areas available to use materials rather than restricting use to one area, that is, blocks in the block area.

Adults should make sure that partitions do not block children's view of available play equipment, and ensure that paths between areas are clear and unobstructed. Ideally, a central storage area will be available for play materials, and adults will regularly draw materials from this area to reconstruct play centers to match children's developing interests and needs.

The playground should be zoned to reflect children's natural play behaviors. For example, preschool children (ages 3 to 5 years) need areas or zones for gross motor activity, construction play, dramatic play, and as they approach 5 years of age, flat, grassy areas and hard-surfaced areas for games with rules and chase games. The arrangement of such spaces requires skill and training and should not be done merely on the basis of tradition. To further enhance the playground, a mix of portable materials (housed in a storage facility or storage buckets on the playground) and large-motor equipment (superstructures) should be skillfully selected. Gardens, nature areas, and sand and water areas complement this overall design.

Variety of Play Materials

The quantity of play materials per child should be considered carefully. Decreasing the quantity of materials may increase both positive and negative social interaction. Increasing the quantity of materials may have an opposite effect. The total amount of available space and the maximum number of children to play in that space must be carefully weighed. Too much material or too many children in a given space leads to behavior problems. All the variables—number of children, space available, quantity of materials—are taken into account when planning a play area. Setting up a play area should be followed by careful observation of children to determine which components need further modification. A constant rule is that good play areas are never finished but need continuous refinement and change as children grow. For this reason, the caregiver should assume the role of participant (not director) as opportunity arises to understand how children are using the play areas and equipment.

Toy Structure and Realism

In order to facilitate children's dramatic play, both indoor and outdoor settings should be provided with low-structure and low-realistic materials that serve as props for transforming the real world into the fantastic and magical one which meets children's imaginative play needs and interests. Low-structure (not intended to suggest a play theme) or low-realistic materials such as blocks, sand, and water, are not always sufficient in themselves to activate higher levels of dramatic play among younger children, due to the absence of theme suggestion or specificity in the materials.

For optimum development of dramatic play, environments for young children should include high-structure, realistic materials such as play houses, dolls, toy vehicles, dress-up clothes, and so on, along with low-structure and low-realistic materials. As children enter primary school, their play needs are changing and their interests shift increasingly to organized games and socializing activities. This means, of course, that play environments, indoors and outdoors, must be constantly examined and modified to ensure age and developmental appropriateness.

Layout and Design

In designing (zoning and equipping) optimal outdoor settings for play, there are fundamental factors to consider. A sufficient variety of materials and equipment should be available to provide for the diverse interests and abilities of children. Zones should be created to facilitate children's play and they should be defined by functional and visual boundaries. Outdoor environments must include areas for active and passive activities as well as social areas that enhance group activities. Good playgrounds are never finished and must be constantly modified to meet the rapidly growing needs of children for novelty, complexity, and challenge.

Children's Television Viewing

The influences of television programs on children's play are profound. Television heroes are replacing parents and public leaders as role models (U.S. News and World Report, 1985), and watching television violence leads to aggressive behavior in children. However, few adults prohibit or regulate children's television viewing, and it has become a major source of information and enjoyment.

The reasonable solution is ensuring balance in children's television viewing by providing alternative, creative activities, and consistent guidance by parents in children's television viewing (Frost, 1992). In other words, adults should ensure that children have many rich, real-world experiences through active participation and facilitation. They should communicate with children about the programs they watch on television and regulate the quantity and type of programs that children view. Parents should also take a responsible role in providing alternative, developmentally appropriate activities to balance children's television viewing. Finally, getting children out of the house and taking the family to good play environments are an effective antidote for the temptation of television viewing. Family recreation through play effectively promotes prosocial behaviors, motor skills, cognitive development, and, simultaneously, serves a therapeutic role for children in a high-pressure world through family bonding.

CONCLUSION

Collectively, the research on indoor and outdoor play environments reveals a pattern of neglect especially regarding the impact of the physical environment on nurturing children's play culture and play behavior. The research also provides considerable guidance in designing, maintaining, and using play spaces. At the present time, a revolution is emerging in play environment design with special attention to play value and safety.

Growing concerns for children's safety in playgrounds has resulted in national franchise chains of indoor pay-for-play settings. These franchise play environments are typically limited in play value. They emphasize profit over substance and entertainment over play by featuring junk food, birthday parties, violent video games, and gross motor equipment with little attention to creative play. The developers and sponsors of these mega-chains would be well served by carefully studying the impact of physical play environments on children and implications of play for child development.

Play is not merely important for physical development and fun. It sustains children's basic social, cognitive, and emotional development. The materials and equipment provided for play do not have to be expensive.

Rather, they should reflect wise selection and arrangement based on research and observation of children at play.

The key issues in quality physical play environments are play value, safety, adult playleadership, zoning and layout, novelty and complexity, structure and realism, and quantity and flexibility of space. Finally, the factors that influence the nature of play, for example, family life, television, books, and community experiences should be carefully assessed to ensure that children have a constructive range of experiences to bring to their play.

To assist in ensuring that children have reasonably safe, developmentally relevant play environments, adults must be trained in playleadership. Adults assume primary responsibility for the quality of children's physical environments. Appropriate roles include adults' responsibilities, providing adequate time, space, and materials and in identifying qualities of the physical play environment that enhance or detract from the benefits of play. Currently, there are no formal playleadership training programs in the United States. Professionals can learn from the programs in England and other European countries where play training is an integral facet of professional qualifications for those who work with children.

REFERENCES

Anastasi, A. (1958). Heredity, environment, and the question of "how?" *Psychological Review, 65*, 197–208.

Auerbach, J., Lerner, Y., Barasch, M., & Paalti, H. (1992). Maternal and environmental characteristics as predictors of child behavior problems and cognitive competence. *American Journal of Orthopsychiatry, 62*(3), 409–420.

Barker, R. G., & Wright, H. F. (1955). *Midwest and its children.* New York: Harper & Row.

Bateson, G. (1987). *Steps to an ecology of mind.* Northvale, NJ: Jason Aronson, Inc.

Bathiche, M. E., & Derevensky, J. L. (1995). Children's game and toy preferences: a cross-cultural comparison. *International Play Journal 3*(1), 52–62.

Bell, M. L., & Walker, P. (1985). Interactive patterns in children's play groups. In J. L. Frost and S. Sunderlin (Eds.), *When children play* (pp. 139–144). Wheaton, MD: Association for Childhood Education International.

Berk, L. E. (1994). Vygotsky's theory: The importance of make-believe play. *Young Children, 50*, 30–39.

Bloch, M. N. (1989). Play: A cultural-ecological framework. In M. N. Bloch and A. D. Pellegrini (Eds.), *The ecological context of children's play* (pp. 120–154). Norwood, NJ: Ablex.

Bloch, M. N., & Pellegrini, A. D. (Eds.). (1989). *The ecological context of children's play*. Norwood, NJ: Ablex.

Borman, K., Laine, C., & Lowe, D. (1993). Conflict and context in peer relations. In C. Hart (Ed.), *Children on playgrounds* (pp. 44–84). Albany, NY: State University of New York Press.

Boulton, M., & Smith, P. (1993). Ethnic, gendner partner, and activity preferences in mixed-race schools in the U.K.: Playground observations. In C. Hart (Ed.), *Children on playgrounds* (pp. 210–238). Albany, NY: State University of New York Press.

Bronfenbrenner, U. (1975). Reality and research in the ecology of human development. *Proceedings of the American Philosophical Society, 119*, 439–469.

Bronfenbrenner, U. (1979). *The ecology of human development: Experiments by nature and design*. Cambridge, MA: Harvard University Press.

Brown, J. G., & Burger, C. (1984). Playground designs and preschool children's behaviors. *Environment and Behaviors, 16*, 599–626.

Bruner, J. (1990). *Acts of meaning*. Cambridge, MA: Harvard University Press.

Bruya, L. D. (1985) The effects of play structure format differences on the play behavior of preschool children. In J. L. Frost and S. Sunderlin (Eds.), *When children play* (pp. 115–120). Wheaton, MD: Association for Childhood Education International.

Bruya, L. D., & Langendorfer, S. J. (1988). *Where our children play: Elementary school playground equipment*. Reston, VA: American Alliance for Health, Physical Education, Recreation, and Dance.

Bryant, D. M., Burchinal, M., Lau, L. B., & Sparling, J. L. (1994). Family and classroom correlates of head start children's developmental outcomes. *Early Childhood Research Quarterly, 9*, 289–309.

Bubolz, M. M., Eicher, J. B., and Sontag, M. S. (1979). The human ecosystem: A model. *Journal of Home Economics, 71*, 28–31.

Campbell S. D. and Dill, N. (1985). Impact of changes in spatial density on children's behaviors in a day care setting. In J. L. Frost and S. Sunderlin (Eds.), *When children play* (pp. 115–120). Wheaton, MD: Association for Childhood Education International.

Campbell, S. D., & Frost, J. L. (1985). The effects of playground type on the cognitive and social behaviors of grade two children. In J. L. Frost & S. Sunderlin (Eds.), *When children play* (pp. 81–88). Wheaton, MD: Association for Childhood Education International.

Choat, E., & Griffin, H. (1986). Young children, television & learning: Part I. The effects of children watching a continuous off-air broadcast. *Journal of Educational Television, 12*, 79–104.

Christie, J., & Johnsen, E. (1983). The role of play in social-intellectual development. *Review of Educational Research, 53,* 93–115.

Christie, J. F. and Johnsen, E. P. (1989). The constraints of setting on children's play. *Play and Culture, 2,* 317–327.

Clements, D. H., & Nastasi, B. K. (1993). Electric media and early childhood education. In B. Spodek (Ed.), *Handbook of research on the education of young children* (pp. 251–275). New York: Macmillan.

Corsaro, W. A. (1985). *Friendships and peer culture in the early years.* Norwood, NJ: Ablex.

Crnic, K., & Greenberg, M. (1990). Minor parenting stresses with young children. *Child Development, 61,* 1628–1637.

Cunningham, C., Jones, M., & Taylor, N. (1994). The child-friendly neighborhood: Some questions and tentative answers from Australian research. *International Play Journal, 2*(2), 79–95.

Deacon, S. R. (1994). *Analysis of children's equipment choices and play behaviors across three play environments.* Unpublished doctoral dissertation, University of Texas at Austin.

deMarrais, K. B., Nelson, P. A., & Baker, J. H. (1994). Meaning in mud: Yup'ik Eskimo girls at play. In J. L. Roopnarine, J. E. Johnson, & F. H. Hooper (Eds.), *Children's play in diverse cultures* (pp. 179–209). Albany: State University of New York Press.

Dempsey, J. D., & Frost, J. L. (1993). Play environments in early childhood education. In B. Spodek (Ed.), *Handbook of research on the education of young children* (pp. 306–321). New York: Macmillan.

Dixon, R. A., & Lerner, R. M. (1992). A history of systems in developmental psychology. In M. H. Bornstein & M. E. Lamb (Eds.), *Developmental psychology: An advanced textbook* (3rd ed.) (pp. 3–58). Hillsdale, NJ: Lawrence Erlbaum.

Dodge, M. K., & Frost, J. L. (1986). Children's dramatic play: Influence of thematic and nonthematic settings. *Childhood Education, 62,* 166–170.

Donaldson, M. (1978). *Children's minds.* New York: Norton.

Duyme, M. (1988). School success and social class: An adoption study. *Developmental Psychology, 24,* 203–209.

Einon, D., & Barber, F. (1994). Those who use more space to play as children are less field-dependent as adults: A preliminary study. *International Play Journal 2*(3), 208–214.

Elder, G., Caspi, A., & Burton, L. (1988). Adolescent transitions in developmental perspective: Sociological and historical insights. In M. Gunnar and W. A. Collins

(Eds.), *Development during the transition to adolescence: Minnesota symposia on child psychology, 21.* Hillsdale, NJ: Lawrence Erlbaum.

Elder, J. L., & Pederson, D. R. (1978). Preschool children's use of objects in symbolic play. *Child Development, 49,* 500–504.

Elgas, P. M., Klein, E. L., Kantor, R., & Fernie, D. E. (1988, Fall–Winter). Play and the peer culture: Play styles and object use. *Journal of Research in Childhood Education, 3*(2), 142–153.

Englebright-Fox, J., & Dempsey, J. (1996). Swings in the outdoor play environment: A worthwhile investment for young children. *International Play Journal 4*(1), 39–50.

Eron, L. D. (1982). Parent-child interaction, television violence, and aggression of children. *American Psychologist, 37,* 197–211.

Eron, L. D. (1986). Interventions to mitigate the psychological effects of media violence on behavior. *Journal of Social Issues, 42,* 155–169.

Eron, L. D., Huesmann, L. R., Lefkowitz, M. H., & Walder, L. O. (1972). Does television violence cause aggression? *American Psychologist, 27,* 253–262.

Escobedo, T. H. (1992). Play in a new medium: Children's talk and graphics at computers. *Play and Culture, 5,* 120–140.

Fagot, B. I. (1977). Variations in density: Effects on task and social behaviors of preschool children. *Developmental Psychology, 13,* 166–167.

Field, T. M. (1980). Preschool play: Effects of teacher/child ratios and organization of classroom space. *Child Study Journal, 10,* 191–205.

Fishbein, H. D. (1984). Evolution, culture, and socialization. In H. D. Fishbein (Ed.), *The psychology of infancy and childhood: Evolutionary and cross-cultural perspectives* (pp. 47–100). Hillsdale, NJ: Lawrence Erlbaum.

Fishbein, H. D., & Burklow, K. (1993). Age-related changes in object-use and verbalization among pre-school children in a free-play setting. *International Play Journal 1*(1), 27–44.

Fitt, S. (1974). The individual and his environment. *School Review, 83,* 617–620.

Fox, J. E., & Tipps, R. S. (1995). Young children's development of swinging behaviors. *Early Childhood Research Quarterly, 8,* 235–251.

Friedrich, L. K., & Stein, A. H. (1973). Aggressive and prosocial television programs and the natural behavior of preschool children. *Monographs of the Society for Research in Child Development, 38* (4, Serial No. 151).

Friedrich, L. K., & Stein, A. H. (1975). Prosocial television and young children: The effects of verbal labeling and role playing on learning and behavior. *Child Development, 46,* 27–28.

Frost, J. L. (1979). *Children's play and play environments.* Boston: Allyn & Bacon.

Frost, J. L. (1992). *Play and playscapes.* Albany, NY: Delmar.

Frost, J. L., & Campbell, S. D. (1985). Equipment choices of primary-age children on conventional and creative playgrounds. In J. L. Frost & S. Sunderlin (Eds.), *When children play* (pp. 89–92). Wheaton, MD: Association for Childhood Education International.

Frost, J. L., & Jacobs, P. (1995). Play deprivation: A factor in juvenile violence. *Dimensions, 23*(3), 14–20, 39.

Frost, J. L., & Strickland, E. (1985). Equipment choices of young children during free play. In J. L. Frost and S. Sunderlin (Eds.), *When children play* (pp. 93–101). Wheaton, MD: Association for Childhood Education International.

Garrett, P., Ng'andu, N., & Ferron, J. (1994). Poverty experiences of young children and the quality of their home environment. *Child Development, 65,* 331–345.

Getz, S. K., & Berndt, E. G. (1982). A test of a method for quantifying amount, complexity, and arrangement of play resources in the preschool classroom. *Journal of Applied Developmental Psychology, 3,* 295–305.

Ginsburg, H. J. (1975). *Variations of aggressive interaction among male elementary school children as a function of spatial density.* Paper presented at the meeting of the Society for Research in Child Development, Denver.

Goelman, H., & Jacobs, E. V. (Eds.). (1994). *Children's play in child care settings.* Albany: State University of New York Press.

Golomb, C. (1977). Symbolic play: The role of substitutions in pretense and puzzle games. *British Journal of Educational Psychology, 47,* 175–186.

Gramza, A., Corush, J., & Ellis, M. (1972). Children's play on trestles of differing complexity: A study of play equipment design. *Journal of Leisure Research, 4,* 303–311.

Grubbs, G. A. (1994). An abused child's use of sand play in the healing process. *Clinical Social Work Journal, 22*(2), 193–209.

Guerra, M. (1989). Verbal swaggering: Lunchtime grotesqueries in the child care center. *Play and Culture, 2,* 197–202.

Hagekull, B., & Bohlin, G. (1990). Early infant temperament and maternal expectations related to maternal adaptation. *The International Journal for the Study of Behavioral Development, 13,* 199–214.

Hagekull, B., & Bohlin, G. (1995). Day care quality, family, and child characteristics and socioemotional development. *Early Childhood Research Quarterly, 10,* 505–526.

Hart, C., Dewolf, M., & Burts, D. (1993). Parental disciplinary strategies and preschoolers' play behavior in playground settings. In C. Hart (Ed.), *Children on playgrounds* (pp. 271–314). Albany: State University of New York Press.

Hart, C. H., DeWolf, M. Wozniak, P., & Burts, D. C. (1992). Maternal and paternal discipline styles: Relations with preschoolers' playground behavioral orientations and peer status. *Child Development, 63,* 879–892.

Hart, C. H., & Sheehan, R. (1986). Preschoolers' play behavior in outdoor environments: Effects of traditional and contemporary playgrounds. *American Educational Research Journal, 23,* 668–678.

Hartle, L., & Johnson, J. E. (1993). Historical and contemporary influences of outdoor environments. In C. H. Hart (Ed.), *Children on playgrounds* (pp. 14–42). Albany: State University of New York Press.

Hartup, W., & Larsen, B. (1993). Conflict and context in peer relations. In C. Hart (Ed.), *Children on playgrounds* (pp. 44–84). Albany: State University of New York Press.

Hartup, W., & Moore, S. (1990). Early peer relations: Developmental significance and prognostic implications. *Early Childhood Research Quarterly, 5,* 1–7.

Haskins, R. (1986). Social and cultural factors in risk assessment and mild mental retardation. In D. C. Farran & J. D. McKinney (Eds.), *Risk in intellectual and psychosocial development.* Orlando, FL: Academic Press.

Hayward, D., Rothenburg, M., & Beasley, R. (1974). Children's play and urban playground environments: A comparison of traditional, contemporary, and adventure playground types. *Environment and Behavior, 6,* 131–168.

Heath, S. B. (1990). The children of Tracton's community: Spoken and written language in social change. In J. Stigler, R. Shweder, & G. Herdt (Eds.), *Cultural psychology: Essays on comparative human development* (pp. 496–519). Cambridge: Cambridge University Press.

Heine, M. K. (1991). The symbolic capital of honor: Gambling games and the social construction of gender in Tlingit Indian culture. *Play and Culture, 4,* 346–358.

Henniger, M. L. (1985). Preschool children's play behaviors in an indoor and outdoor environment. In J. L. Frost & S. Sunderlin (Eds.), *When children play* (pp. 145–150). Wheaton, MD: Association for Childhood Education International.

Herman, J. F., Shiraki, J. H., & Miller, B. S. (1985). Young children's ability to infer spatial relationships: Evidence from a large familiar environment. *Child Development, 56*(5), 1195–1203.

Heusser, C. P., Adelson, M., & Ross, D. (1986). How children use their elementary school playground. *Children's Environments Quarterly, 3*(3), 3–11.

Holmes, R. M. (1991). Categories of play: A kindergartner's view. *Play and Culture*, *4*, 43–50.

Honig, A. S. (1983). Research in review: Television and young children. *Young Children*, *38*, 63–76.

Howe, N., Moller, L., Chambers B., & Petrakos, H. (1993). The ecology of dramatic play centers and children's social and cognitive play. *Early Childhood Research Quarterly*, *8*, 235–251.

Howes, C., & Stewart, P. (1987). Child's play with adults, toys, and peers: An examination of family and child-care influences. *Developmental Psychology*, *23*, 423–430.

Hurtwood, L. A. (1968). *Planning for play*. Cambridge, MA: MIT Press.

Hutt, C., & Vaizey, M. J. (1966). Differential effects of group density on social behavior. *Nature*, *209*, 1371–1372.

Isbell, R. T., & Raines, S. C. (1991). Young children's oral language production in three types of play centers. *Journal of Research in Childhood Education*, *5*(2), 140–146.

Jacobs, P. (1994a). *Teacher role's with children on the playground*. Unpublished manuscript, University of Texas at Austin.

Jacobs, P. (1994b). *An exercise in freedom on the playground*. Unpublished manuscript, University of Texas at Austin.

Jacobs, P. (1996). The teacher's role in the playground. In M. Guddemi, T. Jambor, & A. Skrupselis (Eds.), *Play: An intergenerational experience* (pp. 24–26). Little Rock, AR: Southern Early Childhood Association.

James, N. C., & McCain, T. A. (1982). Television games preschool children play: Patterns, themes and uses. *Journal of Broadcasting*, *26*, 783–800.

Johnson, J. E. (1983). Context effects on preschool children's symbolic behavior. *Journal of Genetic Psychology*, *143*, 259–268.

Johnson, J. E., Christie, J. F., & Yawkey, T. D. (1987). *Play and early childhood development*. Glenview, IL: Scott, Foresman & Company.

Johnson, M. W. (1935). The effect on behavior of variation in the amount of play equipment. *Child Development*, *6*, 56–68.

Kantor, R., Elgas, P. M., & Fernie, D. F. (1993). Cultural knowledge and social competence within a preschool peer culture group. *Early Childhood Research Quarterly*, *8*, 125–147.

Kelly-Byrne, D. (1989). *A child's play life: an ethnographic study*. New York: Teachers College Press.

Kemerer, F., & Walsh, J. (1994). *The educator's guide to Texas school law* (3rd Ed.). Austin, TX: University of Texas Press.

Kinsman, C. A., & Berk, L. E. (1979). Joining the block and housekeeping areas: Changes in play and social behavior. *Young Children, 35*, 66–75.

Kritchevsky, S., Prescott, E., & Walling, L. (1977). *Planning environments for young children: Physical space.* Washington, DC: National Association for the Education of Young Children.

Kyrios, M., & Prior, M. (1990). Temperament, stress, and family factors in behavioral adjustment of 3–5-year-old children. *International Journal of Behavioral Development, 13*, 67–93.

Ladd, G., & Price, J. (1993). Playstyles of peer-accepted and peer-rejected children on the playground. In C. Hart (Ed.), *Children on playgrounds* (pp. 130–161). Albany: State University of New York Press.

Lancy, D. (1991). The autotelic learning environment revisited: An exploratory study. *Play and Culture, 4*, 124–128.

Lerner, R., & Kauffman, M. (1985). The concept of development in contextualism. *Developmental Review, 5*, 309–333.

Liben, L. S., Moore, M. L., & Golbeck, S. L. (1982). Preschoolers' knowledge of their classroom environment: Evidence from small scale and life size spatial tasks. *Child Development, 53*, 1275–1284.

Lincoln, Y., & Guba, E. (1985). *Naturalistic inquiry.* Newbury Park, CA: Sage.

Loo, C. M. (1972). The effects of spatial density on the social behavior of children. *Journal of Applied Social Psychology, 2*, 372–381.

Luster, T., & Dubow, E. (1990). Predictors of the quality of the home environment that adolescent mothers provide for their school-aged children. *Journal of Youth and Adolescence, 19*(5), 475–494.

Lyle, J., & Hoffman, H. (1972). Explorations in patterns of television viewing preschool age children. In E. A. Rubenstein, G. A. Comstock, & J. P. Murray (Eds.), *Television and social behavior: Television in day-to-day life: Vol. 4. Patterns of use.* Washington, DC: U.S. Government Printing Office.

Martini, M. (1994). Peer interaction in Polynesia: A view from the Marquesas. In J. L. Roopnarine, J. E. Johnson, & F. H. Hooper (Eds.), *Children's play in diverse cultures* (pp. 73–103). Albany: State University of New York Press.

McCartney, K. (1984). Effect of quality of day care environment on children's language development. *Developmental Psychology , 20*(2), 244–260.

McCord, J. (1988). Parental behavior in the cycle of aggression. *Psychiatry, 51*, 144–153.

McGhee, P. E., Ethridge, L., & Benz, N. A. (1984). The effect of level of toy structure on preschool children's pretend play. *Journal of Genetic Psychology, 144,* 209–217.

McGowan, R. J., & Johnson, D. (1984). The mother-child relationship and other antecedents of childhood intelligence: A causal analysis. *Child Development, 55,* 8810–8830.

McKee, M. (1993). Summer in the city. *International Play Journal 1*(3), 169–178.

McLoyd, V. C. (1983). The effects of the structure of play objects on the pretend play of low-income preschool children. *Child Development, 54,* 626–635.

Mergen, B. (1991). Ninety-five years of historical change in the game preferences of American children. *Play and Culture, 4,* 272–283.

Miller, S. M., Fernie, D., & Kantor, R. (1992). Distinctive literacies in different preschool play contexts. *Play and Culture, 5,* 107–119.

Minuchin, P. P., & Shapiro, E. K. (1983). The school as a context for social development. In E. M. Hetherington (Ed.), *Handbook of psychology: Vol. 4. Socialization, personality, and social development* (pp. 197–274). New York: Wiley.

Montes, F., & Risley, T. R. (1975). Evaluation traditional day care practices. *Child Care Quarterly, 4,* 208–215.

Moore, E. (1986). Family socialization and the IQ test performance of traditional and transracially adopted black children. *Developmental Psychology, 22,* 317–326.

Moore, G. T. (1986). Effects of the spatial definition of behavior settings on children's behavior: A quasi-experimental field study. *Journal of Environmental Psychology, 6,* 205–231.

Moore, M. (1992). *An analysis of outdoor play environments and play behaviors.* Unpublished doctoral dissertation, University of Texas at Austin.

Moore, R. (1989). Diversity as an ecological measure of quality. In M. N. Bloch and A. D. Pellegrini (Eds.), *The ecological context of children's play* (pp. 191–213.) Norwood, NJ: Ablex.

Moore, R. (1990). *Childhood's domain: Play and place in child development.* Berkeley, CA: MIG Communications.

Naylor, H. (1985). Design for outdoor play: An observational study. In J. L. Frost & S. Sunderlin (Eds.), *When children play* (pp. 103–113). Wheaton, MD: Association for Childhood Education International.

Nicholson, S. (1971). The theory of loose parts. *Landscape Architecture, 62*(1), 30–34.

Nicolich, L. (1977). Beyond sensorimotor intelligence: Assessment of symbolic maturity through analysis of pretend play. *Merrill-Palmer Quarterly, 23,* 89–99.

Ninio, A. (1990). Early environmental experiences and school achievement in the second grade: An Israeli study. *International Journal of Behavioral Development, 13,* 1–22.

Ogbu. J. U. (1981). Origins of human competence: A cultural-ecological perspective. *Child Development, 52,* 413–429.

Ogbu, J. U. (1990). Cultural model, identity, and literacy. In J. Stigler, R. Shweder, & G. Herdt (Eds.), *Cultural psychology: Essays on comparative human development* (pp. 520–541). Cambridge: Cambridge University Press.

Olweus, D. (1993). Bullies on the playground: The role of victimization. In C. Hart (Ed.), *Children on playgrounds* (pp. 85–128). Albany: State University of New York Press.

Parten, M. (1932). Social participation among preschool children. *Journal of Abnormal and Social Psychology, 27,* 243–369.

Peck, J., & Goldman, R. (1978). *The behaviors of kindergarten children under selected conditions of the physical and social environment.* Paper presented at the meeting of the American Educational Research Association, Toronto, Canada.

Pellegrini, A. D. (1985) Social-cognitive aspects of children's play: The effects of age, gender, and activity centers. *Journal of Applied Developmental Psychology, 6,* 129–140.

Pellegrini, A. D., & Davis, P. D. (1993). Relations between children's playground and classroom behavior. *British Journal of Educational Psychology, 63,* 88–95.

Pellegrini, A. D., & Perlmutter, J. C. (1989). Classroom contextual effects on children's play. *Developmental Psychology 25*(2), 289–296.

Pettit, G., & Harrist, A. (1993). Children's aggressive and socially unskilled playground behavior with peers: Origins in early family relations. In C. Hart (Ed.), *Children on playgrounds* (pp. 240–270). Albany: State University of New York Press.

Pinciotti, P., & Weinstein, C. S. (1986). The effects of a tire playground on children's attitude toward play time. *Children's Environments Quarterly, 3*(3), 30–39.

Phillips, R. (1945). Doll play as a function of the realism of the materials and the length of the experimental session. *Child Development, 16,* 123–143.

Plomin, R., McClearn, G. E., Pedersen, N. L., Nesselroade, J. R., & Bergman, C. S. (1988). Genetic influence on childhood family environment perceived retrospectively from the last half of the life span. *Developmental Psychology, 24,* 738–745.

Preiser, W. F. E. (1972). Work in progress: The behavior of nursery school children under different spatial densities. *Man Environment Systems, 2,* 247–250.

Proshansky, E., & Wolfe, M. (1975). The physical setting and open education. In T. G. David & B. D. Wright (Eds.), *Learning environments* (pp. 30–48). Chicago: University of Chicago Press.

Pulaski, M. A. (1973). Toys and imaginative play. In J. L. Singer (Ed.), *The child's world of make-believe* (pp. 74–103). New York: Academic Press.

Reimer, B. (1993). When the playground enters the classroom. In C. H. Hart (Ed.), *Children on playgrounds: Research perspectives and applications* (pp. 316–343). Albany: State University of New York Press.

Riegel, K. F. (1975). Toward a dialectical theory of development. *Human Development, 18*, 50–64.

Roberts, C., Pratt, C., & Leach, D. (1991). Classroom and playground interaction of students with and without disabilities. *Exceptional Children, 57*(3), 212–225.

Rohe, W. M., & Nuffer, E. L. (1977). *The effects of density and partitioning on children's behavior.* Paper presented at the meeting of the American Psychological Association, San Francisco.

Roopnarine, J. L. Johnson, J. E., & Hooper, F. H. (Eds.). (1994). *Children's play in diverse cultures.* Albany: State University of New York Press.

Roper, R., & Hinde, R. A. (1978). Social behavior in a play group: Consistency and complexity. *Child Development, 49*, 570–579.

Rubin, K. H. (1977). Play behaviors of young children. *Young Children, 32*, 16–24.

Rubin, K. H., & Caplan, R. (1992). Peer relations in childhood. In M. Bornstein & M. Lamb (Eds.), *Developmental psychology: An advanced textbook* (3rd Ed., pp. 519–578). Hillsdale, NJ: Lawrence Erlbaum.

Rubin, K. H., & Seibel, L. G. (1979). *The effects of ecological setting on the cognitive and social play behaviors of preschoolers.* Paper presented at the annual meeting of American Educational Research Association, San Francisco.

Sameroff, A. J. (1975). Early influences on development: Fact or fancy? *Merrill Palmer Quarterly, 21*, 269–294.

Sanders, K. M., & Harper, L. V. (1976). Free-play fantasy behavior in children: Relations among gender, age, season, and location. *Child Development, 47*, 1182–1185.

Scarr, S. (1988). How genotypes and environments combine: Development and individual differences. In N. Bolger, A. Caspi, G. Downey, & M. Moorehouse (Eds.), *Person in context: Developmental processes* (pp. 217–244). Cambridge: Cambridge University Press.

Scarr, S. & McCartney, K. (1983). How people make their own environments: A theory of genotype-environments effects. *Child Development, 54*, 424–435.

Schluderman, S. & Schluderman, E. (1983). Sociocultural change and adolescents' perceptions of parent behavior. *Developmental Psychology, 19*, 674–685.

Serbin, L., Marchessault, K., McAffer, V., Peters, P., & Schwartzman, A. (1993). Conflict and context in peer relations. In C. Hart (Ed.), *Children on playgrounds* (pp. 162–183). Albany: State University of New York Press.

Shapiro, S. (1975). Preschool ecology: A study of three environmental variables. *Reading Improvement, 12*, 236–241.

Sheehan, R., & Day, D. (1975). Is open space just empty space? *Day Care and Early Education, 3*, 10–13.

Shin, D. (1994). *Preschool children's symbolic play indoors and outdoors.* Unpublished doctoral dissertation, University of Texas at Austin.

Shin, D., & Frost, J. (1995). Preschool children's symbolic play indoors and outdoors. *International Play Journal, 3,* 83–96.

Sholtz, G. J. L., & Ellis, M. J. (1975). Repeated exposure to objects and peers in a play setting. *Journal of Experimental Child Psychology, 19*, 448–455.

Simmons, R., Burgeson, R., & Carlton-Ford, S. (1987). The impact of cumulative change in early adolescence. *Child Development, 58*, 1220–1234.

Singer, J. L., & Singer, D. G. (1976). Can TV stimulate imaginative play? *Journal of Communication, 26*, 74–80.

Singer, J. L., & Singer, D. G. (1981). *Television, imagination, and aggression: A study of preschoolers.* Hillsdale, NJ: Lawrence Erlbaum.

Singer, J. L., & Singer, D. G. (1986). Family experiences and television viewing as predictors of children's imagination, restlessness, and aggression. *Journal of Social Issues, 42*, 107–124.

Smilansky, S. (1968). *The effects of sociodramatic play on disadvantaged preschool children.* New York: Wiley.

Smilansky, S. & Shefatya, L. (1990). *Facilitating play: A medium for promoting cognitive, socio-emotional and academic development in young children.* Silver Springs, MD: Psychosocial and Educational Publications.

Smith, M. W. & Dickinson, D. K. (1994). Describing oral language opportunities and environments in Head Start and other preschool classroom. *Early Childhood Research Quarterly, 9*, 345–366.

Smith, P. K., & Connolly, K. J. (1976). Social and aggressive behavior in preschool children as a function of crowding. *Social Science Information, 16*, 601–620.

Smith, P. K., & Connolly, K. J. (1980). *The ecology of preschool behaviors.* Cambridge: Cambridge University Press.

Smith, P. K., & Dodsworth, C. (1978). Social class differences in the fantasy play of preschool children. *Journal of Genetic Psychology, 133*, 183–190.

Sprigle, H. A. (1972). Who wants to live on Sesame Street? *Young Children, 28*, 91–109.

Steele, C., & Nauman, P. (1985). Infant's play on outdoor play equipment. In J. L. Frost & S. Sunderlin (Eds.), *When children play* (pp. 121–127). Wheaton, MD: Association for Childhood Education International.

Steinberg, L. (1986). Stability (and instability) of type A behavior from childhood to young adulthood. *Developmental Psychology, 22*(3), 393–402.

Steinberg, L., Elmen, J. D., & Mounts, N. (1989). Authoritative parenting psychosocial maturity, and academic success among adolescents. *Child Development, 60*, 1424–1436.

Strickland, E. (1979). *Free play behaviors and equipment choices of third grade children in contrasting play environments.* Unpublished doctoral dissertation, University of Texas at Austin.

Stroufe, A. (1988). The role of infant-caregiver attachment in development. In J. Belsky and T. Nezworski (Eds.), *Clinical implications of attachment.* Hillsdale, NJ: Lawrence Erlbaum.

Teets, S. (1985). Modification of play behaviors of preschool children through manipulation of environmental variables. In J. L. Frost & S. Sunderlin (Eds.), *When children play* (pp. 265–271). Wheaton, MD: Association for Childhood Education International.

Tizard, B., Philps, J., & Plewis, I. (1976). Play in preschool centers II: Effects on play of the child social class and of the educational orientation of the center. *Journal of Child Psychology and Psychiatry, 17,* 265–274.

United States Consumer Product Safety Commission. (1991). *Handbook for public playground safety.* Washington, DC: Author.

Ungerer, J. A., Zelazo, P. R., Kearsley, R. B., & O'Leary, K. (1981). Developmental changes in the representation of objects in symbolic play from 18 to 34 months of age. *Child Development, 52,* 186–195.

U.S. News and World Report. (1985). What entertainers are doing to your kids. October 28, 46–49.

van Andel, J. (1986). Physical changes in an elementary schoolyard. *Children's Environments Quarterly, 3*(3), 40–51.

Vittachi, A. (1989). *Stolen childhood: In search of the rights of the child.* Cambridge, MA: Blackwell.

Vygotsky, L. V. (1962). *Thought and language.* Cambridge, MA: MIT Press.

Vygotsky, L. V. (1978). *Mind in society: The development of higher psychological processes.* Cambridge, MA: Harvard University Press.

Wall, S. M., Pickert, S. M., & Gibson, W. B. (1989). Fantasy play in 5- and 6-year-old children. *Journal of Psychology, 12*(3), 245–256.

Wallach, F., & Afthinos, I. D. (1990). *An analysis of the state codes for licensed day care centers: Focused on playgrounds and supervision.* New York: Total Recreation Management Services.

Wallach, F., & Edelstein, S. (1991). *Analysis of the state regulations for elementary schools: Focused on playgrounds and supervision.* New York: Total Recreation Management Services.

Weinberger, L., & Starkey, P. (1994). Pretend play by African American children in Head Start. *Early Childhood Research Quarterly 9,* 327–343.

Werner, H. (1957). The concept of development from a comparative and organismic point of view. In D. B. Harris (Ed.), *The concept of development.* Minneapolis: University of Minnesota Press.

White, F., Hargraves, L., & Newbold, C. (1995). The midday playground experiences of five and six years olds: Mixed messages and neglected opportunities. *International Play Journal 3*(3), 153–167.

Wilson, R. S. (1983). The Louisville twin study: Developmental synchronies in behavior. *Child Development, 54,* 298–316.

Winn, M. (1977). *The plug-in drug.* New York: Viking.

Winter, S. M. (1985). Toddler play behaviors and equipment choices in an outdoor playground. In J. L. Frost and S. Sunderlin (Eds.), *When children play* (pp. 129–138). Wheaton, MD: Association for Childhood Education International.

Wohlwill, J., & Heft, A. (1987). The physical environment and development of the child. In D. Stokols & I. Altman (Eds.), *Handbook of environmental psychology* (pp. 281–328). New York: Plenum.

Wolfgang, C. H. (1985) Preschool children's preferences for gender-stereotyped play materials. In J. L. Frost & S. Sunderlin (Eds.), *When children play* (pp. 273–278). Wheaton, MD: Association for Childhood Education International.

Woodson, R. H., & da Costa-Woodson, E. M. (1984). Social organization, physical environment, and infant-caretaker interaction. *Developmental Psychology, 20*(3), 473–476.

Wortham, S. C., & Frost, J. L. (1990). *Playgrounds for young children: National survey and perspectives.* Reston, VA: American Alliance for Health, Physical Education, Recreation and Dance.

Chapter 14

Real and Not Real:
A Vital Developmental Dichotomy

Brian Vandenberg

Why do children play? From an evolutionary perspective, play is a puzzle. Play serves no obvious biological need; it is an activity that is divorced from immediate adaptive concerns, and it is done for the fun of it. Furthermore, it is children who most actively engage in play, which can involve considerable risk and a suspension of concerns about reality. There must be adaptive benefits to such a high-risk activity that children seem compelled to perform, yet none are obvious. One explanation that has been offered is that the adaptive functions of play are indirect; that through play, important cognitive and social skills are stimulated (Rubin, Fein, & Vandenberg, 1983).

Another answer to why children play has been offered by Freud (1960) and Piaget (1962), who argue that play serves important functions in childhood, but the growth of reason results in the disappearance of play as an important factor in thought. In Piaget's terms, the play of young children reflects the distorting influence of the dominance of assimilation over accommodation. With development, assimilation and accommodation become more differentiated and integrated, creating a more stable cognitive structure. Under these conditions, assimilatively dominated activity is less distorted, and play is more adapted to realistic goals and activities. Or, as Freud indicates, "play is brought to an end by the strengthening of a factor that deserves to be described as the critical faculty or reasonableness" (Freud, 1960, p. 128). These theories are compatible with the way that adults usually view children's play. Children outgrow their tendency to engage in playing house, school, and other fantasy themes, and their belief in fairy tales and myths, such as Santa Claus, erodes as the children come to see their logical shortcomings (e.g.,

"How can Santa fly around the world in one night?"). Childhood fantasy play and children's myths are developmentally idiosyncratic phenomena that disappear once individuals begin to develop these critical faculties.

PLAY AND MYTH

Fantasy, Belief, Reality

These approaches, which have dominated contemporary thinking about children's play, assume that play is secondary to other, more salient developmental functions. Play is a epiphenomenon that stimulates more important cognitive or social skills, or it is a childish activity that is usurped by reason. But what if we began our investigation by asking, "What are the features of a being that is capable of creating theories of play and interpreting their experience from these various vantage points?" This turns the process of investigation on end. Theories of play, instead of providing the assumptive framework for gathering data, become important data in themselves. The answer to this question is that humans are myth-making beings who create reality through belief in stories they have constructed about reality. By myth, I don't mean mistake, as the word is sometimes used, but myth as a lived-in belief system that orders and gives meaning to life.

Thus, humans are myth-believing beings for whom reality is a trusted fantasy. To be human and to live in a meaningful way within a culture requires that we live in and through a sophisticated, abstract system that is largely imaginary. To be incapable of fantasy is to be barred from human culture. Children's fantasy play is an expression of this human capacity to create imaginary worlds that structure, energize, and give meaning to experience. Play is a manifestation of the fundamental properties of myth-making, and cognitive, social, and symbolic abilities are concomitant aspects of this process. The myths and fantasies of childhood are not eroded by the onset of reason; rather, they are replaced by more sophisticated adult myths about the importance of reason. Ironically, the mythical belief in reason by adults has led to the myth that adults have no myths.

Our reality is grounded in the myths, assumptions, beliefs, and ways of saying that compose intersubjective mutuality. Culturally sanctioned myths about what constitutes reality, if they are believed, create the reality. In Bateson's words, "propositions . . . about the world . . . are not true or false in a simple objective sense; they are more true if we believe and act upon them, and more false if we disbelieve them. Their validity is a function of our belief" (Ruesch & Bateson, 1968, p. 217). Or, as William James asserts, "truths cannot become true till our faith has made them so" (James, 1956, p. 96). So, for example, egos, motives, crime, interest rates, GNP, money, God, or, for that matter, cognitive processes, social roles, play, and human development are abstractions that carry considerable ontological weight that is derived from the way they are embedded in the web of cultural assumptions about the nature of reality, and from the beliefs about their status as real entities (Miller, 1973). When these concepts are evoked, they serve to order, orient, and organize us in a particular way to ourselves, to others, and to our world.

This does not mean the reality is a solipsistic fantasy, or that the world simply can be wished away. The world has a tangible presence that is ignored at our peril. However, myths and beliefs about the world can vary greatly, and they influence the nature of our understanding and relation to it. For instance, the belief that "trees are for wood" engenders a much different experience and stance toward the world than "trees are for worship"; through our belief, we create the reality of our experience of trees. Cross-cultural comparisons reveal that there are a wide variety of myths and beliefs. Unfortunately, this insight is often overlooked, as we are prone to relegate the beliefs of others to the realm of fantasy, and reify our own as Reality. As Sutton-Smith (1980) points out, "the cosmic constructions of ideology and religion are seen as ultimate meanings without which none of the rest makes sense. Other people's religious or ideologies are, of course, often designated as mere "fairy tales," mere "child's play" (p. 12).

The Real and the Not Real

While various cultures will use different myths and beliefs to organize experience, it is essential that individuals within a culture share a common ground of understanding, and be able to discern what is real from what is not (within the shared framework). Failure to accurately and consistently distinguish the real from the not real has serious consequences. In Vygotsky's (1978) words, "to behave in a real situation as in an illusory one is the first sign of delirium" (p. 102). Thus, it is not enough to have the capacity for imaginative involvements; individuals must also be grounded in the myths, beliefs, and ways of communicating that form the basis of intersubjectivity that enables appropriate distinctions between real and not real.

But what is real and what is illusory? Bateson's (1972) analysis of play suggests that what distinguishes the playful from the serious, the "real" from the "not real" is the metacommunication, "This is play." Metacommunication lifts thought out of the immediate welter of signals, creating a new level of communication. The reality of an exchange is not simply what a signal communicates, but is determined by the metacommunication about how a signal is to be interpreted. The message, "This is play," is not expressed by a particular signal, but rather is a "way of saying," whereby actions are exaggerated, repeated, jumbled, or transformed in some unusual or unique way (Miller,

1973; Schwartzman, 1978); the "saying is the playing" (Garvy, 1977). Play can be *anything*, said playfully. Playful saying is integral to the ongoing stream of communication that slides from the serious to the playful and back. The playful and the serious, the "real" and the "not real" are distinguished by the ways that communication is punctuated. The dynamic tension between "real" and "not real" is a necessary consequence of metacommunication, which assigns ontological value to signals. Metacommunication and increasingly complex linguistic and metalinguistic communications evoke an imaginary world, where what is real, what is play and what is madness is determined by how messages are framed and understood. Reality is an interpretative act.

Development is not simply the acquisition of information about a given world. Rather, it involves becoming grounded in an uncertain world that is beyond understanding (Vandenberg, 1991). This is achieved through enculturation into the meanings, myths, rituals, social practices, and assumptions that order, orient, and organize individuals in common ways and provide a sense of reality that allows for confident action in the world. What is real and what is illusory is not an obvious, directly perceived dichotomy but is based upon discerning conventional markers of communication. The challenge for children is to learn the appropriate ways of interpreting and punctuating communication, so as to properly share the appropriate communicative ground of intersubjective meanings and to dwell within the sociocultural reality that is constituted from this common ground. It is crucial that children know what is serious and what is not, and that they understand and trust the regularities and particularities of communication that are essential for appropriate participation in intersubjective mutuality.

However, this is not easily achieved. The complexity of adult communication, with the layers of metacommunicative, linguistic and metalinguistic signification, and levels of abstraction is stupefying to the uninitiated. Children, who are the uninitiated, gradually enter the assumptive world that is embodied in reflexive gestures, meanings, and ways of saying that provide a sense of grounded reality. Children are capable of distinguishing play from not play, but their appreciation of what is "real" and what is "not real" is labile and lacks the sophistication found in adult members of the culture.

BECOMING GROUNDED

There is a close association between the development of capabilities to become involved in increasingly complex communicative exchanges, and becoming grounded in increasingly sophisticated beliefs, myths, and intersubjective mutuality. The developmental path of play is particularly revealing of the increasing capacity for sophisticated imaginative involvements and for complexly nuanced distinctions between the real and the not real. The following discussion will provide a brief overview of this developmental path of play and communication. There are, of course, wide individual differences and variations across contexts, so what is offered is meant simply as a general guide, not a universal proscription.

The first period, infancy, is marked by participation in intersubjective mutuality that requires coordinating actions with others using trusted signals that enable cooperation and understanding. During this time the basic coordinates of intersubjectivity are established, as are the essential skills for communicative exchanges; recognizing that a signal is a signal, learning to coordinate and sequence signals with another, adjusting communications based on feedback, establishing common referents, and repairing, clarifying, and correcting messages. Objects begin to be understood within the context of intersubjectivity, as the "environment" becomes imbued with sociocultural significance (Vandenberg, 1995). Adults are essential for the being of infants, and infants are exquisitely attuned to "being with" adults. Adults serve as an executive function, regulating and orienting infants experiences and prompting and shaping their expressions. Infants' communication and memory are limited to the behavioral plane, but mastery of this level is essential to the development of later, more complex and abstract communications. Communication is expressed through bodily movements, gestures, and vocalizations. By knowing the acceptable ways of expressing and interpreting intentions, the common ground of intersubjectivity becomes part of infants neuromusculative (Vandenberg, 1995). Thus, reality is limited to the behavioral plane, is largely organized and structured by adults, and therefore is quite labile. But infants' communicative achievements also roots them, in a primordial way, within the web of sociocultural intersubjectivity. These developments are reflected in the play of infants. Infants are capable of complex communications on the behavioral plane; they are capable of play, saying, "This is play," about certain actions and objects (Rubin, Fein, & Vandenberg, 1983). This metacommunicative ability suggests that infants are capable of lifting themselves out of the stream of ongoing activity; they are not stimulus bound, but are free from the welter of necessity.

Infancy gives way to early childhood, which is marked by the emergence of language, and the communicative tasks accomplished in infancy on the behavioral plane must now be learned on the more abstract, linguistic plane. Words are instruments of great power, allowing for significance within a vast horizon of sociocultural intersubjectivity. Language serves important intermental functions, as it is used as a tool for social influence and cooperation. It also affects a transformation of intramental functions, which become abstract, conceptual, logical, measured, and selective. Thought has been freed from the immediate properties of the perceptual field and children have gained access to the complex intersubjectivity of adult communication (Vygotsky, 1978). However, they are not stabilized in this world, or, rather, their stability is externally influenced and grounded. Children have not yet internalized their own voice, their attention is two-dimensional and fluid, and they are unable to assume executive control of their own thought—they must rely on the authoritative voice of others (Wertsch, 1991).

The growing complexity and lability of children's reality is reflected in their play. Children during this age engage in a great deal of fantasy play, and it has been called the age of play. A central question is whether they really believe their imaginative involvements are real (e.g., Harris, Brown, Marriott, Whittal, & Harmes, 1991; Singer & Singer, 1990; Woolley & Wellman, 1993). While the research is not definitive, the fact that the question is even asked, and it is asked repeatedly, reflects uncertainty about how children view the ontological status of their believed-in imaginings and whether they have yet learned to secure the boundaries between reality and illusion. Regardless of the research results, it is clear that in actual practice, adults allow younger children considerable leeway in their assumptions about what is real and what is illusory; few adults would be concerned that 5-year-old children may be taking their stuffed animals or imaginary playmates too seriously.

Children's transition to middle childhood is characterized by greater communicative sophistication and stability of thought. During this time, inner speech becomes fully internalized and provides a means for self organization and influence. But inner speech serves more than simply a cognitive-organizational function. Children appropriate the voices of authority for themselves, acquiring the valuings and ways of saying that confer power and a sense of grounding. Their self-organizing valuings embody the authority derived from the appropriated voices. It is also during this time that children become intensively involved in a context that shapes thought and behavior in ways that are highly valued by the culture: school. In school, children learn to decontextualize experience, acquire skills of literacy and to think rationally, all of which are critically important for participating in the realities of the culture (Wertsch, 1991).

This is also a time when childhood and adulthood are straddled. Children become capable of self-direction, are beginning to acquire a sense of authority about their own voice, becoming capable of abstract thought and beginning to confront expectations about a cultural reality that is objectified and rational. It is an age where the playful can include imaginary playmates—or chess—and children are still allowed leeway in their imaginings; an age where the boundaries between the real and the illusory are not completely secured.

Adolescence marks a time of great change, as children enter puberty and must confront growing expectations and demands to become a more integral member of the culture. Childhood fantasies and imaginative involvements receive less leeway, and play becomes more realistic, rule-bound, and rational

(Rubin, Fein, & Vandenberg, 1983). There is a change in adult evaluations of the reality of imaginative involvements, and there are increased expectations to be anchored in the realities of adulthood. When children between 4 to 8 years old have imaginary playmates, adults are not usually concerned, but after 12 years of age, imaginary playmates are likely a source of deep consternation for adults. Indeed, it may be a sign of mental illness, a sign that the adolescents have failed to properly assign ontological status to the appropriate communications. It is noteworthy that the diagnosis of schizophrenia is difficult and rare before the age of 8, one reason being that some of the most telltale clues of a "thought disorder," which is part of the diagnosis of schizophrenia and involves an inability to distinguish reality from fantasy, are ever present aspects of the thoughts of young children (Russell, Bott, & Sammons, 1989). There are greater expectations, and far greater consequences for adolescents (and adults) to properly distinguish reality from illusion. Considerable emphasis is placed on reason, rationality, and detached objectification, and there is suspicion and fear associated with fantasy, irrationality, and imaginative involvement.

Development, then, can be said to be a process of "hardening of the categories."[1] The distinction between the real and the illusory becomes of utmost importance. There are increasing expectations that these boundaries will be understood and honored, and there are considerable sanctions for the failure to do so. Boundaries and demarcations between the real and the illusory are essential, as they allow for shared assumptions and values that are necessary for cooperative action, and it is crucial that individuals come to share this intersubjective grounding. Children acquire this grounding gradually, and the expectations for them to navigate the subtle and complex layers of messages of varying ontological status increases with development. Play offers insight into the complexity of the paths of becoming grounded in the myths, beliefs, assumptions, and ways of saying that define reality.

The preceding discussion suggests that reality is composed of trusted myths invested with belief, that the demarcation of the real from the not real is of critical importance in becoming grounded, and that the developmental path of play reveals an ever increasing complexity and significance of distinguishing real from not real, investing belief, and becoming grounded. The period of early childhood is a particularly salient time when play involvements flourish. The following discussion will explore several implications of this view of play for young children.

PLAY IN EARLY CHILDHOOD

An essential feature of young children's play is their ability to communicate their intent to play, and to enter into appropriately playful exchanges with peers that require a mutual understanding of what is real and what is not. For example, a child who wishes to play with others must learn how to communicate, "This is play," "I would like to play," and "May I join you in your play?" These are supercharged overtures, for they require the signaling of understanding of what is to constitute the real and the not real, the manner in which the play is to proceed in relation to others, and one's role in the playful exchange. The watching child trying to negotiate entry into an ongoing play round is a paradigmatic event that reveals important features of human life. For such a child, an invitation into the playing group is more than just an opportunity to play; it is an issue of existence. To be outside the group is to be a nonentity, to join the play is to be accorded an officially sanctioned identity and status within a group of trusting and trusted players. This is at the heart of the process of coming to be grounded; to share a common myth framework, and to trust that others will also. In doing so, one derives meaning through play, and a sense of belonging and rootedness by sharing the trust of others. The play of preschoolers is one of the early steps in learning to negotiate one's place with others in joint, cooperative involvements.

Play in the preschool years can be about anything, said playfully. The act of transforming something from real to play is an act of lifting experiences out of the ongoing context of everyday involvement, highlighting them and making them the object of investigation. Play affords children the opportunity to make visible, inspect, and understand experience that is otherwise hidden. The act of play is different from that which the playful act enacts. This is evidenced in an example, cited by Vygotsky (1978), of two young girls, who are sisters, who are playing at being sisters.

> They are playing at reality. The vital difference . . . is that the child in playing tries to be what she thinks a sister should be. In life, the child behaves without thinking that she is her sister's sister . . . as a result of playing, the child comes to understand that sisters possess a different relationship to each other than to other people. What passes unnoticed by the child in real life becomes a rule of behavior in play. (Vygotsky, 1978, pp. 94–95)

Signaling, "This is play," is a transformational act. Real experiences are rendered "not real," the serious made playful, thus allowing for it to be seriously reconsidered.

Many contemporary perspectives on play consider it a means for the acquisition of information, exercising cognitive functions, or elaborating social skills. But such explanations do not fully explain why play is so passionate, so thrilling, and so riveting for children. The emotional demeanor of play is in dramatic contrast with that usually associated with acquiring information, exercising functions, or practicing skills. Play is exciting because it flirts with an existential dichotomy of being and not being, real and not real. This vitality of playing at the real, without consequences, allows children to dwell within possibilities, to try them out without suffering the penalties that would otherwise accompany such actions.

Dwelling within possibilities is contrary to the Freudian notion of play as mastery of past traumatic events. This is not to argue that children don't play out and play over past events. But the salience of these past events, the reason why they emerge in the present, is because of the way they influence, constrain, and structure children's anticipations of their future. Past, present, and future are not separate, self-contained features of time that exist independently. Rather, they are intimately linked to an organic temporality whereby children's playful involvements reflect their present, indwelling projections about their future that is based on their experience. Thus, the passion of play is a result of playing with the vital dichotomy of real and not real that has significance for how children anticipate their future.

But this is not all. The excitement of play results from the sheer exercise of freedom over necessity. For example, dramatic play, such as playing house, is a common form of play among preschoolers. In such play children enact common meanings associated with family membership, and there is undoubtedly a component of hopeful projection of future possibilities. However, the children play with the script, new twists and alternatives are introduced and the script is bent to the desires of the children; perhaps more favorable child-oriented behaviors are assumed by the mommy and daddy players, or the children in the family are more angry, demanding, and powerful. The children are uncovering the power and limits of public meanings, and at the same time exercising their sense of freedom over them. It is thrilling to transform the real to the not real, to journey into forbidden areas of darkness behind the public mask of conventionality, and to become aware of one freedom to do so in the process. The ease with which the real can be rendered not real, by the simple signal, "This is play," reveals the contingency and fluidity of the social construction of reality. Young children's play is a frolicking in this fluid contingency.

Children play with the social "facts" of their lives, but their play is also shaped by cultural factors, and there have been important changes that have altered the context of their play. During the first two-thirds of this century, children's first encounter with schooling was kindergarten, which frequently was only half-day, and not aimed at developing academic skills. However, during the past several decades, there has been a dramatic increase in the number of mothers who have entered the workplace, and children are now being placed in day care and preschools. Children's institutional life is beginning much earlier. Furthermore, there has been an increase in concern that children acquire the requisite cognitive and social skills needed in an increasingly complex, technological world (Garbarino, 1989). This has created a dilemma for how to approach this new class of institutionalized children. They are too young, by traditional wisdom, to be subjected to rigorous tutoring, but they should begin to acquire some of the necessary skills for academic survival.

Play is a particularly attractive solution to these dilemmas, for it preserves the mythic, playful aspects of childhood, yet at the same time, it offers the possibility of enhancing valued cognitive and social skills. What results is a "play curriculum." Toys are selected, play activities planned, adult tutoring and guidance offered that are aimed at very specific payoffs and goals. Adults, of course, have the responsibility to organize and guide children's activities in ways they think is most appropriate. The danger of play curriculum, however, is that the focus on adult intentions renders the activity as no longer playful; that the concern for imparting educational lessons in play destroys the child's freedom, joy, and passion realized at the boundary of real and not real.

The changing historical conditions, which are forcing a redefinition of the meaning of early childhood, pose questions to early childhood educators; are we to value play, joy, and frivolity for their own sake, even if they never lead to desired developmental outcomes? How much do we want our children to learn, and how early? At what expense? What are the role of institutions in the lives of young children? Confronting these issues brings a sharper appreciation of our values about play in the lives of our children . . . and in our own.

NOTE

1. I am grateful to William Conroy for suggesting this phrase.

REFERENCES

Bateson, G. (1972). *Steps to an ecology of mind.* New York: Ballentine.

Freud, S. (1960). Jokes and their relation to the unconscious. In J. Strackey (Ed.), *The standard edition of the complete psychological works of Sigmund Freud* (Vol. VIII). London: Hogarth.

Garbarino, J. (1989). An ecological perspective on the role of play in child development. In M. N. Block & A. D. Pellegrini (Eds.), *The ecological context of children's play.* (pp. 16–34). Norwood, NJ: Ablex.

Garvey, C. (1977). *Play.* Cambridge, MA: Harvard University Press.

Harris, P. L., Brown, E., Marriott, C., Whittal, S., & Harmes, S. (1991). Monsters, ghosts and witches: Testing the limits of the fantasy—reality distinction in young children. *British Journal of Developmental Psychology, 9,* 105–123.

James, W. (1956). *The will to believe.* New York: Dover.

Miller, S. N. (1973). Ends, means and galumphing: Some leitmotifs of play. *American Anthropologist, 75,* 87–98.

Piaget, J. (1962). *Play, dreams and imitation in childhood.* New York: Norton.

Rubin, K. H., Fein, G. G., & Vandenberg, B. (1983). Play. In E. M. Hetherington (Ed.), *Handbook of child psychology: Vol. 4. Socialization, personality and social development* (pp. 693–774). New York: Wiley.

Ruesch, J. & Bateson, G. (1968). *Communication: The social matrix of psychiatry.* New York: Norton.

Russell, A. T., Bott, L., & Sammons, C. (1989). The phenomenology of schizophrenia occurring in childhood. *Journal of the American Academy of Child and Adolescent Psychiatry, 28,* 399–407.

Schwartzman, H. B. (1978). *Transformations: The anthropology of children's play.* New York: Plenum.

Singer, D. G., & Singer, J. L. (1990). *The house of make-believe.* Cambridge, MA: Harvard University Press.

Sutton-Smith, B. (1980). Children's play: Some sources of play theorizing. In K. H. Rubin (Ed.), *New directions for child development: Children's play* (pp. 1–16). San Francisco: Jossey-Bass.

Vandenberg, B. (1991). Is epistemology enough? *American Psychologist, 46,* 1278–1286.

Vandenberg, B. (1995). Infant communication and the moral matrix of human life. *Family Process, 29,* 21–31.

Vygotsky, L. S. (1978). *Mind in society.* Cambridge, MA: Harvard University Press.

Wertsch, J. V. (1991). *Voices of the mind.* Cambridge, MA: Harvard University Press.

Woolley, J. D., & Wellman, H. M. (1993). Origin and truth: Young children's understanding of imaginary mental representations. *Child Development, 64,* 1–17.

Contributors

Robert J. Coplan, Assistant Professor of Psychology, Carleton University, obtained his baccalaureate at McGill University (1990) and his doctorate at the University of Waterloo (1995). Research interests focus on social, emotional, and personality development. He has recently published manuscripts in child development and development and psychopathology and has contributed chapters to *Developmental Psychology: An Advanced Textbook* (Bornstein & Lamb, Editors, 1992) and *Advances in Clinical Child Psychology* (Ollendick & Prinz, Editors, 1995).

Judy S. DeLoache (Ph.D., Illinois, 1973) is Professor of Psychology at the University of Illinois at Urbana-Champaign. Her research focuses on children's understanding of symbolic relations.

Susan Engel is Professor of Psychology and Director of Graduate Studies at Bennington College. Dr. Engel received her Ph.D. in 1985 from the CUNY Graduate Center. Her research interests include language development, creativity, memory, and narrative. She is also actively involved in education reform. Dr. Engel is the author of *The Stories Children Tell: Making Sense of the Narratives of Childhood,* 1995.

Joe L. Frost is Parker Centennial Professor in Early Childhood Education at the University of Texas at Austin. He is Past President of the Association for Childhood Education International and Past President of the American Association for the Child's Right to Play. His most recent book is *Play and Playscapes,* published by Delmar in 1992. He consults with government agencies, schools, cities, attorneys, and architects on issues of playground design and child safety.

Fergus Hughes is a Professor of Human Development and Psychology at the University of Wisconsin–Green Bay, where he regularly teaches a course on children's play. His books include *Human Development: Across the Life Span* and *Children, Play and Development*, which recently appeared in a second edition. His latest published article is "A Program of Play for Infants and Their Caregivers", which appeared in the January 1995 issue of *Young Children*. He is currently completing work on a book entitled *Child Development*, which will be published in 1996 by Prentice Hall, and is working on an article dealing with children's play in the twenty-first century.

Paul J. Jacobs is an instructor in child development and early childhood education. His doctoral dissertation addresses issues of play leadership and the adult's role in a free play environment. He is a play leader and playground consultant in Texas and a member of the International Association for the Child's Right to Play and the National Association for the Education of Young Children.

Robert D. Kavanaugh is Hales Professor of Psychology at Williams College. Dr. Kavanaugh received his Ph.D. in Developmental Psychology from Boston University in 1974. He is interested in the development of reasoning and imagination in young children. With Paul Harris, he is the co-author of "Children's Understanding of Pretense," *Monographs of the Society of Research in Child Development*, 1993, and co-editor, with Steven Fein and Betty Zimmerberg of *Emotion: Interdisciplinary Perspectives*, 1993.

Jennifer Lasker is an undergraduate student in the Department of Child and Family Studies at Syracuse University.

Angeline Lillard is an Assistant Professor in the Department of Psychology at the University of Virginia. She has held a National Science Foundation Visiting Professorship at the University of California at Berkeley, and her dissertation received the 1992 American Psychological Association Division 7 Outstanding Dissertation Award.

Donald P. Marzolf (Ph.D., Illinois, 1995) is Assistant Professor of Psychology at Louisiana State University. His research focuses on children's mapping and transfer of spatial relations.

Susan B. Neuman is an Associate Professor in the Curriculum, Instruction and Technology in Education Department and Urban Education at Temple University, where she teaches undergraduate and graduate courses in literacy. Her research interests include early literacy across languages and cultures, family literacy, and technology. She has authored three books, and many articles which have appeared in the *American Educational Research Journal, Reading Research Quarterly, Reading Teacher*, and *Early Childhood Research Quarterly*.

Anthony D. Pellegrini is a Professor of Early Childhood Education and a Research Fellow of the Institute for Behavioral Research at the University of Georgia. He received his Ph.D. in 1978 from Ohio State University and has been at Georgia since 1979. He has also taught Head Start and elementary school. His current areas of research include social influences on early literacy development and developmental functions of children's play. Recent publications include: *School Recess and Playground Behavior* (State University of New York Press, 1995), *Observing Children in Their Natural World: A Primer in Quantitative Observational Methods* (Lawrence Erlbaum, 1996), and with L. Galda, B. Shockley, and S Stahl, "The Nexus of Social and Literacy Experiences at Home and at School: Implications for Early Literacy," *British Journal of Educational Psychology, 65,* 273–285.

Sophia L. Pierroutsakos (M. A., Illinois, 1994) is a graduate student in the Department of Psychology at the University of Illinois at Urbana-Champaign. She is studying infants and toddlers' understanding of photographs.

Kathleen Roskos is a Professor at John Carroll University, where she is Chair of the Education Department. Her research interests include early literacy and teacher education. She has written widely on these topics and her research has appeared in *Reading Research Quarterly, Elementary School Journal, Reading Teacher, Young Children,* and *Early Childhood Research Quarterly.* She is currently a co-editor of *Reading Teacher,* published by the International Reading Association.

Jaipaul L. Roopnarine, was born in Guyana, South America; he was educated under the English system there before pursing a B.A. degree in psychology and a Ph.D. in child studies from the University of Wisconsin–Madison. He is currently Professor of Child Studies and Inclusive Early Childhood Education at Syracuse University in New York. His area of research has been on peer and parent-child relationships across cultures and he has conducted research in India, Malaysia, Taiwan, and the Caribbean, and on African American and Puerto Rican fathers. He is the co-editor of *Approaches to Early Childhood Education* and *Parent-child Socialization Across Cultures* and is currently working on a book on multicultural early childhood education. He has published extensively in early childhood and developmental psychology journals.

Kenneth H. Rubin, Professor of Human Development and Director, Center for Children, Relationships, and Culture, University of Maryland, obtained his baccalaureate at McGill University (1968) and doctorate at the Pennsylvania State University (1971). He has been Treasurer, Secretary, and Membership Secretary of the International Society for the Study of Behavioral Development; Associate Editor, *Child Development;* Coordinator (President) of the Developmental Section, Canadian Psychological Association; and Member-at-Large, Developmental Section, American Psychological Association. Research interests focus on social, emotional and personality development and developmental psychopathology. Books *include The Development and Treatment of Childhood Aggression* (1991, with Debra Pepler) and *Social Withdrawal, Inhibition, and Shyness in Childhood* (1993, with Jens

Asendorpf). He has contributed two chapters to the *Handbook of Child Psychology*—"Play" (with Fein & Vandenberg, 1983), and "Peer Interactions, Relationships, and Groups" (with Bukowski & Parker, in press).

Megan Sachs is an undergraduate student in the Department of Child and Family Studies at Syracuse University.

Olivia N. Saracho is Professor at the University of Maryland. She taught Head Start, preschool, kindergarten, and elementary classes in Brownsville, Texas, and was Director of the Child Development Associate Program at Pan American University. Her current research and writing is in the area of cognitive style, academic learning, and teacher education in relation to early childhood education. She is co-author of *Foundations of Early Childhood Education* (Prentice Hall), *Right from the Start* (Allyn & Bacon), and *Individual Differences* (Longman), and co-editor of *Professionalism and the Early Childhood Practitioner* and the Yearbook Series published by Teachers College Press.

Dongju Shin is Associate Professor of Early Childhood Education at Duksung Women's University in Seoul, Korea. Her doctoral dissertation addressed children's symbolic play and was the basis for an article in the *International Play Journal* in 1995.

Francine Smolucha, Professor of Psychology, Moraine Valley Community College, Palos Hills, IL (1976–); Visiting Lecturer, The School of the Art Institute of Chicago, Department of Art Education and Art Therapy (1991–); Ph.D., Educational Psychology, University of Chicago (1991). Conference presentations (APA, NRCD, NAEA, UN/INSEA, AERA, British Psychological Association) and numerous journal articles, in the U.S. and Europe (psychology of art/creativity). Frequent contributor to U.S. Dept. of Education's ERIC Documents Collection; co-author (with husband Larry) of *Developmental Psychology: A Synergistic Approach* (forthcoming from Brooks-Cole, 1996). Author/educator, play researcher, and Russian translator of Lev Vygotsky.

Larry Smolucha, Visiting Lecturer at the School of the Art Institute of Chicago, Department of Art Education and Art Therapy (1992–). M.A., psychology, University of Chicago (1992); M.F.A., sculpture, University of Chicago (1978). Conference presentations and journal articles, in the United States and Europe (psychology of art/creativity). Frequent contributor to U.S. Dept. of Education's ERIC Document Collection. Selected Publications: "Levels of Discourse in Psychotherapeutic Interactions", *Journal of Literary Semantics, 23*(1) (1994); *The Visual Arts Companion* (Simon & Schuster/Prentice Hall, 1995); co-author (with wife Francine) of *Developmental Psychology: A Synergistic Approach* (forthcoming from Brooks-Cole, 1996). Primary research interests: psychopathology and inner speech.

Catherine M. Smith (M. A., Illinois, 1993) is a graduate student in the Department of Psychology at the University of Illinois at Urbana-Champaign. She is studying how young children understand representations of their own bodies.

Bernard Spodek is Professor of Early Childhood Education at the University of Illinois, where he has taught since 1965. He received his doctorate in early childhood education from Teachers College, Columbia University, then joined the faculty of the University of Wisconsin–Milwaukee. He has also taught nursery, kindergarten, and elementary grade classes. His research and scholarly interests are in the areas of curriculum, teaching, and teacher education in early childhood education. Dr. Spodek has taught and lectured extensively in a variety of places in the United States, Australia, Canada, China, Israel, Japan, Korea, Mexico, and Taiwan. From 1976 to 1978 he was President of NAEYC, and from 1981 through 1983 he chaired the Early Education and Child Development Special Interest Group of the American Educational Research Association. He is widely published in the field of early childhood education. His most recent books are *Professionalism and the Early Childhood Practitioner* (Teachers College Press, 1988), *Foundations of Early Childhood Education* (Prentice Hall, 1987), and *Today's Kindergarten: Exploring its Knowledge Base, Expanding Its Curriculum* (Teachers College Press, 1986).

Marshall Stores is an undergraduate student in the Department of Child and Family Studies at Syracuse University.

Georgene L. Troseth (M. A., Illinois, 1996) is a graduate student in the Department of Psychology at the University of Illinois at Urbana-Champaign. She is studying young children's comprehension of video representations.

David H. Uttal (Ph.D., Michigan, 1989) is Assistant Professor of Psychology at Northwestern University. His research focuses on early symbol understanding and the development of spatial cognition.

Brian Vandenberg is Professor of Psychology at the University of Missouri, St. Louis. His interests include historical and theoretical perspectives on human development, and he has a long-standing interest in play.

Subject Index

A

abused children, 182
Articulation of the Body-Concept Scale, 249
assessment, 220
Association for the Study of Play, 197
attachment, 119, 124
attention deficit hyperactivity disorder, 179
autism, 180

B

beliefs, 17
block play, 248

C

child-defined activity, 220
cognitive growth, 240
cognitive style dissonance, 249
cognitive functioning, 244
cognitive style, 241, 244
computer program, 271
contemporary playgrounds, 271

correcting, 108
cultural learning styles, 209

D

delayed language, 175
demonstrations, 108
developmental changes, 83
direct observation, 226
disabilities, 171
dramatic play, 247
dual representation hypothesis, 67

E

ecological sensitivity, 228
Embedded Figures Test, 249
emergent literacy, 100
ethological theory, 123

F

fantasy play, 296
field independence, 241
field dependence, 241
Froebel, Freidrich, 4

Author Index